Critique of Rights

Christoph Menke

Critique of Rights

Translated by Christopher Turner

polity

First published in German as *Kritik der Rechte* © Suhrkamp Verlag, Berlin 2015
This English edition © Polity Press, 2020

This publication was supported by the DFG funded Cluster of Excellence "Normative Orders" at Goethe University Frankfurt am Main.

Polity Press
65 Bridge Street
Cambridge CB2 1UR, UK

Polity Press
101 Station Landing
Suite 300
Medford, MA 02155, USA

ISBN-13: 978-1-5095-2038-1
ISBN-13: 978-1-5095-2039-8 (pb)
A catalogue record for this book is available from the British Library.

Library of Congress Cataloging-in-Publication Data

Names: Menke, Christoph, 1958- author.
Title: Critique of rights / Christoph Menke ; translated by Christopher
  Turner
Other titles: Kritik der Rechte. English
Description: Cambridge, UK ; Medford, MA : Polity, 2020. | Includes
  bibliographical references and index. | Summary: "The declaration of
  equal rights arguably created the modern political community. But this
  act of empowering individuals caused the disempowering of the political
  community. Exposing this, Menke opens up a new way of understanding
  rights that no longer involves the disempowering of the political
  community"-- Provided by publisher.
Identifiers: LCCN 2019024007 (print) | LCCN 2019024008 (ebook) | ISBN
  9781509520381 (hardback) | ISBN 9781509520398 (paperback) | ISBN
  9781509520428 (epub)
Subjects: LCSH: Civil rights--Philosophy. | Liberalism.
Classification: LCC JC571 .M425513 2020 (print) | LCC JC571 (ebook) | DDC
  323.01--dc23
LC record available at https://lccn.loc.gov/2019024007
LC ebook record available at https://lccn.loc.gov/2019024008

Typeset in 10 on 12pt Sabon by
Servis Filmsetting Ltd, Stockport, Cheshire
Printed and bound in Great Britain by TJ International Limited

The publisher has used its best endeavours to ensure that the URLs for external websites referred to in this book are correct and active at the time of going to press. However, the publisher has no responsibility for the websites and can make no guarantee that a site will remain live or that the content is or will remain appropriate.

Every effort has been made to trace all copyright holders, but if any have been overlooked the publisher will be pleased to include any necessary credits in any subsequent reprint or edition.

For further information on Polity, visit our website: politybooks.com

CONTENTS

MARX'S PUZZLE

The bourgeois revolutions that since the eighteenth century brought down the regimes of traditional domination [*Herrschaft*] are first of all declarations of equal rights: they declare the rights of the human being and of the citizen.[1] Regimes of traditional domination were regimes of inequality. In such regimes, the power to exercise political judgment and rule was distributed in a radically unequal manner. In contrast, bourgeois revolutions establish equality, and to them equality signifies equal rights. Equality and equal rights amount to the same thing, in the revolutions' view. However, they are not the same. Equality *does not mean* rights. Instead, equality of rights is a specific formal determination of equality. The decisive act of bourgeois revolutions is therefore not the decision in favor of equality. Rather, it is the decision to give equality the form of rights.

This decision is puzzling. In his analysis of "The Declaration of the Rights of Man and of the Citizen," Marx writes:

> It is puzzling enough that a people which is just beginning to liberate itself, to tear down all the barriers between its various sections, and to establish a political community, that such a people solemnly proclaims (*Declaration* of 1791) the rights of egoistic man separated from his fellow men and from the community. ... This fact becomes still more puzzling when we see that the political emancipators go so far as to reduce citizenship, and the *political community*, to a mere means for maintaining these so-called rights of man, that, therefore, the *citoyen* is declared to be the servant of egotistic *homme*, that the sphere in which man acts as a communal being is degraded to a level below the sphere in which he acts as a partial being.[2]

1

According to Marx, the revolutionary declaration of equal rights is puzzling because of the contradiction in the subject, namely the antithesis between the political subject who declares rights and the social or private subject (the two are equivalent in civil society) who is authorized by rights, and thus between the basis and the content of rights. The declaration of rights is a political act; it is *the* political act. In declaring rights, the political community creates itself in opposition to regimes of traditional domination. Because politically declared rights authorize the apolitical ("egoistical") human beings of civil society, however, the declaration of rights is at the same time the degradation of politics, its debasement to a mere means. It places the political community – which is "the true content and end"[3] – into the service of "egoistic man separated from his fellow men and from the community." The puzzle of the bourgeois declaration of equal rights is the puzzle of a self-reversal: it is the political act that authorizes apolitical human beings and thereby politics' deauthorization of itself – the politics of depoliticization. The revolutionary declaration of rights is the first and last political act: the relinquishing of political power by means of politics – politics for the last time.

Marx believes that "The puzzle is easily solved."[4] This solution amounts to the claim that "Political revolution is a revolution of civil society."[5] And this means that "Political emancipation was at the same time the emancipation of civil society from politics."[6] The puzzle is that the bourgeois revolution degrades political community into a means for the rights of apolitical human beings. The solution to this puzzle is the fact that bourgeois [*bürgerliche*] politics emancipates civil [*bürgerliche*] society from politics through the declaration of rights. Bourgeois politics assumes civil society as its "natural basis" and henceforth operates "on the presupposition of its existence."[7] It is governance as the administration of society. In other words, bourgeois politics is the "police."[8]

Marx seeks the – simple – solution to the puzzle of the bourgeois revolution in its effect, which he views as its secret goal. With the declaration of rights, the bourgeois revolution "degrades" politics into a means because it wants to make civil society the presupposition for politics and thereby to free it from politics. This simple solution, however, is too simple, because the puzzle of the bourgeois revolution does not merely consist in understanding why it degrades politics, but rather – and more fundamentally – in *how* it does this. In other words, the puzzle of the bourgeois revolution consists in understanding how it degrades politics *through the declaration of rights*. According to Marx, the equal rights declared by the bourgeois revolution are the decisive mechanism for politically producing civil society. It is therefore this mechanism, the

2

mechanics of rights, that must be understood if the puzzle of the bourgeois revolution is to be solved. Neither its ill effects – civil society with its new forms of domination (exploitation and normalization) – nor its good intentions, which, conversely, liberalism opposes to these ill effects, namely dignity, autonomy, self-determination, and so forth, can provide a solution to the puzzle of the bourgeois revolution. This puzzle requires an examination of the form of rights: of rights *as form*.

My thesis is that we cannot grasp the content, aims, and effects of the bourgeois declaration of rights without having understood how it operates. The "how" of rights has precedence over its "what," "why," and "to what end." The form of rights comes before their content, goal, and effect,[9] because this form is not neutral.

Rights are a specific form of normativity: to have a right means to have a justified and therefore binding claim. And to declare a right means to grant a justified and therefore binding claim. The bourgeois declaration of rights understands this to mean that a justified claim can only be a claim as equal. That is not all, however. For at the same time, it understands this normative justification of a claim in such a way that the claim is thereby transformed into something "factual" that is prior to and separate from the political community. This holds for everything to which we have a right: for example, by giving us rights, the bourgeois state allows "private property, education, occupation, to act in their way, i.e., as private property, as education, as occupation, and to exert the influence of their special nature. Far from abolishing these real distinctions, the state only exists on the presupposition of their existence."[10] For Marx, this is the basic feature of the mechanism of bourgeois rights. Contrary to what Marx repeatedly says (and something for which he was repeatedly criticized),[11] this mechanism does *not* consist in the justification of egoism (in general, egoism is not a category of legal theory or social criticism but rather an ethical category, a category of morality). Instead, this mechanism is the *naturalization of the social* (its transformation into something factual, the act of presupposing it), which happens when it becomes the content of legal claims.

The equal rights declared by the bourgeois revolution are a particular, completely new kind of normative mechanism: they combine normativity and facticity. They are normatively regulative in securing equality, but they do this by – actively – presupposing factual conditions that they thereby remove from political governance. The normativity of bourgeois rights consists in their creation of a pre- and extra-normative facticity. The form of bourgeois rights expresses an upheaval in normativity's mode of being. *As a result*, the declaration of rights is the mechanism that (as Marx maintains) gives rise to civil society and in so doing degrades politics into the police, into administration. In order to solve the puzzle of the bourgeois revolution – the puzzle of the political self-degradation of politics, the puzzle of the emancipation of civil society from politics through the emancipation of politics – we must understand the peculiar mechanism of bourgeois rights. We must understand the radical, onto-logical redefinition of normativity that lies at the basis of the bourgeois form of rights.

It is therefore the puzzle posed by Marx, and not his "simple" solu-tion, that leads the way for our inquiry: it leads the way to an analysis of the bourgeois form of equal rights. As we proceed, we will have to subject liberalism to critical analysis,[12] since liberalism is based on the insight that the declaration of equal rights is absolutely constitutive for the bourgeois revolution's redefinition of politics and society. Yet, at the same time, liberalism is unable to understand that – and how – the bourgeois form of rights precisely degrades politics into the police and produces the "actual inequalities" of society. Liberalism counters the actual social and political effect of rights with its good ("moral") inten-tions. This is what liberalism calls criticism, namely confronting existing conditions with good, justified claims. With this superficial notion of criticism, it skips the analysis of form. It is through form, however, that intentions produce effects.

Marx calls this kind of criticism vulgar: "Vulgar criticism falls into ... [a] *dogmatic error*." It criticizes by "*fighting* with its subject matter." "True criticism, by contrast, shows the inner genesis" of the things it criticizes. It "describes the act of its birth, ... it *explains* them, it compre-hends their genesis, their necessity."[13] The true analysis and true criticism of bourgeois rights are one and the same. True analysis is simultaneously true criticism because it discerns the – ontological, and not historical – genealogy of bourgeois rights. It confronts bourgeois rights not with their moral intention, but with their genesis, their basis. This means, however, that criticism is able to discover the other of bourgeois rights in their basis. According to this thesis, the basis of the bourgeois form of rights is the modern upheaval in the ontology of normativity. According to the program of true criticism, the ontological upheaval of modern law must therefore simultaneously call the form of bourgeois rights – which it establishes – into question; indeed it must undo and destroy this form. True genealogical criticism reveals a contradiction in the modern upheaval of law: it establishes *and* denies bourgeois law. True criticism, which proceeds genealogically, develops a radical objection *to* the exist-ing conditions *out of* the existing conditions.

4

Criticism of the bourgeois form of rights consists in demonstrating the claim that it cannot grasp its own basis. In being traced back to its ground, the bourgeois form of rights gets buried as a result. A new right then becomes possible: a right of new, other rights; a right of rights that do not presuppose anything; rights that do not depoliticize what they entitle. It is true that the bourgeois revolution "resolves civil life into its component parts, without revolutionising these components themselves or subjecting them to criticism."[14] The rights of new right, in contrast, are revolutionary because they transform what they entitle. Critical understanding must lay the ground for this transformation.

* * *

The way to achieve this goal proceeds in four steps that can be summarized in four theses:

1 The modern form of rights breaks with the tradition of classical law. Classical rights are fair shares, while modern rights are legal claims to natural claims. The modern form of rights opens law up to the non-legal. Rights are situated at the limit of law.

2 The modern form of rights expresses a fundamental upheaval in the ontology of law. If all law is defined by the difference between form and matter, modern law is the materialist self-reflection of its form, establishing the difference between law and non-law within the law.

3 The bourgeois form of rights is law's self-reflection in the mode of its denial. This constitutes the positivism of bourgeois rights, namely that they reify law's non-legal substance into something positively given. Bourgeois rights authorize the subject's private self-will and thereby engender bourgeois society's new forms of domination.

4 A new revolution of rights that breaks with their bourgeois form must overcome their positivism: it must carry out the self-reflection of modern law [Rechts] dialectically. It thus establishes a new right [Recht]. The dialectic of activity and passivity in political judgment forms its basis: new right is the right of counter-rights.

This book will proceed by combining historical description and conceptual argumentation. On the one hand, it is a matter of grasping bourgeois law [Recht] today through readings of relevant texts. On the other hand, it is a matter of clarifying the basic concepts of the philosophy of law and developing them dialectically. The description of bourgeois law is prominent in parts I and III: part I explicates the historical difference between the classical and modern conception of rights; part

III examines the ideological presuppositions and social consequences of their bourgeois form. In contrast, parts II and IV foreground conceptual reflection: part II analyzes the relation of form and matter that is constitutive of law, and elucidates the concept of its modern self-reflection; part IV outlines a theory of the judgment that establishes rights by reflecting on the structure of political subjectivity. The social-historical description of bourgeois law and the conceptual unfolding of the dialectic of law are distinct projects. However, they refer to each other. Their connection is the critique of rights.

Part I

History: The Legalization of the Natural

> Here we find ourselves in the "Copernican" moment of the history
> of the science of law, at the boundary between two worlds. A new
> social order is born, whose nucleus will become an individual right
> that is developed entirely from the concept of *potestas*, elevated to
> the dignity of a right.[1]

Modern legal theory and philosophy of law were the first to speak of
rights that belong to the individual and which the individual can exercise
for his or her own ends. For this reason, rights here are also first characterized as a person's property, endowment, or capacity. It is only at this
point that talk of "subjective" or "individual" rights could flourish. At
the same time, rights are an essential way of formally defining private or
civil law. Rights are primarily defined as claims that enable one person to
impose an obligation on another person. The form of rights is therefore
as old as the institution of civil law: they have existed ever since there
were contractually regulated exchange relations. Both of these observations must be borne in mind at the same time. Together, they define the
historicity of rights: rights are a form that can only be understood in
historical terms.

We are concerned with the modern form of rights. This modern form
cannot be understood by merely considering the continual formulations
expressed by civil law regarding the normativity of exchange relationships that, beyond mere family arrangements, pervade all societies: the
modern form of rights alters social exchange relationships so fundamentally that no concept of their normative regulation – obligation, freedom,
equality, authority [*Herrschaft*] – is able to retain its traditional meaning.
Nor can the modern form of rights be understood by attempting to derive

it directly from the basic concept of modernity's normative order, from the concept of the self-determining, autonomous subject: the modern form of rights does not exist because there are autonomous subjects, but autonomous subjects exist because the modern form of rights does. The modern form of rights results from a radical transformation of law. This transformation is radical because it concerns the *meaning of law*. With the modern form of rights, the concept of law, indeed the concept of normativity, acquires a new, fundamentally different meaning. The transformation in the conception of rights, which were traditionally expressed in terms of private law, thus does not remain restricted to this domain: "law" *as such* thereby comes to mean something else, and hence rights in their modern form only exist beyond private law.

A radical transformation of law takes place in the modern form of rights. The de-moralization [*Entsittlichung*] of law expresses this in negative terms: traditionally, law is the moral or rational order of the fair share in which each receives his or her own – his or her right. The modern administration of rights, however, must be defined in positive terms. It consists in the reconfiguration of the basic relation between the legal and the pre- or extra-legal, between norm and nature. In the modern form of rights, law becomes the process of juridification: rights are the mechanisms of an incessant legalization of the natural.

— 1 —

A PHILOSOPHICAL HISTORY OF RIGHT'S FORM

Historians debate who should be regarded as the first author responsible for formulating the new – contemporary or modern – way of talking about a right as a person's "power" [*Macht*]. In a series of influential essays, the legal historian Michel Villey maintains that William of Ockham was the first to have systematically understood a right in this manner. Ockham thus claims that:

> a right of using is a licit power [*potestas licita*] of using an external thing of which one ought not be deprived against one's will, without one's own fault and without reasonable cause, and if one has been deprived, one can call the depriver into court.[1]

> Lordship [*dominium*] is a principal human power of laying claim to and defending some temporal thing in a human court. "Human power" separates this lordship from the divine lordship.[2]

Villey's critics have cast doubt on whether these formulations by Ockham already amount to a break with tradition – something which is only supposed to have occurred with later authors.[3] At the same time, these critics have pointed out that similar formulations can already be found in "men who rediscovered the Digest and created the medieval science of Roman law."[4] However we date this break, though, it is undeniable that a distinction was established in the ideologically formative phase of modernity, between medieval nominalism, late scholasticism, and rational natural law. Indeed, Thomas Hobbes already invokes this terminological distinction as a frequently overlooked and yet obvious conceptual fact. Reviewing its history two hundred years later, Friedrich Carl von Savigny again cites it as a common, self-evident insight.

9

This distinction involves two different meanings of the term "right" [*Recht*]: the difference between *right* [*Recht*] as a justified or prevalent regime of laws and *a right* [*Recht*] as a person's claim. In explaining the title of his *The Rights of War and Peace*, Hugo Grotius formulates this distinction as follows:

> For Right in this Place signifies meerly that which is just, and that too rather in a negative than a positive Sense. . . . There is another signification of the word right, different from this, but yet arising from it, which relates directly to the person. In which sense, right is a moral quality annexed to the person, justly entitling him to possess some particular privilege, or to perform some particular act [C.M. - *qualitas moralis personae competens ad aliquid juste habendum vel agendum*]. This right is annexed to the person.[5]

Francisco Suárez explains the two "different meanings of the term 'right'" in a similar way:

> Sometimes "right" means an ethical claim [C.M. – *moralem facultatem*] to a thing or the right to a thing, whether we are dealing with an actual right of ownership or merely with the right to share in something. Right, in this sense, is the proper object of justice. . . . But "right" also characterizes law, which is a norm for ethically good action and which establishes a certain consistency in things. In this sense . . . , "right" coincides with "law." To put this concisely, we can call the first meaning "useful right" [*ius utile*] and the other meaning "ethical right" [*ius honestum*], or the first meaning could be called "real right" [*reale*] and the second meaning "lawful right" or "legal norm" [*legale*].[6]

Hobbes draws on a terminological distinction between law and right to capture the same conceptual difference[7] – a distinction that Hobbes introduces as a translation of the Roman distinction of *lex* and *ius*, getting to the heart of the decisive contrast, for him, between right as binding law and *a right* as freedom:

> For though they that speak of this subject use to confound *Jus* and *Lex*, *Right* and *Law*, yet they ought to be distinguished, because RIGHT consisteth in liberty to do, or to forbear; whereas LAW determineth and bindeth to one of them: so that Law, and Right, differ as much, as Obligation and Liberty; which in one and the same matter are inconsistent.[8]

> I find the words *Lex Civilis* and *Jus Civile*, that is to say, *Law* and *Right Civil*, promiscuously used for the same thing, even in the most learned authors; which nevertheless ought not to be so. For *Right* is *Liberty*, namely that liberty which the civil law leaves us: but *Civill Law* is an

Obligation, and takes from us the liberty which the law of nature gave us. ... Insomuch as *Lex* and *Jus*, are as different as *Obligation* and *Liberty*.[9]

Since German has no equivalent for this terminological distinction, "Let us call" what others refer to as *ius* or right[10] "a right of this person synonymous with privilege; some call it right in a subjective sense," as Savigny puts it two hundred years after Hobbes.[11] Right [*Recht*] "in the objective sense" is law [*das* Recht]: right [*Recht*] as governing statute [*Gesetz*]. Right in the subjective sense is *a* right, in other words, a claim that a person or "subject" can make which is normatively binding or, as Kant puts it, the "moral capacity for putting others under obligations."[12]
None of the modern authors who distinguished between right as law [*Gesetz*] and right as claim considered this distinction to be a new conceptual insight. Indeed, for the most part they never even maintained that a terminological innovation was involved. They instead presented the distinction as though it were already established by Roman legal practice or by Aristotelian-Scholastic legal theory. Yet such a distinction had never been made explicitly in practice or in theory, prior to modern legal thought. The distinction between right and a right, between law and right,[13] between right [*Recht*] as law [*Gesetz*] and right as claim, "right" [*Recht*] in the objective and in the subjective sense, seems as ancient as it is modern: ancient in *what* it says, in its content; but modern to the extent *that* it is said, that this content is explicitly formulated and established. On the one hand, it seems as if the distinction between right as law and right as claim is always already given. On the other hand, to *make* this distinction is to do something fundamentally new, with far-reaching consequences. In other words, this distinction is more rhetorically than semantically novel, more an act of distinguishing than an issue of content. In that case, however, can it still be the same distinction?

The Reversal of Primacy

Leo Strauss firmly declared Hobbes to be the original author of the distinction between law [*Gesetz*] and claim. Accordingly, Hobbes' distinction between "law" and "right"[14] – despite its derivation from the Roman distinction between *lex* and *ius* – must be regarded as a radical "innovation" that enabled him to definitively differentiate "modern" politics from its "ancient" understanding.[15] Strauss' argument for Hobbes as the original author of the modern distinction between law and right [*Anspruch*] (and

11

thus not Grotius, whom he viewed as still bound to tradition on this critical question) maintains that Hobbes was the first to understand it as "fundamental." In other words, Hobbes was the first to understand that this distinction concerns the *basis* of the legal system. For Hobbes "fundamentally distinguished" law and right to indicate precisely that "modern political philosophy takes 'right' as its starting point, whereas classical political philosophy has 'law'" (while Grotius still thought that the "moral quality by virtue of which a person has a right to or can do something [*ius proprie aut stricte dictum*]," which he distinguishes from right as law, "presupposes *lex*"[16]):

> Because Hobbes was the first to distinguish with incomparable clarity between "right" and "law," in such a way that he sought to prove the State as primarily founded on "right," of which "law" is a mere consequence [. . . .] – Hobbes is for that very reason the founder of modern political philosophy.[17]

Strauss' historical argument for Hobbes as the original author of the distinction between law and right [*Anspruch*] is thus based on his thesis concerning the *point* of this distinction: the reason for making it is to "subordinate law to right."[18]

Regardless of what we think about Strauss' suggested chronology, it forms the systematic substance of his interpretation of Hobbes. In distinguishing law and right [*Anspruch*], we are thus concerned with nothing less than a new response to the question of priority, and hence with the question of basis: at issue is "the supplanting of the primacy of obligation [C.M. – which the law imposes] by the primacy of claim."[19] By isolating the claim [*Anspruch*] in this manner, *over and against* obligation and law, it becomes the "fundamental moral fact" *prior to* law.[20] According to Strauss, this therefore means that modern politics begins by drawing the distinction between law and claim. To make this distinction *is* the modern act of revolution: "The fundamental change from an orientation by natural duties to an orientation by natural rights."[21]

Leo Strauss sees the basic process of liberalism at work in the reversal of primacy between law [*Gesetz*] and claim, between law [*Recht*] and rights.[22] Liberalism means thinking law, or the legal system, on the basis of rights, or from the individual. Liberalism is "that political doctrine which regards as the fundamental political fact the rights, as distinguished from the duties, of man."[23] Liberalism views the distinction between law and a right as the revolutionary act that separates modernity's political order from tradition, because, with this distinction, the right as claim is first *set apart* from law as statute (the legal claim is no longer an effect of the legal system, as it traditionally was, but stands alone), so as to ultimately become *prior* to this system.[24] The semantic content of the distinction between *ius* and *lex*, or "law" and "right,"[25] may be an ancient one and merely analytical, a distinction between two modes or perspectives in which we can speak of "right." However, the rhetorical *meaning* or *purpose* of the distinction between law and a right – as Leo Strauss interprets liberalism, whose history accordingly begins with Hobbes – is to establish the claim as the basis of law [*Gesetz*], or rights as the basis of law [*Recht*].

But how can there be a legal claim that is able to normatively bind others *before* and thus independent of law's legal order? Is not the idea of *a* right before *law* "nonsense upon stilts,"[26] as Jeremy Bentham said of the rights of man, or, as Raymond Geuss puts it, "white magic"?[27]

Along with Strauss, Hans Kelsen has also objected to the concept of rights, arguing that liberalism establishes a "dualism" – of claim and law – which supposedly reverses the explanatory relations between them:

> The original intention of the dualism of objective and subjective right [*Recht*] expresses the thought that the latter precedes the former both logically and temporally: subjective rights emerge first (such as private property, the primary prototype of a subjective right), and only later do we also find objective right as a state order that protects, recognizes, and secures the subjective rights that have emerged independently from it.[28]

Subjective right precedes objective right, the claim precedes law. For Kelsen, this basic thesis of liberal dualism has an obvious "ideological function": it is supposed "to conceal the socio-economically decisive function" of capitalist private property.[29] However, the priority of claim over law is also conceptually incoherent. It encapsulates the aporia of modern natural law [*Naturrechts*] that lies at the basis of liberal dualism: the paradox of a natural legal claim – the idea of a claim that is supposed to naturally occur of its own accord *and* at the same time is supposed to be obligatory.

The idea of a natural right [*Rechts*] is paradoxical because it is the idea of a right [*Rechts*] before law [*Recht*]. "Rights before law," however, either (i) are *not rights* at all, or (ii) do *not* really exist *before law* at all.

(i) Either the following is valid: if claims, as natural, are supposed to precede law, there are no rights. This is clearly Spinoza's position: the talk that I have a natural "right" can only negatively mean that no one else has the right to hinder me – not because others are obligated to refrain from hindering me due to my legitimate claim, but because we stand beyond or, better, *on this side of* law *and* obligation. Natural right

13

before law is the semblance of a right because it has no corresponding obligation:

> [Everyone] always endeavors as far as in him lies to preserve his own being and (since every man has right to the extent that he has power), whether he be wise or ignorant, whatever he endeavors and does, he endeavors and does by the sovereign right of Nature. From this it follows that Nature's right and established order under which all men are born and for the most part live, forbids only those things that no one desires and no one can do.[30]

"There is no normativity in nature,"[31] and for this reason, too, there are no natural rights.

(ii) Or the following is valid: if rights are supposed to be natural claims, then they do not precede law. This is how Kant understood the matter: on his account, individuals admittedly already have "private" rights prior to the positive legal system of the "civil constitution." "What belongs to each is only secured, but not actually settled and determined" by such a constitution. ". . . Prior to a civil constitution (or in *abstraction* from it), external objects that are mine or yours must therefore assumed to be possible."[32] The existence of private rights here has a "provisional"[33] character (in the literal sense of the word): it remains in force "as long as it does not have the sanction of public law, since it is not determined by public (distributive) justice and secured by an authority putting this right into effect."[34] Private claims on what is mine or yours are thus pre-juridical (and in this sense natural) insofar as they are not under the legal protection of a public authority. In the crucial normative sense, however, they are already constituted by right [*Recht*] as law [*Gesetz*]: "for the obligation here arises from a universal rule."[35] Even natural rights are based on law, according to Kant: on a law that exists prior to and independent of all public legislation.

Either natural rights that precede law [*Recht*] do not yield any obligations, and for that reason are not really rights at all, and therefore not law's basis. *Or* natural rights that precede law are actually rights that are binding, but in this case are constituted according to a legal rule and thus, again, not the basis of law.

The corollary of this critique of the liberal "dualism" of a right and of law, which first renders rights independent from law and then explains the latter's basis, is expressed by Kelsen as the insight that rights only exist in *juridical relationships*:

> Thus if the concept of subjective right and the subjective bearer of rights reveals any ideological function . . . , all that emerges are juridical

relations between human beings, or more precisely between statements of fact regarding human behavior that are connected to each other by the juridical norm, as its content. The juridical relationship is a relation between two statements of fact, one of which is a human behavior defined as a juridical obligation, while the other is a human behavior defined as an entitlement.[36]

Juridical relationships are the starting point, not rights. This means, first, that rights exist *in relation to* obligations; rights designate positions in a relationship that also includes other corresponding normative relations or, to put it simply: positions of obligation.[37] And, at the same time and contrary to how they are understood in terms of natural law, this means that entitlements can also only be grounds for obligations *within* particular juridical relationships: where juridical relationships exist, it is possible to say that on their basis someone is obligated to behave in a certain way *because* someone else is entitled to expect such behavior and to demand it. Where juridical relationships exist, rights can be the basis for obligations. *That* juridical relationships *do exist* – the premise of this relational basis – does not for its part depend on the existence of a rule or a law [*Gesetz*] that links the two kinds of behavior to each other in this specific normative way. According to Alexandre Kojève, it is only "the intervention of a third human being, C, impartial and disinterested" as representative of the "legal rule" which forms the "necessary or 'essential' constitutive element":

> This intervention [Tr. – of a third human being] is the specifically juridical element. It is this which confers a juridical character to the situation as a whole. . . . In this case, and in this case alone, we will be able to say the following:

> a) A *has the droit* [Tr. – the right] to act as he does; his action and the effect of this action constitute his *subjective right*, and he himself is the *subject* of this *droit*, [and] therefore a *subject of droit* in general (or a *juridical person*, either *physical* or *moral*).[38]

Rights only exist in juridical relationships, and juridical relationships only exist under laws [*Gesetzen*]: thus Kelsen's twofold move here – similar to Wittgensteinian linguistic therapy – traces rights back to their logical or grammatical place in our juridical discourse. The revolutionary claim of a liberalism founded on natural law, which on Strauss' interpretation is supposed to be expressed by the distinction of "right" and "law,"[39] is that rights are the basis of law [*Recht*] or statute [*Gesetz*], and this claim is therefore rejected by Kelsen as ungrammatical and meaningless. To put Kelsen's thesis into sharper contrast: rights can never be the basis of law, since they are only normatively binding, and thus obligatory, on the basis of law.

As a result, Kelsen concludes that the conception of subjective right as an independent category must be abandoned: subjective right is only a "reflex of legal obligation." It can be "reduced to objective [right], attributed once more to objective [right]."[40] For Kelsen, to distinguish subjective right from objective right amounts to claiming that the former is the basis of the latter. Because that claim is meaningless, we can dispense with subjective right (in other words, a claim that is conceptually distinct from law) as a legal category – a misleading construction with ideological intentions.

However, this conclusion is wrong. For Kelsen's alternative – subjective right as ultimate basis *or* as mere reflex – is a false dichotomy: it misses crucial insights into the modern distinction between *ius* and *lex*, right and law,[41] between *a* right and law [*Recht*], between claim and law [*Gesetz*]. To understand this distinction, we must grasp its precise significance and the reason for this significance, namely that it frees the legal claim from the derivative position of being a mere reflex, *without* at the same time attributing an authoritative force to it that would form the basis for rights. We thus require a different understanding of the modern declaration of the primacy of rights over law, which Strauss justifiably considered to be the principle that inaugurates modern politics: an understanding that does *not* view the "priority of right over law" (Strauss) to mean that the claim forms the normative basis for law. For, conversely, Spinoza's argument is that a claim does not have any normatively binding force *prior to* law, and thus we arrive at Kant's argument that any claim has normatively binding force only *by virtue of* law.

The basic thesis of this alternative understanding is that the modern priority of rights over law is a redefinition not of law's basis, but of its form. The modern distinction between *a* right and law is the revolutionary act of modern politics: not because it prioritizes rights as the basis of law, but because it radically transforms law. The modern distinction between a right and law expresses a *revolution of legal form*. It defines law as *the right of rights*.

A New Form of Government: "Modern Roman Law"

This is already the meaning of Savigny's distinction between the two conceptions of right, right in the subjective sense and right in the objective sense. For Savigny himself, and not merely his critics, also

16

understood subjective right in relational terms. The basic concept of Savigny's legal theory is the juridical relationship, and not subjective right.[42] Thus for Savigny, the concept of subjective right is not at all supposed to designate a prior ground at rest in itself, on which the legal system can be established. Rather, Savigny employs the concept of subjective right to characterize the specific new form of currently existing juridical practice.

The "Roman Law" to which Savigny's title refers (in what follows, this will be capitalized [Tr. – and in quote marks] to distinguish it from the juridical era of Roman law, or law in ancient Rome) is civil or private law, which he sharply distinguishes from public law: "The first has for its object-matter the state, that is the organic manifestation of the people; the second the totality of jural relations which surround the individual man."[43] Private law is the "jural relation . . . as a relation between person and person, determined by a rule of law."[44] It is only here that we find "right in the subjective sense." There can be no individual rights here, and public law is operative as the obligation-imposing statute, since "in public law the whole appears as the end, the individual as subordinate."[45] In contrast, the private juridical relationship between persons is a matter of rights as an individual person's power, quality, competence, claim, or freedom. These (subjective) rights are based on an (objective) legal rule. According to Savigny, the distinction between the two usages of the term "right" should thus not be understood to mean that both are considered to be normatively independent of each other, which would then entail that the claim has normative priority over law. Rather, Savigny is concerned with differentiating two *domains* or *types* of law that are sharply distinct in their basic relations: on one side, public law, the only place where the normative structure of law and obligation prevails; on the other side, private or civil law, in which mutual equals have claims on and obligations to each other. While rights cannot exist in the individual's public or political relationship to his or her community (since in this relation of membership there is no reciprocity or opposition: the community is just the person him- or herself in another form), private law is the domain of rights: for Savigny, private law is the form of law that is exclusively concerned with the rights of individuals. While the community is the individual's goal in public law, in private law the individual's claim becomes the goal of the legal system.

In restricting rights to the domain of private law, we can clearly see the limits of Savigny's line of thought: he misconstrues the logic and dynamic that were inscribed in the modern conception of rights *from the very beginning* and simultaneously driven beyond the domain of private

17

law. In what follows, this will be shown in detail.[46] At the same time, however, Savigny defines modern private law in such a way that the concept of law is utterly transformed. Private law's power to transform law itself is a direct consequence of its new social significance. For modern "Roman Law" is already distinguished from traditional law by the fact that it defines not merely a limited domain, but the totality of society and its normatively regulated relations. "Private law exists in all societies," explains Franz Böhm, it is "an element of the most diverse social orders. But it is only one element, not the whole of social order."[47] In contrast, private law in modernity comes to define the whole of society; this is why Böhm calls modern civil society "private-law society." Bourgeois society's totalization of private law, making it into the fundamental principle of society, also simultaneously generalizes the functional definition of private law, something emphasized by Savigny: the securing of the individual's rights becomes the new *functional definition of law in general*. Law now *exists so that* rights may be secured.

For this reason, Savigny's "Modern Roman Law" is not merely a special domain of law that is concerned with the claims of individuals. In fact, through its social totalization, it fundamentally reinterprets the category of the claim as a legal concept. This revolutionizes the concept of law, making manifest the modern distinction between *a* right and law: the modern declaration of the primacy of the claim – the primacy of the claim over law [*Gesetz*] – signifies a *redefinition* of law [*Recht*]. Distinguishing between claim and law [*Gesetz*] as two meanings of "right" [*Recht*] amounts to establishing a new concept of law *and* of claim: a new understanding of the *relation* between claim and law [*Gesetz*]; an understanding in which claim has priority over law or precedes law, because now the task, indeed *the function of law in general, is to secure claims*.[48]

The modern primacy of rights is thereby understood in a manner that is *rechtsimmanent* (Niklas Luhmann) [Tr. – "immanent to law"]. Strauss and Kelsen understood the ideological program of natural law liberalism to be its wish to base law on rights and to base rights on the subject; "the basis of rights was now the individual, conceived of as subject."[49] In contrast, Savigny's choice of the title "Modern Roman Law" provides a perspective from which we can understand the primacy of rights functionally, rather than normatively and thus concerned with grounding rights. The "rupture of subjective and objective right" is therefore a matter not of the "*source* of law" but of "legal *protection*,"[50] a matter not of the basis, but of the meaning and function of law. "Primacy of rights" means that law [*Recht*] – right [*Recht*] in general – is now a matter of safeguarding and securing rights. Law operates solely by safeguarding and securing juridical claims.

The talk of "natural rights" thereby comes to have a different meaning as well. If we understand the primacy of rights normatively, rights are deemed "natural" because they are supposed to precede law [*Gesetz*] and form its basis. Yet, as we have seen, modern natural law, in Spinoza or Kant, never grasped the connection between a right and law (even if both Strauss and Kelsen attribute this position to modern natural law and criticize it as the ideological primacy of rights). For this reason, talk of the natural when it comes to rights means something completely different from a source of right before law. Instead (as in the thesis we are about to consider), it is the *contents* of a claim that are natural, the aspirations that bourgeois private law, socially totalized, exists to safeguard and secure, according to Savigny. This thesis runs as follows: if the primacy of rights is to be understood functionally and not normatively, then natural rights are not law's basis but its matter. Aspirations and actions are natural, when law has functionally provided for their safeguarding and securing. To say that – according to its new modern definition – there is *nothing more* to law than rights means that law is a matter of *normatively* securing prior and given *natural* aspirations and actions (that is, ones existing before law). The primacy of rights is functional, not normative, but the functional understanding of the primacy of rights simultaneously entails a new conception of the normativity of law. It entails defining the normativity of law [*Recht*] by its *relation to* natural claims. The normativity of the modern right [*Recht*] of rights has the structure of a *legalization of the natural*.

Savigny's examination of "Modern Roman Law" focuses on the historical upheaval in private law. This is related to the thesis that private law today creates a *new concept of (subjective) right or the claim*: the "natural rights" talked about in modern theory are not a new class of rights. Above all, they are not pre-juridical rights that form the basis for law, but signify a radically new way to understand what rights are.

This new understanding combines two features:

(i) The *functional totalization of the claim*. The definition of modern law (as such or in general) is *the securing of rights*.
(ii) The *naturalization of the content* of rights. The modus operandi of modern law consists in the *legalization of the natural*.

The modern totalization of private law creates (i) a new understanding of law (all law secures rights), which (ii) implies a new understanding of rights: all rights legalize the natural. On Savigny's view, this new understanding of law and of rights begins in private law, but – contra Savigny – it is not limited to it. Modern private law establishes a new understanding of law [*Recht*] and of rights that is impelled beyond private law *according to its own concept* and from its own internal logic, since it inverts the meaning of law [*Gesetz*] in general by granting claims primacy over law. As I will show in the third part of this book, the modern conception of rights definitively includes private *and* public rights. As remains to be shown, however, we can only understand the new modern *meaning* of the concept of rights if we understand it on the basis of the historical upheaval of private law that marks the beginning of modernity.

Excursus: The Politics and History of Civil Law (Weinrib)

Why is the distinction between the two meanings of "right" [*Recht*] – between law [*Recht*] and a right – so fundamental in the modern conception of law? Because drawing this distinction means determining the modern conception of rights by radically redefining the relation between law [*Gesetz*] and claim. This redefinition is radical because it involves the relation of norm and nature (and because this relation, as will be shown, is constitutive of law[51]). – We thus have our question, and a provisional answer that remains to be further developed in what follows.

This answer is critical of two other common ways of defining law as claim. *First*, it clearly rejects the idea that the concept of a right (in the subjective sense of the word, namely a right which one has and exercises) can only be understood on the basis of a subject who is the bearer of rights: rights as claims are not a property of the subject, which the subject asserts and establishes. *Second*, however, rights are also misunderstood if, because of this, they are merely defined as a moment in the legal relationship between two persons. The step from rights as a property of the subject to rights as a moment in a relationship is correct, but insufficient. To stop here amounts to a depoliticization and a dehistoricization of the concept of rights.

This thesis is opposed to a theory that – in Ernest J. Weinrib's pointed formulation[52] – seeks to protect the "autonomy" of "the idea of private law" from its economic functionalization and from sociological critique. The goal of this theory is to conceive the legal relationship between a person who is entitled to something and a person who is correspondingly obligated as an independent relationship. In other words, this theory

20

aims to conceive such a legal relationship in the juridical "form" that it has itself established. It thus characterizes this relationship as a "direct," "immediate" relation between two persons, which is defined by a "correlation" of entitlement and obligation. Thought in purely immanent terms, this relation's "unity" is to be found in the correlation of law and duty, since this correlation entails that the basis for one person's responsibility, for that person's having to do something (having an obligation), and the basis for another's claim to something (having a right), is *the same*. On Weinrib's thesis, this is why the private legal relationship can only be understood on its own terms.

One aspect of this thesis is the irreducibility of legal obligation. In even their most elementary forms, private legal relationships between persons (such as relations of exchange) must become autonomous, independent of the motives that inclined individuals to enter into them (and of the social functions that fulfill their exchange relations). Exchange cannot exist without the normative correlation of entitlement and obligation, which bridges the distance, however minimal, between individual actions. To exchange something is completely different from handing things over at the same time. "It was here," writes Nietzsche on contractual relationships, "that *promises* were made."[53] The breeding of animals that can (and therefore may) promise is thus presupposed. To enter into exchange with someone always already means to recognize the equal normative status of that person (or, in other words, to recognize the other person as an equal). Instead of merely being an individual distinct from me, the other becomes a person equal to me, because she has something at her disposal that I want from her, and I have something at my disposal that she wants from me. Mutual recognition or the equality of persons is the necessary condition for the correlation of rights and obligations in the private legal relationship.

The recognition or equality of persons, however, which is presupposed in exchange, simultaneously exceeds every act of exchange: it is not merely relative, between the two of us, but general. In exchange, the normative status that I recognize in another is based not on *my* act of recognizing *you*, but on the application of a general rule that precedes this act. We are both equally subject to this rule, whose particular cases we thus equally constitute. The exchange relationship is a *private* legal one because it is a matter of the entitlements and obligations in a relationship between *individual* persons (who, as particular individuals, have different motives for entering into it). The exchange relationship is only a private *legal* one, however, because the persons bound to each other by entitlement and obligation fall under a general rule, which confers on

21

them their normative status as *equal* persons.[54] In a relationship between mere individuals, there are no entitlements and obligations at all. Such a relationship has no normative content on its own. Normativity (in the interactions between individuals) signifies equality, and equality requires generality: a rule or a law [*Gesetz*].

The force of obligation, which first makes one person's claim on another into an entitled claim, is therefore *not* to be explained (as Weinrib believes) on the basis of the "immediate," "direct" relationship between the two parties. In other words, this relationship (and thereby right in the subjective sense) is not autonomous: it is based on right [*Recht*] as law [*Gesetz*] (right in the objective sense).[55] Right as claim cannot be understood at all – claim is not understood as a *right* – without understanding that it is based on right as law. It only achieves its normativity on this basis. Savigny formulates this relationship, in which a basis is established, as follows:

> The decision upon the individual right [C.M.- in the subjective sense] is only possible by a reference of the particular matters of fact to a general rule by which the particular rights are governed. That rule we simply call *law* [Tr. – *Recht*] or law in general: some term it law in a general sense.[56]

One person's rights and claims vis-à-vis another are only possible on the basis of law, that is, on rules that are generally valid. In other words, a person's private rights vis-à-vis another are based on both persons' subjection to law [*Gesetz*]. As the correlational theory demonstrates, rights only exist in the legal relationship, but legal relationships only exist in normative orders whose generality is able to give rise to equality. The normativity of the private legal relationship is thus not autonomous, as the correlational theory claims, but is something that is done, an effect of law [*Gesetz*]. The normativity of the private legal relationship therefore has a political basis. For the relationship between the individual and law [*Gesetz*] is "political" because it is a relationship of membership, in which the individual takes part in a general order. This is the basis of private law. Private law is also called civil law, *ius civile*, because it is the law [*Recht*] of citizens who are equally under the law [*Gesetz*]; private law is political.[57]

If legal relationships between persons, in which rights exist as individual claims, are therefore political insofar as they arise on the basis of right as law, then the question of the form of the rights that individuals have over against each other leads to the political question of the form of the administration of law over individuals. Why does the legal system

grant an individual's claim on another? How does the legal system understand the normative force of the claim that it secures for a person in his
relation with another, and on what basis? To put this more generally and
fundamentally: *Why does law rule so as to give rise to rights? How does
law rule by giving rise to rights? And what gives rise to law – what kind
of politics, society, subjectivity – by giving rise to rights?*
This question concerns the relation between the legal system and
the claims of individuals against each other: it is concerned with how
the legal system understands what is at issue in the claims individuals
make against each other and therefore why these claims occur. This
question, however, has been answered in a variety of ways over the
course of history. The program of identifying *the one* suprahistorical
"idea of private law" (Weinrib)[58] can only refer to the abstract aspect
of the correlation of rights and duties within an already constituted
legal relationship. In contrast, the political question of how law rules,
in giving rise to such legal relationships with their legal claims, can
only be answered by noting that, in private law too, there are various
historical ways in which law rules, which must be conceptually distinguished from each other. As Savigny's reference to "the *Modern* Roman
Law," in contrast to correlational theory, succinctly makes clear, the
politicization of private law implies its historicity. *Law rules differently
in history*, it entitles differently in traditional and in "Modern Roman
Law."
It is important to note, however, that this differentiation is concerned
neither merely with content nor only with the goal of lawful creation
of legal claims. The historical differentiation indicated in Savigny's title
instead concerns *the form of rights* or *rights as form*. If, according to
Weinrib's definition, the form of rights is their essence; and if the essence
of rights consists in the normative force of claims (with Kant: the "capacity for putting others under obligations"), then we cannot define the
form of rights without grasping the nature of this normative force. The
normative force of rights, however, is based on *law* [*Recht*] and thus on
the individual's ("political") subjection to law [*Gesetz*]. To *only* analyze
rights by way of their correlative relations to obligations is thus not really
formal at all, but a mere formality. Such an analysis speaks of rights,
without grasping their normative force. For it wishes to speak of right
while excluding politics – an exclusion that Weinrib considers merely an
external agenda.[59] If, or *since*, their normative force is an essential feature
of the form of rights and since their normative force is political, because
it is based on law [*Gesetzes*] ruling over individuals, the form of rights
also changes with the historical transformation in the basic structure of

such rule. "The meaning of a term such as *a right* is theory-dependent [C.M. – and thus practice-dependent]": the form of rights changes with the theory and practice of juridical rule.[60]

* * *

There are three interpretative hypotheses for the modern character of rights:

1 The modern distinction between law and a right, between right as law [*Gesetz*] and as claim, declares the *primacy of rights* over law [*Recht*]. This constitutes its rhetorical, performative sense: the distinction of law [*Gesetz*] and claim wishes to invert this relationship or revolutionize law [*Recht*].

2 The declaration of the primacy of rights concerns the function of law, not its basis. The primacy of rights thus does not involve a substantive redefinition of the basis for laws [*Gesetze*], but radically redefines the *form of juridical normativity*.

3 By declaring the primacy of rights, the redefinition of the normativity of law revolutionizes the *relation of norm and nature*. The truth of modern natural law is to be found in the fact that the modern character of rights is concerned with the relation between natural claims and legal rules.

These three hypotheses suggest that we should initially (and for as long as possible) follow Niklas Luhmann's guideline for interpretation: subjective right should *not* be conceived on the basis of its reference to the subject, since it is doubtful "if naming the secret already reveals whether the function of this characteristic of law in subjective rights has anything to do with reference to the subject."[61] If Luhmann suggests that we instead see this function in a new way, as law's "self-regulation,"[62] this will be understood in what follows to mean that the modern primacy of rights indicates an upheaval in the basic relation of law to that which it regulates. The primacy of rights concerns the *way in which law is administered*: *how* law rules and *over what*. The subject, whom the modern formula ("subjective rights") regards as having rights, is the effect of this new way of administering rights – not its basis.

From Athens to London

According to Luhmann, the introduction of the modern category of rights "modifies the awareness of law" by breaking with the traditional idea of "right, or the just" (*ius sive iustum*). On this traditional view, law is "that which is justified by an objective order. Therefore, it is also interpreted as a derivative of *iustum*."[63] Luhmann explains this as follows:

> The sanction available via law is only a supplementary apparatus for an already existing order. *Ius*-semantics adheres to these guidelines and therefore interprets *ius* as justice to be administered. As a result, justice, in concrete terms, is that in a position which is due to *another*. In this specific positional *and* social sense, it is *relatio, mensura, commensuratio, aequalitas, adequatio*.[64]

Traditional law defines relations of reciprocity between entitlements and obligations that are themselves defined by essentially different positions in a stratified social order. In it, "diverse contributions, for example, those of the guardian and of the ward, those of the prince and of his advisers, coalesce into a legal relationship."[65] Claims and rights are here contributions, determined by social positions, to a relationship that is reciprocal, and to this extent just. If, in contrast, legal claims in modern times are "defined as *facultas*, as capability, as formative power,"[66] they are thereby released from such relations of reciprocal justice. The modern character of rights is unjust (according to the standard of traditional law). It has the character of a thoroughgoing de-moralization of law.

Luhmann describes this process by distinguishing two types of law: traditional moral law and modern law. Yet we can better understand the specific difference of the modern category of rights if we expand our view to include a third regime that carries out the *transition* between moral and modern law. In the history of philosophy, this occurs in Roman law. For Roman law indeed adopts the traditional moral code as *ius sive iustum*: "Justice is the constant and perpetual wish to render everyone his due [*jus suum cuique*]."[67] This is not the whole story, however. If we follow the argument that Michel Villey developed in a series of essays, it becomes clear instead that a de-moralization of law already begins in Roman law itself. This does not at all mean that Roman law should be understood as a prototype of modern law. Contrary to a (specifically German) tradition of legal criticism from the early Hegel to Heidegger, which plays off Athens against Rome, and thereby combines law in Rome with law in Western European modernity into a complex whole, Villey's work aims to clarify the radical difference between Roman and modern law – which for him, including the idea of human rights,[68] seemed to be a decline in the Roman awareness of law. The Roman de-moralization of law does not anticipate the modern conception of rights, but, conversely, first allows us to recognize them in their radical innovation.

To demonstrate this, in what follows I will develop a sharply stylized outline of three regimes of private law, which can be situated in three distinctive locales in the history of philosophy: Athens, Rome, and London. In doing so, I am concerned not with historical accuracy (I am therefore not claiming that *this is how it was* in these three places at a certain time), but with the conceptual distinction of three models of private law. I draw this distinction with one goal in mind, namely to allow the specific feature of that legal system which has become central in the modern category of rights to emerge. I am therefore concerned with the upheaval in the form of law, the upheaval in its normativity and rule, which the modern character of rights brings about and expresses. This character provides a completely new answer to two questions: how (and what) apportions or distributes law? And how (or to what extent) does law rule and is law enforced? The modern character of rights revolutionizes how law is distributed and rules: the modern right of rights *enables self-preservation* (chapter 2) and *allows choice* (chapter 3).

— 2 —

INTEREST IN SELF-PRESERVATION

To understand different legal systems, we should first ask: how is law apportioned or distributed? To put this more precisely: what does it mean to say that law safeguards the respectively obligation-imposing claims of individuals? And how does law understand the nature of these claims? How does such safeguarding define the equality of law [*Recht*]? And how does this determine the concept of law [*Gesetz*]?

From Share to Power

1 *Athens*

Greek legal theory grasps the concept of a right – as Aristotle puts it in the fifth book of the *Nicomachean Ethics* – in its definition of "corrective" justice, "corresponding to the two classes of private transactions, those which are voluntary and those which are involuntary."[1] It is essential that transactions regulated by corrective justice involve a relationship between equals. Such justice does not involve the relationship to an "officer."[2] Corrective justice constitutes the field of private law and applies to both voluntary and involuntary transactions. In other words, it applies to "the interchange of services . . . in the form of Reciprocity," in which the parties concerned exchange goods with one another. And it also applies to transactions in which one party has injured another, and where the resulting damage must now be corrected.

What justice means here is revealed in this second case, in the rectification of damage or loss: establishing or securing a state of equality, a "mean by way of arithmetical proportion between the greater and the

27

less." "And thus . . . Justice in Rectification will be the mean between loss and gain."[3] This rectification of equality can also be described as a way for each to receive *his share* – or, to put it simply, *his right* [Tr. – *sein Recht*]:

> Thus the just is a sort of mean, inasmuch as the judge is a medium between the litigants. Now the judge restores equality: if we represent the matter by a line divided into two unequal parts, he takes away from the greater segment that portion by which it exceeds one-half of the whole line, and adds to it the lesser segment. When the whole has been divided into two halves, people then say that *each "has their share,"* having got what is equal.[4]

Aristotle's conception of one person's right vis-à-vis another is that a person has the right to *his own*. In the case of loss, a judge corrects this right by awarding restitution to the aggrieved party, so that the latter thereby recoups his just or equal share:

> to have more than one's own is called gaining, and to have less than one had at the outset is called losing, as for instance in buying and selling, and all other transactions sanctioned by law; while if the result of the transaction is neither an increase nor a decrease, but exactly what the parties had of themselves, they say *they "have their own"* and have neither lost nor gained. Hence Justice in involuntary transactions is a mean between gain and loss in a sense: it is to have after the transaction an amount equal to the amount one had before it.[5]

The right that one party has is his own as equal share. The individual's claim is the just share, which is due him according to the rules of equal distribution.

This is just as applicable to the voluntary transaction between persons in exchange, in which justice does not exclusively require providing restitution for a loss, but can also be satisfied by simply engaging in a quid pro quo with the other party. To be sure, equality cannot be understood here in arithmetical terms (as is the case in restitution, where the loss suffered is rectified: "For it makes no difference whether a good man has defrauded a bad man or a bad man a good one").[6] Proportional justice, however, which determines the exchange of different goods, has precisely the same meaning: it produces a *state of equality* – a state in which it can be said that, with his just share, *each has received his own*.

> There will therefore be reciprocal proportion [C.M. – in exchange] when the products have been equated, so that as farmer is to shoemaker, so may the shoemaker's product be to the farmer's product. And when

28

they exchange their products they must reduce them to the form of a proportion, otherwise one of the two extremes will have both of the excesses; whereas *when they have their own*, they then are equal, and can form an association together, because equality in this sense can be established in their case.[7]

The demands that individuals make on each other are legal claims, which they are entitled to make against one another, if the goal is for each to "have their own." Similarly, in contract and indemnity law, both exchange and restitution require a state of equality that defines individuals' respective entitlements. "Thus attention to the equality of gain and loss in corrective justice [C.M. – likewise with the equality of rendering a service and receiving the same in return in contract law] presupposes the notional equality of initial holdings,"[8] which is either compensated for in restitution or realized in exchange. Equitable distribution determines what this equality of shares or "initial holdings" (as Weinrib puts it) consists in, however, and thereby determines each person's own: right as one's own is what is commensurate or corresponds to each person as he is. Just as the arithmetical equality of rectification presupposes that distribution disrupted by loss was rectified,[9] so the proportional equality of exchange consists in the realization of goods and rendering of services according to their relative significance in the life of the community – in the satisfaction of needs whose regulation is the state's political responsibility. The fair share is the basis for corrective equality and for the equality of exchange. Right [*Recht*] as an individual's claim is based on law [*Recht*] as just order. The proper ordering of persons and objects whose regulation, production, and safeguarding is a political matter, and forms the basis for any private claim that one individual is entitled to make vis-à-vis another.

2 Rome

Roman law adopts, virtually unchanged, the basic definition of the legal claim, which was framed by a moral understanding of law in Athens. In Rome, the fact that someone has a right, and thus a justified claim on someone else, also means that such a claim is his own, that it rightfully belongs to him, and that, in particular, it is his fair share of something. Justice – in other words, a state of affairs in which persons and things stand in a relation of equality – is the basis of rights. Cicero is drawing on this when he reproaches "the friends of the people," who push for a redistribution of land and the eviction of previous owners:

29

[They are] undermining the foundations of the commonwealth: first of all, they are destroying harmony . . . , and second, they do away with equity [C.M. – or equality: *aequitatem*], which is utterly subverted, if the rights of property are not respected. For, as I said above, it is the peculiar function of the state and the city to guarantee to every man the free and undisturbed control of his own particular property [*suae rei cuiusque custodia*].[10]

Anyone deprived of his own suffers an injustice. In contrast, those who make it their business "to look after the interest of the state" see to it that "every one shall be protected in the possession of his own property by the fair administration of the law and courts."[11] Laws founded on right [*Rechtsgesetze*] articulate what constitutes relations of justice or equality, and what is appropriate for each person in such just relations is his own. This is his right: the right that a person has is his own, and justly belongs to him. "To each his own: *suum tribuens*. . . . It is the task of justice to apply to each and every thing *the legal provision that corresponds to it*."[12] Equitable distribution precedes an individual's right, and is the subject matter of legal practice. "*Ius* is the share that is awarded to someone, the result of distribution. . . . The word [C.M. – *ius*] designates the fair share": one has a right according to the standard of justice [*Gerechtigkeit*] and hence only to something equitable [*Gerechtes*].[13] The individual's right is his fair share.

If we characterize this as the alignment of Roman law with moral law (their alignment in the basis, namely as the foundation of rights in justice), then on Villey's interpretation such an alignment is different from moral law due to its abstractness: Roman law abstracts from morality in the exercise of rights. First of all, this indicates how equality is understood in the civic relationships that establish law. The Roman citizen's right is also his own fair claim to a share equal to anyone else's. "The reason for making constitutional laws" is "to hold the higher and lower classes in an equality of right"; right must correspond to "equality of rights before the law . . . otherwise they would be no rights."[14] From now on, however, this equal share consists in the abstract fact of being a free Roman citizen. He is an equal citizen insofar as he bears the title of *pater familias*: master in his own house, able to freely dispose of matters there. He possesses a "sphere of independent activity; the Roman is only responsible for the manner in which he exercises his rights over his property, his family."[15] Because this abstract position of equal civic status shapes the crucial regard for equitable distribution, citizens can no longer be guided in their association with each other by an orientation to an authoritative hierarchy of value when they contribute to or satisfy needs deemed politically important in the state, as they were on the Aristotelian model. If each person's own only consists in being a free citizen like all other citizens ("an *equality* in which *all* count as the *same*, i.e. as *persons*"),[16] the standard of their exchange cannot, indeed must not, be left up to them. However the quantitative ratios turn out, exchange is only considered just because (or when) each person is regarded as a property owner. One's own, which equitable distribution allots to each person, consists in being a property owner.

This stage of abstraction in Roman law leads to misunderstanding (something contested by Michel Villey, in particular), insofar as it introduces a new concept of law as justified claim. The categorical difference that separates Roman law [*Recht*] from modern law (this is why Villey contests such an understanding), however, is thereby blurred, indeed it even vanishes from sight. This misunderstanding consists in conflating the Roman citizen's right [*Recht*] as property owner or his right *as* ownership with a right *over* his property. On this view, that which is one's own, which equitable distribution allots to the Roman citizen, is understood to be the power to use one's own things. This is a misunderstanding because "*ius* is not *subjective*, in the meaning this word comes to have in scholastic language, it is *objective*. . . . A share in things and not power over things."[17] Right [*Recht*] as fair share and private power, which on the Roman view enables the paternal property owner to dispose over what is his own, are indeed related to each other. However, "If any *ius* has as its practical consequence the exercise of a *potestas*, then it is not this *potestas*, because ultimately law itself has by no means authorized me to exercise an arbitrary and unlimited power in my domain."[18] My right is my fair share in a thing, not my power to dispose over this thing. Roman law [*Recht*] secures one's own for each, but how and why someone uses what is his own is not its concern. In Rome, the use of law is private, not a matter for legal provisions. "Law has nothing to say" about usage:

> [Law] draws the boundaries for domains, but is not concerned with what happens in each domain, the relations of the property-owner to his domain, which has been bestowed on him. The absolute power exercised by the Roman master over his affairs is generally not a legal matter; it is passed over in silence, falling into law's gap.[19]

Roman law is in transition, since it associates the traditional moral justice of distribution and of the share, the definition of a right as fair share, by abstracting from citizens' usage of their rights.

31

3 London

Villey's words immediately make clear how the various authors whose formulations have laid the groundwork for the modern form of rights (which Savigny calls "right in the subjective sense") proceed in fundamentally different ways. As we have seen, the modern revolution of rights reverses the priority between *a* right and law, between right as claim and right as law. This revolutionary reversal, however, is only possible because the conception of the legal claim itself is completely reformulated. This reconception involves the relation between possession and use, the "(fact) that" and the "for what purpose" of the legal claim – the juridical and the pre- or extra-juridical.

On the Roman view, a person's legal status and their extra-juridical power are strictly distinguished from each other. Equal legal status consists in each person having their own, or an equal, fair share of a thing. In addition, legal equality in Rome involves the capacity for legal actions, above all, the commencement of *actiones*.[20] A rightsholder's power or freedom *over* his own, in the use of his fair share, is something radically different. The power (*potestas*) exercised by a person over his domain is private, or to put this more precisely, it is *natural*, because it precedes the legal system, only existing outside of it. "Freedom, from which men are said to be free, is the natural power of doing what we each please, unless prevented by force or by law."[21] In Rome, "for a jurist, power is an external condition, a *prejuridical* concept."[22] There is no connection between legal status – the fair share, one's own – and private power or the natural freedom to dispose over a domain that is one's due. A clear line divides the two, separating law from the pre-juridical.

In contrast, the juridical and the pre-juridical are linked to each other in the modern conception of rights. This is why Ockham calls right [*Recht*] "power," and his successors call it "capacity," "quality," "competence," or "freedom."

Excursus: Ockham's Defense of Poverty (Villey)

According to Michel Villey, the modern development that will shatter the Roman separation of juridical share and natural power begins with William of Ockham's observations in defense of the Franciscan vow of poverty against the pope's critique (though, again, this is not primarily a matter of historical fidelity, but has to do with the conceptual content of his argument).[23] The goal of the papal critique consisted in "compelling the Franciscans to accept the title of property owners – which was a scandal."[24] The pope's argument was that the Franciscan approach to poverty is self-contradictory, insofar as, on the one hand, it rejects any property, but on the other hand it also claims to be allowed to use things – food, clothing, shelter, and so forth. For a use of things that is not to be unlawful appropriation must always be based on a fair share of something (in a *ius* as previously defined). Contrary to their own self-conception, the Franciscans are therefore not outside the law, since in their use of things they unwittingly assume that they have a right to such things, and thus that they deserve a fair share. "The claim that the Franciscans have no rights is mere fiction;" "the claim to live outside the law is absurd."[25] The possession of a right is always already presupposed in the use of a thing. Thus runs the pope's argument, which is in complete accord with tradition.

In contrast, Ockham argues that the legitimate (which here only means: not unlawful) use of things does not assume *any* property, any legal claim, indeed does not assume any right: if there is a community in which everything is held in common by all (*omnia communia*), then it will also be the case, in such a community, that "use of fact can be separated."[26] To be able to rebut the papal objection that the Franciscan vow of poverty is self-contradictory, however, he must understand (as Villey critically observes) the concept of the legal claim in a completely different way from how it is understood in the papal objection: Ockham must introduce a fundamentally new conception of the legal claim.

> Right [*le droit*], in the technical sense of the term, no longer refers to the good that is justly due to something (*id quod iustum est*), it refers to a much narrower concept: the power that one holds over a good.[27]

Ockham can plausibly claim that the right claimed by Franciscans in their use of things is *not* a fair share in something (which the papal criticism claimed was a prerequisite for any legitimate use), but right as an individual's *power*: not merely a person's power for lawful actions as they deal with something of theirs in relation to other persons, such as selling it to someone, or obtaining compensation for a loss in court. Instead, right as *power to* (in fact or by nature) *use things* (*potestas licita utendi re extrinsica*) is the basis and goal of every lawful action vis-à-vis other persons.[28] Ockham, in his defense of the Franciscan vow of poverty against the pope's traditional legality that right [*Recht*] is the fair share that someone has in a thing, surreptitiously inaugurates the modern conception of rights as a claim to the power and the freedom to dispose over things (this is the grim point that Villey's account wishes to make).

Ockham thus establishes the legal basis for a reorganization of social (and economic) relations that ultimately undermined the Franciscan way of life. In the Franciscans' attempt to establish a use of things that was outside the law, they in fact initiated a transformation of law [*Recht*] that, according to Villey, severed the traditional connection between right [*Recht*] and justice: by defining right as a claim *to* natural, extra-legal use.

Giorgio Agamben has spoken of the "subtlety of Ockham's strategy" against the papal critique, which allowed for "holding oneself both outside and before the law."[29] However, while in Ockham this strategy aims at the "possibility . . . of pursuing an existence outside the law,"[30] it actually – as Villey interprets Ockham's position in the history of law – yields a fundamentally new image of law, through which law is opened up to its outside and thereby integrates what is outside the law into law. The Franciscan "right, not to have any rights"[31] is historically realized in the modern right [*Recht*] to not be right: as the right to be willing and acting outside the law [*Recht*]. The very same thing holds true for the modern character of rights.

If Ockham calls right [*Recht*] a "power" and then goes to call it "capability," "quality," "competence," or "freedom," this is not merely a terminological innovation, but a conceptual revolution, because the two categories that were separated by the Romans – legal status and pre-juridical, natural power – are merged into *one* paradoxical complex. If, since Ockham, the right that someone has is characterized as their power, then the legal claim that such a person has on another is thus determined by the individual's pre-juridical, private use of what is his own, in carrying out his natural activities. The concepts by which the legal claim has been explained since Ockham – power, capability, quality, competence, or freedom – are characterized by a constitutive ambiguity or bipolarity. They connect what was kept apart in Roman law: the legal and the extra-legal, legal validity and private or natural use. Claim can only be defined *as* power because power, conversely, has become "an ambiguous term," as Leo Strauss summarized this fundamental change with reference to Hobbes: "It stands for *potentia*, on the one hand, and for *potestas* (or *jus* or *dominium*), on the other. It means both 'physical' power and 'legal' power. The ambiguity is essential."[32] The power that from this time forward is understood to be right as claim is the *legal power* to exercise *pre-legal power*.

According to Villey, this alteration of the concept that Ockham unwittingly proposed in his defense of Franciscan poverty is ratified by seventeenth-century natural law, when it conceives rights created by order-establishing contracts (initially, therefore, the rights of the sovereign and then, in the exercise of these sovereign rights, the rights of the subject in *Ius Civile* or Right Civil)[33] on the basis of natural rights. On Hobbes' view, natural right consists in "the Liberty each man hath, to use his own power, as he will himselfe, for the preservation of his own Nature; that is to say, of his own Life."[34] As Spinoza puts it, "each individual thing has the sovereign right to do everything that it can do, or the right of each thing extends so far as its determined power extends."[35] Every creature is naturally entitled to take "anything that he believes useful to himself," in which he therefore sees the preservation of his existence:

> And since it is the supreme law of nature that each thing strives to persist in its own state so far as it can, taking no account of another's circumstances but only of its own, it follows that each individual thing has a sovereign right to do this, i.e. (as I said) to exist and to behave as it is naturally determined to behave.[36]

In the state of nature, talk of a "right" to the exercise of power for self-preservation is obviously only meant in a negative sense, because no one else has a right, opposed to mine, to hinder the exercise of my power. There are no normative obligations here – only external hindrances, including the power of others – that could be invoked against my right to, and therefore against the exercise of my power for, self-preservation, at my own discretion. For normative obligations are only present when, in exercising the natural right to self-preservation, the contract that establishes society includes a limitation on, and therefore defines the purpose of, this unlimited right.

Because, however, this contract, which establishes society and which simultaneously creates normativity and sovereignty, occurs in each individual's exercise of natural right, and therefore because it is based on securing the natural power for self-preservation, this also remains its goal:

> The Final Cause, End, or Designe of men, (who naturally love Liberty, and Dominion over others,) in the introduction of that restraint upon themselves, (in which wee see them live in Commonwealths,) is the foresight of their own preservation, and of a more contented life thereby.[37]

Obviously, the natural right to self-preservation cannot yield a counter-right or opposed right *against* the sovereign. Yet there is no need for this, either. For the laws [*Gesetzen*] that the sovereign enacts, according to his "sovereign law and right" and thus according to his own conception,[38]

35

can only be a matter of that very power of self-preservation that constitutes the content of natural right. Hobbes expresses this in an awkward manner, in a negative way, when he writes that "The Liberty of a Subject, lyeth therefore only in those things, which in regulating their actions, the Soveraign hath praetermitted."[39]

He then provides a list of examples, however: "such as is the Liberty to buy, and sell, and otherwise contract with one another; to choose their own aboad, their own diet, their own trade of life, and institute their children as they themselves think fit; & the like" – *including* freedom of faith and thought, insofar as they remain "inner."[40] The Hobbesian sovereign safeguards bourgeois civil or private right, whose central line of thought was formulated by Spinoza:

> We can mean nothing by the civil right of the citizen other than the freedom of each person to conserve themselves in their own condition, which is determined by the edicts of the sovereign power and protected by its authority alone.[41]

Private right, which is now centered on property,[42] is thus nothing but a transformed natural right: natural right that has been limited by law and is thereby secured; a power for natural self-preservation that is limited by law and thereby secured. The conceptual link between right (or claim) and power remains in force even for the categorical break at the state's contractual foundation. Natural power is the content of rights safeguarded by the state. The rights that citizens of a state have vis-à-vis each other have a natural content. The natural rights established in a state have *the same content* – which is not to say, of course, that they have the same scope – as natural rights. The pre-juridical state of nature persists in the juridical state in the form of bourgeois rights. Indeed, the pre-juridical state of nature *is validated* in the juridical state. The safeguarding of the pre- and extra-juridical, and therefore of the natural, becomes the basic definition of law.

Above all else, the break with tradition made by the modern form of rights thus consists in what Roman law passed over in silence; what, in Rome, falls into the "gaps of law" (Villey): pre-juridical private or natural activity now becomes something which law talks about in order to enable such activity or to safeguard it, and therefore truly becomes a legal matter, the goal of law. A juridically entitled claim that obligates others is a claim *to* what is non-juridical, indeed to what is pre-juridical, to the natural. What, in Rome, was outside the law (things and the ways in which they were used) now becomes its essential content: what is outside of law becomes inside, indeed becomes the heart and soul of law. The modern form of rights inscribes the natural and thereby the pre-juridical into law.

Modernity calls a right a claim or a power because it is the claim to realize claims, the power to exercise power. Rights are (juridical) claims to (natural) claims, the juridical authorization of natural power.

Right to the Extra-Juridical

We now begin to see why the distinction between the two usages of the term "right" [*Recht*] – right as law [*Gesetz*] and right as claim – is so crucially important for legal thought on its way to modernity. Since Ockham, right has been defined in a new way. This does *not* simply consist in the insight that we should distinguish between legal claim and juridical law, because there is at least one type of laws whose purpose is to define claims. This insight is as old as the institution of private or civil law [*Privat- oder Zivilrechts*], since we are here concerned with claims that one person is entitled to make vis-à-vis another person under a law [*Gesetz*] that is valid for both. In making the distinction between legal claim and juridical law, modern theory since Ockham has instead defined the legal claim, as well as how claim and law interact, in a fundamentally new way. Indeed, it has fundamentally redefined how law's [*Rechts*] normativity is to be understood in general.

In Athens, as in Rome, "a right" indicates a claim that one person has over against another as regards his own fair share in some matter. As in Athens, this fair share can be understood to mean that, in exchange for their own work, a person receives a share in another's work that is proportionally commensurate to the politically determined significance of their respective work and activity for the community. Alternatively, as in Rome, the fair share can be understood to mean that both persons are free citizens who are equal to each other, insofar as both are patriarchal owners with mastery over their portion of people and things. As different as Roman equality of citizens is from the Aristotelian grounding of justice in the proportional value of works and contributions, they both remain bound to the basic definition of *right as justice*. In Athens *and* Rome, a legal claim is just because it is a claim *to something just*, to a share that is determined by just distribution and equalization between persons.

In London, however, with the modern character of rights, the legally binding claim that a person makes is a matter not of something just – the fair share – but of something pre- or extra-juridical: the power or

37

freedom to engage in an activity that is independent of law and thus already prior to law. To this extent, we can call such a claim "natural," which implies that the natural is the social (the theme of part III). The legal claims of one person over against another are claims not to something just, but to something natural and therefore prior to law. Legal claims now exist not to assess what belongs to each, what each person's fair share in something is, but to secure or enable each person's carrying out of their own natural activities. Rights stand *on the boundary* between law and the pre- or extra-juridical. As Talcott Parsons says of modern law in general, rights are the "mediating 'interface'" between law and that which is outside the law.[43]

Modern rights essentially define the claim by combining what is categorically different. The content of a right is something extra-juridical. A right is a claim to the power or freedom to engage in a natural activity. The content of a legal claim is a pre-legal claim. The pre-legal claim's content only becomes a right, or a justified claim that can obligate others, however, when it submits to an external condition. A legal claim emerges from the claim's pre-juridical content by restricting its scale and scope. This is now the definition of the law of right [*Rechtsgesetz*]. Law [*Gesetz*] is no longer the just prescription of ethical action, but the external demarcation of domains of natural activities over and against one another. The mechanism by which legal claims emerge from natural claims is not their *transformation* into moral claims, but their demarcation over and against each other from outside – *substantively unchanged*. Rights exist when each person, in Hobbes' suggestive formulation, is "contented with so much liberty against other men, as he would allow other men against himselfe."[44] In Kant's reformulation of this thought: "What end anyone wants to set for his action is left to his free choice. The maxim of his action, however, is determined a priori, namely that the freedom of the agent could *coexist with* the freedom of every other in accordance with a universal law."[45] Law [*Gesetz*] realizes the equality of each person (and thereby yields legal claims) by demarcating pre-legal claims – which, as natural, are boundless and thus incommensurate – from each other and thus allowing them to exist alongside each other. The new conception of law presupposed by the modern character of rights is now one in which law is the outer limit of what is unlimited in itself, not the authoritative postulation of an inner measure.[46]

Only through its structural externality does law [*Gesetz*] obtain the egalitarian content that is the distinctive feature of modern law [*Recht*]. In Athens and Rome, just division measures what is each person's own, according to what each is for their community. The legal claim is based on – is proportional to – the individual's moral existence. And this is essentially variable. In contrast, natural claims, whose demarcation enables the law [*Gesetz*] of modern right [*Rechts*] to yield legal claims, are essentially equal. They have no inner measure that links and distinguishes them. For this reason, law does not judge them, does not distinguish them into high and low, dignified and undignified, but demarcates them from outside: law considers them equal. The egalitarian redefinition of justice in the modern law of right reflects the "actual . . . equality" of the natural,[47] the pre-juridical, to which law [*Recht*] has bound itself.

While in Athens and Rome the legal claim's entitlement or obligation is therefore guaranteed (it is a justified claim because it is a claim to something just; the claim's just content is the basis for its normative, legally binding force), the claim only receives justification or becomes binding in the modern character of rights through the demarcation of equality, which externally subordinates what is claimed. The reason why a claim's legality is no longer able to coincide with its content is that its content is pre-juridical or natural: the legal claim's content is no longer just, and therefore moral, but the natural activity of a human being. This natural content can never have binding force by itself, but only obtains it through its external demarcation. The claim's normative power here stems no longer from its content, from what it is, but from the extent and magnitude of its application. The content and the force, the substance and basis of rights diverge with the naturalization of the claim's content in the modern character of rights.

At the same time, however, this means that extra-juridical, natural content and the claim's legally binding force are *connected* to each other *as distinct* in the modern character of rights: the legal claim is linked *back* to the facticity of a natural striving. Only because it *is* the case that the human being "strives to persist in his own being"[48] can there also be a right to the juridically defined exercise of the power of self-preservation. Natural striving lies at the basis of rights: rights to the natural power of self-preservation, which laws [*Gesetze*] grant and administer, presuppose that this power and its orientation to self-preservation is the human being's fundamental natural "quality" or "determination."[49] One doctrine of modern natural law is that rights *cannot be derived from natural facts*: they do not need to be artificially established by communal contract to have normatively binding force. Another doctrine of modern natural law is that rights *are based on natural presuppositions*: the establishment of rights proceeds from natural, factual strivings that are prior to law. It is by means of such external demarcation that law [*Recht*] yields entitled and obligatory claims. The modern character of rights realizes the unity *and* difference of establishment [*Setzung*] and presupposition [*Voraussetzung*], of normativity and nature.

Excursus: Rights and Interests (Raz)

The so-called interest theory of rights provides us with one way to reformulate this doctrine of modern natural law. According to Rudolf von Ihering's famous redefinition, which is opposed, on utilitarian grounds, to the traditional idealist theory of the will, "rights are legally protected interests."[50] Concerning the theory of the will (which he traces back to Hegel), Ihering writes that "This view's mistake consists in the fact that it allows the concept of subjective right to be subsumed under that of the will. Its final goal is to define the will, and law, as a demarcated portion of willing substance."[51] He opposes to this view the following thesis: "Utility forms the substance of law, rather than the will or power."[52] Ihering himself already pointed out the deliberate one-sidedness, indeed the inadequacy of this definition, which is only able to conceive the "substantial" moment of rights, but unable to conceive their "formal" moment and thus unable to distinguish between someone who is benefited and someone who is entitled. Nevertheless, the interest theory of rights has often been adamantly defended.[53] This is because interest theory, influenced by utilitarianism, is able to express an essential feature of the modern character of rights that is missed in the idealist theory of the will. This feature is the implicative relation between natural and legal claims, which defines the modern conception of rights – and only this conception.

According to Joseph Raz, the central insight from which interest theory proceeds indicates that we can only define the concept of rights by locating them within a network of grounding and justificatory relations. "Rights" define the form of a specific kind of normative argumentation. In this regard, rights are *first* grounds for – and not what corresponds to – obligations:

> the right is the ground of the duty. It is wrong to translate statements of rights into statements of "the corresponding" duties. A right of one person is not a duty on another. It is the ground of a duty, ground which, if not counteracted by conflicting considerations, justifies holding that other person to have the duty.[54]

Second, this grounding of duties by the establishment of rights happens in such a way that a person's interest is invoked – instead of referring to an imperative or a law [*Gesetz*]:

A right is based on the interest which figures essentially in the justification of the statement that the right exists.[55]

The interests are part of the justification of the rights which are part of the justification of the duties.[56]

This has two different implications: the fact that a person has a specific interest is not sufficient on its own (it is only a necessary "part") for recognizing this person's right to that in which they have an interest. For this reason, we need an additional argument, which finds authoritative expression in laws [Gesetzen]. Rights are therefore based on interests only under laws, in a normative order. At the same time, however, the *fact* that a person has a specific interest is a necessary condition for (an *essential* part of) recognizing that person's right. This is the crucial conceptual insight offered by interest theory – however we answer the question of utility or freedom. It entails that the normative force of rights is connected to the facticity of natural strivings that exist prior to law, and thus to *the fact that* persons *have* interests. Interests are simultaneously defined by where they are conceptually located in the grounding of rights and by their factual, empirical existence. They link rights back to facts.

To sum all of this up: Leo Strauss has interpreted the introduction of the modern conception of rights as "the supplanting of the primacy of obligation [C.M. – which the law imposes] by the primacy of claim." This thesis is absurd, if we understand it to mean that there cannot be legally binding claims without law [Gesetz]: rights only exist under a law. Spinoza writes "This is precisely what Paul is saying when he acknowledges that there is no sin before law is established, i.e., as long as men are considered as living under the government of nature."[57] At the same time, however, on the modern understanding, rights *are referred back* to the fact of natural strivings prior to law, whose fulfillment in activities they legalize. It is therefore true of the modern character of rights that law [Gesetz] "did not *create* [C.M. – rights], it only *authorized* [them]."[58] To put this more precisely: law [Gesetz] creates rights *by* authorizing something that exists prior to law [vorrechtlich]. The form of the creation of rights is the *legalization of the natural*.

The locus of rights is paradoxical: they stand on the boundary that connects law [Recht] and what is outside the law, normativity and nature, to each other, by dividing them from each other. Law and what is outside the law are separated from each other *and* linked to each other in the modern character of rights. They are divided from each other in order to then link what has been divided. The modern form of rights is a paradoxical characteristic of juridical normativity: it fixes normativity and facticity in place, without resolving normativity into facticity. The normative force of a legal claim, the fact that it is binding on another, is not a consequence of a factual, naturally existing interest (it cannot be derived merely from what is already there) but it does follow *upon* this interest. Rights cannot only be oriented to interests, they *must* relate to interests, which means, in particular, that they *rest* on interests, their basis is the natural.

Niklas Luhmann defines the composition of modern law in terms of "*normative closure* and *cognitive openness.*"[59] According to Luhmann, law can therefore be regarded either normatively – in which case it is regarded as closed – or cognitively – in which case it is regarded as open. This choice between alternatives misses the decisive feature in the modern character of rights. Luhmann's thesis, which we oppose, is that "the distinction between norms and facts" in modern law "kept . . . early writings on the sociology of law . . . at a distance from other legal theory,"[60] because the "blending" of the two distinct sides is *not* "avoided."[61] It is in fact quite the reverse: the modern form of rights *carries out* the distinction of norms and facts in such a way that they are distinguished from each other *and* linked to each other. In this way, normativity is distinguished from and bound to facticity: rights – *only* – entitle us to what is natural; we can only be entitled to something natural. The normativity of rights enables, secures, and safeguards the natural. The normativity of rights makes the norm's other – nature – into its interior, its presupposition, and thus its goal.

— 3 —

INNER CHOICE

The first axis around which the distinction of three historical legal systems – Athens, Rome, London – revolves is the legal claim's essential character (by which one person is able to obligate another). In all three regimes, law gives rise to individual claims in two fundamentally different ways: by dividing what is common *or* by legalizing the natural. This immediately involves a second axis of distinction, however. It concerns the essence of juridical governance – the meaning of the "legality" [*Gesetzlichkeit*] that defines law: why, to what end, and over what does law rule in giving rise to claims? In these three regimes, how does law understand the fact that it must rule, in order to safeguard claims? And how does it understand the fact that the claims of individuals against each other only exist under the rule of law?

From Paideia to Sovereignty

Law rules all: legal regulations are based on the capacity for coercion. Such regulations bear the threat of coercion. The oldest doctrine of law is that the relation to law must remain a relation of "awe" [*Ehrfurcht*], indeed one of "fear" [*Furcht*], so that law can be the institution of justice.[1] In the *Eumenides*, Aeschylus formulates it as the insight that a right which is only established to express the equality of citizens (and which is thus distinguished from personal rule [*Herrschaft*]) requires subjection to the threatening ruling power that everyone wields over the individual. Athena thus proposes a new system of law for her city since it will closely fuse equality and rule. For "But who that traineth not his heart in fear, be it State or be it man, is like in the future to reverence

43

justice as heretofore? Approve thou not a life ungoverned nor one subjected to a tyrant's sway."[2] Law holds sway [*herrscht*], it binds its rules to the capacity for coercion, since it reckons with human beings who are not lawful – who do not do, of their own accord, what law must hence prescribe for them. This is true of all law, but in a fundamentally different sense for each of the three legal systems.

1 Athens

Aristotle examines law's mode of being from the perspective of the virtues, namely by examining the conduct of the person administering justice. Justice as equality (which we have already considered), and thus the virtue of seeing that each person receives his own, is justice "*in the particular sense*," since it is only "a part of universal justice."[3] Here, justice means realizing equality in the distribution within a community and in the dealings of individuals with each other, and therefore giving each his own. Justice in the universal sense is different from this. *In its universal sense*, it is a special regard not merely for equality, but for doing what one is supposed to: doing what is right. Laws [*Gesetzen*], however, stipulate what the right thing to do is. Justice in general, or "universal justice," is thus the virtue of obeying laws – the virtue of the "lawful."

Aristotle also says that the universal justice of lawfulness is "perfect virtue,"[4] since it is doing what is right. To exercise the virtue of lawfulness, and therefore to fulfill the requirements of law [*Recht*], simply means to enact *the* virtues, because they are precisely what the laws require: doing what is virtuous. As Werner Jaeger summarizes this break with the agonal, heroic definition of the virtues, sealed by Aristotle's conception of lawfulness, virtue *consists* "in . . . [the] voluntary submission to the new authority of the law."[5] At the same time, however, Aristotle limits the scope of this concept, by arguing that justice as lawfulness is "perfect virtue, though with a qualification."[6] This has two meanings.

The first meaning is that lawfulness is "perfect virtue . . . [insofar as] it is displayed toward others."[7] The virtue of lawfulness is simply a matter of the relation to other persons. This indeed narrows the domain of lawfulness:

> This is why Justice is often thought to be the chief of the virtues, and more sublime "than the evening or the morning star"; and we have the proverb –
>
> In Justice is all Virtue found in sum.

44

And Justice is perfect virtue because it is the practice of perfect virtue; and perfect in a special degree, because its possessor can practice his virtue *towards others* and not merely by himself.[8]

The virtue of lawfulness, although (or precisely because) it is not "perfect virtue," can be viewed as the highest virtue, since it consists in enacting virtue not merely in "one's own affairs" but "toward others." Conversely, this is called the virtue of lawfulness, and thus of obeying the law, because its rules simply express how to behave virtuously in our conduct toward others. "Laws are designed to regulate and order relations between human beings: no more and no less."[9]

The claim that the virtue of lawfulness is not "perfect virtue," however, has another, second meaning. This is evident in *how* it stipulates laws [*Gesetzen*] and therefore also in what it alone *can* stipulate:

> the law prescribes ... the conduct of a brave man, for example not to desert one's post, not to run away, not to throw down one's arms; that of a temperate man, for example not to commit adultery or outrage; that of a gentle man, for example not to strike, not to speak evil; and so with actions exemplifying the rest of the virtues and vices.[10]

Law stipulates virtuous *deeds* – and therefore does not stipulate the disposition that is virtue. Justice as lawfulness and (perfect) virtue are "the same quality of mind, but their essence is different." Only "what as displayed in relation to others is Justice, as being simply a disposition of a certain kind is Virtue."[11] The virtue of lawfulness is thus not "perfect virtue" because it *can only* refer to virtuous deeds, and this is why we can distinguish a virtuous disposition and virtuous deeds within lawfulness. The virtue of lawfulness only includes the capacity for a virtuous disposition, since it also includes the capacity for a sham virtue, the enacting of *feigned virtue* – the virtue-less accomplishment of virtuous deeds.

The lawfulness of law [*Gesetzlichkeit des Rechts*] is defined by its limitation to deeds, and thus defined by its ignoring of disposition. For Aristotle, however, this is a matter simply of the modality of legal rules and their fulfillment, but not of their *meaning*. It is a matter of their "how," but not their "why." The legal rule refers to virtuous deeds, but it *aims at* disposition. Law [*Recht*] links deeds and disposition in the same way that education does:

> The virtues ... we acquire by first having actually practised them, just as we do the arts. We learn an art or craft by doing the things that we shall have to do when we have learnt it: for instance, men become builders by building houses, harpers by playing on the harp. Similarly we become

45

just by doing just acts, temperate by doing temperate acts, brave by doing brave acts. This truth is attested by the experience of states: law-givers make the citizens good by training them in habits of right action – this is the aim of all legislation, and if it fails to do this it is a failure; this is what distinguishes a good form of constitution from a bad one.[12]

Education signifies habituating ourselves to act in certain ways so as to give rise to a disposition that is realized in these actions, whose deeds are these actions. Actions and deeds therefore precede disposition: "The virtues ... we acquire by first having actually practised them."[13] Education is a process that leads through actions to capabilities and dispositions. The creation of an interior and one's own necessarily proceeds through externality:

> Persons in the states mentioned repeat propositions of geometry and verses of Empedocles; students who have just begun a subject reel off its formulae, though they do not yet know their meaning, for knowledge has to become part of the tissue of the mind, and this takes time.[14]

Moral education must proceed through the repetitive performance of deeds in order to create a virtuous disposition, just as a student learns by repeating words, by speaking them as though he would and could speak them – such students "talk in the same way as actors speaking a part."[15] An external rule and its externally repeated fulfillment in actions where we *feign* action are required to complete the process of education.

This is precisely where we can situate the Greek conception of law: law is the sustained moment of externality through which every educational process must proceed. The Greek conception of law is pedagogical: "it will be important for the legislator to study how and by what courses of training good men are to be produced, and what is the end of the best life."[16] Law is an authority for moral education. On the Greek view, this orients and thus justifies law's externality, including the violence that it uses and the fear that it provokes. Law has an "educational mission."[17] Its "lawful" human being is the incipiently virtuous human being.

2 Rome

While the telos of Greek law is education in virtue, an essential feature of the Roman conception is to stretch the link between law and virtue so much that the externality of law obtains a positive existence. Roman law also presupposes "moral rules or Roman religious rules,"[18] but it no longer views law [*Recht*] itself as able to *create* morals – certainly not all by itself, as Aristotle thought.

46

Cicero thus describes the difference between the Roman conception of law [*Gesetz*] and that of the "great philosophers," and therefore of the Greeks, as follows:

> Philosophers have taken their starting point from law [*a lege*] ... , they think that its name in Greek [*nomos*] is derived from "giving to each his own" [*nemein*], while I think that in Latin [*lex*] it is derived from choosing [*legere*]. They put the essence of law in equity, and we place it in choice [*delectus vim*]; both are attributes of law.[19]

Cicero views choice as the normative act of distinguishing between right and wrong ("Law, therefore, is the distinction between just and unjust things")[20] and emphasizes how it tends to both establish and command. Law does not already exist, it does not have being, but is made or must be made. Thus "it should be clear that in the interpretation of the word 'law' itself there is the significance and intention of choosing something just and right [*vim et sententiam iusti et iuris legendi*]."[21] The content of law is justice and the dictum its mode of being: it operates with the *power to establish*.

According to Cicero, law's power to establish is not subjective or arbitrary at all. On his view, the command indeed defines law's effect, but not its creation. The Roman understanding of law does not consider the command to be "the basis of the essence of domination,"[22] as Heidegger thought. For the basis of law is reason. If, in the question of the "principles of right," the "great philosophers" have taken law as their starting point, then according to Cicero they did this on the justified assumption that "as these same people define it, law is the highest reason, rooted in nature, which commands things that must be done and prohibits the opposite. When this same reason is secured and established in the human mind, it is law."[23] The sequence of steps leading from the nature of right to its reason and then to its law runs as follows:

> Those who have been given reason by nature have also been given right reason, and therefore law too, which is right reason in commands and prohibitions; and if they have been given law, then they have been given justice too. All people have reason, and therefore justice has been given to all.[24]

Right as law is establishment, command – and, at the same time, it has been *given* to all people through their "right reason" (because "we are born for justice and ... justice is established not by opinion but by nature"[25]). How are these claims supposed to be compatible?

They are no longer compatible as they were on the Greek conception.

For the Greeks, there was *one* perspective on the political governance of the community, from which law's justice (as distributive) was able to be thought together with its externality (as educative). This is the political "synthesis of reason and subjectivity, of nature and artificiality" in the moral-pedagogical conception of law.[26] In Rome, on the other hand, with Cicero, the two aspects of law [*Recht*], that it is established and natural, a command and something reasonable to do, are associated with different perspectives, are given different roles, *personae*. To be sure, Cicero also firmly declares that "law ought to correct vices and encourage virtues." As a result, "the knowledge of how to live should be drawn from it." The "function of law" is "to persuade rather than to compel all things through force and threats."[27] This education, however, does not take place *through* law [*Gesetz*] in its juridical manifestation, as establishment or command. It occurs due to its natural-rational basis or content, and happens outside of the institution of law [*Recht*]: in the philosophical contemplation *of* law. Philosophy, as "parent and teacher" of the human being who comes to know himself [*sich selbst erkennenden*], is oriented to the "eternal law" that is prior to any "written" one.[28] Law has morally educative power only if, and insofar as, philosophy is able to *recognize* [wieder*zuerkennen*] what is natural and not established in law that has been established. "When [reason] in a human being ... is brought to maturity, [it resides] in the mind of wise men:"[29] *mere* law, if it exists for itself and remains unconceptualized in a philosophical sense, *is* mere establishment, mere command.

Cicero's linking of law's rational content to philosophical awareness [*Erkenntnis*] gives its externality a different sense than it had on the Greek model. Its externality is no longer viewed as transitory, as the moment in which education is passed on, but is understood in perspectival terms. The externality of law is now its necessary mode of appearance – law as it appears from its *own* perspective. The sublation of law's externality becomes one-sided: it only happens in the special (in a twofold sense) perspective of philosophy. Conversely, externality persists in law's operation itself. Natural reason manifests itself in law [*Gesetz*] as "the power of command [*imperium*], without which no home or state or nation or the whole race of mankind can survive, nor can nature or the world itself."[30] From law's [*Recht*] non-philosophical perspective, a commanding externality is unavoidable, because natural reason is absent by nature, because the human being's deviation from natural reason has become second nature:

> The justice of which I speak is natural, but ... such is the corruption of bad habits [*corruptelam malae consuetudinis*] that it extinguishes what

48

I may call the sparks given by nature, and that contrary vices arise and become established.[31]

life is sought because it keeps us in the state in which we were born.[32]

Because the merely natural striving for self-preservation has taken the place of natural reason and corrupted it, a law that commands is necessary. While philosophy spreads the view that "justice is desirable on its own account [*per se*],"[33] law which no longer educates but commands accepts the striving for self-preservation as a given. Natural law's surpassing of political paideia, which based law on the rational nature of human beings instead of placing it under community control, yields the conception of a right that, by externally commanding, creates a non-juridical, non-lawful nature that is opposed to it.

Human nature is at the same time freed from moral teleology, since, in Rome, law can no longer be legitimated by claiming that its coercion is neutralized, insofar as it is educative. It is therefore freed because law here no longer fulfills the task of education in the virtues, indeed entirely renounces this task and the strictness of its rules. Law's overt domination has anthropological implications. If the lawfulness of law is inscribed into a teleology of education, human nature appears to be in principle capable of morality, indeed to aim for it. Educative law's conception of nature is teleological: the natural human being to whom the legal rule, as it has been legally established, refers is someone who has yet to become virtuous or to be made virtuous, and is therefore the virtuous human being in the imperfect mode of having a capacity that is not yet developed enough to be actualized. Roman law's severing of the teleological connection between nature (as disposition) and virtue (as goal) in the operation of its commands (or more precisely: its excluding virtue from law and delegating it to philosophy) also means that it is no longer able to explain their relation by referring to the ontological hierarchy of possibility and actuality. *From law's perspective*, and in terms of how it operates, nature and morality, self-preservation and virtue, have the same ontological status: they are both equally possible. For Roman law, virtue becomes merely *one possibility* – and the natural inclination to self-preservation becomes another possibility. Both the "right reason" of virtue and the natural "mental error"[34] of self-preservation are equally possible.

3 London

Faced with a striving for self-preservation that had become a second, corrupt nature, the only choice left for Roman law was to command by giving orders and to rely on the achievement of education, which takes place not in and through law, but somewhere else and in some other way. Law and morality are different; they operate in distinct ways, without being opposed to each other. This is why, on the one hand, law is the merely external rule of "right reason" over corrupt nature's errors in judgment, but does not ensure the normative "choice" of reason over nature in the educative transformation of nature into reason. And, on the other hand, this is why the merely external rule of law over nature is no problem. If asked to justify itself, law [*Recht*] can certainly no longer refer to *its* educational goals – it has lost the right [*Recht*] to do so here. It can, however, point to philosophy, the virtuous human being's "parent and teacher," which de-problematizes what is problematic in law – since all establishment is a problem.

The modern sovereign, who has been created by contractual appointment, is no longer able to establish: its dominion is nothing more than its commands, including legal rules. To be sure, its dominion is "absolute" or "unlimited," because "Sovereign Power . . . is as great, as possibly men can be imagined to make it."[35] This is precisely because the human beings whom it rules have *made* it, however; because it is the expression of a "skill," which "consisteth in certain Rules, as doth Arithmetique and Geometry; not (as Tennis-play) on Practise onely."[36] Using this skill, human beings have made the sovereign itself, and because they have made it, because they are its "authors," anything the sovereign does by virtue of its authority cannot be an injustice against them, and is therefore always justified. A sovereign only appears external to its subjects, merely establishing and coercing, if they forget its basis, and therefore if they forget themselves, their act of establishing it. The sovereign's power over its subjects, exercised in establishing and administering law, is unlimited: the sovereign may do what it likes, precisely because its authority is not its own (just as the sovereign is not its own author, so too its authority is conferred on it).

The sovereign, however, may only do what it likes in conformity with the goal or "end" that it is there to accomplish: "the Peace and Defence of them all." "The end of Obedience [C.M. – and thus of sovereignty] is Protection."[37] This goal of the state does not grant the individual any right against the state: the fact that the state's goal is individual self-preservation defines the form, and not the content, of its sovereignty. For only the sovereign's decision can determine the meaning of "protection" and "self-preservation," and therefore determine how one is to safeguard self-preservation. (And this, too, again follows from the state's goal: we cannot ensure the protection of each person if everyone wants to define what protection means for themselves.[38]) In making such a decision, the sovereign is wisely oriented to familiar anthropological facts such as "natural timorousnesse" and exercising "discretion."[39] The exercise of sovereign rights has not merely pragmatic but also logical conceptual limits – and therefore limits that follow from the formal definition of sovereignty, due to its purpose: protection. There are limits to what the sovereign may do because, according to the concept of sovereignty, there are some things the sovereign *cannot* do.

This includes all actions in which a human being *is opposed to himself*:

> If the Soveraign command a man (though justly condemned,) to kill, wound, or mayme himselfe; or not to resist those that assault him; or to abstain from the use of food, ayre, medicine, or any other thing, without which he cannot live; yet hath that man the Liberty to disobey.
>
> If a man be interrogated by the Sovereign, or his Authority, concerning a crime done by himselfe, he is not bound (without assurance of Pardon) to confesse it; because no man (as I have shewn in the same Chapter) can be obliged by Covenant to accuse himselfe.
>
> Again, the Consent of a Subject to Soveraign Power, is contained in these words, *I Authorise, or take upon me, all his actions*; in which there is no restriction at all, of his own former naturall Liberty: For by allowing him to *kill me*, I am not bound to kill my selfe when he commands me. 'Tis one thing to say, *Kill me, or my fellow, if you please*; another thing to say, *I will kill my selfe, or my fellow*. It followeth therefore, that No man is bound by the words themselves, either to kill himself, or any other man.[40]

The variety of different cases that Hobbes enumerates (actions that the sovereign cannot require of us) share one basic feature: the sovereign cannot require a subject to perform an action that assumes or expresses an intention opposed to that subject's own striving for self-preservation. The sovereign may not prohibit its subjects from striving for their self-preservation. For if the sovereign were to do so, it would thereby demand that its subjects violate the first law [*Gesetz*] of nature, according to which "a man is forbidden to do, that, which is destructive of his life, or taketh away the means of preserving the same."[41] The fact that the sovereign cannot forbid the striving for self-preservation therefore does not imply that it is unable to forbid such a thing (for instance, because, in contrast to the Greek model, it has lost the power to educate). Instead, the implication is that the sovereign cannot wish to do so: this is not a question of efficacy, but of the sovereign's essence, and thus of its existence (which is owed precisely to the laws of nature). The sovereign cannot forbid its subjects from striving to preserve themselves without self-contradiction. This is why it would not be unjust for his subjects to refuse such a command – although determining what is just and unjust is up to the sovereign alone.

This insight into the structure of sovereignty has two implications for law [*Recht*], the most important medium of authority [*Herrschaft*]. First, law is defined *negatively*, as a being-free-to or a being-permitted-to: law can never forbid subjects from striving for their self-preservation, which it must always allow or accept. This is the other side of the positive authorization of the natural by the modern character of rights, which we have already examined (see chapter 2). The internalization of the natural in law, the opening of law to the natural, is here understood to mean that the natural power of self-preservation forms the goal of law: law *is intended to* enable the interest of subjects, to enable their striving for self-preservation. This obviously includes the power to define and restrict their interest (so that everyone has equal opportunity). At the same time, however, it should now be evident that legal power has its fundamental limit, its unreachable counterpart, in the interest or striving for self-preservation: it must assume that this striving is a fact and *allow* it.

Second, this means that the legal system *distinguishes* between the striving for self-preservation – which is always allowed – and its fulfillment – which law [*Recht*] must always restrict. The sovereign may not demand that a human being violate his own law [*Gesetz*], the nature of his striving or volition – that he turn his will against himself or turn himself against his will "in such a way that he ceases to be a human being."[42] This means, however, nothing less than that the sovereign should *not* interfere *at all* in its subjects' volition if it does not wish to end up contradicting itself, to end up contradicting why it was established and its justification. What the sovereign's subjects wish and strive for, and how they do this, is their concern, since it is a natural matter – the kind of natural fact that constitutes the basis because it is the starting point for the creation of the sovereign. The natural, the striving for self-preservation, which the sovereign must authorize because he is authorized by it, therefore becomes *internality*, which systematically eludes his rule. The interior of the sovereign's subjects is external to law and therefore law must remain external to it. Permission of the natural signifies law's self-restriction in the face of internality and thereby its restriction of itself to exteriority.

Hobbes has very clearly formulated the distinction between a legally governable exterior and a legally ungovernable interior in religious matters (whose conception in the modern era results from this distinction). Just as only the sovereign can determine what is just or unjust (since there is no justice and no normativity prior to the contract that establishes it), so too only the sovereign can say "what is, or what is not the Word of God" in a "Christian Common-wealth."

> From whence may be concluded this first point, that they to whom God hath not spoken immediately, are to receive the positive commandments of God, from their Soveraign ... And consequently in every Common-wealth, they who have no supernaturall Revelation to the contrary, ought to obey the laws of their own Soveraign, in the externall acts and profession of Religion. As for the inward *thought*, and *beleef* of men, which humane Governours can take no notice of, (for God onely knoweth the heart) they are not voluntary, nor the effect of the laws, but of the unrevealed will, and of the power of God; and consequently fall not under obligation.[43]

This line of thought clearly aims to distinguish the inner (thought or belief) from the outer (actions and declarations). The sovereign *must* regulate the latter and prescribe or forbid, in order to fulfill the goal that forms its *raison d'être*: protection, peace, defending everyone. Conversely, the sovereign is not supposed to regulate the former, to impose or forbid thought or belief, because he *cannot do* this. Deviating from the architecture of his theory, Hobbes nevertheless argues, on epistemological grounds, that the sovereign cannot do this (because thought or belief cannot be perceived by a human ruler), which he goes on to give a theological twist (because thought or belief can only be perceived by a divine ruler).[44] Yet the actual Hobbesian argument for the claim that the sovereign cannot and should not regulate his subjects' internality, their thoughts and beliefs, is precisely the same one that he makes for the claim that the sovereign must regulate their exteriority, their actions and declarations. The sovereign's incapacity is not epistemological, but a matter of legitimacy, and thus essential. A consequence of this is that legitimacy, and thereby the essence of the sovereign, consists in the sovereign's legalization of the extra-legal, which it must simultaneously preserve and protect (in positive terms) and leave alone and put up with (in negative terms).

In his study of Hobbes' *Leviathan*, with its juxtaposition of anti-Semitic resentment and brilliant insights, Carl Schmitt has called the divergence between a legally regulated exterior and a legally unregulated interior the "seed of death" for the sovereign as conceived by Hobbes himself in the image of the Leviathan.[45] As soon as this divergence occurs, all it takes, according to Schmitt, is "a small intellectual switch emanating from the nature of Jewish life"[46] to bring about the bourgeois liberal constitutional state:

53

Only a few years after the appearance of the *Leviathan*, a liberal Jew noticed the barely visible crack in the theoretical justification of the sovereign state. In it he immediately recognized the telling inroad of modern liberalism, which would allow Hobbes' postulation of the relation between external and internal, public and private, to be inverted into its converse. Spinoza accomplished the inversion in the famous Chapter 19 of his *Tractatus Theologico-Politicus*, which appeared in 1670.[47]

Schmitt's account of the consequences of Hobbes' restriction of sovereign commands to the external actions of its subjects is completely right: the Hobbesian sovereign is ultimately undone by this restriction. To put this more precisely: with the Hobbesian sovereign's self-restriction to the external, the sovereign is deprived of the power to administer the rule of law over corrupt nature. This was the Roman view, which Hobbes wishes to uphold but no longer can, according to Schmitt. The Romans abandoned the Greek idea of moral education, in which law's externality only seems to be a transitional moment. For Schmitt, this image of moral paideia is a later projection of political Romanticism. In contrast to the Greek idea of education in law, Roman law accepts the externality of law as an inevitable condition, since it corresponds to the reality of a corrupt nature. The fact that law is external to the human being's natural reality here means that law rules over those against whom force must be used. Understood in Roman terms, the externality of law is enforced as domination [*Herrschaft*]. A sovereign who represents political unity with his person is required for this imperative conception of law. It is only as a sovereign person that the legal system is able to rule over the natural.[48] For Schmitt, this is Hobbes' dilemma, the contradiction inherent in his thinking: first, with the image of the leviathan, he evokes a personal sovereign, able to dominate mere nature, and yet, at the same time, with the sovereign's self-restriction to only ruling over its subjects' external actions, Hobbes has planted its "seed of death." For in recognizing the distinction of inner and outer, willing and acting, the sovereign no longer represents political unity. He no longer rules over the naturalness of human beings, but legalizes their natural strivings. This is now the only way for him to acquire his authority. The Hobbesian sovereign, as established or simply agreed to, is a sovereign who restricts himself, a sovereign who has already resigned when it comes into office. Such a sovereign experiences a "metamorphosis from 'Realism' to 'Nominalism'" and what Ernst Kantorowicz observed of Shakespeare's *Richard II* holds true of him: "The Universal called 'Kingship' begins to disintegrate; its transcendental 'Reality', its objective truth and god-like existence, so brilliant shortly before, pales into a nothing, a *nomen.*"[49] Instead of dominating the natural, it is accepted. The resigned consequence of law's externality is its own self-externalization. The sway of sovereign law, by its own inner logic, has become law whose essence is permission or authorization [*Befugnis*].[50]

Permitting Freedom

The self-restriction of law, and thus law's own restriction of itself, consists in the fact that law cannot interfere with the natural striving for self-preservation, because this striving is law's basis (and hence its goal). Law's basis is simultaneously its limit: law must permit the natural striving for self-preservation. The conception of legal permission thereby obtains a new meaning. For what is thereby permitted is essentially undefined, indeed is indefinable, *for law*: law does not permit a particular kind of striving for self-preservation in a particular sense, but permits striving for self-preservation in general, or undefined striving.

In his argument for self-restricting the legal regulation of religion to external actions and declarations, Hobbes describes this indefinability in epistemological terms: rulers cannot "take notice of . . . the inward *thought*, and *beleef* of men," since these are "the effect of the . . . unrevealed will, and of the power of God."[51] The indefinability of the inner is the human understanding's inability to recognize its causality. The more radical and promising interpretation gets by without such assumptions, and conceives indefinability in practical terms – in other words, as freedom. On the question of whether "the report [of miracles] be true, or a lie," Hobbes thus writes:

> In which question we are not every one, to make our own private reason, or conscience, but the public reason, that is, the reason of God's supreme lieutenant, judge. . . . A private man has always the liberty, *because thought is free*, to believe or not believe in his heart those acts that have been given out for miracles. . . . But when it comes to confession of that faith, the private reason must submit to the public; that is to say, to God's lieutenant.[52]

The self-restriction of law's governmental power to external actions signifies nothing but the permitting of freedom: the permission to think and believe whatever one wants, whatever one deems it right to think and believe. Legal permission sets judgment free.

Freedom is predicated of thought ("because thought is free"). The reason for this and the way in which freedom is thereby understood becomes evident if we take up the perspective adopted here by Hobbes: the perspective of rule by law. On this argument, rule by law must permit that natural striving which forms its basis (and thus its goal). Thought, of which Hobbes predicates freedom, is legally permitted and therefore natural thought: "reason" (of which Hobbes speaks in the above-cited passage) that pertains to the striving for self-preservation; thinking *about* the natural striving for self-preservation, which everyone is occupied with *in* their own natural striving. Hobbes proceeds on the assumption that the striving for self-preservation occurs under natural laws [*Gesetzen*] that we adhere to in our reasoning. If, however, Hobbes next goes on to make clear that these "are not properly laws, but qualities,"[53] then this implies that the freedom of thought enjoyed in carrying out the natural striving for self-preservation *is not subject to any normative laws at all*: it is free (in this sense) because it is lawless – free from any kind of normativity. Spinoza concludes that the freedom of natural thought only follows "the rules determining the nature of each individual thing by which we conceive it is determined naturally to exist and to behave in a certain way"[54] – and therefore does not follow the rules of "sound reason."[55] "But since we are here discussing the universal power or right of Nature, we cannot acknowledge any difference between desires that are engendered in us by reason and those arising from other causes."[56] Natural thought is free precisely insofar as it is also able to be a thought without reason, indeed a thought that can be opposed to reason. The (natural) freedom of (natural) thought is the freedom to think rationally *or not* to think rationally. It is *this* freedom, the freedom of indifference between reason and unreason, "which the civil law leaves us."[57]

The full meaning of this definition becomes evident when we note the question to which it responds. It becomes evident, in particular, when we note that the question which Hobbes answers by introducing freedom of thought and belief is a question of how (not a question of whether), since it is clear that subjects have to obey the sovereign's legal commands as regards religious matters. These commands establish which creed holds sway in a state and, consequently, how one should worship (including which reports of miracles are to be declared true). These commands of the sovereign must be obeyed, but not because subjects view them as right; the sovereign's commands may not demand this. Human beings have established the sovereign precisely in order to authorize it to give commands that must be obeyed *regardless* of what subjects think of them. It does not matter *why* subjects obey such commands: they neither require, nor do they ever expect, an understanding of their correctness.

Laws [*Gesetzen*] leave the bases for complying with them up to us. The modern sovereign's resignation from the inner lives of its subjects, to which it has no access, follows from its realization that it cannot *want* their inner compliance at all, because of what the sovereign is – instituted and authorized by those over whom it rules. In recalling its basis in the will of its (future) subjects, the sovereign, in its laws, recognizes its subjects' freedom to want what it wants *or not* to want this.

This is completely opposed to the Greek idea of education in law, the view that law exists *in order to* influence its bases in an external manner that cancels itself out and to engender a moral disposition of having the capacity for the right bases. In its operation, Roman law breaks with this idea by considering morality *and* immorality, sound reason *and* merely natural striving to be equally possible. Law in Rome concludes from this that its externality is not a temporary expedient in the educational process that is later dispensed with, but something which is just as impossible to get rid of as the corruption of human nature, which law must rule with its commands. Even here, therefore, law still judges in a moral sense – law imposes sound reason against merely natural striving – but it no longer *proceeds* in a moral manner since it no longer educates us to reason soundly, but instead rules. With the modern form of rights, in contrast, law [*Recht*] does not simply resign itself to the possibility that it might be internally repudiated and view this as ineradicable (and for this very reason in need of commands). Instead, law allows and indeed enables it – as *possibility*. The externality of law (which is an essential part of its conception) thereby has its *meaning* radically transformed: it has become an externality that is opposed to an internality whose inaccessibility to law signifies freedom from law.

Excursus: Legal Choice (Kant)

Kant's conception of legality is defined by the claim that there is an internal connection between law's externality and permitting freedom. Legality and morality are two forms of lawgiving, which Kant distinguishes "with respect to the incentive": on the one hand, there is "The mere conformity or non-conformity of an action with law, irrespective of the incentive to it," and on the other hand, there is "that conformity in which the Idea of duty arising from the law is also the incentive to the action."[58] Kant also formulates this distinction as follows: "Ethical lawgiving (even if the duties might be external) is that which *cannot* be external; juridical lawgiving is that which can also be external."[59] Since juridical lawgiving stipulates not why but how we are supposed to act, it only regulates "the external and indeed practical relation of one person to another, insofar as their actions, as facts, can have (direct or indirect) influence on each other."[60] Juridical lawgiving does not provide any reasons for why we are supposed to act in such ways. This can be formulated in positive terms: since juridical lawgiving only considers external actions, and not the inner reasons for such actions, and because actions, viewed in this way, are acts not of the will (of the capacity for desire, "whose inner determining ground . . . lies within the subject's reason"), but of choice (of "the capacity for *doing or refraining from doing as one pleases*"),[61] the restriction of juridical lawgiving to actions entails setting choice free, within legal limits. "No account at all is taken of the *matter* of choice, that is, of the end. . ." but right judges "the *form* in the relation of choice on the part of both, insofar as choice is regarded merely as *free,* and whether the action of one can be united with the freedom of the other in accordance with a universal law."[62] The "universal principle of right" is a consequence of the externality of juridical lawgiving precisely because "Any action is *right* if it can coexist with everyone's freedom in accordance with a universal law, or if on its maxim the freedom of choice of each can coexist with everyone's freedom in accordance with a universal law."[63] Of course, another consequence is that juridical lawgiving can never require "that this principle of all maxims be itself in turn my maxim":[64] if right leaves the basis for action up to us, then it also leaves up to us the basis for those actions that we are required to do in order to comply with it.

Kant proceeds to give an emphatic interpretation of legally permitted choice: it forms a person's "innate" right to the freedom "of being *his own master (sui juris)*."[65] Equality, which is likewise innate, follows immediately from this single basic right to choice, as does the presumption of innocence, as well as the authorization "to do to others anything that does not in itself diminish what is theirs" – including "such things as merely communicating his thoughts to them, telling or promising them something, whether what he says is true and sincere or untrue and insincere (*veriloquium aut faliloquium*); for it is entirely up to them whether they want to believe him or not."[66] The legally permitted "inner" sphere, which Hobbes restricts to thoughts and beliefs, includes for Kant all utterances that do not "harm" anyone. Right must leave it up to our choice, and must therefore leave our choice up to us not merely in an invisible and inaccessible inner sphere, as with Hobbes, but also in everything we say that does not harm others. This decisive step beyond Hobbes, however, follows from the logic of Hobbes' own argument: the claim that right cannot concern itself with reasons that form the basis for action. If a person can bend the knee while engaged in religious worship, then one person can tell another person something true (or untrue). When lawgiving (in the more recent, modern sense) is external, there cannot be a legal prohibition on lying.[67] The only thing that is legally relevant is how "their actions, as facts, can have (direct or indirect) influence on each other."[68] In other words, what counts is whether such an influence "harms" others because it transgresses the limits of equality. In this case, however, as Kant turns Hobbes' thoughts against Hobbes himself, we would be unable to regulate not merely belief but also profession of faith, not merely thoughts but also declaring such thoughts – insofar as such actions do not harm others in the specified manner. Legal obligation must remain external: it is the external regulation of the merely external, and thus the setting free of everything not external. This is the basis for the Kantian right to freedom. It is not "innate" because it results from human nature, but because it is a consequence of the conception of right as external lawgiving.

What, however, is the basis for the externality of juridical lawgiving, and in what does it consist? Kant explains such externality as follows: "No external lawgiving can bring about someone's setting an end for himself (because this is an internal act of the mind)."[69] Right must set internality free, *because* it gives laws in an external manner. Our review of the Greek conception of educative law [*Recht*] and the Roman conception of law as dominion [*Herrschaft*] has revealed that this conclusion is incorrect – or circular. Setting internality free is only a consequence of law's externality if we have already surreptitiously placed it there. Law's externality can also be understood in a completely different way: as educative or oppressive, for instance. Law's externality, which defines its form in general, law as such, is therefore not the basis for the distinctive way in which the modern form of rights permits freedom: the form of modern rights is not a – simple or direct – consequence of law's form. Hence the question of *why* modern law construes and establishes its externality so as to permit freedom of choice. This question remains unanswered in Kant's conception of legality; indeed, it is not even posed. We need a different conception of legality, as the specific feature of modern law, to grasp its connection with the modern character of rights.

We will call this different understanding of modern legality the *self-reflection of law*. The relation between the form of law and the form of modern rights is not immediate, but mediated: it is mediated by law's self-reflection.[70]

* * *

Modern law rules by restricting itself. It rules in such a way that, with its regulations, it validates the natural will's choice. It validates the will prior to law's regulation: this is the second definition of the modern character of rights. In substance (in performative or functional terms),[71] it is opposed to the first definition – the first enables, the second permits – but it is a direct consequence of that definition. Permission is the other, negative side of how law positively enables the natural.

Spinoza formulates the juridical setting free of internality as the maxim that law may not rule in such a way that those who are ruled thereby cease *to be human beings.*[72] Strauss and Schmitt follow him when they interpret the resignation of the sovereign in Hobbes' theory as the birth of liberalism – thus taking liberalism at face value. In this case, setting the natural free from legal rule means setting the human being free from state rule: to understand the term "liberal" in such terms is to view law's self-restriction (to the external as opposed to the internal) as the liberation of the individual. This is a misunderstanding of both legal permission and the liberal form of governance, however. The modern character of rights does not set the individual free from law, but sets internality, which cannot be regulated, free from legally regulated externality. The modern character of rights establishes the difference of inner and outer. It establishes this difference, however, *in* the individual (who thereby becomes a subject). Modern law's externality becomes the modern subject's internality: the modern subject must exercise law's external governance of the natural will *in (and by) itself.* The modern subject must externally rule itself.

Modern law's break with Greek paideia does not therefore mean – as a simple liberal interpretation supposes – freeing the individual from the claims of legal regulation. It never entails that law has no normative claim on the being or ontology of the legal subject. Now, however, this claim no longer means that the individual develops the disposition of justice and becomes moral. The claim of modern law on the subject now amounts to the claim that the subject will become able to internally maintain external rule over the natural – over itself as natural. It also entails that the subject acquire power over itself to split itself into legal volition and natural volition, so that its legal volition simultaneously restricts and sets its natural volition free. In other words, modern law no longer educates, but *disciplines.*[73] It does not transform the individual's nature, which is governed by law [*Gesetz*], into a virtuous disposition, but produces the subject of self-discipline: the subject who can itself govern its own nature.

— 4 —

ANTAGONISM OF PERFORMANCE

Having gone through the history of the regime of private law twice, we now have two accounts of the modern form of rights: first, rights *enable* the realization of natural striving by restricting such striving according to the law of equality. Second, rights *permit* natural striving by setting it free internally. The modern form of rights is defined by its performance – by what it *does* in relation to the non-juridical. It legalizes or, in other words, secures the natural. This performance has a dual form: it enables and permits. Enabling and permitting define how modern law governs. Modern law's governing is a matter of enabling and permitting. In contrast, prohibiting and imposing, the performances of traditional (according to Foucault, sovereign)[1] law, have a derivative status. The way in which law rules has thereby been fundamentally transformed – obviously without ceasing to be the "other form" (Marx) of social domination.[2]

The two achievements (or performances) of the modern form of rights were introduced in order to refer to two different dimensions. Legal enabling refers to *why* rights are being *exercised* – as well as how law applies to actions in which rights are being exercised: law enables the realization of natural claims. In contrast, legal permission refers to *why we should comply with* legal obligations – to how law relates to the reasons why the legal stipulations of rights are complied with: law permits discretionary natural volition. These two dimensions of the modern form of rights correspond to the two versions of the history of their emergence. Both versions have three stages: from moral law (in Athens: Aristotle) to natural law (in Rome: Cicero) and then on to modern law (in London: Hobbes).

The *first version* of this history is concerned with a fundamental

61

upheaval in how law yields obligatory claims. In moral law, rights are the share, what belongs to one, what each deserves in a just division. Rights are conceived on the basis of a just order, which is the basis for any claim that one person is entitled to make over against another. This also remains true of Roman law [Recht]. At the same time, right [Recht] here is still what each has as his own, but is no longer a share in moral practice. Roman law abstracts from the morality of exercising rights; "it is passed over in silence, falling into law's gap" (Michel Villey).

The modern form of rights should now be unmistakable. The modern form of rights is not silent on the question of why rights are being exercised or used, but gives a radically new answer to this question: right enables the completion of "natural" activities. "Natural," in this sense, means pre- or extra-juridical: every action not oriented to law's [Rechts] normativity is natural. Modern law *produces* the naturalness of the non-juridical, or the non-juridical as natural.[3] Law secures the opportunity for natural action.

The *second version* of the history of how the modern form of rights emerged is concerned with how law establishes and ensures compliance. Moral law conceives and organizes its compliance in pedagogical terms: education is the point of complying with law. Law is prescriptive because it can only be focused on the works, and not the disposition, of virtue. Yet this is precisely how it engenders virtue as disposition. In Roman law, in contrast, the establishment of law is depoliticized into an establishment of natural reason, and is thereby depoliticized into enforcement against ubiquitous unreason, the corruption of the human being. In breaking with Greek paideia, external dominion in Roman law presupposes the continual possibility of unjust conduct.

Once again, there is no way to mistake the modern form of rights for this Roman characterization. For in its modern form, the enforcement of legal obligations is limited to the "external," to actions and their effects on each other, in such a way that the internality of subjects, their volition, is not merely grudgingly accepted, but *permitted.* Modern law establishes the compelling obligation to obey it precisely by allowing us the freedom to come up with reasons to obey it. The modern form of rights is concerned with freedom of choice: the natural freedom of law through law.

The performance of the modern form of rights is the legalization of the natural. This – and not because they exist by nature and are therefore valid "before law" (Spinoza) – is *why* they are called "natural" rights. Their performance consists in securing the pre-juridical status quo, natural action and volition. The modern form of rights is concerned with securing the natural. They achieve this in an irreducibly dual way: as enabling and as permission. What constitutes the necessity and thus the unity of this dual form?

In the nineteenth century, the modern theory of rights developed two basic conceptions whose opposition shaped the discussion until well into the twentieth century: interest theory and will theory (or a theory of choice). Each theory formulates one of the two performances of the modern form of rights in a one-sided manner and suppresses the other. Interest theory claims that all rights aim to ensure the equal realization of natural striving. The basic types of such striving are interests, whose realization is to be secured by rights. In contrast, the will theory of rights emphasizes that all rights aim to secure domains in which we can focus our natural striving at our own discretion. Choice prevails in such domains of legal non-regulation. According to interest theory, law is concerned with ensuring that specific goals can be reached. It is therefore concerned with the opportunity to carry out actions that satisfy interests, actions which are focused on goals and which can thus be identified by their goals. According to will theory, in contrast, law is precisely the reverse, aiming instead to secure the natural will's capacity to be exercised free from legal considerations. This theory is therefore concerned with the opportunity for optional achievements – regardless of the goals aimed at and, consequently, regardless of the reasons why we attempt such achievements. The enabling of interests and the permitting of choice must address the natural, which they wish to secure, in opposite ways: as determined and as indeterminable. Interest theory and the theory of choice have contrasting conceptions of nature.

Excursus: The "Formal" and the "Material" Side (Ihering)

In the conflict between the interest and the will theory of subjective rights, Rudolf von Ihering joined the first party – for interests, against choice – and then attempted to resolve the conflict by reconciling the two sides. Ihering sharply criticizes German idealism's theory of the will and its basic acceptance of a utilitarian conception of law's use and purpose. Yet he also develops a model in which both interest and choice, enabling and permitting, are supposed to be compatible. As Ihering argues against Kant, Savigny, and Hegel, rights cannot simply be understood as the permitting of free choice, since in that case there would be nothing "good" about them at all and they would have no "content." "Rights grant nothing useless: the substance of law is *usefulness*, not the *will*." "A right

63

without a corresponding opportunity for satisfaction is an absurdity."[4] This is why rights must be conceived as "legally protected interests," since otherwise they could not be claims to *something* specific.[5] Ihering polemically developed this line of thought in detail. At the same time, however, and conversely, he identified the reason why the interest theory of rights, as it was formulated, cannot account for the modern conception of a right on its own. His basic (and influential) argument is as follows: the interest theory of rights cannot properly account for a right because the protection of interests can be a mere "reflex effect" of legal regulations, without such regulations having to take the form of legal enablement – without the protection of interests being an *entitlement*. However, if law does not merely protect interests indirectly, as a "reflex," but aims to enable them, in the form of rights, then we must recognize the *willing* of these interests and their realization: the protection of interests is not supposed to be "completely independent of . . . what is willed or not willed."[6] The legal protection of interests must include authorizing the will to have recourse to this protection (or not), depending on whether we actually have a certain interest (or do not). Legal protection necessarily entails the recognition of willing or striving.

This not only means that interest and choice must be thought together, but also that their connection must be conceived just as Ihering represents it. Interest and choice, enablement and permission, emerge together in this way because they form the "substantial" and "material" moment of any right:

> There are two moments that are constitutive for the conception of right, a *substantial* moment, in which right's practical goal is a substantial one, that is, the use, advantage, or gain that right is supposed to ensure, and a *formal* moment, which is related to every goal merely as means, namely, legal protection, *taking legal action*.[7]

Georg Jellinek reformulates this attempt to resolve the conflict of interest theory and will theory as follows:

> An individual will is only transformed into a subjective right when the former's authority over the existence and scope of interest is recognized. Will and interest or good therefore necessarily belong together in the conception of right. . . . Willpower is the *formal*, good or interest the *material* element in the subjective right.[8]

Ihering's and Jellinek's solution to the problem of how interest and choice are to be thought together in defining rights is as follows: interests define the "what" and "to what end," while the will defines the "that" and "how" of the right's respective claims.

The price that Ihering and Jellinek must pay for this solution – a consequence of their general anti-idealist program – is a fundamental curtailment of choice and thereby permission in their conception of a legal claim. For law does not permit choice simply because it grants the protection of interests, in the form of rights, so that this protection can be freely exercised (or not), and so that "it is up to individuals whether they decide to make use of their rights or not."[9] Instead, law's allowance for the protection of interests so that this protection can be freely exercised (or not) – as Kant's following through of Hobbes' argument to its logical conclusion already showed – exempts the reasons for willing something from consideration *in general*. It therefore permits choice, and this permitting of choice cannot be limited to the mere decision to demand the protection of interests. On the contrary, in the modern conception of rights, the right to a claim is only a *consequence* of the right to choice, which is inscribed in the form of legal claims.[10] If the modern form of rights is (co-)defined by the permitting of choice, since, as Ihering convincingly argues, we cannot otherwise distinguish between advantage and entitlement (in other words, between the protection of interests as a mere "reflex effect" of a law [*Gesetz*] and the legal claim), then choice is not merely a matter of how we make a claim but forms part of the *content* of entitlement. The legal claim does not merely entitle "willing or not-willing" (Ihering), and therefore the choice to make a claim. The legal claim only permits an interest that is protected by right, and even permits us not to pursue this interest, because it is already left up to choice to *have* this interest or *not* to have it.[11] The permitting of choice cannot be linked to the enabling of interest by simply distinguishing the different aspects of entitlement – formal and substantial entitlement (Ihering) or material entitlement (Jellinek) – because the permitting of choice does nothing less than call into question a fundamental assumption, without which legal enablement is inconceivable: the assumption that interests which have been enabled actually exist and are being pursued.

On the one hand, it is true that enabling interests and permitting choice are two aspects of the legalization of the natural in the modern form of rights, since every right is *always simultaneously both*. On the other hand, however, the performance of the modern form of rights *cannot* both enable *and* permit *to the same degree in each case*. For enablement and permission are structurally opposed ways in which the natural is legalized. Since legal enabling is concerned with safeguarding the realization of interests, and since interests are basic types of natural striving, law must *define* them: it must define what an interest is, which interests exist, and what it means to realize interests – what counts as

65

realization. The conceptual locus of interest is to be found precisely where law in itself attempts to illustrate the distinctions that are relevant for natural action. Interests only exist in modern law as enabling of the natural. Since legal permission, on the contrary, is concerned with safeguarding the exercise of choice, and since choice is the capacity to select an option without having to provide reasons for one's selection, law can only legalize choice by *not defining* it: law must blind itself to the different reasons we may have for doing things that fall outside of its scope. The conceptual locus of choice is characterized by the fact that it is situated where law ignores distinctions that are relevant in natural striving. As is the case with interests, choice only exists in modern law by permitting the natural.

Law is enabling in its intention to safeguard our ability to accomplish something important for natural striving, and thus something definite. Law is permissive in its intention to safeguard our natural striving's capacity to refer to something that is up to us, and thus something indefinite. Legal enablement and legal permission imply nothing less than two different understandings of the natural, of the pre- or extra-juridical, which rights in their modern form legalize. Enablement understands the natural as fundamentally determined (and determinable) by law, while permission, in contrast, understands the natural as indeterminate (and indeterminable) with respect to law. These two contrasting conceptions of nature define modern law as (i) economic law and (ii) anthropological law:

(i) Due to its positive enabling performance, modern law is immediately *economic*. It facilitates the natural striving for self-preservation by providing the necessary means for such striving.

(ii) Due to its negative permissive performance, modern law is immediately *anthropological*. It creates the natural human being, in distinction from the citizen, by relieving the latter of morality.

* * *

These two performances of law, positive and negative, enabling and permitting, are two aspects of the legalization of the natural carried out by the modern form of rights. Their relation is here defined in a dual manner:

On the one hand, it is true that the enabling of interests and the permitting of choice must occur together in any law. The enabling of interests, formative for law, is linked to whether we do or do not will a claim to them, while the permitting of choice, likewise formative for law, is linked to the specification of a perspective or a good. Rights in their modern form secure interests and choice *at the same time*.

On the other hand, it is true that the enabling of interests and the permitting of choice are opposed to each other. The enabling of interests presupposes that law defines natural striving. The permitting of choice presupposes that law cannot determine natural striving. In the modern form of rights, the securing of interests and the securing of choice are *diametrically opposed*.

In the modern form of rights, the dual performance of its legalization of the natural, enabling (of interests) and permitting (of free choice), are inextricably and simultaneously conceived as both unity and opposition. The modern form of rights is defined by this simultaneous unity *and* opposition of definitive enablement *and* liberatory permission for the natural. This constitutes the *formative antagonism* of its performance: due to the form of rights, the unity of modern law only develops in the opposition of mutually exclusive performances. This opposition forms the specifically modern version of "The Struggle for Law" (Rudolf von Ihering).[12]

Part II

Ontology: The Materialism of Form

A darned stocking is better than a torn one. Not so with law.[1]

The modern form of rights is to be understood by starting not with its bearer, the subject, but with the structure of law: this is the basic methodological thesis of the readings of the history of philosophy outlined in part I. These readings follow the conservative interpretations of the modern form of rights provided by Leo Strauss and Michel Villey, who interpreted this form as the expression of an upheaval in the conception of law. In the modern form of rights, a revolutionary transformation occurs in the conception of law, in the conception of juridical normativity, indeed of normativity in general. This transformation affects the fundamental relation in which law stands to its other, to pre- or extra-juridical nature.

Strauss and Villey have clearly indicated and precisely described the fact that the modern form of rights amounts to a revolutionary upheaval in the concept of law. They are unable to comprehend it, however. To them, modern law is sheer decline: Strauss and Villey strongly emphasize the radically new structure of normativity in modern law – as a normativity based *on* and thus related *to* facticity – but they are unable to conceive this structure in its positivity. They are unable to conceive the "*positive* history" of modern law, its original "type of rationality," or its "juristic experience,"[2] since they completely misconstrue the operation that allows us to understand the normativity of modern law and thus the modern form of rights. It is this operation alone that allows us to raise the question of whether an alternative to it, beyond the nostalgic invocation of tradition, is possible, namely whether and how there can be a *renewed* transformative revolution of rights. This basic operation is

69

the self-reflection of law. The modern form of rights is the form of law's self-reflection – law in the form of its own self-reflection.

In this regard, "self-reflection" is an ontological category. It designates modern law's mode of being: what (and how) modern law *is*. Modern law is self-reflective or is not modern law at all. At the same time, this implies that "modern law" is not a historical concept, but a structural one. Modern law is law that is self-reflective. It is therefore law which *is* the *way* it is: it reveals what and how law essentially is. "Self-reflection" here is not only an ontological category because it designates modern law's mode of being. Rather, it is an ontological category because it explains modern law's specific mode of being *on the basis of law's being*. The fact that modern law, in the form of rights, is law's self-reflection means that this is the – only – form in which what law is can be represented and performed.

The form of rights can therefore only be *evaluated* by considering this ontological definition of modern law. It is the foundation for the critique of rights, since the critique of rights assesses this form to determine whether – and how – it allows modern law's self-reflection to be carried out.

— 5 —

LEGALITY'S GAP

Let us now review the basic insight into the structure of modern law that we have obtained with the modern form of rights. We can summarize it by elucidating the Kantian term for this new understanding of juridical normativity. This term is "legality."

Legality denotes the freeing of what is juridically established from a previous idea of justice, whether this is understood in moral-political terms (Athens) or in terms of natural law (Rome). Legality signifies that what is juridically established has now become autonomous. Autonomy here means that law must create its own normativity. In other words, law's normativity is only its own if it is created – without being based on a moral politics or natural reason. Law's legality consists in the self-creation of its own normativity or, to put this slightly differently, legal right [Recht], considered in terms of morality or natural law, is always "any given legal norm" [beliebiges Recht].[1]

This, however, is only the negative side of legality in the modern era, its break with traditional just law. The fact that law's autonomy simultaneously implies the modern form of rights – and just how this occurs – is crucial. The positive side of legality in the modern era consists in the fact that autonomous law [Recht] is the right of rights [das Recht der Rechte].[2] Why is that? We can answer this question by going through the history of rights and attending to both sides.[3] They provide two answers to the question of legality's structure.

The *first answer* claims that law's legality consists in the operation of legalization. The autonomous act of establishing, on which law's normativity depends, is not something instituted without presuppositions, not a case of something arising from nothing. Instead, precisely to the contrary, the establishment of law takes place in a process of (re-)

71

forming what already exists. The autonomous normativity of legal right [*Recht*] is based on facticity or nature. In this respect, nature designates everything that exists before or outside of the legal system, as a normative order: something is natural *for law* because it exists independently of and prior to law, and is thus to be validated by law. The legal system regulates the natural. It therefore proceeds on the basis of strivings that it treats as facts. It does not attempt to intervene in such strivings, to educate or suppress, but attempts to enable them (at the very least limiting, and at best promoting them) from outside, accepting their givenness, according to a law [*Gesetz*] of equality. This is the first sense of the modern form of rights: they entitle – legalize – natural strivings that are considered to be facts. This becomes clear in interest theory (chapter 2): interest theory understands the normative content of rights as the entitlement to realize a natural striving, a natural drive, within the bounds of equality. Interests belong to the sphere of nature or facticity, which simultaneously precedes and is presupposed by law. For admittedly, striving as natural fact cannot yield a legal claim all by itself, but law can (and should and wants to) only legalize that striving as a natural fact which already exists prior to it. This occurs in the modern form of rights: rights entitle or enable the realization of pre-existing natural strivings.

The *second answer* claims that if autonomous law [*Recht*] is the right [*Recht*] to the factual (as the first answer maintains), then its normativity is based on presuppositions that it cannot have at its own disposal. Sovereign law in London is distinguished from moral law in Athens just as much as it is from imperative law in Rome by its connection to the awareness that law cannot wish to intervene in the facticity of natural striving. The same normativity that establishes itself cannot ensure that its bases are shared, since autonomous law knows that its normative order is merely obeyed, and indeed is established, because it is conducive to natural striving as fact. This is why autonomous law must free natural striving as fact. We thus arrive at the second sense of the modern form of rights: they permit – legalize – natural striving as fact. This gets to the heart of the theory of free will [*Willkürtheorie*] (chapter 3): a legal system that, as autonomous, is aware of the limits of its (educational or ruling) power is a system that must free the striving which it regulates, as something presupposed by it that lies outside its scope. The legal system must leave choice [*Willkür*] alone, must put up with what appears (from the perspective of law and *its* bases) to be arbitrary discretion. This occurs through the modern form of rights: rights entitle or permit the arbitrary contents and modes of natural strivings.

The form of rights therefore has two basic definitions:

(i)   By enabling, rights *base* law on natural strivings as facts.
(ii) By permitting, rights *restrict* law to natural strivings as facts.

These two basic definitions must be brought together: the form of rights always both establishes *and* restricts law. The restriction and establishment of law are held together in the form of rights. In basing law on natural strivings as facts, law is restricted, because it can only validate – or enable – what already exists prior to it as fact. Furthermore, in restricting itself to natural strivings as facts, law forms its own basis, because it must thereby validate – or permit – what already exists prior to it as fact. And by restricting itself to natural strivings as facts, it establishes itself, since it must thereby validate – must permit – what already exists prior to it as fact. Contrary to the liberal self-misunderstanding, rights cannot be defined by the fact that they "set limits on the sovereign will of the political legislator."[4] For their limiting is not "external" to what is limited, but "essential." Such an approach "starts from . . . the de facto limits that can be set to this governmentality . . . precisely in terms of the objectives of governmentality."[5] There is no contradiction between law's self-establishing and self-limiting. The establishment of law *is* its limitation, the limitation of law *is* its establishment.

For both sides have the same basis: there are two sides to law's relation to nature, juridical normativity and natural facticity. This relationship defines and constitutes the form of rights. Rights are the way in which the difference between law and non-law (or nature), the difference between normativity and facticity, is enacted within law. The modern form of rights is the form of difference. In other words, the modern form of rights constitutes a paradox. It enacts the difference *between* law and non-law *in* law. The form of rights is therefore processual (and thereby political). The modern form of rights takes the form of a process – the process of legalization: the juridification of the natural, the creation of law on a natural basis. And the form (or dynamics and energetics) of this process is the difference between normativity and facticity. The difference between law and non-law becomes the form of law in the form of rights.

Excursus: The Rule of Law (Neumann)

The concept of legality combines two features: the autonomy of law's creation and its constitutive reference (back) to what precedes law,

73

"nature." In his examination of the modern (or bourgeois, liberal) conception of law as "rule of law," Franz Neumann has shown how these two features are closely connected and mixed together, but cannot be isolated from each other. Neumann writes:

> This state, in which laws and not men were to rule (the Anglo-American formula) – that is, the *Rechtsstaat* (the German formula) – has rested upon force and law, upon sovereignty and freedom. . . . Both elements are indispensable. There is no modern theory of law and state which does not accept both force and law, even if the emphasis accorded to each of these components has varied in accordance with the historical situation.
>
> Juridical terminology expresses this actual contradiction in the two concepts of objective law and subjective rights (in German, both terms can be covered by the term *Recht*). "Objective law" means law created by the sovereign, or, at any rate, law attributable to the sovereign power; subjective rights are the claims of an individual legal person. The one negates the autonomy of the individual; the other presupposes and affirms it. Various theories have attempted to reconcile the contradiction expressed by these two terms. . . . All of these solutions are only apparent solutions, since they misconstrue the fact that both elements, norm and legal relationship, objective law and subjective rights, are original data of the bourgeois legal system.[6]

The history of bourgeois law is the history of the confrontation between these two sides – the two sides of legality: between the sovereignty or autonomy of the establishment of law [*Recht*] and law's reference to what precedes it, the subject's natural freedom. The critical theorist's task consists in thinking the equiprimordiality of both moments together, and therefore in not deriving the one from the other, but grasping their tense unity.

Neumann sees this unity in the idea of law's [*Gesetz*] universality: "We have, therefore, arrived at the conclusion that the central idea of the liberal legal system is that of the generality of the law."[7] He arrives at this conclusion because the "central idea" under consideration simultaneously holds two things to be true: on the one hand, law is "the positive law of the state, and not any kind of natural law as distinguished from it." Universal law, on the other hand, because it is a law of freedom, is "a new material law . . . [that] is thus confronted with law in a formal sense."[8] The puzzle of the modern idea of legality consists in how the autonomy of ("sovereign") lawmaking can be conceived together with the ("material") reference back to what precedes law. This is the puzzle of the concept of law.

To solve this puzzle, everything depends on how we understand the materiality of general law ("a new material law . . . [that] is thus confronted with law in a formal sense"). Neumann offers two entirely different explanations of this materiality that indeed contradict each other. In his first explanation, Neumann – like Carl Schmitt in the latter's *Constitutional Theory*,[9] on which Neumann is drawing – defines the materiality of bourgeois law as substantive ethical content. According to Neumann, it stands in a "tradition of scholastic and secular natural law" that "is not completely lost; it is still alive in the postulate of the generality of the law."[10] In this first explanation, the autonomy and the materiality of bourgeois law confront each other as alien: the autonomy of establishing bourgeois law is externally restricted by its ethical-substantive content. This external restriction leads to a situation in which the ethical substance that established bourgeois law "has lost its evident quality" and all that remains of the "bourgeois Rechtsstaat's ideal foundation" is a "helpless formalism,"[11] as is the case today on Carl Schmitt's diagnosis.

The second explanation is entirely different: here the materiality of law [*Gesetz*] is supposed to consist not in its concrete or substantive connection to normative contents, but in *how law [Recht] proceeds* – in the autonomous creation of its own normativity. Neumann thus explains the material content by drawing on the idea of the separation of powers: "The conception that the general law, as the material law, is distinct from law in a formal sense is decisively influenced by Montesquieu's theory of the separation of powers." For the crucial element of this doctrine is not merely the assumption "that it is possible materially to distinguish various functions of the state . . . therefore, that legislation, jurisdiction, and administration . . . are themselves substantially different." Rather, much more fundamental is the fact that

His [Tr. – Montesquieu's] theory further assumes a sphere of freedom of the individual which is fundamentally unlimited, so that any intervention of the state must be based upon general laws and must be controlled by independent judges, who do not create, but only declare, the law. The elements of the system are, therefore, pre-state liberty, interference with this liberty by material laws and execution of the laws by independent judges; with the consequence of the separation of powers.[12]

The materiality of law [*Recht*] therefore consists not in its translation of normative contents into laws [*Gesetze*], but in its assumption of a natural fact: the "material" assumption that *there is* "a sphere of freedom of the individual which is fundamentally unlimited." It assumes that natural

75

freedom, prior to law, is a fact. On Neumann's second explanation, modern law [*Recht*] is material because of the way in which, by autonomously generating itself, it refers back to a material that it must validate as prior to it and thus "natural." The universality of law [*Gesetz*] serves this purpose, precisely because it is purely formal. In other words, it does not articulate a substantial (for instance, moral) idea of justice. If the materiality of bourgeois law [*Recht*], as it was explained in its second sense, is understood to be its constitutive reference to an assumed factual freedom, it will for this reason no longer restrictively confront the formal universality of law. Instead, the materiality of bourgeois law can only be realized in the form of universal laws [*Gesetze*], with laws of merely formal generality or equality.

How we answer the question of the materiality of the bourgeois "rule of law" [*Gesetz*] is also crucial for answering the question of how law in the authoritarian state acts in relation to it. On Schmitt's diagnosis, when we interpret the authoritarian state as resulting from the internal disintegration of bourgeois law, we end up with a "political concept of law" [*Gesetz*] (law as sovereign establishment) that is only extrinsically connected to and mixed together with a "constitutional concept of law" (law as freedom-securing universality), but cannot be internally linked on conceptual grounds. The authoritarian state only ratifies the internal contradiction of the bourgeois "rule of law": "The two elements of the concept legal order are then dissolved into independent notions and thereby testify to their conceptual independence."[13] In an authoritarian state, the political order rids itself of traditional ethical contents – such as individual freedom and equality – that provided a more than merely formal meaning to the universality of bourgeois law. At the same time, the authoritarian state's political order thereby frees itself to establish and enforce a different political equality of the people, one which is no longer formal but "substantial" and which is opposed to the universality of bourgeois law.[14]

Neumann's explanation of bourgeois law's inner unity of formality and materiality yields a completely different interpretation of the relation between the bourgeois rule of law and the authoritarian state, which is indeed opposed to the first. For with Schmitt's ideas for the reconciliation of a "strong state and sound economy" in mind, Neumann claims that politics in an authoritarian state does not become truly autonomous or sovereign at all. Instead, the state that realizes the "totality" is simultaneously supposed to secure private property: "The realm of economics is left free. It is satisfied with providing regulations for the 'political' sphere."[15] This is precisely why the authoritarian state realizes the legal order's "material" reference to something factually prior to law as directly and immediately as possible. It does so under "renunciation of the general character of the law [Gesetz],"[16] which, in bourgeois law [Recht], is worn as a "mask" to disguise relations of social and economic domination. The authoritarian state's legal order is not politically autonomous or sovereign at all, as Schmitt believes, but functions economically; "all restraints are abolished which parliamentary democracy, even when functioning badly, had erected against the unlimited execution of the requirements of monopolies."[17] If the materiality of bourgeois law [Recht] is understood to be its ethical-substantive content, which is externally opposed to the modern autonomy of the establishment of law, then the authoritarian state is the necessary result of a crisis in which the rule of law's two sides separate from each other; such is Schmitt's interpretation. If, in contrast, the materiality of bourgeois law is understood to be its reference to something factual, which it presupposes, then bourgeois law and the authoritarian state are two fundamentally different modes of operation *that share the same structure.* Both validate the facticity of what precedes law and is naturally given (and of the social relations into which this natural facticity develops): bourgeois law does this under the mask of universal law [Gesetz], while the authoritarian state does it with brutal openness and directness.

A two-part question thus arises. First: how are we to understand law's [Recht] reference to the factual or natural? On what basis is this reference established? Second: is there another way to proceed than through either laws or authoritarianism? Is there an alternative to the alternative of bourgeois and authoritarian state?

* * *

What constitutes the basic structure of law, whose self-reflection results in the paradox of rights? Why does law's self-reflection lead to *this* form, in which the natural and the factual validate what is beyond law in law (and which thus appears to be a paradox)? Because the self-reflection of law is nothing but the expression and formation of a gap that is to be found at its very heart. Self-reflection here means to expose the gap in law, the gap that constitutes law [Recht]; not to mend the tear in right [Recht], but to affirm it.

Distinction and Self-Reference

There is a gap in the heart of law [*Recht*] – of all law: Niklas Luhmann has formulated two insights that lead to this thesis, which forms the basis for understanding the modern self-reflection of law. The first insight is that (i) law – as form – is characterized by two different distinctions. The second insight is that (ii) both of these distinctions in law – as system – are linked by their self-referentiality.

(i) *The twofold difference of form*: Everything that law does is defined by its use of a specific form. In other words, everything that law does is defined by its use of a form that is specifically unique to it. In other words, it is defined by its making of a specific distinction, since "the form of the form is . . . a distinction."[18] In law [*Recht*], this is the distinction of legal and illegal [*Recht und Unrecht*]. Law uses this distinction to do what only law (and law alone) can do: identify something as legal or illegal. Law is to be found wherever and whenever the distinction of legal and illegal is operative. "[T]here is no other authority in modern society which can proclaim: this is legal and this is illegal."[19]

Anywhere law is used in this form and something is identified as legal (or illegal), there will thus be an "outside": for what is legal, this will be the illegal; and for what is illegal, it will be the legal. "Now we have to consider yet another outside, namely, the outside of the difference between [legal] and [illegal], that is, the outside of the unity of this difference, the outside of [law]. This would then be the world."[20] Law is constituted by using its form "in a certain domain . . . that becomes . . . *its* environment."[21] Law distinguishes between legal and illegal. This distinction simultaneously leads to another distinction, however. Alongside the distinction between legal and illegal, there now emerges the distinction between distinguishing legal from illegal and not distinguishing legal from illegal: the distinction of legal and *non*-legal.

As with any form, so for law's form, too, both distinctions always occur together. Yet they are fundamentally different. The first is normative and symmetrical: it distinguishes between two sides that are normatively opposed to each other – as positive (legal) and negative (illegal) side – but are two sides of the same coin; both are "values" (Luhmann). The second distinction is structural and asymmetrical: its two sides are the form as it is used in law and the world as law's outside, the non-legal; legal form and matter that is indifferent to law and thus – from law's perspective – formless.

(ii) *Self-Reference*: The first distinction, between legal and illegal, is

78

present in law in such a way that one or the other side of the distinction is used to identify something (as legal *or* illegal). In contrast, the second distinction, between legal and non-legal, occurs in law where (and because) it identifies something with such distinctions and at the same time refers *to itself*: law must distinguish between legal and non-legal, between itself and world, because law does not exist without self-reference. For in order to be able to legally refer to anything and identify it as legal or illegal, law must refer to other occurrences of distinguishing and be able to identify these as legal, too. And to do this means to identify them as legal *and not* non-legal, and therefore to employ the distinction of legal and non-legal. Law cannot merely be defined by its distinguishing between legal and illegal, since there could then only be a single legal act, a single use of the distinction between legal and illegal. Every use of the distinction between legal and illegal repeats the use of this distinction, however. Law therefore requires not only the identification of something as legal or illegal, but also the identification of other acts as such that use the distinction of legal and illegal or that do *not* use it – and thereby, at the same time, law requires the use of the distinction between legal and non-legal.

We can also formulate the same argument, drawing on H.L.A. Hart, that law cannot merely consist of primary rules. The "step from the pre-legal into the legal world" is only taken when there is (at least) a secondary "rule of recognition" that allows us to say when we are dealing with a legal rule of the primary type and thus with a legal occurrence.[22] Law can only contain primary *rules* if it does not consist exclusively of *primary* rules. For law cannot operate without "basal self-reference": its operation "requires a minimum 'similarity' in the elements."[23] Every act of judicial decision or of legislation thus relates to other such acts and in doing so achieves the "forms of identification" for law (as law).[24] Law [*Recht*] operates on two levels at the same time: it *uses* the distinction of legal and illegal (to identify something as legal *or* illegal) and it *refers to* this distinction (to identify something as legal and not non-legal).

Luhmann has formulated the logical form of law [*formlogische Gesetz*] at work here in a general way, as follows:

Each form has two sides that it distinguishes. Those two sides, however, do not participate in the shaping of the form in an equal manner. The operational use of the form can only proceed from one of its two sides. The operational use has to begin somewhere, for it would otherwise be unnecessary to distinguish the two sides at all. The distinction is made with the pragmatic intent to designate one side but not the other. What is distinguished, therefore, has to be distinguished from the distinction itself. Such a formulation might be dismissed as a mere rhetorical trifle.

79

... Yet ... the problem remains. We cannot begin with the operation as long as the distinction [C.M. – in other words, using the distinction] between distinction and indication (signification) is not copied into the distinction.[25]

In law's simultaneous reference to the distinction that it uses, in its only being able to use this distinction in such a way that it must at the same time refer to it, the distinction is distinguished from the act of using it. And because this occurs in law itself, we can also say that the distinction used by law is "copied into" law or that the "distinction ... recurs in itself."[26] In using the distinction of legal and illegal, and referring to it, law simultaneously uses the distinction of legal and non-legal. Law uses both distinctions, and this two-level use of distinction is internally connected. Law is the doubling, indeed the separation *and* connection of decision *and* self-referral, practice *and* self-reference.

Gap, Violence, Exception

The meaning of distinguishing, the meaning of "distinction" [*Unterscheidung*], is radically different on these two levels. The distinction between legal and illegal is a distinction between two values that are mutually exclusive, both of which are defined by law, however. The distinction between legal and non-legal, in contrast, is a distinction between legal distinction and legal non-distinction (or non-legal distinction). It is a distinction between law and the "world" as a zone of indeterminacy, from law's perspective. The fact that these two distinctions are fundamentally different does not mean, however, that they cannot work together. Indeed, they must work together. The world beyond law, the non-legal, is the "'unmarked space' ... [that] cannot be distinguished but can only be brought into a form by making a distinction."[27] Law does this by leaving the world (the non-legal) behind, but not as "the infinite space of otherness" opposed to it.[28] Instead, law leaves the world (the non-legal) behind by establishing the distinction between legal and illegal. The legal is distinguished *from* the non-legal in such a way that the distinction between legal and illegal is drawn *in* it – and is thus drawn where the distinction between legal and illegal has not (yet) been made. And it is thereby transformed into a legal distinction.

This means that, when it distinguishes between legal and illegal, in the legal decision, there is nothing at all that is non-legal, and therefore no world *for law*. To regard something as illegal and thereby a "trigger for legal operations"[29] means precisely to treat it as belonging no longer to the world, but to law. In this regard, it is already (always already) an element or process in law. "In other words, the legal system creates its own territory by its own operations (which are at the same time social operations). Only when doing so does it develop a social environment of law within society."[30] The fact that the world, as an unmarked space of the non-legal, is "brought into a form" (Luhmann) by the drawing of legal distinctions does not therefore mean that, in law's operation, a form is externally applied to a non-legal, extraneous matter. We thus need to break with the metaphysical "tradition" that "teaches us to conceptualize form as one side of a distinction whose other side can then be designated in various ways – such as form/matter, form/substance, or form/content."[31] The legal only exists *in* the process of law: law is legal from the beginning, all the way down to its matter, its material. Legal proceedings thus refer not to events and agents in the "world," but to their legally formative representatives. A legal process is impossible without representation.[32] In every legal proceeding in which there is a distinction between legal and illegal – as far back as we can imagine – we also find a preliminary procedure included, in which elements that can be legally processed were generated. This preliminary procedure, which has been included [*eingeschlossen*], is at the same time (so it seems) *con*cluded [ab*geschlossen*] by being "brought down . . . .to a fall." "Thereby the fallen are not destroyed but are in a certain way raised up again – within the limits fixed by the dominating ones."[33] There can be no pre-legal material at all that would still have to be made a legal matter in the legal process. Any such material is or has always already been a matter of law. The fact that the world is "brought into a form" by law is therefore not a step that is taken now, in the sense of carrying out a lawful act in the present moment, but something that must have been carried out always already, so that the legal process will have existed.

At the same time, however, the absence of the non-legal world in the operation of legal form is never guaranteed. The achievement, and thus the conclusion (temporally: the pluperfect) of the pre-legal preliminary procedure, is never assured. Here, however, this can only mean that the non-legal world, which is opposed to its own legal representation, can always *adversely* impact a legal proceeding, as commotion, murmuring, distraction, obstinacy, disorder, refusal, violence.[34] The non-legal world *can* reveal the limits of the legal process's power of juridification, since the criminalization of opposition as unjust ("contempt of court" and the like) is ineffective. This, however, is not something that can be established on the basis of experience. On the contrary, the concept of law must establish the potential for this experience: the basis for the

81

non-legal interruption of law is to be found in law itself. This basis is nothing but the distinction of legal and non-legal. Law uses this distinction in referring to itself, in order to confirm itself. Because law can only do this in such a way that it distinguishes itself in itself from non-law, however, reference to *what – and where – it is not* is inscribed in its own self-reference. In being aware of itself, law is aware of non-law. Law is therefore aware that something eludes its distinguishing – since this is what non-law *means*. To be sure, law, as it proceeds, can never experience the non-legal as such, as non-legal. In proceeding, law can never identify something as non-legal (since all legal identification is identification as legal). Because it is familiar with non-law (or is at least aware of it), however, law recognizes the possibility that something which it cannot resolve is opposed to its procedure. It does not have a conception of non-law, but has one of the possibility of non-law. This possibility manifests itself as an experience of the limits of experience: in the identification of (or as) something that it can identify neither as legal nor as non-legal. Something is *non-legal* precisely insofar as it is neither legally nor non-legally *defined*.

If law, however, in referring to itself, irresolvably ascribes to itself the possibility of experiencing what is irreducible to legal terms, it also thereby destabilizes the existence or presence of the legal decision. If there is a legal process, if there are legal distinctions, this *is* a legal decision about the legal. *That* there is a legal process, that legal distinctions are being made here and now, is not a given fact. "[T]here is never a moment that we can say *in the present* that a decision *is* just."[35] Because law uses the distinction of legal and illegal in such a way that it refers to this distinction and thereby distinguishes itself from non-law's non-distinction, law, in itself, refers to what is outside of it. The formless world, the world as unformed, whose absence is presupposed in law's operation, is present in law as absent. The "murmuring rush of our surroundings" is audible in law. "Law is thus not something still, but a murmuring rush."[36]

The procedure of law is therefore faced with two opposed demands:

On the one hand, if the legal is all that there is in the legal process, then the non-legal has *always already* become legal, so that there can be no distinction between legal and illegal.

On the other hand, the preliminary procedure of juridification is *always still* underway, because the "infinite otherness" of the non-legal can never conclusively be given legal form.

In other words, the distinction of legal and non-legal is simultaneously present and elsewhere in law:

On the one hand, it is *necessary* that the difference between law and non-law is absent in law. It cannot exist in law (or if it does, law ceases to exist).

On the other hand, it is *possible* that the difference between law and non-law is operative in law. Law cannot be protected from non-law's intrusion (which is why it is unclear whether legal decision occurs here and now).

Law's *gap*, which is not to be closed, yawns between this alternative.

How is the gap in law torn open? By its self-reference, and therefore by its duplication into decision and self-reference. To put this more precisely: the gap in law is opened by the legal decision's self-duplication into the identification of something as legal or illegal and into reference to other, similar acts of identification (qua secondary rules).[37] For law thereby refers to itself in distinction to non-law and sees itself confronted with the – irresolvable – problem of operating with this distinction. This problem is "irresolvable" – since law cannot resolve it. Law can only operate with the distinction between legal and illegal, while the distinction between law and non-law dims, becoming inoperable. If form emerges in form, if law's distinction is replicated in law's necessary reference to its own form, a paradox thus arises: "the form of the form is a paradox. . . . A paradox is a form that contains itself."[38] For what form, in this case law, contains in itself is precisely the distinction of law and non-law, *which it cannot contain* – as long as it wishes to be law, making distinctions between legal and illegal and thereby making decisions (or as long as law must be this: because it would otherwise not be law, and therefore not exist at all or be nothing). Form's re-entrance into form is formless: murmuring rush. The paradox is that law's reference to its own form is necessary or constitutive of law – without it, law does not exist at all – *and* impossible, leaving law itself exposed – since it refers law to the non-legal, with which law can do nothing.

The violence of law dwells in this gap.[39] This explains why – and in what sense – law not only employs violence as an external instrument, but also structurally inscribes violence into its own operation. Violence thereby signifies the potential and efficacy of an effect, on this side of normative logic. Violence is sheer factual enforcement. In its decisions, law operates beyond violence. It breaks with violence, because here its effectiveness is normative. To decide a legal case is to apply a normative distinction that corresponds to the parties in dispute as legally described and defined entities. This is law's presupposition: in its normative operation, law must presuppose that it – only – deals with the legal, with legal matters and legal persons. At the same time, in its self-reference, law is aware of another side, the non-legal. It is thereby also aware that it is itself only the other side over against the non-legal. This is why law is also aware that its presupposition is not guaranteed and given. The possibility of a paradox thus emerges, namely a legally impossible situation: that law finds itself confronted with a situation which cannot exist at all for law, a situation in which law is exposed [*ausgesetzt*] to the effect of the non-legal and must therefore turn its presupposition [*Voraussetzung*] into something that it establishes itself. In this situation, law must establish [*setzen*] its "pre-" [*sein Voraus*].[40] In other words, law must enforce [*durchsetzen*] itself in the non-legal against the non-legal. To be able to operate legally or normatively, it must therefore operate in the non-legal: law must become non-legal. It must obliterate its legal form and function non-legally so that it can be law.

This situation is the exception:

> Every general norm demands a normal, everyday frame of life to which it can be factually applied and which is subjected to its regulations. The norm requires a homogeneous medium. This effective normal situation is not a mere "superficial presupposition" that a jurist can ignore; that situation belongs precisely to its immanent validity. There exists no norm that is applicable to chaos. For a legal order to make sense, a normal situation must exist, and he is sovereign who definitely decides whether this normal situation actually exists. *All* law is "situational law."[41]

The logic of the exception is the logic of law's violence. The exception is the moment in which law's gap is revealed – the moment when it is torn open, because it shows that law's presupposition of normality, the assumption that it is a decision about something that is already a legal matter and can thus operate in a purely normative fashion, is incorrect. It is the moment in which law must establish itself for the first time and always again. In this moment, "law splits into a pure being-in-force [*vigenza*] without application (the form of law) and a pure application without being in force: the force-of-~~law~~."[42] Law's fate, its splitting of itself in itself from itself and its effectuation as mere "force," and thus the violence of enforcement, is the fundamental way in which the persistence of the non-legal (as distinct from law) in law (and therefore against law) is exhibited: law's fate is that the distinction between law and non-law cannot remain external to law, but must become operative in law.

* * *

At the same time, it has become evident that the question of the legal form's other, of the un-formed, is not as easy to resolve as its system-theoretical definition seems to suggest. This definition holds that all legal operation, because it can only operate by distinguishing legal and illegal, is the use of a form. Such a definition is directed against a tradition that understands form as *one* side in a distinction, "such as form/matter, form/substance, or form/content,"[43] and therefore understands the use of form to be its application onto a matter that is distinct from it. This is a metaphysical tradition with oppositions that are simultaneously binary and hierarchical. It understands form and its other as opposed to each other (and then defines their relation by the priority of form, which is imprinted or inscribed onto matter).[44] The systems-theoretical theory of form raises a question against this understanding:

> what happens if the other side of the distinction . . . is simply omitted from consideration and form as such becomes the main focus of reflection and manipulation? What happens if "formal logic" is pursued as an attempt to ground all distinctions in themselves – an endeavor Gödel eventually halted? What happens when we raise the Derridean question of what the form, as a precondition for being form, makes appear as "present," and furthermore what is thereby excluded from consideration?[45]

When this happens, however, it is *not* (as Luhmann would also say) the case that forms or distinctions "are only . . . the play of differences among themselves."[46] It is not at all the free play of forms, but the re-entrance of the distinction of form *from its other* into form, which opens a gap in law and produces the paradox. The other side of the distinction cannot "simply be omitted." It is not so easy to dispense with this distinction. Rather, the other side returns in form's self-reference, and therefore in its interior. However, it returns as another other side: it is no longer matter as "substance" or "content" that achieves presence through form (as its essence), but matter that achieves presence as form's other; matter as the unmarked or formless, as the unformed (in form).

Self-Reflection

Law's self-reference tears open a gap, since "we end up facing a paradox with every attempt we make to observe the unity of the world in the world, that is, the unity of a distinction on which an observation is based."[47] There are various ways to avoid this paradox. Law can attempt to close the gap by doing something itself – and can believe itself able to accomplish this. Law can also *recognize* that this gap cannot be avoided, and can *reform* itself in light of this recognition, radically changing its form, the form of its form. Law can reconcile this paradox in an illusory manner, or perform it self-reflectively. This is the alternative of traditional and modern law. Law can operate in two ways with regard to its structural gap or paradox (and thus to its violence): it can patch it or it can deepen it – by tearing *itself* open. The motto of modern law is:

> A darned stocking is better than a torn one. Not so with self-consciousness. [C.M. – or: Not so with law.]⁴⁸

Law in Athens and law in Rome are two examples of the first possibility, the attempt to close its internal gap.⁴⁹ Both understand law as a specific form of distinguishing that refers to itself and thereby distinguishes itself from non-law. Both again wish to sublate the distinction of law and non-law in an encompassing unity and thus neutralize it, however. Both attempt to patch the tear in law. This is evident in how they deal with law's aspect of establishment, with law as an institution.

To understand law as an institution means to trace it to an act of establishment, of institution, from which it has emerged and which it must perpetually reiterate, practice, and orchestrate, in order to continue existing. In doing this, law breaks with the mythical conception of justice as fate. Anaximander formulates this conception of law in the following dictum:

> Whence things have their coming into being there they must also perish according to necessity; for they must pay a penalty and be judged for their injustice, according to the ordinance of time.⁵⁰

Justice straightens things out "according to necessity," in having them "pay a penalty," by passing away, for the injustice of their coming into being. Mythical justice is justice as the prevalence of fate. Law as an institution thus begins by presenting itself as a kind of (pre)history, the history of its institution. Law is an institution because or when it remembers (and therefore claims to remember) that it has been instituted and therefore must have been enforced: against others, in or against a world in which there is not yet a difference between legal [*Recht*] and illegal, in or against a world *before law* [*Gesetz*]. If, however, there is a world before law, there can also be a world after law: if law first had to be instituted, the possibility always exists that it could disappear again. This could occur, for instance, because other interests and concerns cloak themselves in or supplant the juridical distinction of legal and illegal. (This is the situation in which Oedipus finds himself in the beginning of his tragedy: the Thebans think they have something more important to do than atone for the murder of their king. Oedipus reinstitutes law with the statement that puts an end to this situation, by declaring himself to be a judge in this matter: "Well, *I* will start afresh and once again / Make dark things clear."[51]) Law is an institution because it views justice not as self-evident, something that enacts itself, but rather as something to be done. Law is justice that has been instituted. And the fact that law is instituted means that it must be opposed to non-law, that it must be enforced against non-law. By acting to institute itself, law exists in a difference – the establishment of law is the establishment of the difference between law and non-law, which it can neither accept nor overcome. This is what tears open the gap in law, namely the gap between what it must do and what it can do.

Models of traditional law attempt to close law's gap by minimizing the distinction between law and non-law, by reducing it to a mere moment. Pedagogical law in Athens understands the institution and enforcement of law to be a transitory moment in the teleologically oriented process of moralization. In this process, the violence of establishment is just as legitimate as it is unavoidable and useful. It is in the service of education and thus obtains its meaning as well as its justification from the idea of its own self-sublation. Non-law is the possibility of law, while law is the truth or reality, the telos, of non-law. Rational law in Rome adheres to this model, on other grounds, but it diminishes the moral integration of law and nature into a mere perspective, one that is beyond the law, and ignores the other perspective – the inner or proper perspective for law – of its continual opposition. The convergence of nature and law is here the result no longer of (moral, "political") education, but of philosophical insight that presupposes law, although – or even because – it is ineffective *in* law. Law relies on the perpetual possibility of striving for mere self-preservation. Yet, at the same time, philosophy knows that this is the self-lapsing of our true nature. If law's relation to non-law in Athens is *integrative* (law's power over the non-legal is merely a passing stage in the formation of a moral disposition that is no longer to be opposed to law, so that law itself has vanished), in Rome it is *imperative*: law's power over the non-legal is the expression of a split in human nature that cannot be overcome. Both, however, are models that are supposed to minimize the (bad) infinity of the violence of establishment, which law as an institution is exposed to from outside via moral education or philosophical insight: Athens' moral, pedagogical law did this by construing non-law as *not-yet*-law, as the possibility of law, and thereby construing law as the truth of non-law. Imperative rational law in Rome did this by construing non-law as *no-longer*-law, as a state of corruption or decline.

The distinction between law and non-law, which tears open the gap, is conceived either teleologically in reference to its (future) sublation or privatively on the basis of its absence or lapse.

Modern law begins with the decline of these attempts at minimization. Modern law is law that no longer thinks its distinction from non-law – in the absence of which law would not exist since there would be no institution of justice – from an afterwards, from its no-longer, or from a before, from its not-yet, but exists in the present moment of this distinction. Modern law *is* therefore law in crisis; modern law does not exist beyond or before its crisis. Modern law is law whose gap is its essence, whose essence is its gap. It is law *as law*, law *established* (as law): law that is nothing but law (in the terminology used above: the law of "legality"). Law's self-establishment as law radicalizes its self-reference into its self-reflection.

Law's self-reference – by which it constitutes itself in identifying different occurrences as *also* legal occurrences and thereby identifying every application of the distinction of legal and illegal as a reiteration of this distinction – simultaneously introduces a (second) distinction between law and non-law. For identifying itself as law implies not understanding itself as non-law. In its self-reference, law merely operates on one side of this distinction, but it can only do this by referring to non-law, however implicitly. This is why the possibility of experiencing a gap, violence, and the exception is a conceptual characteristic of law. Law's self-reflection consists in nothing but making explicit this simultaneity of self-reference and reference to something different, which must always remain implicit in law's operation.

> We will speak of [*self-reflection*][52] when the basic distinction is between system and environment ... It is an operation by which the system *indicates itself in contrast to its environment* [C.M. – my emphasis]. This occurs, for example, in all forms of self-presentation that assume the environment does not immediately accept the system in the way it would like itself to be understood.[53]

Self-reflection is the stage in which it becomes evident in law (exactly how this happens remains to be shown) that law can only refer to itself (or that law can only exist) by referring to itself in distinction to non-law or referring to non-law as law's other.

This stage of self-reflection characterizes the basic feature of modern law, through which it is opposed to both models of traditional law. From modern law's perspective, its self-reflection is based on identifying a simple truth that is ignored by both the Greek educational program and the Roman program of dominion. This simple truth is that non-*law* is *non*-law. In other words, non-law is neither *not-yet* law (thus the teleological interpretation in pedagogical law: the natural tendency *to* law, law in the mode of its still unrealized possibility) nor *no-longer* law (thus the interpretation in imperative law that theorizes degeneration: natural corruption, nature as the loss of reason or nature as the loss of its very self). Rather, nature is law's other insofar as it is the radical *absence* of the distinction between legal and illegal: nature neither as the possibility of education for virtue nor as the corruption of reason, but as the epitome of processes that are *not* oriented to this distinction *at all*. We therefore arrive at a conception of nature in the modern sense: nature is conceived as innocence by Spinoza, as a time and place "before law," in which there is thus "no sin," no wrong, because there is no law.[54] Likewise, for Pascal, nature is conceived as a time and place without "any proportion," which means that in our experience of nature "Nothing stays for us."[55] Law's self-reflection therefore begins to think non-law from the perspective of law: to think nature as radically external. And the self-reflection of law which thus begins consists in conceiving itself in distinction to non-law as its other.

There are two aspects to this, which signify:

(i)   law's recognition of non-law's externality: law's self-reflection as *(pre-)establishment* [Voraus-setzung] *of non-law*.

Because, however, law establishes non-law in advance, it simultaneously signifies:

(ii) the recognition of law's externality over against non-law: self-reflection as *law's self-externalization*.

Excursus: Sovereignty or Play (Agamben)

The (modern) alternative to law's (modern) self-reflection is sovereignty. According to Carl Schmitt's definition,[56] the category of sovereignty designates the power to "definitely" decide that the "normal everyday frame of life," which presupposes the legal norm for its validity, does not obtain. It is not limited to this, however. In addition, it is the power to *create* the normal situation. It is not merely the power to declare the state of exception, but also to – temporarily – end it by making its declaration. Sovereign power is bound to a "goal" whose attainability defines

89

it. Otherwise, it would not have this goal (its attainability thus "makes it superfluous").[57] Its goal is to close law's gap. Law is torn between what it must always already presuppose as given and what it can perform itself. Law is essentially powerless. The situation in which this essential power-lessness manifests itself is the situation that Schmitt calls the "exception." The sovereign's supra-legal power consists in its ability to guarantee the presupposition of law in this situation. The sovereign transforms what traditional law regarded as ensured by morality or reason into its own achievement, its own establishment. In this regard, law is modern.

Schmitt's figure of the sovereign, however, is also already modern insofar as it has the concept of the exception at its disposal, since this precisely means that it sees the basis for its gap between establishment [*Setzung*] and presupposition [*Voraussetzung*] in law's constitutive self-reference. The basic definition of sovereignty is therefore awareness of law's gap. This is where the truth of the idea of sovereignty is to be found. Yet it becomes false precisely when it claims a supra-legal power that allows it to close this gap, even if this only ever happens in an ad hoc manner (which results in the gap repeatedly reopening): the capacity to produce the normality presupposed by law. As Walter Benjamin shows, contra Schmitt's baroque staging of sovereignty, such power cannot be finite. The sovereign, who is supposed to ensure the institution of law, must "topple over, 'heavy with crowns.' Kings must *pro*-pose [vor-*tra-gen*] the occasionally grotesque discrepancy between signs and that of which the latter are supposedly signs."[58] The gap that the Schmittian sovereign wants to close resurfaces in its innermost depths, namely between what it wants (because it must want it) and what it can do.

The Schmittian sovereign begins with a reflexive insight: insight into law's gap. And it ends in unreflective blindness: it is itself faced with the gap that constitutes it. For this reason, it looks somewhere else – to liberals and Jews – for the guilty party that has infected it with the "seed of death."[59] The Schmittian sovereign's reflexivity comes to a halt before itself. It does not see why it has always already failed. And because it considers itself to be the solution, it leaves law, to whose aid it comes, unchanged when it gets involved in the limits of law: law's form, the form of its normativity, the structure of the distinction between law and non-law (which results in law's gap) remains internally unchanged by the sovereign's additional external involvement. The sovereign is only an external supplementation of law. In this regard, law's self-reflection is opposed to the idea of sovereignty. Law's self-reflection is not merely cognitive (it does not merely consist in the awareness of law's gap, which the sovereign also has), but practical. Law's self-reflection changes the form of law. In other words, law's self-reflection changes the form of its normativity.

In so doing, law's self-reflection also simultaneously stands in contrast to the consequence that Giorgio Agamben has drawn from Benjamin's critique of the Schmittian solution. This consequence consists in a use of law that is no longer adjudicative:

> What opens a passage toward justice is not the erasure of law, but its deactivation and inactivity [*inoperosità*] – that is, another use of the law. This is precisely what the force-of-~~law~~ (which keeps the law working [*in opera*] beyond its formal suspension) seeks to prevent. Kafka's characters – and this is why they interest us – have to do with this spectral figure of the law in the state of exception; they seek, each one following his or her own strategy, to "study" and deactivate it, to "play" with it.
>
> One day humanity will play with law just as children play with disused objects, not in order to restore them to their canonical use, but to free them from it for good. . . . And use, which has been contaminated by law, must also be freed from its own value. This liberation is the task of study, or of play.[60]

Study and play are two ways of using law that "deactivate" its normative claim. For this reason, they are non-violent (since law's violence is the other non-normative side *in* its normativity). This is only possible, however, because, in their case, there is no outside or other against which law must be instituted and enforced. Study and play are worldless. If the traditional models sublate the difference between law and non-law in political morality or natural reason (and thereby limit its violence), and if Schmitt's doctrine of sovereignty consigns this violence to a supra-legal power (without acknowledging the melancholy of its groundlessness), Agamben simultaneously gets rid of the difference between legal and illegal as well as the difference between law and non-law, in the oblivious absorption of play and study.

But what happens the moment we wake up? If the difference between law and non-law emerges once more? Are we then only left with outmoded traditional models of reconciliation or the affirmation of sovereignty?[61] In contrast to this, the concept of self-reflection conceives a radical transformation of law: an inner transformation of the form of law itself.

A survey of its modern history yields two fundamental features of the concept of self-reflection that are vitally important for further clarifying this transformation of law:

(i)   It is clear from the outset that self-reflection is not to be conceived as an act of self-consciousness – if consciousness is to be understood

91

as knowledge of present objects. For that would lead to an insoluble problem: consciousness, in which the self becomes its own object, cannot be consciousness of the self *by the self*, as a self.[62] Instead, self-reflection has the structure of transcendental reflection, since it carries out the *"synthesis"* that "is not given through objects but can be executed only by the subject itself, since it is *an act of its self-activity*."[63] The subject constitutes itself in reflecting on the "act" of self-activity wherein the subject constitutes its objects. Self-reflection is the (re-)enactment of *self-creation*. In other words, law's self-reflection is nothing but the reflection of the self-creation of law.

(ii) It is equally clear from the outset that the process of self-reflection cannot be equated to "self-grounding" or "self-forgetfulness."[64] At the same time, to reflexively carry out the constitutive act of self-creation means "to designate the boundaries" of the self and "to leave open a space" in which there is no self.[65] If self-reflection must therefore be understood as self-limitation, then space for the other, as a limit on the reflexive self, does not exist independently of it. It is its own (pre-)supposition [(*Voraus-)Setzung*]. The self that limits itself *"points beyond itself"* but does so in itself: it contains the other, over and against which it limits itself, in itself.[66] And because the self, understood reflexively, only consists in the process of its own self-creation, self-creation is the self's establishment [*Setzung*] as (pre-)supposition [*(Voraus-Setzung)*] of the self's other. The self's other is immanent to its self-production: it is "heterological."[67] Non-law is not what is external to law, but what, as external, *is operative in law's innermost depths*.

Excursus: Reflection and Ritual. When is Modernity? (Douglas, Turner)

The central feature of classical theories of modernization is the claim that normative orders are reflexive. Accordingly, modern normative orders are distinct from traditional ones because they keep their own creation in mind. They are distinguished by their finitude in a radical, structural sense: not merely by the improbability of their genesis and not merely by the possibility of their disappearance. Rather, they are characterized by the essential crisis of their existence, which is due to the fact that every order stands in an irresolvable relation to its other – and that modern orders are aware of this.

Is this not also true, however, for those orders that modern ones claim to have left behind as traditional? Indeed, is this not even much more true for such traditional orders than for modern ones? Traditional orders are aware that they are exposed to an uncontrollable other. Are not modern ones, in comparison, defined by the loss of self-reflection – the supersession of self-reflection by strategies of self-grounding? Since (at least) Arnold van Gennep's study of rites of passage,[68] it has become evident that the rituals of premodern societies are a matter not merely of their own self-presentation and self-affirmation, as Durkheim believed, but of a practiced transgression. Such transgression leads neither to a sphere above the social nor beyond such a sphere, as in later religions, but leads back to a state prior to the social: rituals are concerned with the transition *to* the social, with the "threshold" *between* nature and society or culture. Rituals are "liminal" (Victor Turner).[69] For rituals are those cultural practices that reiterate their establishment in themselves, in being exposed to a confrontation with their other, with unformed, unarticulated, and disorderly nature. Even more than this, rituals are not merely those cultural practices in which a culture creates itself from and in opposition to a state of disorder, of "wild impulses" (Turner), but are those cultural practices whereby a culture simultaneously creates a state of otherness that stands in contrast to it. Rituals *create* the impure, the indistinct, by involving a cultural order in an endless adventure of self-creation:

> Thus a cycle has been completed. Dirt was created by the differentiat-
> ing activity of mind, it was a by-product of the creation of order. So it
> started from a state of non-differentiation; all through the process of
> differentiating its role was to threaten the distinctions made; finally it
> returns to its true indiscriminable character. Formlessness is therefore
> an apt symbol of beginning and of growth as it is of decay.[70]

Rituals are modes of practiced (or "performative") reflexivity – "a condition in which a sociocultural group . . . turn[s], bend[s] or reflect[s] back upon [itself],"[71] in returning to the threshold of its being, the *limbus* of the pre-cultural, the impure state of indistinction.

Modernity's distinguishing of itself through its self-reflection is therefore groundless. The cultural-critical argument that it is precisely modernity that has forgotten reflection is more promising: modernity no longer has a cultural place for the practiced confrontation with the no-place [*Unort*] of the natural, as the indistinct, from which each respective culture is created, while remaining perpetually exposed to its threat. It is precisely this cultural placelessness of the confrontation with culture's other, however, that undermines modernity's reflexivity in comparison to the rituals of traditional cultures. Such placelessness at the same time provides a unique opportunity for its radicalization, since the ritual placement [*Verortung*] of culture's performative reflexivity limits its power: it is inscribed in an economy of conservation; it functions as compensatory and thus as stabilizing. Ritual reflects a society's normative order, but because it takes place alongside that order, it leaves everything within it as it is: "The *liminal* phases of tribal society invert but do not usually subvert the *status quo*, the structural form of society."[72] In contrast, modernity de-ritualizes its self-reflection and thereby becomes placeless. In doing so, it becomes potentially ubiquitous: modern self-reflection stakes its claim in the normative order's innermost depths. It overthrows the normative order from within.

Self-reflection is not a privilege of modernity. On the contrary, modernity undermines practices of cultural self-reflection by de-ritualizing them. At the same time, however, it thereby transforms self-reflection from a ritual into a potential, namely a potential to transform the normative structure's basic order itself. The critical question, both decisive and to be decided, is thus: how can reflexivity be internally established in a normative order without conveying its transformative power via this internalization?

— 6 —

MATERIALIZATION

Law's self-reflection consists in its being regarded (and performed) in distinction to non-law. In this respect, the self-reflection of law is doubled in itself: law's self-reflection in distinction to non-law simultaneously entails non-law's self-reflection in distinction to law. As comparison with models of traditional law has shown, non-law in distinction to law only *exists* through law's self-reflection. In other words, only here – and thereby through law's self-reflection (which in this sense is modern) – does what is not defined by the form of law – law's environment or "nature" – have the status of law's other. Law's other, the being-other of non-law, is an effect of its self-reflection. For in law's self-reflection, non-law is likewise reflected, experienced and constituted as that which neither was nor will be juridical, but is precisely that which is not law. Law's self-reflection triggers non-law's – *own* – self-reflection (as *non*-law). Self-reflection is therefore not only doubled into two forms, but also doubled into two relations between both forms. Law's self-reflection is double and single at the same time: double as the self-reflection of law *and* the self-reflection of non-law; single, insofar as non-law's self-reflection only occurs *through* law's self-reflection.

Even in the doubling of the self-reflection of law and non-law, their relation thus remains asymmetrical: law is the form, non-law the formless – *relative* to law's form. Non-law is the formless that only exists if or because law as form exists. In other words, law and non-law are linked by *one* process of formation, which simultaneously creates that which precedes form in the establishment of form, namely the formless, which must repeatedly be "brought into a form"[1] and thereby never achieves form – properly or entirely. (To put this more precisely: the formless must repeatedly be brought into the form of the normative distinction

95

between legal and illegal, but is never itself defined by this form and is hence always opposed to this formation; this is the basis for the "gap in law.") If form's other can be called matter, and if matter is nothing but form's other here, then the two sides of self-reflection linked to each other, law and thereby non-law, can be characterized as follows:

(i) The self-reflection of non-law consists in its claim, in opposition to its formability, that it is non-form, indeed un-form, or matter.

(ii) The self-reflection of law consists in its rendering matter operative as non-form or un-form, in its formation.

The twofold, double-single movement of self-reflection therefore signifies:

(i) First, the *naturalistic self-withdrawal* of non-law, since the insight that matter dissolves all forms in its abyss is naturalistic.

(ii) Second, the *materialist processualization* of law, since the insight that all forms are co-produced by matter's driving forces is materialist.

The Naturalization of the World

If the form of law, in its self-reflection, is defined as non-law's other, then it thereby defines non-law as form's other (not only provisionally and from its perspective, but continuously and fundamentally). In this regard, law's self-reflection amounts to a radical redefinition of the relation of form and matter, and of matter's status therein. Matter, non-law, achieves independence, even precedence, over against form through the self-reflection of law's form. Form reflecting on itself presupposes non-law as matter. Form's self-reflection turns matter into form's presupposition. Form's self-reflection is simultaneously the presupposition of matter.

There are two implications here: the presupposition [*Voraussetzung*] of matter occurs through form, but is opposed to form – the presupposition of matter is a pre*supposition* and a *pre*supposition. In law's *pre*supposing of non-law as its other, however, it presupposes precisely what eludes it, indeed what opposes it. This means that matter too simultaneously becomes self-reflective in form's self-reflection, though in a different way. In being presupposed by self-reflective form, matter is established [*setzt . . . sich*] *as* non-form or non-norm: as what does not have the form of law on its own and is always still to be brought into the form of law. In other words, matter is established as what does not follow from law's normativity of its own accord, but must always still be assimilated and realized in it. The matter of law – the matter of non-law, as defined by modern law's self-reflection – will thus never have become form. It is the non-*form* that establishes itself as *non*-form. Modern self-reflecting law accordingly defines non-law as "nature": nature is established indifference, the indifferent establishment of form or norm.[2] Matter's self-reflection – which occurs in, indeed because of, form's self-reflection – is its (self-)*naturalization*.

The fact that nature signifies naturalization, because it is an effect of self-reflection, already includes a first indication of how we should *not* understand naturalness, which, for modern law, is a feature of non-law: its naturalness is not the positivity of events under laws [*Gesetzen*], which is how modern natural science defines its subject matter. The naturalness of law's non-legal matter cannot be understood scientifically. Hannah Arendt characterizes modernity by referring to "the latent . . . conflict between the two possible methods to be derived from Galileo's discovery, the method of the experiment and of making on one hand and the method of introspection on the other."[3] In this conflict, "the latter was to achieve a somewhat belated victory," which leads to *another* "naturalism." Arendt demonstrates that self-reflection also naturalizes,[4] but in a different way from scientific cognition, since the naturalness of self-reflective law's non-legal matter is not the sheer, static, positive absence of its form or norm (the realm of causality). Rather, non-legal nature is the *lack of a norm*. To put this more precisely: non-law, reflecting on itself and establishing itself as natural, is matter that defines itself as the absence of a norm.

The first, groundbreaking articulation of this structure of self-reflective naturalization or naturalizing self-reflection is found in the concept of the "natural will," which forms the basis for modern natural law's construction of a state that guarantees rights, as a starting point – even if this is conceived so as to only draw the consequences of the natural-scientific cognition of human willing and acting's law-like regularities [*Gesetzmäßigkeiten*], from which laws of right emerge and to which, enabling and permitting, they are referred.[5] The concept of willing, which remains on this side of its attribution to a subject, thereby designates the dynamic, striving, "orectic" basic tension that defines the non- or pre-juridical. There are no states of affairs or events that exist prior to or outside the law, in nature, but rather strivings and their realizations in directed movements. These can be the activities of a subject, although they do not need to be. Because this striving is natural, the causal determination of each and every thing in nature is evident ("because every act of mans will, and every desire, and inclination proceedeth from some

97

cause, and that from another cause, in a continual chain"[6]). However, this mechanism of causal determination – which is the point of the "natural will" – must be conceived from the immanent perspective of striving, from its self-reference. And from this perspective, naturalness signifies precisely the opposite of pervasive determination, which is what it seems to be from the perspective of an omniscient observer: namely "an innumerable number of chains, joined together,"[7] which, as *innumerable*, yield no determinacy and hence no certainty. The natural will is causally determined without itself knowing how, whereby, and to what end. In the natural will, to be natural means to be aware of itself as natural. And to be aware of itself as natural means to be aware that it is itself determined, but without knowing anything determinate. The natural will's awareness of itself is indeterminate. The natural will is aware that it is indeterminate for itself.

The point of this conception of nature, for the Enlightenment, is to resolve the teleological illusion that striving is concerned with something beyond itself. "There is no such *Finis ultimus*, (utmost ayme,) nor Summum Bonum, (greatest Good,) as is spoken of in the Books of the old Morall Philosophers"[8] for striving, defined as natural. Ancient, Aristotelian moral philosophy considers the knowledge of striving for an ultimate aim or greatest good to be conceptual, and not empirical, knowledge. Hobbes, however, wants to say not only that such knowledge of an ultimate aim or greatest good is impossible, in principle, but also that the natural will, in its self-reference, through the form of its self-awareness, calls such knowledge into question, indeed rules it out: knowledge of ultimate aims or greatest goods may exist, but not in and by the will itself (of whose aims or goods it is supposed to be knowledge). For since "natural" causation means being causally determined, but, from an internal perspective, signifies indeterminacy, it also follows that natural striving cannot know what it is striving for. Natural striving is therefore not simply a-teleological, but is defined as a-teleological by its natural non-knowledge, or by the non-knowledge of its nature. Natural striving is striving that reflects itself as natural – that identifies or establishes itself as natural. Such striving defines itself as essentially indefinite for itself. In other words, it defines itself not merely as striving that is unable to know its causes, but as striving that is unable to know what it is after because it cannot know its causes. This means that such striving is not definitive, but only exists here and now and is thereby provisional. The positive knowledge that there cannot be any *ultimate* aim or any *greatest* good corresponds to the will's natural non-knowledge of itself. "Natural" signifies exceedance of telos, a break with teleology.

The temporality of the natural will, reflecting on itself, is therefore defined as infinite seriality. The claim that the will has no ultimate, greatest aim, that it is a-teleological, is a statement about the status of its aims. Natural striving is unable to come to an end and fulfill itself in any of its aims. The basic formal definition of natural aims is that natural striving, and thus striving that is aware of and defines itself as natural, is negation and therefore the transgression of any – supposed – ultimate aim or greatest good. For ancient moral philosophy did not view the greatest good as only some further good that was merely greater, and did not view the ultimate aim as only some further aim that was merely more important, but viewed the greatest good as the unity of all goods, and the ultimate aim as the totality of all aims. This is what natural striving repudiates and undermines: natural striving is the negation and transgression of unity, of the totality of all natural aims. A will that has no higher aim than a natural one, or a simply a-teleological will, is a will aware that its aims cannot be unified. This knowledge determines its willing: natural willing is the establishment of aims beyond the unity of previous aims. It is a willing that wills on and on, that wills beyond: "Felicity is a continuall progresse of the desire, from one object to another; the attaining of the former, being but still the way to the latter."[9] Natural willing is willing that is always ahead of itself – an indeterminate or boundless willing. In other words, it is a formless willing; a willing against and beyond every form.[10]

The Materialism of Form

Through the act of self-reflection, something that was suffered becomes one's own free doing. Self-reflection changes the fate (or the tragedy) of law not by giving law a form that would no longer be exposed to that fate, but by absorbing law's fate into its concept and thereby into its performance. Law's self-reflection consists precisely in the resolute realization of the immanence of fate, namely that the tragedy of law is not external to it, but lies at its very heart.

Law's fate is its gap: it can only establish itself in such a way that it presupposes its other, and must again be externally enforced in opposition to its other. Law's fate is thus its violent institution and enforcement, which endlessly reproduces the unsurpassable externality of its form. Law's self-reflection begins with the insight that it is therefore the form of law itself which renders it belated vis-à-vis its other. The externality of form is its own doing, or the shadow of its own doing: form's act of presupposing its other, matter. The first stage of law's self-reflection consists in recognizing that *form itself* – and not any powers that mar or hinder it from outside – is the deferral of form. In law's [*Recht*] self-reflection, the law [*Gesetz*] of form becomes the form of law [*Gesetz*]. How is this form to be understood?

The basic definition of self-reflective law that we have now arrived at is that it is the self-externalization of law as presupposition of non-law. This is the basic definition of modern law from its beginning. Only by starting with it can we understand the basic redefinition of the form of rights (through both of law's performances, enablement and permission).[11] The redefinition of the idea of rights, which distinguishes modern from traditional law, is simply the expression of its self-reflection. Modern law, however, only achieves an adequate understanding of self-reflection, which it constitutes all along, later in its history. The reconceptualization of modern law thus forms the decisive step that, from the end of the nineteenth century, in the wake of social criticism of the liberal regime of private law, has been discussed under the misleading – or, as will be shown, ambiguous – heading of "materialization."

The basic insight of this reconceptualization can be formulated by contrasting it with the interpretation of law's self-reflective structure that immediately precedes it, and which it contests, but which remains influential to this day and forms the basis for eighteenth- and nineteenth-century (private law) liberalism. Liberalism interprets modern law's self-reflection as *law's resignation*: law, which views itself as irresolvably distinct from non-law, no longer claims to transform non-law for educational purposes, as traditional law did, or to be able to govern it on the basis of reason. For law, to reflect on itself in its difference from non-law means to resign in the face of non-law's externality, which thereby frees non-law to develop its own uncontrollable dynamic.[12] Law's self-reflection amounts to its abdication (and abdication means resignation), since it begins by experiencing its own powerlessness, its powerlessness as the defining feature of its power. The enforcement of legal form runs into a factual limit: the norm is limited by the factual, whose countervailing power it reproduces, indeed reinforces, with each attempt to transform or control it.

Law reacts to this experience of its own limitation – on liberalism's understanding of the transformative power of self-reflection – by limiting *itself*: liberalism is law that limits itself to the externality and otherness of factual relations. If (bourgeois) "society" is the name for the totality of these factual relations that are external to law, then liberal law is the law of bourgeois society: law [*Recht*] that allows bourgeois society to come into its own [*zu ihrem Recht kommen*] (against and through law). In liberalism, law's self-reflection consists in affirming its limitation and thereby voluntarily surrendering power, which, in its experience, it does not have anyway. On Hegel's early diagnosis, liberalism's experience of law's powerlessness in the face of the (social) "system" of externality leads it to conclude that:

> Thus it is necessary that this system be consciously adopted, recognized in its rightfulness, excluded from the class of the nobility, and be given a class of its own for its realm, where it can make itself secure and develop its whole activity in its own muddle and the superseding of one muddle by another.[13]

On the liberal interpretation, the self-reflective performance of the distinction between law and non-law consists in its "conscious separation." As a result, "each of them is done justice" [*erhält jedes sein Recht*] – law *and* non-law *as opposed to* law *through* law. Law's self-reflection is its "reconciliation" with its fate:

> This reconciliation lies precisely in the knowledge of necessity, and in the right which ethical life concedes to its inorganic nature, and to the subterranean powers by making over and sacrificing to them one part of itself. For the force of the sacrifice lies in facing and objectifying the involvement with the inorganic. This involvement is dissolved by being faced; the inorganic is separated and, recognized for what it is, is itself taken up into indifference while the living, by placing into the inorganic what it knows to be a part of itself and surrendering it to death, has all at once recognized the right of the inorganic and cleansed itself of it. This is nothing else but the performance, on the ethical plane, of . . . tragedy.[14]

The liberal model's basic thesis of resignation claims that law's self-reflection is – nothing but – its self-limitation. The problem with this thesis is its inconsistency.

The liberal model understands law's relation to non-law as something performed through law itself. In this regard, it is a model of law's self-reflection: law's relation to what it is not is performed through and thus in law itself. Law's liberal resignation is its *self*-restriction to non-law's otherness, which is therefore present in it. On the liberal conception, however, this is only supposed to be negative, only a limit. Here is where we find this model's inconsistency: it ignores the simple dialectical insight that every drawing of a limit, and thus every self-restriction, implies transcendence of that limit. "Something is already transcended by the very fact of being determined as a restriction."[15] If law can only limit itself in such

101

a way that, in itself, it can only refer to non-law as its other or as external, then in doing so law has not only limited itself and freed non-law from it, but has *established* [*gesetzt*] non-law. Liberal self-limitation is by no means merely negative. As law's (pre-)supposition [*(Voraus-)Setzung*] of non-law, it is positive: the positing and positivization of non-law. If self-reflection means that the external is within, then what is external to law does not merely stand externally opposed to it, and law's merely negative self-limitation is impossible. The liberal self-limitation of law has always already transcended itself. It does more than it claims, and *establishes* – positivizes – the non-legal. This requires a radicalization of law's self-reflection beyond its merely negative, liberal form.

This radicalization initially occurs in "tendencies" that Max Weber observed in the law of his time, and for which he employed the ambiguous concept of "material rationalization," since they are tendencies that are "favorable to the dilution of legal formalism."[16] At first sight, it seems that Weber is thus conceptually encapsulating very different changes that were occurring in the law of his time, ones that not only concerned law in various ways, but which Weber also assessed very differently. The reason why the materialization of law yields a radically new, indeed anti-liberal conception of self-reflection, however, can only emerge if we see the inner unity of these changes.

First, Weber uses the concept of material rationalization to describe changes in the "technical character" of the legal process: for instance, the fact that rendering a verdict and arguing before the court are no longer solely oriented to legal bases, but also begin to consider the reactions of interested parties, especially their (economic) commercial interests or their (ethical) attitudes, in "the free evaluation of proof." According to Weber, "in precisely this manner it introduced an individualizing and relatively material factor into legal formalism."[17] For in doing so, law's own formal logic – whose ever-purer development Weber views as Western law's history of rationalization – is split by "the recognition of such attitudes which are held by the average party concerned with the case, i.e., a general and purely business criterion of an essentially factual nature, such as the average *expectations* of the parties in a given transaction. It is this standard which the law has consequently to accept."[18] Reference to the extra-legal, which is regarded as fact in legal findings, takes the place of formally concluded legal argumentation.

Second, and above all, however, Weber also characterizes those changes in the law of his time that assumed the form of "ethical" demands, due to intensified class struggle in the nineteenth century, as "material rationalization of law":

102

New demands for a "social law" to be based upon such emotionally colored ethical postulates as "justice" or "human dignity," and directed against the very dominance of a mere business morality, have arisen with the emergence of the modern class problem. They are advocated not only by labor and other interested groups but also by legal ideologists. By these demands legal formalism itself has been challenged.[19]

Materialization in this second sense is evident, for example, in the fact that the legal assessment of contracts no longer solely refers to the concordant expression of the wills of legal persons, as in bourgeois-liberal private law, but also includes reference to their social conditions and the impact of such conditions. According to Weber, however, this compels law to include material considerations in its judgment:

> Such a concept as exploitation, or the attempt to treat as immoral, and thus as invalid, a contract because of a gross disproportion between promise and consideration, are derived from norms which, from the legal standpoint, are entirely amorphous and which are not juristic or conventional or traditional in character but ethical and which claim as their legitimation material justice rather than formal legality.[20]

Materialization in its second sense thus designates the fundamental process of transformation that breaks through the model of liberal private law with "both the social demands of democracy and the welfare ideology of monarchical bureaucracy" and compels law to consider the "entirely amorphous ... norms" of "material justice."[21] The "ethical postulates" of justice and human dignity that were previously used to critically assess law from outside thereby become operative in law itself.

The first type of materialization, materialization of a "technical character," is pragmatic: "the recognition of such [C.M. – economic or ethical] attitudes which are held by the average party concerned with the case" serves to ensure their acceptance in the legal process. The second type of materialization, law's exposure to external political – (social-)democratic and welfare-state – demands, is ethical-political: through it, law is subject to "ethical postulates" and thereby deprived of its formal consistency. While Weber notes the first form of materialization in a neutral way, his rejection of its second form is overt. Much more important than the question of how Weber assessed ethical-political materialization, however, is the question of how he conceived it, in describing it as a version of the *same* process that he had previously demonstrated in the technical materialization of law. Here we find the – implicit, but crucial – thesis of the concept of materialization: two entirely different changes that only vaguely seem connected by their anti-formalism are rightly subsumed under the same concept of materialization because they are structurally similar reactions to *the same basic problem.*

The basic problem that is first recognized and elaborated in the materialization of law is one that concerns the concept of law itself, because it is inscribed in it. According to Weber, this problem consists in the fact

> that the expectations of parties will often be disappointed by the results of a strictly professional legal logic. . . . The expectations of the parties are oriented towards the economic or the almost utilitarian meaning of a legal proposition. However, from the point of view of legal logic, this meaning is an "irrational" one. For example, the layman will never understand why it should be impossible under the traditional definition of larceny to commit a larceny of electric power. It is by no means the peculiar foolishness of modern jurisprudence which leads to such conflicts. To a large extent such conflicts rather are the inevitable consequence of the incompatibility that exists between the intrinsic necessities of logically consistent formal legal thinking and the fact that the legally relevant agreements and activities of private parties are aimed at economic results and oriented towards economically determined expectations. It is for this reason that we find the ever-recurrent protests against the professional legal method of thought as such, which are finding support even in the lawyers' own reflections on their work.[22]

Materialization responds to the problem of the "disparity" between law and non-law. To put this more precisely: the problem is that, due to this disparity, law, in its operation, has – negative, distorting, unacceptable – effects on non-law, which can in turn lead to "protest" against law. The materialization of law is nothing but law's taking these self-triggered effects and protests into consideration, an insight that is self-reflective insofar as it registers that such protests against law are triggered by law and must for this reason be considered in law.

This is just as true for consideration of "the average party concerned with the case" as it is for progressive "ethical postulates." Whether it involves technical-legal instruments such as the free evaluation of proof or ethical-political conversion into a social right, in both forms of materialization law reacts to its own effects on non-law. The materialization of law is hence nothing but the consistent form of its self-reflection. To put this more precisely: it is the *positive form* of law's self-reflection in distinction to non-law. The unity of these two changes, which Weber assesses differently, though he uses the same term for them, lies in the fact that they yield a right that no longer merely relates negatively to itself, in its difference from non-law, by limiting itself to this difference, as the liberal right does, but positively, by responding to it and thus taking responsibility for the consequences of its effects in the field of non-law. As a result, the concept of materialization, with which Weber wished to criticize changes to law in his time, mainly by describing the formation of social law as a challenge to the centuries-long Western labor of formalizing and rationalizing law, actually accomplishes something entirely different. The materialization of law is a way to characterize its radicalized self-reflection: from (negative) self-limitation to (positive) self-responsibility. Materialized law is law that responds or responsible law: self-reflective law as "responsive" law.[23]

Yet how can law responsively relate to non-law at all? How can law, in responding, and in taking responsibility for itself, relate to non-law, without thereby undermining the distinction between law and non-law and thus undermining the distinction of non-law from law? The question is thus: can responsivity – in Weber's terminology, "recognition" of the non-legal – be a mode of law's self-reflection in distinction from non-law?

This can only be the case if we do not understand such responsivity as "something external to the law against which legal decisions can be measured." Responsivity can only exist "within the law."[24] The material, responsive "recognition" of the non-legal in law cannot mean that non-legal factors – such as economic interests or ethical beliefs or even the ethical postulates that Weber argues play a role in different types of materialization – obtain *validity* in law. The juridical distinction between legal and illegal can only ever have (immanently) legal bases in law, even in materialized law, and economic interests, ethical beliefs or postulates are not legal bases. However, this does not make law into a purely "immanent order," to which non-law's other can only externally stand opposed. Non-law, as law's other, does not stand "structurally 'outside' of the law."[25] Materialization opens law to non-law, without thereby making the non-legal into legal bases. For non-law is not valid, but operative, in law, its absence in responsive law is not normative, but effective: drive (or force), not basis. For this reason, materialized law's responsivity does not contradict its autonomy. Materialization, conceived as self-reflection, instead demonstrates that the formalistic concept of law's autonomy is false: law's responsivity is precisely the way in which its autonomy is self-reflectively performed.[26]

The way in which the concept of materialization redefines law's self-reflection is now evident: self-reflective law's responsivity must be understood as its processualism and its processualism must be understood as its responsivity. If law's self-reflection signifies its materialization, then self-reflective law's rulings and decisions only exist so as to be made in the process of responsivity. Self-reflective law is nothing but law in

105

the process of its self-creation. According to the thesis of the concept of materialization, however, law's self-creation can only take place by essentially referring to non-law. The self-creation of law is a "process of closed openness."[27]

The progressive determination [*Fortbestimmung*] of legal self-reflection in the concept of materialization combines two basic aspects: first, the materialization of law entails understanding law as essentially processual. Self-reflective law is law that creates itself as it is performed; *materialization means processualization*. Second, however, and at the same time, this means understanding the processuality of law as essentially material, in both senses of the term.[28] *Processualization means materialization*, and matter in process is not stuff, object, or material (that on which the process operates from outside), but drive or force: that which is operative in the process, which drives the process on and forward.[29] Law's self-creation is its self-transformation, and its self-transformation [*Selbstveränderung*] is its *self-othering* [Selbstveranderung]: law itself effects the effectiveness of its other.

The self-reflection of law is:

(i)   the *entry of* law's *basis* into law: the processualization of law.
(ii)   the *entry of* law's *other* into law: the materialization of law.

The two processes are one and the same. Law's self-grounding and self-transformation are the same.

Excursus: The Justice of Self-Reflection (Teubner)

If we understand law's self-reflection as its materialization (and its materialization as its self-reflection), then this dual process characterizes modern law's idea of justice, since we cannot understand modern law's justice as the realization of specific moral content. Rather, its justice solely consists in how it acts on itself. For law, "justice has to do with the self-observations and self-descriptions of the system."[30] In law, justice is the disposition (or virtue) to transform or relativize itself.

To begin with, this means that law, in order to be just, must be essentially *changeable*. To put this more precisely: law's justice consists in its *establishing* each one of its definitions as subject to change. Law's justice consists in recalling the processes in which it was changed, and thereby in anticipating the processes in which it will change. In other words, it consists in the awareness and disposition – which, in this regard, are

106

precisely an expression of self-reflection – "that all legal norms and decisions, all reasons and arguments can take a different form:"[31] in the awareness and disposition of contingency. Justice is self-reflective law's "formula for contingency" (Luhmann). Just law is law that potentiates itself: law that exposes itself to the possibility of its being-otherwise.

The insight of the concept of materialization is that, in this process, law's self-reflection cannot cease, since materialization means that there is no change without the other's effect. Change [*Veränderung*] means othering [*Veranderung*]:

> Justice as law's contingency formula explicitly goes beyond internal consistency. It is located at the boundary between the law and its external environment and means both the historical variability of justice and its dependency on this environment. Invoking justice – and this is the core of the contingency formula – makes explicit law's dependency on its ecologies, on its social, human and natural environment. Thus, beyond formal consistency, substantive aspects of orientation come into play. In the definition "adequately complex consistency of legal decisions" the crucial aspect is ecological adequacy as against internal consistency. Justice's intention is not to maximize doctrinal consistency but to respond sensitively to extremely divergent external demands and to strive at the same time for high consistency. Justice as contingency formula is not immanent to the law but a justice that transcends the law. Internal consistency plus responsiveness to ecological demands – this is the double requirement of juridical justice.[32]

To be contingent means that self-reflective law, in order to be able to contingently establish something, must at the same time be willing to be responsive. For it can only transform itself if it can inwardly "transcend" (Teubner) itself: if it can allow law's other to be operative in law itself. Weber defined the materialization of law in precisely this manner. Materialization is the transformation of law by non-law's "protest." Self-reflective, just law as "a discursive praxis . . . subverts itself in a self-propelling cyclical process. Justice becomes self-subversive when, after protesting against positive law, it returns to legal positivisation."[33] The process that constitutes law's justice is the efficacy of the non-legal in law.

The Basis of Rights

We have seen that the self-reflection of law is the self-reflection of its form in distinction to non-law, to "natural" matter that withdraws from and contradicts form. This definition of self-reflective law combines two

107

features: (i) *processuality*, which means: the form of self-reflective law is form that creates or changes itself; and (ii) *materialism*, which means: the matter of non-law is operative in the form of law that creates itself.

Yet how and where are we to find the law's self-reflection in law? How does law accomplish its self-reflection? Gunther Teubner describes how this happens in the following passage:

> [The law] begins to establish norms for its own operations, structures, processes, boundaries, and environments – indeed, for its own identity [C.M. – :] Law begins to reproduce itself in the strict sense of the word if its self-referentially organized components are linked in such a way that norms and legal acts produce each other reciprocally and process and dogmatics establish some relationship between these.[34]

Above all and fundamentally, law draws a *formal* consequence from its self-reflection, however. This consequence is the modern form of rights. Law reflects on itself through its form. *The form of rights is the self-reflective form of law.*

As was shown in part 1, modern rights are processes of juridification become form: the legalization of the natural (in two basic ways, enablement and permission). The modern form of rights signifies the opening of law to non-law, law's emergence from non-law – the process of responsivity. Our discussion of the concept of self-reflection here has now shown *why* and *how* modern law develops this form. For we have seen that the natural, which is enabled and permitted through rights, is operative in law, in its material processuality. The modern form of rights enables and permits the non-legal *because* and *in how* self-reflective law *allows* the non-legal to be operative within it, in other words, by affirming its effectiveness in law. The self-reflection of (legal) form signifies the establishment and thereby the affirmation of (non-legal) matter. And the modern form of rights is nothing but the formation and definition of this affirmation of non-law in law.

Both definitions of self-reflective law, its processuality and its materialism, are at the same time basic definitions of rights, because the form of rights results from law's self-reflection; because the form of rights expresses and carries out law's self-reflection. Rights are therefore:

(i)   processual: rights are the result of processes and they are the start-
       ing point and subject matter of processes. For this reason, rights are
       always other rights. *Every right is a new right*: a right that has come
       to be and hence a right that comes to be. The (modern) form of rights
       is the form of law that changes itself and is therefore *historical*.

108

(ii) material (or materialist): rights are an expression of the effectiveness of non-law's matter in law. *Rights are therefore always obtained through struggle*: they result from non-law's protest against the existing state of law. The (modern) form of rights is a contentious form of law, and thus *political*.

The assertion of rights, their declaration, is therefore essential to their form. The declaration of rights presents rights as decreed and, in this regard, traced back to experiences – of suffering and of struggle – from which they have resulted.[35] The fact that the modern form of rights is the form of self-reflective law is thus only another formulation of the fact that it is *the form of revolutionary law*: rights are the permanent revolution of law as form.[36] At the same time, however, this is where we find the contradiction that ruptures this form. The critique of rights consists in demonstrating this contradiction.

* * *

The basis of rights – the operation that yields the form of rights – is law's self-reflection as affirmation of non-law's efficacy in law. Self-reflective law *wills* non-law. This is a consequence of the legal will's self-reflection. To claim that law's will is self-reflective means that it is the will willing itself: the legal will that wills legal willing. The fact that the legal will wills itself or wills its willing, however, means precisely that it wills the efficacy of the non-legal, of matter. Law wills non-law because it wills non-legally (in a non-legal manner), because its willing is processual and material. The material process or the processual materiality of self-reflective law is the basis of the form of rights. This is the thesis we have been discussing so far.

The unity of law's basis and form is the basic modern principle of legitimacy, which was first formulated in contract theory during the modern era. Contract theory wants law to be based on nothing but what is enabled and permitted by its form: what law entitles us to in the form of rights, and to what end, and therefore the content of this form; and how and for what reason law itself is entitled to do this, and thus the basis of rights – these two definitions, to what end and for what reason, are supposed to be one and the same. Contract theory is unable to conceive this unity, however. It is not resolved by how contract theory substantively defines it, since the content inscribed in the form of rights is natural striving. Law, however, is only able to become instrumentally, and not normatively, binding on the basis of natural striving alone, however rationally it may be understood and performed: contracts are

109

then only concluded and adhered to because, and for as long as, the contracting parties believe that doing so is useful for their natural striving. In contract theory's declaration that natural striving, the content of the form of rights, is simultaneously the basis of law, it therefore only arrives at a right-as-if, a "quasi-right."[37]

The idealist theory of law begins with this critique of contract law. The consequences of such a critique are that natural striving (with its instrumental rationality, at best) cannot be the basis of law, but that freedom as practical reason must be. Freedom is the "substance and destiny" of law,[38] its why or whence and – only – for this reason also the end toward which it aims. The idealist theory of law thereby runs into a problem that is precisely the converse of, and thus structurally identical to, the problem faced by contract theory. For just as contract theory cannot explain how the natural striving entitled by modern law is supposed to simultaneously establish law, so the idealist theory of law cannot explain how entitlement to natural striving is simultaneously supposed to follow from the practical reason established by law. The idealist theory of law is faced with the same irreconcilable contradiction as the contract theory that it criticizes, namely that between the basis of law and the content of rights. It glosses over this contradiction by calling both "freedom." Yet both are freedom in an unconnected, indeed opposed, sense: rational freedom as autonomy is the basis of law, while natural freedom as choice is what is entitled by the form of rights. The idealist response to contract theory harbors an aporia: that of the unity of autonomy and choice, normative reason and natural striving. This observation allows us to suggest two distinct ways forward that point in different directions.

Jürgen Habermas takes one direction. The idealist theory of law wishes to explain the modern form of rights by arguing that "the legal subject's private autonomy" has "a foundation in the moral autonomy of the person." According to Habermas, however, this idealist "bond . . . between freedom of choice and the person's autonomous will" is "severed" – the purported unity of autonomy and choice is no longer convincing and cannot be restored.[39] In other words, its unity is aporetic. Habermas concludes from this that the unity of (law's) basis and content (of entitlement) – the unity that constitutes the modern form of legitimacy – should not be abandoned but must be *loosened*. The unity of basis and content is indirect – it is fractured and mediated by an external condition that predefines it, which introduces a difference into it. This condition is the modern form of rights. The form of rights prescribes the content of entitlement. Rights legalize the non-legal, the choice and interest of natural striving. According to Habermas, however, this formal requirement cannot itself be derived in turn from law's basis, freedom as practical reason or autonomy. Rather, it results from the "language" or the "code" of (modern) law, in which autonomy is supposed to be realized.[40]

Yet why should we lend credence to the claim that "an autonomous association of free and equal citizens can be constructed only by means of modern law and on the basis of individual rights that deserve recognition because they are generated by discursive means"?[41] According to Habermas, the answer to this question is "part of a *functional* explanation and not a normative justification of law. The legal form is in no way a principle one could 'justify', either epistemically or normatively."[42] The claim that there is a modern form of rights, and thus the claim that modern law enables and permits natural striving and that all legitimately created law has *this* form and hence *this* content is not a normative claim, but a functional and systemic imperative. It is therefore an imperative derived from the structure of a modern, functionally differentiated society, and is thus to be *accepted*. Habermas resolves the idealist aporia of the unity of autonomy and choice, of practical reason and natural striving, by positing a third factor between the basis of law and the content of entitlement. This third factor is the form of rights introduced in functional terms, which is supposed to externally mediate the other two.

The other route consists in not resolving the idealist aporia but, on the contrary, deepening it. The aporia in which the idealist theory of modern law becomes stuck implies that only autonomy, as practical reason, can be the basis of law, but that the content of rights is natural striving. If neither of this aporia's two theses can be abandoned, practical reason must therefore establish natural entitlement, in other words, it must establish a non-normative, a-rational striving. Turning against Habermas, we could say with Wellmer that communicative rationality itself establishes nothing less than "a *right not* to be rational."[43] Practical reason, however, is only *able* to establish non-rational entitlement if it already contains the non-rational *in itself*: if practical reason itself is the aporetic "unity of a-rationality and rationality."[44] The other route for dealing with the idealist aporia is to deepen the aporia *between* law's basis and content so that it becomes an aporia *in* the basis of law. The thesis then holds that law can and must entitle the natural, the a-rational, because the natural and a-rational are already operative in law's basis. *Because* all practical reason also has natural striving operative within it, because all autonomy has choice operative in it, any right *of* autonomy must simultaneously be a right *to* natural striving.[45]

111

The concept of law's self-reflection points in this direction. The form of rights can be neither normatively established nor functionally declared. Instead, the form of rights results from the self-reflective performance of law – the self-reflection of its constitutive distinction between law and non-law, between form and matter. The distinction between form and matter thereby becomes a distinction in form and in matter. Both matter and form draw the distinction between form and matter in themselves, but in distinct ways. For one side, that of law's form, this means that natural striving, self-reflective law's matter, is operative in the production of its form (*without* implying that natural striving's operativity is able *by itself* to produce law's form; the idealist theory of law's critique of contract theory's reductionism remains valid in law's self-reflection). The materialism of self-reflective form consists in this mediated operativity. Only this materialism of form or norm establishes the modern form of rights: the form of rights is defined by entitling, enabling, and permitting natural striving. Law does this not for functional reasons, however, but because it has always already, in its inner performance, allowed natural striving to become operative and has affirmed it.

This demonstrates why Habermas only has recourse to a functional explanation of the modern form of rights, when faced with the idealist theory of law's aporia – the claim that the right of autonomy entitles the freedom of natural striving. He has recourse to only this explanation because the self-reflection of law is not conceived radically enough. For Habermas, law's self-reflection only means its processualization, the "proceduralization" of autonomy as the basis of law.[46] At the same time, however, self-reflective proceduralization signifies its materialization: without the operativity of material drives and powers, without the operativity of non-law in law, there can be no autonomous process of self-creation. Habermas is therefore unable to solve [*lösen*] the aporia, but can only functionally *dis*solve [*auflösen*] it, because he still conceives the basis of law in an idealist manner, as only autonomy, even if proceduralized. The basis of rights, however, can only be conceived in a materialist manner: by the materialism of self-reflective law.

Excursus: The Biopolitical Context (Agamben)

According to Giorgio Agamben, the "inscription of an outside the law within the law" is "the original structure in which law encompasses living beings by means of its own suspension": it is the logic of the state of exception, in which the violence that is essentially inscribed into law manifests itself.[47] In the state of exception, law's validity is "suspended" precisely to thereby put it into "power," or, in Schmitt's words, to thereby create the normal situation that once again makes it possible to apply legal norms. This suspension of legal validity means that, in the state of exception, law no longer judges life according to its norms and no longer subjects life to them. According to Agamben, however, this is precisely how it includes life in itself. Suspending the subsumption of life under law signifies precisely the interiorization of life into law. For in performing its normalization of life, which suspends validity, law itself becomes life (or *like* life): it sheds its normative form. The normalizing inclusion of life into law is the conversion of law into life. Law opposes the anomie of life, but can only do so in such a way that it creates a zone of anomie in itself, in such a way, indeed, that it becomes anomic itself. The fact that "law applies itself to chaos and to life only on the condition of making itself, in the state of exception, life and living chaos" becomes evident in the "anomic tendency" within law's interior.[48]

Agamben elsewhere describes this twofold relation between law and life, in the state of exception (law that no longer provides norms for life but normalizes it is thereby converted into life), as the emergence of a zone of undecidability between norm and fact. This is a

> zone in which de facto proceedings, which are in themselves extra- or antijuridical, pass over into law, and juridical norms blur with mere fact – that is, a threshold where fact and law seem to become undecidable . . . at which *factum* and *ius* fade into each other.[49]

Agamben, however, thereby describes the state of exception in the very same way that modern law as a whole is to be understood – as an order of "legality." For as we have seen, this order, as legalization of the natural, signifies nothing less than a fundamental reformatting of the relation between the normative and the factual. The modern order of legality is nothing but the process from fact to norm and from norm to fact, and the representation of this process is the (modern) form of rights.

Agamben concludes from this that the modern order of rights and the violence of the state of exception, which is generalized in forms of totalitarian domination, are internally related:

> The fact is that *one and the same* affirmation of bare life leads, in bourgeois democracy, to a primacy of the private over the public and of individual liberties over collective obligations and yet becomes, in totalitarian states, the decisive political criterion and the exemplary realm of sovereign decisions.[50]

According to Agamben, the modern form of rights and the state of exception have the same structure: they are both forms of law's inclusion of life – and, at the same time, of the normalization of life through law and its conversion into life. In other words, they are both forms of the same biopolitical definition of law.[51]

Agamben's relativization of the difference between the modern form of rights and its totalitarian repeal, in the name of their biopolitical similarity, pertains not to their value, but to their ontology. According to Agamben, they are the same in their basic constitutive structure: in how they define the relation of law [Gesetz] and life, norm and fact, law [Recht] and non-law, form and matter. However, this ignores the fact that they are opposed to each other in this utterly fundamental relation, and therefore ontologically opposed. The fact that both are defined as an "inscription of an outside the law within the law" (Agamben) actually means something structurally, fundamentally different in these two cases. It is the difference between law before and after its self-reflection: the difference between two entirely distinct modes in which law refers to the experience of its gaps.

We have seen above that the experience of law's gap is based on law's self-reference. For through its self-reference (without which there is no law), law obtains the conceptual capacity for, and empirical experience of, non-law – of what eludes the difference between legal and illegal. The consequence drawn by the state of exception is to suspend the norm, while the consequence of the modern form of rights, in contrast, is the norm's self-reflection. Both can be described as "an inscription of an outside the law within the law." In the suspension of the norm, this occurs in such a way that the outside becomes subject to violent normalization through law. In operating violently, and thus not normatively, law simultaneously becomes its own outside. Conversely, in law's self-reflection, the "inscription of an outside the law within the law" is performed in such a way that law allows its outside to become operative in its self-creation, therefore empowering law's outside in law (and in this way "recognizing" it [Max Weber]). The strategy of normativity changes in the normalizing suspension of law: it becomes violent, anomic – its own other. In contrast, the concept of normativity changes in law's self-reflection: in its self-reflection, law's normativity conceives itself as processual and material – as the operativity of the material in the process of formation, or the operativity of the factual in normalization.

The conceptual, and therefore ontological, distinction between the sovereign suspension of law in the state of exception and its materialist self-reflection is that only law's self-reflection draws a conceptual,

114

ontological distinction. The sovereign suspension of law blends norm and fact, but leaves them as they are: externally distinct from and externally opposed to each other. In contrast, law's self-reflection changes the conception of norm and the conception of fact, the conception of form and the conception of matter from within: it understands (and performs) them in such a way that their other is their interior. The sovereign suspension of law is strategically innovative (it joins what was divided, it transfers law's outside to its inside), but conceptually reactionary. It proceeds anomically, but continues to define law as it has always been defined, as a normative order over life. Law's self-reflection, in contrast, carries out a conceptual revolution in law. It creates a new conception of law.

Agamben's equation of the modern form of rights with sovereign violence in the state of exception, due to their same basic biopolitical definition, is therefore unable to conceive the revolution in law. In other words, for Agamben, law has no real history.[52] This separates Agamben's concept of biopolitics, the biopolitical structure of law *as such*, from Michel Foucault's conception. On Maria Muhle's view, biopolitics or biopower in Foucault means a politics that not only has life for its object, but uses life as a "working model." "Biopower not only refers to *life*, but at the same time does this *on the model of life*."[53] Agamben views a politics "on the model of life" as an anomic politics: a politics that reverts from normativity into the anomy of life to ensure normativity's conditions for normality. For according to Agamben, normativity and life are still externally, conceptually opposed to each other precisely where they change into one another in practice. In contrast, Foucault understands a politics "on the model of life" as a radically *new* politics. For Foucault (following Georges Canguilhem), a politics "on the model of life" implies *the model of another normativity*: the "living being's normativity" (as "plasticity," or "being capable of establishing new . . . norms").[54] The modern form of rights can only be grasped by understanding it as the form in which materialist self-reflection performs a radical redefinition of normativity.

— 7 —

THE CRITIQUE OF RIGHTS

Law's self-reflection is the basic operation by which modern law creates itself. This operation forms its essence. The essence of modern law is an *act* – its self-creation through law's act of self-reflection. The basic structure that defines all law as law [*Recht*] emerges in this self-reflection: the opposition of law [*Gesetz*] and nature, the normative and the factual. Furthermore, law [*Recht*] performs the opposition of law [*Gesetz*] and nature, in law [*Recht*], through the act of its self-reflection. Law that reflects on itself thereby becomes another law. It changes its form: the act of self-reflection yields a new, different form of law.

This new form of self-reflective law is the modern form of rights: law's self-reflection consists in internally defining both sides of the contradiction, law [*Gesetz*] and nature, the normative and the factual, through their relation to their other. The modern form of rights consists in enabling and permitting law [*Gesetz*] to refer to the non-legal or natural. Act and form, modern self-reflection and modern rights, thus correspond to each other. To put this more precisely: the modern form of rights, based on law's [*Recht*] self-reflection, on the act of self-reflection, yields the modern form of rights. Modern law's self-reflection is its essence, the modern form of rights its appearance.

This is the *conceptual* definition of the connection between law's self-reflection and the modern form of rights. The way that this connection really works, however, contradicts such a definition. In conceptual terms, the modern form of rights is the realization of law's self-reflection, but in fact, in reality, it is the opposite of this. For in the form that rights actually assume, we find dissimulation, distortion, indeed the blockade of law's self-reflection. This is the reality of rights in *bourgeois law*. Bourgeois law is the only positive form yielded by modern law to this

116

point (since law established by socialist states is not modern law: law in Moscow was not modern, but a medium of education and oppression; it combines elements of law found in Athens and Rome).[1] As bourgeois law, this positive form of modern law rests on a crucial basic definition. This definition – which defines it as bourgeois – states: rights are *rights of the subject*. Bourgeois law defines the modern form of rights as "subjective rights." The definition of modern rights as subjective rights is the basic operation of bourgeois law. Bourgeois law comes into contradiction with itself through this basic operation, however.

For on the one hand, the model of subjective rights is *based* on the modern self-reflection of law, since it is the central definition of bourgeois law, and since bourgeois law is the positive historically and socially prevalent form of modern law. The act of self-reflection, the revolutionary processualization of law, is the basis for subjective rights: this act is the essence of such a form, and this form has the appearance of such an act. On the other hand, however, the model of subjective rights distorts and dissimulates the self-reflection of law, on which it is based: the model of subjective rights is a form of law that *blocks* the act from its revolutionary processualization.

If this is the case, however, if these are its two sides, then the basic model of subjective rights is (self-)contradiction become reality: the contradiction between essence and appearance. On the bourgeois model of subjective rights, essence (the formative act) and its positive, actual content (how a subjective right is composed and operates) are in contradiction. The verdict on bourgeois law results from insight into this contradiction: such law is false because it is a form that contradicts its own essence. The falseness of bourgeois law lies in its incapacity to truly present or manifest what it enables, and what it thereby *is*.

The falseness of bourgeois law is real. It is the falseness of a socially prevalent form of law. It is a falseness that positively exists. This falseness pervades bourgeois law, it applies to all of its elements. Only in being philosophically conceived, however, does it emerge as what it is, as contradiction of essence and appearance. It only becomes evident when we grasp bourgeois law as the *thought* of bourgeois law. We must recognize the fact that such thought "though philosophically erroneous, had to some extent *become true in practice* in modern bourgeois society."[2] What is philosophically false in the thought of bourgeois law should therefore not be understood as a falseness that would be measured by another thought to which it is – normatively – opposed. It is false on its own terms: the standard by which the thought of bourgeois law is false is its own essence, its inner basis. Bourgeois law is false

117

because it contradicts *itself*. To think bourgeois law means to expose its self-contradiction.

Yet even this point can again be understood and made in a false way, namely as a merely normative critique. The essence of bourgeois law is then understood to be its basic normative idea, while its positive content, which stands in contradiction to this, is understood to be its (still) insufficient realization. The essence of bourgeois law is the standard not for its normative critique, however, but for its ontological one: bourgeois law does not fail to be what it is supposed to be, but fails to be *as it is*. It fails to realize its essence. Bourgeois law fails at, indeed dissimulates and blocks, the act of self-reflection that establishes it. Bourgeois law simultaneously presupposes revolutionary processualization *and* annuls it. It wishes to be post-revolutionary and thereby becomes anti-reflective (and anti-revolutionary).

* * *

Bourgeois law and its basic model of subjective rights are ontologically false: this thesis will be developed in part III of the present volume. From the outline sketched to this point, however, we have already obtained an early indication of the *kind* of falsehood that is involved in bourgeois law, namely the error at the basis of the thought of bourgeois law. This error consists in simultaneously presupposing *and* dissimulating the self-reflection of law. Jürgen Habermas has referred to this error as positivism: "That we disavow reflection *is* positivism."[3] The thought of bourgeois law is false insofar as it is a form of positivism.

According to Habermas's definition, positivism is the disavowal of reflection. Positivism is therefore not the sheer, simple absence of reflection. Rather, the disavowal of reflection is itself a (indeed self-contradictory) way of engaging in reflection: it is engaging in reflection *as* or *through* the disavowal of reflection. The basic formulation of law's self-reflection is that non-law become operative in law, that matter become operative in the self-creation of form. This is an understanding and performance of bourgeois law that makes matter into law's basis and therefore into something given prior to law, something that is present for law in advance. In other words, in its basic model of subjective rights, bourgeois law *positivizes* law's material other. As positivism, bourgeois law is a disavowal of *reflection*, because it is law's reference to its other. And it is a *disavowal* of reflection, because it is law's reference to its other as something given to it in advance.

In other words, bourgeois law is the "Myth of the Given" (which Wilfrid Sellars has argued is the basic definition of empiricism) become reality:

One of the forms taken by the Myth of the Given is the idea that there is, indeed *must be*, a structure of particular matter of fact such that (a) each fact can not only be noninferentially known to be the case, but presupposes no other knowledge either of particular matter of fact, or of general truths; and (b) such that the noninferential knowledge of facts belonging to this structure constitutes *the ultimate court of appeals* for all factual claims – particular and general – about the world.[4]

The Myth of the Given is a myth because it authorizes. As something positively given, matter has the "authority" of being the indisputable starting point for everything further, for every development of form and norm.[5] This is precisely how Adorno describes the basic approach of positivism, namely as distortion of the materialist "primacy of the object" into the pre-givenness of something indisputably, opaquely immediate, which is left over as "residue" or "that which remains given after subjective appendages have been subtracted."[6] This subtraction, however, was its own deed. The residue prior to reflection is produced by the (disavowal of) reflection. To apply this to bourgeois law: its positivism is "resignation before individuality,"[7] whose limiting and foundational authority it has itself first produced, and which it establishes as "valid" through the model of subjective rights.

Let us hasten to emphasize just where the error of bourgeois law is *not* to be found: its empiricism or positivism is not reductionism. Bourgeois law's error is not so simple – which is why it is not quickly resolvable and easily preventable. Bourgeois law's *starting point*, the authority of the ultimately given, is not identical to deriving all normativity from something merely factual. Bourgeois law does not derive what should be from something that is, but *constructs it by starting out from it*. (The positively given not only helps establish bourgeois law, but – as Locke carefully puts it – validates it as "foundation,"[8] as the basis that must support its structure, but which cannot determine its form on its own and therefore cannot guarantee its binding power.) Bourgeois law's error occurs *prior to* the question of whether what is can form the basis for what should be. Just as the error is not merely a normative one (not the inconsistent, ineffectual modification of its basic normative idea), so too it is not a logical error, no simple fallacy. Rather, we are once again confronted with an ontological error that occurs in self-reflective law's empirical or positivist definition of matter's mode of being: in its conception of operative material as positively given in law's self-reflective formative process.

In other words, bourgeois law's error is its false materialism. Materialism's insight consists in "passing to the primacy of the object" or in conceiving "matter as such with something like a driving force."[9]

119

Indeed, its insight consists in form's self-reflection. Empiricism under-stands this to mean that the object is something immediate, and its immediacy is considered to be alpha and omega [*ein Erstes und Letztes*]. Dialectical materialism contradicts this empiricist materialism. Adorno's objection to positivism is that matter is not all-important [*Letztes*], but a moment, and this moment is "to be continually sublated . . . by virtue of the process that grasps it."[10] The primacy of the object is not its pre-givenness, but only exists in mediation. Dialectical mediation makes that which it mediates into a moment. Mediation therefore means not external equivalence, but inner, ontological transformation. In it, "the multiplex is immediately annihilated, and is null."[11] The dialectical process succeeds where empiricism (whose "principle" is "multiplex being," and which declares multiplex beings to be something positively given) must forever remain a "failure": it succeeds at "pressing on to the absolute nullity of its qualities."[12] In other words, the dialectical process does not realize the primacy of the object by considering it to be an unchanging given, positive determinacy. On the contrary and in opposition to positivism, it realizes the primacy of the object by allowing material to be operative as nullity, as the radically indeterminate. Empiricist materialism claims the authority of the positive. Dialectical materialism opposes it with the power of negativity: in the dialectical materialism of the self-reflective legal process, matter is not something, not a "something" that is given to form in advance, but is the nullity of form (in other words, matter is force[13]).

Modern law is characterized by contradiction, by political struggle: *one materialism against another*, the negativity of dialectic against the positiv-ity of empiricism. This contradiction affects all elements of self-reflective law: the relation of normativity and facticity, of form and matter; the logic and energetics of its processuality; justice and the political character of law; finally, the concept of revolution that defines self-reflective law as modern. *All* modern law is materialist, processual, a matter of justice, political, revolutionary – otherwise it is not self-reflective, and therefore not modern. This is true in two ways, however, which contradict each other point by point, and therefore stand irreconcilably opposed to one another. They form bourgeois law *and its other*.

The contradiction between bourgeois law and its other is asymmetric: the empirical understanding of law's self-reflection has become a form of reality in bourgeois law – the only real form of modern law that we know. In contrast, law's other is a law that does not exist (yet). It is true law, however. It is the truth, the true form, the self-reflection of law. Bourgeois law is untrue – a realization of juridical self-reflection that

120

simultaneously distorts and represses what it realizes – but does exist. Law's other is true, but not present.

In this situation, the task of critique is to work out the full implications of the contradiction *between* bourgeois law and its other. It does not accomplish this by imagining different law. That is not critique's primary task. Its primary, most important task is to make the contradiction *in* bourgeois law manifest and to thereby intensify it. This only (and already) happens when bourgeois law is comprehended, since to comprehend bourgeois law means grasping it as appearance of its essence. And to grasp its essence means to grasp that which is simultaneously created *and* contested by bourgeois law – that which is simultaneously its basis and adversary. What holds for all true critique holds for the critique of bourgeois law as well: it does not work to better relations, but to "tear open the social abyss," to "deepen and intensify" contradictions.[14] Critique wants to exacerbate and accentuate the crisis of bourgeois law.

Part III

Critique: The Authorization of One's Own

Self-reflection essentially defines modern law. The modern form of rights is based on it. Yet in its *existing* form (the law of bourgeois society: bourgeois law),[3] modern law can only express its self-reflection by dissimulating it. The contradiction of bourgeois law is to be found in this simultaneity of expression and dissimulation. If modern law is essentially defined by its self-reflection, bourgeois law is a manifestation of modern law that dissimulates its own essence. In other words, bourgeois law is appearance – a manifestation that contradicts itself, namely its essence. Bourgeois law is the false realization of modern, self-reflective law – and, at the same time, it is the only realization of that law to this point.

The fact that bourgeois law only carries out its self-reflection in such a way that it simultaneously dissimulates and denies it constitutes its empiricism or positivism. Bourgeois law rests on the Myth of the Given: the non-legal (or "natural"), which the normativity of modern law in itself self-reflectively refers to as its other, is understood by bourgeois law as given. Bourgeois law positivizes law's other, treating it as an unchangeable given. Its positivism or empiricism consists in the presupposition of the non-legal as already given – of the immediate as "the last word" [*Letzten*] (Adorno).

This positivism is inscribed in the bourgeois form of rights. It is the model of *subjective rights*. The model of subjective rights is thus a

123

derivative category. It is based not on the subject, but on law, and indeed on the positivistically distorted self-reflection of bourgeois law. Its self-reflection is "cloaked in the form of subjective rights."[4] Bourgeois law's positivism is subjectivizing, its subjectivism of rights is positivistic. The legal Myth of the Given is realized by the bourgeois legal subject. In other words, the model of subjective rights *fills* the empiricist position of the given with the subject. Since the given is the site of "the ultimate court of appeals," the site of "authority" (Sellars), this defines the subject as the authority [*Instanz*] of authorization [*Autorisierung*]. The proprietary logic of the bourgeois legal subject is based on the claim that every subjective right is "*ius proprium* [*Eigenrecht*]."[5] Bourgeois law transforms the non-legal into something given that functions as an ultimate court of appeals, by understanding the given as what is the subject's *own* [*das Eigene*]. For what is the subject's own is not properties that she objectively has, but what she wills subjectively. The positivism of subjective rights therefore makes the willing of one's own into an authoritative fact: in bourgeois law, that I will something on my own [*mein eigenes Will*] assumes the authority of the given, from which everything normatively established must proceed. This forms the bourgeois subject's "self-will" [*Eigenwillen*] (chapter 9).

It will be necessary to provide a more detailed account of the mechanism by which bourgeois law authorizes the subject or causes it to become the authority [*Instanz*] of authority [*Autorität*] before its structure can be analyzed and its political, normative, and social consequences (chapters 10–12) can be described. This mechanism is legal authorization [*Ermächtigung*][6] (chapter 8).

— 8 —

AUTHORIZATION

Law's granting of individual rights simultaneously confers power on individuals. For it thereby becomes likely "that one actor in a social relationship will be in a position to carry out his own will despite resistance;" all rights are the "*capacity* to obligate others."[1] Someone with a right does not yet thereby have the requisite access to the means for exercising this right effectively. The link between a legal claim (to something, vis-à-vis someone else) and the further right to assert this claim before an impartial authority is complicated.[2] Someone who has a right, however, also has power because such a person (*this* person and no one else) has reason to expect certain behavior from another, and obligates the other to behave in this way. A right is a normative power: an opportunity for action that is normatively secured against others.[3]

This general definition immediately requires us to distinguish two ways in which rights confer power. We can historically determine these two ways in which rights confer power and classify them as different types of entitlement in traditional and modern law.[4] This distinction, however, can also be understood in structural terms and demonstrated within bourgeois law. One mode of the legal ascription of power here consists in the fact that a person only has "legally . . . endowed . . . opportunities" when those "of all the other individuals are reduced to reflexes of his regulations."[5] Legal regulations for general conditions open up opportunities for particular persons to take action. Others do not have these opportunities. For example, protective tariffs provide advantages and opportunities that are shielded from competition. These opportunities, however, are bound to require that our perception of them complies with the goal of general regulation: opportunities here are bound to this goal. Such so-called "reflex rights" function in a manner similar to how rights traditionally functioned. For the legal power that one person has over against another was here tied to the fact that his willing and acting is a mere reflex, a repetition or mirror-image of the legal system's normative content. The traditional right [*Recht*] gives a person power or assures him an opportunity only insofar as his willing or acting corresponds to law's [*Recht*] objective content. In Athens and Rome, this means correspondence with law's moral or rational content. Here, the individual's legal power is nothing but moral virtue or natural reason, which is at the same time objectively embodied by the legal system. Whether the individual has legal power depends on *what* he wants and does. A right as reflex is a right bound to some content and is for this reason a conditional right.

For this reason, Max Weber claims that "no 'subjective right'" is preserved for the individual by a legal "reflex-effect."[6] This is because the power to provide a person with subjective rights (that is, the specific way in which bourgeois law ensures that it provides opportunities for action) is an essentially unbound or indeterminate power:

> Every subjective right is a source of power that can even be used by someone who would otherwise be entirely powerless, through the existence of the relevant legal clause for an individual case. It is thus already a source of entirely new situations in the activity of communities.[7]

According to Weber, subjective rights are a specific mode of normative authorization: the authorization of the new, and thus, negatively, the authorization to act in a way that is not a mere reflex of the existing normative order.

This authorization has two steps. The first step is methodological: "Every subjective right is a source of power." Subjective rights are modes of authorization that confer normative power. In other words, subjective rights are subjective not because a subject has them, but, precisely to the contrary, because they produce a subject. For to be a subject means precisely to be an authority of capacities and opportunities, an authority of power. Subjective rights are subjective because they subjectify.

Second, the power that provides rights is the power to be a "source of entirely new situations in the activity of communities." "New" here means: not stipulated by the legal order, indeed not envisaged by that order. This is what distinguishes it from reflex rights. If legal discourse in the modern era begins with the insight that there is a second sense of right as claim or entitlement, opposed to the first sense of right [*Recht*] as law [*Gesetz*], and if it defines this second sense of right as a person's capacity, capability, attribute, or even power,[8] then its aim is nothing but legally generated power in this specific sense: as power to will and act *otherwise*, the power for a *new* willing and acting that are not defined by virtue or reason, that form the objective content of law [*Recht*]. This constitutes *authorization* by subjective rights.[9]

As we will see, authorization, which defines bourgeois law, has an unavoidably double form. It is simultaneously political power and private power. Authorization by subjective rights signifies politicization *and* privatization: privatization as politicization, politicization as privatization.

The Political Character of Private Rights

Classical private law liberalism has given a simple answer to the question of authorization by subjective rights. It claims that subjective rights secure and guarantee opportunities for action that exist prior to law. This corresponds to the liberal thesis that law does not exist to realize the imperatives of virtue or reason, but must limit itself to being "only a *permission* or *warrant*."[10] Whenever bourgeois law stipulates something, it limits itself "to the negative – *not to violate* personality and what ensues from personality." Hegel concludes from this: "Hence there are only *prohibitions of right*, and the positive form of commandments of right is, in its ultimate content, based on prohibition."[11] We should not understand this to mean that the novelty of bourgeois law consists in only imposing prohibitions. The prohibitive threat with negative consequences is also the rhetorical form of traditional law. What is new is the *meaning* (or goal) of prohibitions: the meaning of bourgeois law's prohibitions is permissive, not prescriptive or normalizing. As a result, here – and only here – everything that is not prohibited is considered permissible. Legal prohibitions limit spheres of activity over against each other and thereby secure the subject's opportunities for action. They create zones of permission by means of prohibitions. In other words, they negatively authorize subjects, namely by securing opportunities to will and to act for subjects opposed to each other (opportunities that such subjects already have at their disposal).

It is therefore evident that the negative, liberal private law definition of legal authorization – as only permission – rests on an antisocial premise. Georg Jellinek reformulates this premise as follows: "If the private law regime governs economic business relations, it does not add a new moment at all to the individual's free movement vis-à-vis another. Legal relations were living relations long before they submitted to legal normalization."[12] The antisocial premise of the liberal private law definition of subjective rights consists in how it understands the *mode of*

127

existence of what is legally permitted. For to define authorization as permission means to refer it to a "physical" ability that exists prior to law. In particular, it means referring it to an ability to which its legal permission can add nothing and from which its legal prohibition can take nothing. "*What should not be done* by no means excludes the physical *ability* to do it."[13] Subjective rights permit, they only legally secure what is already physically possible anyway. The liberal, private law conception of permission naturalizes that which has been permitted.

Jellinek describes this presuppositional logic of legal permission in order not to criticize it, but to relativize it. He wants to show that there is another possibility – an entirely different way in which subjective rights relate to the subject's ability. There is thus a completely different way to legally authorize:

> The legal order can ... also add something to the individual's capacity for action that the latter did not possess by nature ... All definitions that concern the validity of legal actions and concerns establish a *legal ability* explicitly conferred by the legal order. This ability stands in stark contrast to being allowed to do something.[14]

And, furthermore:

> This capacity, however, is not the result of permission, but of being granted it. The legally relevant capacities granted by the legal order form, in their totality, *legal ability*.[15]

Jellinek's argument against private law liberalism is therefore that subjective rights are not to be understood as the mere allowance of free rein for one's natural or physical ability, because such rights themselves *create* an ability; rights are productive. They produce legal ability: the capacity to perform legal actions. This capacity only exists through law, on the basis of "legal stipulations that confer power." "It would be incorrect to say that someone incapable of conducting business *may* not enter into a contract; rather, he *cannot* do this. No matter what such a person does, a contract is not honored. The supposedly legal transaction that he concluded does not exist."[16] For this reason, subjective rights cannot be defined as mere allowance. Someone with a right is not allowed to do something she already can, but can do something that she previously could not. Authorization by subjective rights goes far beyond the negative operation of permission: subjective rights authorize subjects not only by securing and protecting the opportunities and capacities that they already have (which make them subjects), but by expanding such opportunities and capacities, indeed by creating them in the first place.

Jellinek employed the epochal title "subjective public rights" for his step beyond private law liberalism, from legal allowance to legal ability. This includes his thesis that the two types of subjective rights belong to different legal domains: legal allowance belongs to private law, while legal ability belongs to public law. Legal permission protects one person from another. It protects one person's physical ability, limited by permission, in prohibiting another person from infringing these limits. To legally create or warrant, in contrast, is to give persons the "capacity to manipulate legal norms in their own individual interest."[17] And even when one person exercises this new, legal capacity in relation to another person, she at the same time always already stands in relation to the authority that creates and secures her rights: not to another person, but to the person of the other, to the "law-creating whole," or in the modern understanding: the state. "Allowed to the coordinated, enabled over against the state."[18]

For Jellinek, the fact that allowance and ability, permission and production, as basic definitions of subjective rights, are supposed to be strictly distinguished into two legal domains does not also mean that they can be isolated from one another. They are instead internally connected, as distinct. Yet only in one direction: "an ability without an allowance is perhaps possible" – since there can be a public order in which the individual can participate, without the simultaneous existence of a private legal system in which the individual has permission rights vis-à-vis other persons. Conversely, however, "every allowance necessarily presupposes an ability" – since, in terms of private law, to allow something vis-à-vis others always already means to stand in a relation to the whole, to the community or state, in which the individual has the legally created capacity to legal (co-)activity.[19] No private law permission without public law ability. In other words: "The entirety of private law [is constructed on] the basis of public law."[20] Jellinek thereby stands their relation in traditional private law liberalism on its head. It is only for this reason that his talk of "subjective public rights" is epochal. His argument against private law liberalism is not only that there is another type of rights besides private permissive ones, namely rights that publicly authorize and produce ability. Rather, his argument is that traditional private law liberalism, which demanded private legal permission, is self-contradictory if it does not demand public entitlement, and thus does not demand the entitlement to make demands with others. Private law liberalism does not correctly understand itself.

Excursus: The Political Presupposition of Private Law (Savigny)

The basic structure of Friedrich Carl von Savigny's theory of subjective rights is defined by this self-contradiction.

On Savigny's classic definition, the form of the subjective right belongs to the field of "modern Roman law."[21] According to Savigny, a subjective right's form is current or modern when "the original concept of the person or the legal subject coincides with the concept of the human being, and this original identity of the two concepts can be expressed in the following formulation: each individual human being, and only the individual human being, is capable of law."[22] Yet this identity of human being and person – and thereby the essential equality of all human beings as persons – is only valid, according to Savigny, in the field of Roman law, of civil or private law. As we have seen above, he sharply distinguishes it from public or constitutional law: "The first [C.M. – constitutional law] has for its object-matter the state, that is the organic manifestation of the people; the second [C.M. – private law] the totality of jural relations which surround the individual man."[23] Private law defines the "jural relation as a relationship between one person and another defined by a legal rule."[24] This rule specifies rights in the subjective sense, as warrants or claims. Because, however, "in public law the whole appears as the end, the individual as subordinate,"[25] there cannot be any rights here, either. In the public relation between the individual and the whole, law rules and obligation compels.

Savigny offers not a political argument for strictly distinguishing the two domains of law, but a logical or ontological one: the basic relations in the two legal domains are fundamentally different. The first domain, private law, is characterized by a horizontal relation between individuals who are equal to each other; both are persons. The second domain, constitutional law, is characterized by a vertical relation between the individual and the universal or whole, which are not equal to each other: the public or political relation is that of membership. The universal or whole is therefore not another *adversus* against which the individual can have justified claims, but is the individual herself – in another form: as member of the whole. If private law is concerned with a relation between individuals, then political or public law is concerned with a relation between each individual and a third (or the relation of each one to herself as another, as a third). The basic relations in both domains of law follow a different logic (which is why the structure of their normativity must be distinguished): the concepts of law and duty, claim and entitlement cannot mean the same thing in private and in public law.

130

In Savigny (just as in Hegel), the categorical restriction of the form of subjective rights to bourgeois private law is already directed against the increasing tendencies (which have since become common sense) toward a "false transference of civil-legal constructions onto public law."[26] The subject accordingly "has" subjective rights in precisely the same way, regardless of whether these rights are exercised "against" the state or other individuals. In order for the individual to be able to have the same rights "against" the state as she does against other persons, however, the state would also have to be like another person over against the individual. If the state is the community, however, and the individual is one member of it, then the individual is not opposed to the state, but *in* it: its "member" (Hegel). The entitlements of members vis-à-vis the whole, which is the sole basis for their existence, must therefore be completely different from those of the individual in relation to another individual. They do not fall under the same concept.

From the correct argument, that transferring the concept of subjective rights from private law to public law ignores the logical difference of their basic relations, however, Savigny draws the wrong conclusion, that the two types of law are completely independent and can be separated from each other: he defines the private legal relation between individuals on the basis of their equality as human beings who have subjective rights against each other and *at the same time* defines the public or political relation as a relation to a whole, whose purpose renders the individual a mere "subordinate." Savigny was convinced (and thereby only reflects the indecisiveness of German relations in his time) that the introduction of the bourgeois form of subjective rights into the traditional hierarchical structure of the political community would change nothing – it neither must nor should change anything. Like Hegel (the Hegel of the "right Hegelians"), Savigny wants to have his cake and eat it too. To be able to perform this trick, he has to maintain that the radical upheaval in the *concept* of law, signified by the bourgeois form of subjective rights, is politically insignificant. Furthermore, the public relation between the individual and the legal system is supposedly one of mere "subordination." In the political realm, the bourgeois subject of rights is supposed to remain a traditional subject, as someone who has been subdued, *subjectus* as *subditus*.[27]

This simultaneity of bourgeois private law equality and hierarchical politics is contradictory and unstable, however, and collapses. For the radical redefinition of the claim in private law, in the form of subjective rights, also signifies an extensive *change in law's mode of ruling*. In other words, it signifies a change in the way in which law rules over the

131

individual; a change in the ("public" or "political") relation between the legal whole and the individual. In private law, permission is an authorization of subjects in their relations with each other. The fact *that* law authorizes each individual simultaneously, however, involves the legal status of individuals, since law has thereby recognized them as persons. "Personhood" is simultaneously a presupposition of private law and *iuris publici* [Tr. – "of public law"], because "the state . . . establishes personhood."[28] By concerning themselves with equal rights against each other, individuals *have* already accepted the whole's traditional definition as their ultimate purpose and established themselves as the purpose of the whole. "State rule," when and if it establishes the equality of bourgeois private law, "is thus rule over the free, i.e., over persons."[29]

The conceptual-political – conceptual and political – strategy of Jellinek's programmatic titular idea of "subjective public rights" thereby emerges: it exposes Savigny's division of legal domains as incoherent, indeed as self-contradictory. For it reveals that the citizen who is only concerned with her private freedom always already, whether she is aware of it or not, relies on a public "status" (Jellinek) in doing so. The citizen of private law has simultaneously established a different public legal relation.

Jellinek's argument against private law liberalism proceeds in two steps: (i) *in addition* to subjective rights, which permit some physical ability, there are *also* rights that create a legal ability – the capacity to perform legal actions, to "manipulate" law. (ii) Private law's system of permissive rights simultaneously *presupposes* these creative or "granting" rights: it does not exist without them. The political significance of the liberal order of private law is that it can only exist where the individual has achieved a public status, defined by the state's recognition of her "personhood," since granting the legal ability to act affects the relation between the individual and the whole of law, represented in the state. A new and different type of claim is correlated with this development: "Claims . . . against the official subject of power [*Machtsubjekt*]."[30] In other words, a new type of subjective rights, which offer the individual *herself* the capacity to act in cases where such action was traditionally only performed by the "official subject of power": by law's determination, and therefore politically.

Jellinek understands the political presupposition of private law's subjective rights as pertaining to the structure of public law: the individual's legal status in the state whole, and thus the basic structure of state rule and membership, are changed by the introduction of private subjective rights. This is correct, but is not the whole story, for the political presupposition of private rights. They do not merely concern public

law. Jellinek, in his account of private subjective rights, strongly emphasized that they presuppose ability. Yet this presupposed ability actually
extends much further than the field of public law, to which he immediately restricted subjective rights once again. If, therefore, *with* Jellinek,
the political significance of private subjective rights lies in the fact that
they presuppose the creation of a legal ability, then, *contra* Jellinek, the
political element of subjective rights cannot be limited to public law.
For legal ability, which is presupposed in legal allowance, is not only
the capacity to influence state rule. The significance of the political is
also transformed by the political significance of private subjective rights.
Hans Kelsen draws the following consequence from Jellinek's argument:
according to Kelsen, subjective private law is *itself a political right*.

"So-called 'political' rights" are usually defined as "the power to influence the formation of the will of the state; this means: to participate
directly or indirectly in the formation of the legal order in which the 'will
of the state' expresses itself."[31] In democratic states, this is understood as
"participation in legislation . . . by those subjected to the norms." This
is too narrow a conception of political rights, however. For if political
rights, at their core, can be defined as:

> granting individuals the capacity of participating in the formation of
> the will of the state (in the creation of legal norms), *then the rights
> established by private law, the private rights, too, are political rights*; for
> they too allow the entitled individual to take part in the formation of
> the will of the state. . . . To subsume the private right (that is, the legal
> power to bring about by a law suit the execution of a sanction as a reac-
> tion against the nonfulfillment of an obligation) and the political right
> (which, too, is a legal power) under one and the same concept, namely
> the right as the law in a subjective sense, is possible only insofar as both
> express the same legal function: participation of those subjected to the
> law in the creation of the law.[32]

Kelsen's radicalization of the thesis underlying Jellinek's titular formulation, "subjective public rights," claims that all subjective rights, even
those of bourgeois private law, not only make a public or political *presupposition*, but also have a *public or political dimension*. They are
essentially political because they always authorize in such a way that they
not only permit a physical ability, but also create a legal ability. And they
are essentially political because the legal ability that they create is the
capacity to participate in the creation of law. Finally, they are political
because participation in the creation of law is precisely the basic definition of (bourgeois) politics.

The crucial step in this explanation is of course the first one: the claim that even private law's subjective rights authorize in such a way that they do not merely permit physical ability, but create a legal ability. Jellinek himself says this – without drawing the consequences. "In the legal possibility of raising claims against another, allowance manifests itself *in connection with the power to dispose* [or the "power of disposition"] *over law and claim themselves*. It is the distinguishing feature of private law and specific to it."[33] The power of disposition "over law and claim themselves," however, is obviously not a physical ability, but a legal one (which Jellinek would like to restrict to public law). The rights of bourgeois private law also include the legal power "to change legal relations":[34] the capacity "to exercise rights in such a way as to annul attributable legal consequences."[35] The subject of private rights is already the subject of the transformation of rights. In its private relation to another, this subject politically achieves "participation ... in the creation of law" (Kelsen). Bourgeois private law's subjective rights are *immanently* political.

Jellinek's epochal reflection on the creative power of subjective rights, on their power of granting, concludes that private rights have an irreducibly political dimension – a consequence that moves beyond his own theory of public subjective rights. This thesis holds that subjective rights have an immanent political character. It claims that the political element of bourgeois law is not *only* defined by the institutionalized "participation of those subjected to the law in the creation of the law" (Kelsen), and therefore cannot be limited to it. Political authorization thus takes on a dual character through the form of subjective rights.

First, political authorization is *presupposed* in the system of rights. It results from each person's status, granted by the state, and occurs in the form of rights to participate in the creation of, or, more precisely, in the existing state order's "development" and "modification," mediated by mechanisms of representation (since "The original creation of the social order or of the government is not, after all, part of our social experience").[36] Second, political authorization is immanently *contained* in the system of private rights. It results from the negative act of permitting everything that is not prohibited.[37] This takes place through rights of disposition to change legal relations – to change one's own legal relations, which, however, always also has legal consequences not only for other individuals, but for a third: consequences for what is considered valid, and therefore valid for all. Both the authorization presupposed by private law and the one enacted by private law can therefore be called "political" because they are rights to change law, to transform it as normatively valid. The conception of the political, however, at the same time thereby becomes ambiguous. Its ambiguity defines (and ruptures) the idea and the reality of bourgeois politics.

The argument that Jellinek provides for the political presupposition of the bourgeois system of private law, and thus his argument against traditional private law liberalism, can be understood as follows: if law is not a series of commands, but a product of rules or statutes [*Gesetzen*], then all law presupposes an authority that provides, interprets, and administers statutes. This authority simultaneously holds a position of power and one of recognition. It holds the position of judgment: the binding determination of the legally universal. In traditional law, this position is occupied exclusively. Only one or a few are able to judge. In contrast, the bourgeois system of private law equally distributes the legal power to judge, the capacity for legislative thought, without which law cannot exist. This is a consequence of the argument against the liberal conception of private law, a conception that limits such power or capacity to the equality of allowance, to permitting "physical" ability. Such an argument holds that, if (with Savigny) each human being's capacity for law is the foundation of bourgeois private law, which grants rights to each individual over against other individuals, then this simultaneously presupposes that each individual is recognized by the state as a person capable of law. To be a person capable of law here means to be an equal person, means to be on a par with others, and not someone who has been subdued. Not to be subdued means not to be subject to another's judgment, but to be able to judge like anyone else.[38] And, furthermore, it means to legally sit in judgment over law. The equality of entitlement in the private sense (entitled or authorized over against others) thus presupposes equality of entitlement in the public or political sense (entitled or authorized to judge, that is, to participate in legislation). "Rights-bearers" are simultaneously defined as "rights-*thinkers*" (and their thinking of rights is defined as judgment, and therefore as participation in binding stipulation of legislation or in the interpretation of law) through the establishment of the form of subjective rights.[39] The public law political presupposition made by bourgeois private law, with its premise of equality, implies that every recipient of rights of opportunity is therefore entitled to be co-author of law. The significance of the political authorization presupposed in private law is that it is the authorization to (co-)judge what law is.

In contrast, the authorization to participate in the creation of law, which is not merely presupposed but *contained* by the system of private law, involves disposing over law and claim. Bourgeois private law creates a fundamentally new kind of legal ability, which provides the meaning

135

for its permitting of "physical" ability. This new kind of legal ability, which first (and only) exists in the bourgeois system of private law, is the capacity to create new law – and, furthermore, not legislatively, in thinking and judging the universal, but by changing one's own legal position. The basic operation of this capacity is the contract. The central significance of freedom of contract in bourgeois law is to be found here as well. Bourgeois freedom of contract is established by "legal provisions ... which grant to an individual *autonomy* to *regulate* his *relations with others* by his own transactions."[40] These limits are of a technical-legal nature, and are "prescribed for reasons of expediency, especially for the sake of the unambiguous demonstrability of rights, and thus of legal security."[41] This is "fundamentally established ... in general today," although it "was reached only quite late." For it presupposes that the binding of law to political morality or natural reason has fallen apart. What is generally established today is precisely "that any content whatsoever of a contract, in so far as it is not excluded by limitations on the freedom of contract, creates law among the parties."[42] Disposing over one's own legal relations is therefore, once again, a form of *political* authorization (according to Kelsen) because it creates law. Since it does this, every contractual agreement between two parties always binds "*third parties* who were not involved in making the agreement."[43] It does not bind them in judging the universal, and thus *from* the perspective of the universal, however, but only in such a way that *self-will*, whether of the first party or the second, becomes binding on a third.

The ambiguity of bourgeois politics is one of *judging* or *disposing* over law. The simple resolution of this ambiguity consists in dividing its two sides and assigning them different perspectives, understanding them as two different ways of carrying out a "law-creating ... function" (Kelsen).[44] The adjudicative creation of law would then belong to democratic legislation, while the dispositional creation of law would belong to the contractual practice of private law. This division is untenable, however. It is undermined by the form that political authorization assumes in bourgeois law, since bourgeois law again reduces participation in the political process presupposed by the system of private law to the form of subjective rights. Democratic participation in the political process of legislation thereby becomes a mere possibility – something dependent on the subject's disposition, at its discretion. Because the subject has the right to participate, it not only is able to dispose over whether it will participate politically (at its own discretion), but can also carry out its political participation *as* disposing over its own will. Bourgeois politics is therefore in crisis simply because of its form, the form of subjective rights. Bourgeois politics *is* the crisis of politics, the crisis of distinguishing between judging and disposing – a distinction that is the *sine qua non* of any politics. It must presuppose judging in order to create law. It organizes participation in judging, however, as authorization to dispose over one's own right as one chooses.

The collapse of the distinction between judging and disposing is the paradox of bourgeois politics: it is a "politics of privatization."[45] Before this can be more closely described, however, we need to examine a concept that we have already suggested played a central role for the understanding of the bourgeois form of subjective rights: the concept of "arbitrary discretion" or "private self-will,"[46] which is developed in the subject's disposal over its own legal relations.

To that end, we should first offer a preliminary clarification of methodology that indicates the perspective from which we will view discretion. This will be the perspective of legal subjectification, of subjective entitlement as authorization. From this perspective, discretion itself is an ability. To put this more precisely, it is an ability created by law.

The Ability to Exercise Discretion

Jellinek's critique of private law liberalism leads to a systematic expansion of what rights do. All subjective rights authorize because they are concerned with opportunities for action. Jellinek's insight, however, is that they do this in two fundamentally different ways: either by permitting or by granting, and therefore by conceding or by producing. Both of these legal functions of authorization are already linked in complex ways by Jellinek, and even more in the subsequent discussion that greeted his work. For legal permission presupposes the granting of legal opportunities for action while simultaneously entailing them. The bourgeois subject of private rights, as we have already seen, can participate in the creation of law in a twofold way, by judging and by disposing. And this "political" ability is juridically produced.

Even this complexity of permission and granting, however, leaves one fundamental premise of Jellinek's critique of private law liberalism unchanged. This premise maintains that legal authorization is productive *only* in its granting of a legal ability. In contrast, legal permission, allowance by private law, concedes opportunities for action that already exist prior to every law: "physical" ability. The premise of Jellinek's argument is that all ability which produces law is *eo ipso* legal ability (ability of a legal kind, ability for the legal). Conversely, all non-legal ability, that is,

137

all ability that is not drafted into law, is also not legally produced, but exists prior to and independent of law.

These equivalences are fallacious: to be legally created does not mean to be drafted into law – at least not necessarily in a conceptual sense, and therefore not in every case. It is possible to interpret the syntagma "the legal constitution of the subject" in more than one way. We should distinguish between the constitution of the subject by law and the legality (or lawfulness) of the subject thus constituted. The two can diverge.

This already holds for the way in which private law's allowance is the creation of an ability, since this ability is not a legal one – it is not the capacity to engage in legal activities that create or change law and are thus political, whether they involve judging or disposing, activities which private law's allowance presupposes or implies. Instead, private law's permission itself creates an ability that is non-legal or prior to law: it is non-legal, indeed pre-legal, *and* created by law (or an effect of its own invocation, the interpellation of law).[47] Contra Jellinek's premise (the claim that ability produced by law is legal ability), it turns out that the creative, productive authorization by subjective rights extends beyond the domain of law.

Max Weber uses the term "authorization" for only this specific effect that extends beyond law. Unlike Jellinek, he is interested in how mere permission already authorizes: how it already produces what it permits (and which subsequently *manifests itself* as its presupposition, that is, physical, naturally occurring ability). For according to Weber, the subjective rights of private law authorize because they establish the normative expectation "that one may himself engage, or fail to engage, in certain conduct without interference from a third party."[48] Legal authorization is therefore to be found in the authorization of the discretionary: the fact that I may do something or refrain from doing it. For to be allowed this *is* an ability. I am only *able* to will at my discretion if I am allowed to exercise discretion. In other words, the entitlement to do or refrain from doing what is at my discretion is precisely my authorization because it *first gives* me *the power* to will at my discretion or by choice (or "freely," in the negative sense). Under private law, I am warranted to do what I want, at my discretion – to do so is to exercise a potential or power that I *only* possess at all *through this warrant*. Permission is not the concession of a pre-existing ("physical") opportunity for action, but itself creates a new opportunity for action. Contra Jellinek, Weber's conception of authorization, of permission *as* authorization, concludes that legal allowance is also productive. In other words, subjective rights create an ability

138

that is more than merely legal. Law also creates pre-juridical "physical" ability, as the ability to exercise discretion.

Weber views the authorization of discretion as the distinguishing feature of modern law. Only in modern law are we to understand that anywhere law does not command or prohibit something specific, there is still a third option: the authorization of the discretionary, or the subject of discretion. There is no permitting of discretion in the moral law of Athens or rational law of Rome. The permissible coincides with the imperative – (only) virtuous or rational activity is permitted. For Hobbes, in contrast, the claim that a right consists in nothing but the "liberty to do or forbeare" is presupposed as self-evident.[49] Hobbes supposes that this freedom is only to be conceived negatively, as "the absence of exter-nall Impediments."[50] The negative freedom to do this or that at one's discretion, however, includes a positive presupposition. This is the power of the "or": the will's power *to be able* to decide one way *or* another. It is the power to will, where willing means choosing, since to will in such a way – to be willing and able to will in such a way – that willing means choosing at one's discretion is not the natural form of willing, but an artificially produced form. It is the form adopted by the will of the subject of subjective rights.

In defining legal permission as the authorization to act at one's discretion, Weber thereby formulates a line of inquiry that moves a crucial step beyond Jellinek's "political" extension of the concept of subjective rights. The basic thought that Weber draws on in Jellinek is that subjective rights are not rights possessed by a subject (who exists prior to law), but are rights that create subjectivity as the epitome [*Inbegriff*] of ability or power. Subjective rights are therefore "subjective" because they subjectify. Jellinek had demonstrated this in regard to the legal, or, more precisely, the political ability to create law, which is always also created by permission under private law. Weber radicalizes this thought into the thesis that legal permission is already productive: permission creates what is permitted, which it appears to presuppose. The form of subjective rights yields a new form of willing: willing at one's discretion. Making a choice at one's discretion – as a social, cultural, and political model of subjectivity – only *exists* once subjective rights do. It did not exist prior to the entitlement to discretion. The subject of willing as discretion is the bourgeois subject of negative freedom or the subject of choice. Weber's line of inquiry thus hypothesizes that the bourgeois subject is an effect of the power of subjective rights.

— 9 —

SELF-WILL

Bourgeois law creates a new will through its mode of entitlement. It entitles and thereby authorizes the individual to will and to act at her own discretion. In negative terms, this means that the individual voluntarily chooses the will's content. The subjective right severs the individual's legal power from virtue or reason, to which traditional law linked the individual's opportunity for asserting it. This corresponds to the positive determination that subjective rights authorize individuals to have a will of their own, or authorize them to be self-willed. The bourgeois form of rights is "subjective" insofar as the will makes a choice here not because it wills the morally good or naturally rational, but because it is this subject's self-will. What is one's own [*das Eigene*], the realization of which bourgeois law authorizes, thereby replaces "what belongs to one" [*das Seine*], which traditional law distributes to each individual. The individual obtains what belongs to her, as fair share, through the just division carried out by law. Yet in another sense, conversely, the individual has her own [*sein Eigenes*] all by herself: merely by the fact that *I* will, that it is *my* will. That which is the will's own is therefore not some new purpose – bourgeois self-will is not an (egoistical) will that is only ever concerned with its own, but a new mode of validity: willing is now relevant simply because it is one's own willing, willing *by someone*. Bourgeois law thereby simultaneously *creates* a new form of the will. By granting validity to the subject's will merely because it is her will, it yields a new subject: the subject of a new mode of willing.

In lectures examining the semantic upheavals at the origin of bourgeois society, gathered under the title *The Birth of Biopolitics*, Michel Foucault has examined the basic structure of this new subject on the model of English empiricism. "What English empiricism introduces . . . and doubt-

140

less for the first time in Western philosophy, is a subject . . . who appears in the form of a subject of individual choices which are both irreducible and non-transferable."[1] The claim that they are "both irreducible and non-transferable" means that empiricism understands the subject as the ultimate authority for decisions. It does *not* mean that another more fundamental and significant choice made by the same individual might not lie behind an individual decision (Foucault's example, in the spirit of English empiricism, is the decision to exercise), such as to prefer health to illness, or, at an even more basic level, to prefer what is not painful to what is painful. It means, rather, that *the only thing* that can lie behind an individual decision is another individual choice [*Wahl*]. It means that the basis for deciding what to choose is a decision between choices.

> The painful or non-painful nature of the thing is in itself a reason for the choice beyond which you cannot go. The choice between painful and non-painful is a sort of irreducible that does not refer to any judgment, reasoning, or calculation. It is a sort of regressive end point in the analysis.[2]

To be a subject of self-will means that the subject's mere choice, which has nothing more behind it, is the ultimate basis of each individual decision. This is why an individual's voluntary decision is also non-transferable: "It will be made on the basis of my own preference," on the mere "fact" that I have made such a choice. Foucault here describes a subject of self-will who is constituted by the "principle of an irreducible, non-transferable, atomistic individual choice which is unconditionally referred to the subject himself."[3] This is an empiricist conception of the subject insofar as there are no bases that precede the subject's decision, and thus no judgment nor any procedure (or method). It originates from the subject's will alone. There is a *fact* that forms the basis for a decision, yet it is simply *the fact of her own act – her own choice*. The properties attributed to the subject are not her own. The contents of the subject's will, which (or *insofar as they*) are ascribed to nothing but the fact, and thus the act, of her will, are her own.

For empiricism, the (f)act of one's own will is irreducible. Empiricism removes judgment and deliberation from the will's basis, and thereby from its concept, in order to be rid of judgment (and to thereby escape criticism). It understands self-will as a sheer or ultimate given, from which all normative and political regulation must proceed. This can be critiqued as mere ideology: there is no such self-will at all (according to ideology critique's objection). For to will *means* to judge, and to judge *means* to be in the realm of reasons, which includes the possibility for deliberation. Critique objects that the empiricism of self-will is ideology, since it misconstrues and distorts the reality of willing.

In contrast, Foucault's ("genealogical") objection to the "regressive end point" of decision in an ultimate act of willing, which is as irreducible as it is non-transferable, is that individual self-will exists, but is not self-evidently given. Rather, individual self-will only exists by being made – but by being made, it *actually exists*. While the ideological-critical objection reproaches self-will, on conceptual grounds, for abstracting from the moral and social determination of the will (its truth), Foucault conceives this abstraction as real, namely as the real abstraction of the moral, through which self-will makes itself and which for that reason constitutes it. Understood in genealogical terms, self-will *is* the power to abstract from the moral (and at the same time an act of privately appropriating the social).

From this perspective, the bourgeois self-will can be described as follows: to will means to will something good (to this extent, willing involves judgment), and to will something good means to orient oneself to reasons. This is how willing is linked to deliberation. In willing, it is just as much a matter of the morality of one's goal as it is a matter of how one carries one's will out, just as much a matter of what one is intending to do as it is a matter of one's willing itself. The will is normative: willing is concerned with whether what is intended (as the content of willing) is good or bad and with willing's independence or lack of independence (the development of willing). If this is the basic definition of willing, then an act of abstraction underlies individual self-will, as the fact at the basis of all decisions: self-will *wills* without being concerned about whether what is intended is good or bad, and without being concerned about whether its willing is independent or not. Self-will abstracts in willing. Its willing of this or that is at the same time the will to abstract from the will's normativity. Self-will wills abstractly.

This means that self-will wills the content of its willing without regard for whether it is good or bad, since good and bad are equally valid as mere intentions, namely as the positive and negative value of its preferences. This neutralization of the will's content corresponds to rendering the formation of the will invisible. If the will is concerned with good or bad, then how the will came to be formed becomes crucial: whether it has formed itself by its own deliberations or merely repeats what everyone is saying; whether it is independent, autonomous, or not. In contrast, self-will also abstracts from *how* it reached its decisions. The only thing that matters to it is the fact *that* a subject wills something – it is unconcerned with what it wills or how it wills. The self's willing is indifferent, a willing in normative indifference or as indifferent*iation,* as indifferent establishment of the normative.

This corresponds to the repression of the social and, in particular, to the privatism of self-will. Moral contents, the good or goods, are not products of individual preferences, but exist objectively in social practices. They become individual goals when they are appropriated by individuals – adopted, interpreted, transformed, and so on. This is also why the autonomy or independence of willing is not a feature of individual acts of the will. Still less is it a capability that an individual "atomistic" subject can have, but it refers to the process of the individual's appropriation of the social. The morality and autonomy of willing only exists in dialectical processes in which individuals are simultaneously subjectified and socialized. Moral, independent willing is carried out not in the individual, but *between* the individual and the social.[4] Abstraction, through which self-will neutralizes the normativity of what is intended and renders the development of the will invisible, simultaneously leads to the disintegration of the social, namely by reducing the social to the individual. The between [*Das Zwischen*] – willing as a process *between* the individual and the social – becomes the individual's own. "The individual's desire" comes from "that which '*inter-est*', or that which is publicly common for us, in other words, the space of the political."[5] "However, an individual human being does not have any specific interests. Such interests first arise for the individual only in the common space in which it *sympherei,* con-tributes. This is also where the individual's *sympheron* [C.M. – i.e., its interest] is to be found."[6] Self-will ascribes what can only exist in the dialectic between individual and community to itself as its personal accomplishment. For the self-will, willing is something that the individual alone is capable of and does. The abstraction of self-will from normative difference simultaneously entails the private appropriation of "common space" (Hannah Arendt) by individuals.

The effect of this process of fabrication, which can be described in two ways, as indifferentiation of the normative and privatization of the social, is *the positivization of one's own.* Willing that ignores the moral difference between good and bad, and thereby ignores the social constitution of its contents, understands itself and is indeed carried out as the mere establishment of a fact. Self-will is created behind its own back. The indifferent, private will is not a process at all *for itself,* since it is not practical. It understands and carries itself out merely as the registering of that which the subject strives for or desires.[7] Self-will *asserts* itself.

* * *

Foucault, aided by the empiricist model of self-will, characterizes the subject produced by the modern economic, biopolitical regime, the regime of "civil society,"[8] as follows: the empiricist subject is the bourgeois subject. Its planning and calculations are based on a will "that does not refer to any judgment, reasoning, or calculation" (Foucault). The bourgeois subject's existence presupposes its abstraction from judgments, reasoning, or justifications. The human being of bourgeois society is a human being without bases or, more precisely: a human being whose will, as mere fact, is considered a basis, and therefore someone whose will does not require a sound basis to be considered legitimate. Self-will is a category of validity: self-will *is valid* regardless of whether its will is good or bad. It is thereby also valid regardless of the fact that its will can only be formed in a collective space (that its will is therefore never private, its own).

The operation that produces the bourgeois subject (or "homo economicus") and alone can explain its existence is thus evident: the bourgeois subject described by Foucault presupposes a radical upheaval in the normative order of society – an upheaval in the definition of what kind of willing counts or is valid. And the instrument of this normative upheaval is the form of subjective rights: the form of subjective rights authorizes individual self-wills. For law, in the form of subjective rights, legalizes the mere fact that something is the subject's self-will – his choice or interest. Subjective rights validate the fact that a subject wills something. All subjective rights presuppose this fact and proceed on its basis. To be sure, a legally binding claim can only result from this presupposition (of private self-wills for each individual) after we have taken a further step. The fact must be changed into a right. The decisive factor in this change of the form of subjective rights, however, is that it does not require *any transformation of willing*. It is not an internal change, not one of substance, but an external change, one of scope, the limits of each respective self-will. The step from a subject's willing to her right does not consist in the submission of either the content or mode of her willing to a judgment. Were this the case, there would only be a right to moral or autonomous willing. A subject's will, however, becomes a subjective right not on the basis of the morality of its contents or the autonomy of its formation, but only through its external limitation according to a formal law [*Gesetz*] of equality.

Another way to put this is to say that self-will *is valid*: "validity" denotes a concept that only (and precisely) begins its career with modern law. It means grasping normative power as the "essential role" that something given plays for the subject; as an ("ideal") status that some-

144

thing "real" holds for the subject.[9] Something has validity not because of what it is in itself, but in how it is for and through something else. The insertion of validity here occurs through an externally limiting law of equality. The *only* normative standpoint offered by the form of subjective rights in assessing each individual will is that all self-wills can simultaneously exist. This is a consequence of the definition of self-will. For all are equal in the mere fact, and thus merely in the fact, that they will something. The empiricism of self-will grounds the egalitarianism of its validity. The basic principle of the subjective right is that each subject is entitled to her willing – which always exists regardless of whether it is moral or immoral, independent or not. The subject's willing is therefore only "valid" if it adheres to the external limits drawn by the principle of the equality of all subjects.

Excursus: The "Given" – Juridical Empiricism (Kelsen, Schmitt)

Empiricism – by definition – is the "Myth of the Given." Our thesis to this point is that the form of subjective rights is empiricist or positivist because it proceeds on the basis of an individual self-will's act, which is considered to be a fact that is "both irreducible and non-transferable" (Foucault). The form of subjective rights presupposes the subject's individual self-will as given.

From Marx to Foucault, we find the common critique that bourgeois law, in the form of subjective rights, rests on a "Myth of the Given." This critique is as follows: the bourgeois state with human rights turns the bourgeois individual [*den Bourgeois*], as member of civil [*bürgerlichen*] society, into its (supposedly natural) "basis."[10] Furthermore, the basic feature of the "relation between civil society and the state" is its presumption that "society . . . is already given."[11] For this reason, Foucault says that the essence of bourgeois politics is "more a naturalism than liberalism."[12] However, one can just as well, or better, say that a liberalism which presupposes civil society and the bourgeois subject, in the form of subjective rights, *is* a naturalism.

Even the (otherwise diametrically opposed) interpretations offered by Carl Schmitt and Hans Kelsen of the liberal or bourgeois form of subjective rights have this thesis in common. However, an ambiguity in the meaning of the term "given" also becomes evident in their agreement here. This ambiguity pervades the critique of subjective rights and must be resolved if it wants to engage its subject matter.

In his *Constitutional Theory*, Schmitt interprets the character of liberal rights in such a way that "The individual's sphere of freedom is presupposed as something prior to the state" and "the freedom of the individual is presupposed and the state limitation appears as an exception."[13] Kelsen describes the "ideological significance" of the character of subjective rights in similar terms. It is to be found in the "idea . . . of a legal subjectivity that discovers the subjective right, so to speak, whether in the individual or in certain collectives, a subjectivity that this right alone recognizes and must necessarily recognize, if it does not wish to lose its character as 'right.'"[14] In both Schmitt and Kelsen, the term "given" here means: *existing* of its own accord (independent of and thus prior to law and politics). According to both Schmitt and Kelsen, who are in agreement here, the claim that the freedom of individual decision or self-will is a quasi-natural property of the subject, already present independent of law and politics, is inscribed in the form of subjective rights.

This interpretation, however, is wrong: it is an interpretation that, as Jürgen Habermas has demonstrated, is only correct for one "construction of Natural Law, that of bourgeois society," which is a specific Anglo-Saxon liberal construction. It does not apply to the other interpretation, the French republican construction that culminates in the modern welfare state.[15] However, this interpretation is also inapplicable to the Myth of the Given, which is inscribed *as such* in the form of subjective rights, and not merely in one of its ideological constructs. The reason for this becomes evident in Kelsen's suggestion for how we must understand the subjective right so that, on the contrary, "any ideological misuse" is "excluded": the subjective right must be "reduced to the objective, restricted to the objective."[16] Kelsen poses the following alternative: subjective rights are *either* understood in such a way that they presuppose the self-will's individual freedom as a kind of given that exists by nature prior to and independent of law. For Kelsen, as for Schmitt, this is liberal ideology's natural law "dualism." *Or* subjective rights are understood to be a mere "technique" that "law can, but need not, employ," something established by objective right, like any other one of its normalizations.[17] *Either* subjective rights are ideologically referred back to a natural givenness, *or* they are a non-ideological legal technique that does not make any presuppositions at all.

The position left out by Kelsen's alternative, one inconceivable to it, consists in claiming that the freedom of individual decisions is legally produced and, *at the same time*, that law presupposes individual decisions to be facts. This requires us to draw a distinction between two different meanings of the term "givenness" (which are conflated in Kelsen and Schmitt).[18] "Givenness" can mean the *existence* of freedom prior to law, or it can mean the *validation* of individual choices (*by* law). (Only) Anglo-Saxon liberalism offers an ideological thesis which claims that freedom naturally exists prior to law (on Habermas's reconstruction, for instance). This ideology can be, and indeed already largely has been, eclipsed, without thereby dissolving the empiricist myth that defined the form of subjective rights. The French republican social welfare state theory of subjective rights thus continually emphasizes that individual freedom is only a "product" of subjective rights.[19] At the same time, however, it reproduces the juridical empiricism of subjective rights, since this myth is the structure of legal validity: law refers to individual choices as *facts* through the form of subjective rights. They are considered to be valid as accepted facts: irreducible, impervious to judgment, irresolvable, and not something that can be criticized. By means of their form, subjective rights authorize the subject to validate whatever she wishes as factual – they authorize the subject's self-will.

The thesis to this point is therefore that the empiricism of self-will is juridical and the subject of rights is empirical. Empiricism ascribes the subject's decisions to the irreducible fact of her willing. This ascription is not (or not merely) a philosophical operation (and thereby subject matter for ideology critique). It is an operation carried out by law itself when it translates individual entitlement into the form of subjective rights. Furthermore, it is thereby an operation that law authorizes each individual to carry out: subjective rights authorize each individual to ascribe her decisions to the irreducible fact of her own willing. They authorize the mere act of privately willing. In other words, they authorize the subject to abstract from the moral and to appropriate the social. It is precisely this authorization that constitutes a *specific* (specifically *bourgeois*) individualism, inscribed in the form of subjective rights. We can define this juridical or bourgeois individualism, which is to be distinguished from any cultural and moral individualism, as follows: the form of subjective rights is individualistic because it understands the subject's self-will to be a fact and considers it valid. It therefore authorizes the subject to abstract from the morality of willing and to appropriate the social as her own.

Property Before Property

Property, or more precisely, property in its specifically modern, bourgeois form is the simplest and most basic form of the legal authorization of self-will. Bourgeois private property is the basic category of subjective rights, but not because such a category is supposedly the most socially

147

significant and consequential. The subject's competencies in changing legal positions (as in freedom of contract and the right of action) is in fact more socially significant and consequential. Instead, it is the basic category of subjective rights because what holds true for all subjective rights, including competencies, is most clearly evident in bourgeois private property: they presuppose the fact (and thus the *power*) of the subject's own will and legally institute it.

To grasp what is specific to its bourgeois form, we first need a definition of what constitutes the private character of property. Émile Durkheim has proposed that it lies in a person's right to "exclusive use" of something:

> Something to which I have a property right is a thing that only I may use. It is withdrawn from common use and reserved for a single individual. To be sure, I cannot do with it whatever I like, but I am the only person who can use it.[20]

This suggests that we can determine the exclusivity which defines private property through the "powers that the subject has over things which he possesses."[21] Traditionally, there were three ways to designate powers over a thing: the power to use a thing, the power to benefit from it, and the power to change it, up to and including the power to destroy it.[22] As such, however, these powers over a thing do not constitute property at all. A property owner can thus transfer her powers to others (albeit to very different degrees in various historical regimes of private law) by, for instance, renting to them, giving something to them, or otherwise allowing them rights of use, *without* thereby ceasing to be a property owner of the thing in question. A property owner is not someone who wields powers over a thing, but a person who decides what these powers will be. The exclusivity of the private property owner's power [*Befugnis*] lies in the fact that she alone and no one else disposes over something. Property is a power *over* use, not *in* use, not the exclusivity of use but the exclusivity of deciding on use. A property right is an "exclusive right" because it excludes others from deciding on how something will be used, not from using or employing it.

This seems to contradict the traditional designation of property as *ius in re*, or right *in rem*. Even in this regard, however, property is not opposed to *ius in personam* because it is a relation to a thing *rather than* someone else. For there is no such thing as a legal relation to or even with a thing. The fact that "All rights *in rem* are rights against persons"[23] is also true of right *in rem* – except that property is a right not against one or several persons (with whom one is bound by voluntary or involuntary obligations), but against many, indeed, against every other person (in the same legal system). The exclusivity of the power to decide signifies that to have something as my property obligates everyone else over against me and entitles me over against them.

This general definition of the private property owner's exclusivity also holds for traditional moral law in Athens or rational law in Rome. When Aristotle defends the institution of private property against Socrates (or Plato), he thereby defines it by claiming that "each will apply himself to it as to private business of his own" and describes this as each deciding for himself and alone determining the mode of use.[24] At the same time, however, private property is supposed to be regulated by moral law so that there are "common goods . . . for the purpose of use." In "well-administered . . . states," each person has:

> while owning their property privately put their own possessions at the service of their friends and make[s] use of their friends' possession as common property; for instance in Sparta people use one another's slaves as virtually their own, as well as horses and hounds, and also use the produce in the fields throughout the country if they need provisions on a journey. It is clear therefore that it is better for possessions to be privately owned, but to make them common property in use; and to train the citizens to this is the special task of the legislator.[25]

Private property and common use *at the same time*: the property owner *alone*, exclusive of all others, decides what belongs to him, but it is a legislative task, and therefore a task of law, to see to it that he decides in such a way that use is common. "Common" [*Gemeinsam*] here thus does not literally mean a shared use in common, but means usage of what is held in common or in a universal [*gemeinsamen*] sense. It therefore means use according to virtue (or natural reason). In traditional law, the private property owner's right to exclusive decision is nothing but – and extends only so far as – virtue; it is a right from *and to* virtue. The private property owner's entitlement to alone decide over use is conditioned by the fact that his private decision has a legal basis in morality or reason.[26]

The step toward the specifically bourgeois conception of property as a subjective right now consists in establishing property on a basis prior to law. Such a basis is present before law, before the definitions and features of the legal person. John Locke defines this basis as follows:

> though the things of Nature are given in common, yet Man (by being Master of himself, and *Proprietor of his own Person*, and the Actions or *Labour* of it) had still in himself *the great Foundation of Property*.[27]

149

For Locke, the claim that bourgeois private property has a natural basis, prior to law, signifies that it *begins* with an act (which he understands as labor) that exists *before* any legal system. Labor is the foundation and therefore not the basis of property, but its *beginning*.[28] Locke here speaks of how it was "at first," and thus of property as a natural right, in the state of nature (in which property is factually "bounded . . . so that there then could be no reason of quarrelling," where such quarrelling would have to be arbitrated by legal restrictions according to a law of equality). "Man still had in himself" property's "great Foundation," which is *property before property*: before the right of property, the private or exclusive right to decide vis-à-vis anyone else (which can only exist in a social order), there must have been a kind of property by nature that "Man still had in himself." The step from a traditional to a bourgeois conception of property consists in the thesis that property cannot exist *at all* without (natural) property that is *prior to* (legal) property – that the basis of legal property is natural property.

The basic thesis (and structure) that constitutes bourgeois property and radically distinguishes it from traditional property claims that property has a natural foundation, or that property begins prior to property. Like every right, property must be established in a legal system, so that its claim to an exclusivity of decision vis-à-vis anyone else can obtain the status of a normative obligation. According to Locke, however, this establishment of property in a legal system must be understood by tracing it back to and "beginning" with a claim prior to law. The claim that legal property has its "foundation" in the natural property that essentially belongs to the human being entails that the formation of the legal system *pro*ceeds [aus*geht*] from a natural claim prior to law, and hence, additionally, that this claim is *at stake* [um . . . *geht*] in the formation of that system. Natural property is the "foundation" of legal property not because it constitutes legal property, but because legal property rests on it: natural property is the *condition* for legal property's *meaning*.[29] Bourgeois property's radical difference from traditional property lies not in any of its contents, but in its conceptual structure – in the structure of its normativity: while the normative basis and content of traditional property coincide (the property owner is entitled to his private decision because it is the right one: a virtuous work for which the legal order educates us), they diverge in bourgeois property. Bourgeois property is a right *to* (to, not from: natural property is the foundation and not the normative basis) natural property. It is a right that protects and secures natural property.

Locke defines property before property, in which everything legal first "begins," as property in oneself: the *"great Foundation of Property"* is "still in himself" *because* he is *"Proprietor of his own Person and the Actions or Labour of it"*; "every Man has a *Property* in his own *Person.*"[30] The foundation for legal physical property is natural ("self"-) property, which the human being has in his own person.

This way of speaking is odd – to claim that the human being has his person rather than is a person. In Locke, "person" is a "forensic term."[31] A person is an entity to which actions can be attributed and thereby an entity to which responsibility can be ascribed. In law, this usually occurs in an external manner. Locke, in contrast, regards this attribution from within and hence describes the person as an entity *"appropriating* actions and their merit."[32] If the person is the principle for the ascription of actions, then property in the person is the internalization of ascription – the self-ascription of actions, their appropriation as one's own. The person (which Locke therefore designates as the self) is that mode of being a "thing" in which it "attributes to it *self*, and owns all the actions of that thing as its own."[33] Its actions thereby become the expression of its own "concern for happiness," which Locke considers to be the ultimate principle for making decisions.[34] Property in one's own person or self-property goes beyond the merely external attribution of actions and thereby of responsibilities, insofar as it traces actions back to one's own irreducible and non-transferable self-will. Natural property, which according to Locke constitutes the foundation of the legal "in" a person "himself," is nothing but a term expressing the relation between a person's actions and the self's own will as a subject. "Only the human being in its unique capacity – the 'subject' in the emphatic sense – can give that 'stamp' to some object which marks the claim to property."[35] Bourgeois private property secures (by means of formal-egalitarian limitation) the person's natural property in his actions – the self-property of his actions or having them for his own. It secures the individual's claim to be allowed to express whatever he wishes in his actions.

The private character of property (the claim that the property owner alone, exclusive of all others, has the power to decide on the use of something) thereby obtains a radically new meaning: the private, exclusive power to decide is now only a matter of exerting self-will. Bourgeois private property, and this is the only place where Savigny's general definition of the subjective right is applicable in its pure form, is the "domain of the individual will's independent control":[36] in bourgeois law, private property becomes an individual subject's *private sphere.* Interference by others in the property owner's exclusive power to decide, which the property owner has over his thing, is thus here no longer merely a limitation or a challenge to his power (*dominium*) but a self-injuring (or an injury to himself). Illicit interference in my property now becomes something that "would wrong me."[37]

* * *

If bourgeois ownership of things is concerned with what is the subject's own (if it is a matter of exerting one's own will in disposing over a thing), then the moral rules that constitute traditional property become null and void. According to Aristotle, the lawmaker ensures that the property owner's private decision consists in virtuous deeds and that use thereby becomes common. This not only refers to how the private property owner is supposed to handle what belongs to him, but also refers to what can be property at all. If the subject's self-will becomes the foundation of property, then both limitations, on how property is handled and to what end it is used, are necessarily untenable.

We see here the socially transformative effect of the bourgeois reduction of legal property to natural property. This reduction

> removes "the bounds of the Law of Nature" from the natural property right of the individual. Locke's astonishing achievement was to base the property right on natural right and natural law, and then to remove all the natural law limits from the property right.[38]

It is crucial for bourgeois property that the exclusiveness of its power to dispose over no longer exists only vis-à-vis each other individual (the claim that property is private because this power is wielded by the property owner alone), but exists *against everyone else together*, against the community and its moral or rational principles, on which traditional law based private ownership via education or dominion. *Bourgeois property's proprietary principle dissolves the boundaries of possessive power.* This dissolution of boundaries initially concerns what a piece of property can even be: everything as such that is subsumed into the private "domain of the individual will's independent control." Bourgeois property is thereby the juridical instrument for extending the category of the commodity to labor, land, and money that characterizes the beginning of (and condition for) of bourgeois society.[39] Proprietary dissolution of boundaries next concerns what the subject can do in disposing over her own property – everything as such that the subject is able to will – especially allowing others to use her property for something in return. The other is excluded from deciding over her own thing precisely in order to thereby become "internalized" in the private property owner's domain of control: the proprietary exclusion of the other is a matter of the "absorption of the legal 'sphere' into the sphere of property."[40] Bourgeois property authorizes the subject to use her exclusionary power of decision to "restrictively rule" (Ulrich K. Preuß) over others.

Capacity

Locke's formula for bourgeois property is that the "foundation" of legal property is natural property – the subject is legally constituted in appropriation, and this defines it as (bourgeois) subject. Legal property secures and protects "natural" appropriation. This is the basic formal structure of bourgeois private property. It obtains its *content* from the fact that property prior to law, which the subject appropriates, is understood to be a determination of her will: the subject's decisions are her own. *What* the subject wants obtains validity from the fact *that* she wants it. The specific juridical individualism that is inscribed in bourgeois property amounts to the claim that private disposal over something is a matter of exerting one's own will. A popular metaphor for this is the private "sphere" in which the subject can decide simply by making up her own mind.

Locke himself understood his argument from the natural foundation of legal property in a different way. That is, he understood his argument to extend much further: according to Locke, it is not merely the subject's willing that is its own by nature, but also the deeds that give rise to it through the subject's labor to realize its will. "The *Labour* of his body, and the *Work* of his hands, we may say, are properly his."[41] Locke thereby expands individualism of the will into a "possessive individualism" (Macpherson). Consequently, the thing, insofar as it is the result of one's own labor, belongs to the subject *precisely to the extent* that it is validated by the subject's own will. This is why, for Locke, ownership of things is not merely a legal, and thereby artificial, means of securing something, but is itself a *part* of that which I am to appropriate in a natural way (and thereby belongs to the natural *foundation* of law).

Locke's extension of the will's natural appropriation over its labor on the thing, as product, has obvious ideological motivations and consequences: by extending the will's appropriation in this way, he naturalizes the legal allowance to dispose over something, because (or insofar as) it is based on one's own labor. Locke thereby formulates the ascendant bourgeoisie's ideological position, which was initially directed against feudal property (obtained by plunder and inheritance), and at the same time opposed to the claims of those who are unsuccessful, indolent, and superfluous. However, in Locke's extension of the will's natural appropriation

153

of the product, we also find an argument with the ideological and political potential to directly oppose possessive individualism. This argument entails that individualism of the will, which defines bourgeois property, always already contains *more*, *requires* more than the mere idea of a private sphere in which the individual will can develop unhindered. It therefore also entails that bourgeois property may no longer be equated with its classic form as private sphere, but yields a second type of property without calling its own basic structure into question.

This argument's basic structure is that bourgeois property as private sphere is concerned with securing a domain for the subject in which its own will is in "control" (Savigny). The will is only in control through its explicit statements, and thus through its actions. Property as private sphere abstracts from this. It understands action in only a minimal sense, as the exertion of one's own will. In other words, in property as private sphere, the freedom to act is understood in only a negative sense, as the absence of external impediments. To act, however, means to produce something, to create a product; this occurs through labor. Locke therefore plausibly argues that a subject whose authorization is a matter of law cannot merely be a subject who is engaged in willing (and protected in the private sphere), but must rather be understood as a laboring or productive subject: as "an active self with talents and abilities."[42] By means of these talents and abilities, such a subject *can realize* what it wants; as a subject who has the *means* (subjective and objective, abilities and resources) *by* which it can produce something. *If*, however, the subject of rights must be conceived as an active (or as Locke puts it: laboring) subject, then the conception of bourgeois property as mere private sphere under the will's control is inadequate, indeed untenably abstract. For what is such a domain of the will's unimpeded exertion *worth*, without the possibility of letting one's own will actually be in control?[43] And how is the will supposed to be in control other than by using the appropriate means? Locke's convincing step beyond his own definition of property as private sphere requires that we (also) understand property as possession of means.

The formal structure of this argument involves a theory of the will. As we have seen, bourgeois property signifies the securing of self-will. This is the core definition of bourgeois law's juridical individualism. In defining bourgeois property as private sphere, the will, whose exertion is to be secured, is understood as choice. In this sense, choice is the ability to set goals for oneself at one's own discretion. This occurs when we have to select something. By making its choices, the subject sets goals for itself by selecting between different aspirations (wishes, needs, drives) that it already finds within itself. According to Kant's definition, choice is the capacity [*Vermögen*] for selection between pursuits, through which a subject "adopts" them "into his maxims."[44] In choice, pre-existing, natural, or customary aspirations are therefore transformed: they take on the new form of goals that one has set for oneself. The subject *gives* this new form of a maxim to one of her aspirations by exercising her choice – this maxim is not a goal that the subject has but one that she has set for herself.

Subjects do not only choose goals, however. To will goals means to will their realization. Subjects will the appropriate means for their goals. Goals are only realized with means. To will goals entails willing the means to those goals. This includes being able to *see* them *as* means. Something available is only a means *for* a subject who is apt to gauge its usefulness. To will the means for realizing a goal thus involves gauging whether what is available is any good for accomplishing that goal. In other words, it involves evaluating something. Setting goals by willing simultaneously requires establishing values [*Werten*], and values, according to Heidegger, are "posited by aiming and keeping one's sight on what must be counted." Values, and therefore something available that is assessed to be a means, are "conditions of preservation and increase" of "power,"[45] which signifies the ability to realize goals. Evaluating is gauging and willing of means or, in other words, evaluating is the will as "will to power." Values are "the conditions, posited by the will to power itself, of the will to power."[46] The self's inclination to gauge and evaluate means can be called the subject's "interest."[47] Subjects have interests, and these are interests in means, in abilities and resources to realize goals. If choice is the will as selection of goals, then interest is the will as evaluation, and thereby the willing, of means.[48]

If the subject's self-will forms the pre-juridical (or natural) foundation of bourgeois property; and if self-will is to be conceived as authoritative not merely for selection, but also for evaluation, to be conceived not merely as choice, but also as interest, as the willing not merely of goals, but also of means to those goals – then defining bourgeois property as a private domain for the will's unimpeded control is inadequate. In addition to property as private sphere, we must also consider property as private wealth [*Vermögen*]. Property as private sphere secures the exercise of choice. In its private sphere, the subject can choose goals at its own discretion. Property as private wealth, in contrast, ensures the realization of the subject's interests. "Owning some rice gives the person the *capability* of meeting some of his or her nutritional requirements":[49] through its private wealth, the subject *has* the means, the capabilities, and the resources to realize its goals. Wealth makes assets [*Werte*] or means available. The subject of subjective rights is the subject of self-will, and because self-will is simultaneously choice *and* interest, selecting *and* evaluating [*Werten*], such a subject requires control over her own private sphere *and* over her own private wealth. In contrast to the ideology of traditional private law liberalism, the bourgeois subject of rights cannot be reduced to the subject of choice, whose control secures property as private sphere. Individualism of the will, which defines the form of subjective rights, *yields a second model of bourgeois property from out of itself*: safeguarding the realization of interests, or of assets [*Werten*] as means, through private wealth.

Locke understands this argument to mean that the introduction of interest, which the active laboring subject has in his means, forms a chain that leads directly from the natural possession of one's own will to a *just as natural* possession of a thing. The claim that possession of property results from self-possession is the step that leads to the ideology of possessive individualism. This step is supposed to be justified on the basis of labor, since labor signifies the use of one's own means, capabilities, and resources. *Because* the subject set goals not only by selecting, but also by using its own means, which belong to it as naturally as do its own choices, the thing as product of labor also belongs to the subject.

Two steps, which are both implausible, lurk under the surface here – the step from the selecting of goals to the means for labor, and the step from the use of means in laboring to the product. This is obvious in the second step, which, by describing the thing as a work, the "*work* of my hands" (Locke), is supposed to ensure that such things are my own as naturally as my goals and my means are. Yet why, in making something my own, when I produce something by using my means in labor, do I appropriate this thing as my own, instead of losing my means in the thing? Locke believes that a human being who produces something "hath mixed his *Labour* with, and joyned to it something that is his own, and thereby makes it his *Property*."[50] This leaves open the following question, however: "why isn't mixing what I own with what I don't own a way of losing what I own rather than a way of gaining what I don't? If I own a can of tomato juice and spill it in the sea . . . do I thereby come to own the sea, or have I foolishly dissipated my tomato juice?"[51] Yet the mistake made in the first step is more significant: it explains the subject's means to be his own in the same way that the form of subjective rights assumes from his decisions.

The means for realizing goals are internal or external: they consist of physical and intellectual abilities, as well as natural and cultural resources.

156

No one can write a book without having acquired the corresponding abilities. Yet it is also true that no one can write a book without, for the most part, basing what they do on the activities of others who have the necessary external means at their disposal: from the technological means for writing to intellectual means in the form of other books, scholarly exercises, cultural traditions, up to and including physical means such as concentration, financial support, and affinity – and we should not forget economic means, which make such activity possible in the first place. It is obvious that external means or resources are not already of their own accord something that belongs to the subject. They exist prior to and independent of the subject, and in any case only with the aid of others. This is precisely the case, however, for a subject's inner abilities: a subject has *its* means, resources or abilities, external or internal, only so that it can appropriate socially developed means which exist. Individual disposal over means has the form of participation in social means. The subject's participation in society signifies the individual appropriation of social means and thereby defines *how* a subject *has* its means. All means of one's own are social means that have been appropriated. Locke's possessive-individualistic derivation of the appropriation of a product from the appropriation of the means used in making that product is wrong, since the appropriation of means consists in nothing but social participation.

This requires a reformulation of the second model of bourgeois property as private wealth. Private wealth is the legal guarantee of means (or to put this more precisely: the realization of my interest in means – my "assets"). Locke understands this to mean that legal property only secures natural property. This is the principle that underlies the ideology of possessive individualism. In contrast, if all means are social means and thus if one's own means are social means that have been appropriated, or if I only obtain means, resources, or abilities through social participation, then private wealth consists in the *opportunity to participate* in social wealth. Hegel defines "the *possibility of sharing* in the universal resources" as a person's "*particular* resources."[52] Locke's own labor or means argument, with its theory of the will, yields not possessive individualism, but precisely the opposite, the sociality of participation: each person's private wealth as his or her social right of participation or "right of access."[53] The social definition of means – means only *exist* socially, and thus subjects only *have* their means by *appropriating* social means for themselves – requires understanding property in such a way that "it no longer be confined to the individual right to exclude others [C.M. – which corresponds to property as a private sphere of freely chosen goals], but be extended to include each individual's right not to be excluded from the use or benefit of things, or from productive powers, that can be said to have been created by the joint efforts of the whole society."[54] Property as wealth is the right to one's own means, namely the assurance of realizing one's own interests or values. This right is a participatory right, since social participation here signifies participation in social wealth for the purposes of acquiring one's own wealth. It signifies acquiring wealth of one's own by appropriating social wealth. The right to private wealth must be understood as a social right.

The critique of Lockean possessive individualism therefore leads to the concept of social rights, which has become the basis for a new legal system, the social welfare state, since the end of the nineteenth century, in which the labor movement struggled against a predominant, bourgeois private law liberalism.[55] For this reason, it signifies a fundamental innovation for both the practice and theory of law. The "periodization" of the history of modern law that has become common sense (which was Thomas Marshall's understanding, too, with the caveat that we "obviously should not take" this classification "too seriously") claims that "civil rights came first ... .Political rights came next, and their extension was one of the main features of the nineteenth century ... .Social rights ... began with ... the twentieth century."[56] This sequence should be understood to signify not only an extension of the contents of rights, but a transformation in their conception: social rights define rights *in general* as rights to "membership." They refer to a "status bestowed on those who are full members of a community."[57] For that very reason, however, an interpretation of social rights that posits a radical break between eighteenth-century bourgeois rights and social rights in the twentieth century is too limited in scope, indeed misses what is essential here. Instead, the *same* basic idea of subjective rights, and therefore the basic idea of bourgeois right, is interpreted in an entirely different way on the two models. On Axel Honneth's interpretation of the history periodized by Marshall, the "successive expansion of basic individual rights," from the private bourgeois right to the social right of participation, continues to refer back to "its guiding idea ... that was there from the start."[58] The critique of possessive individualism, which introduces the idea of social rights, does not lead beyond bourgeois right, but interprets it in a different way.

This is primarily a historical thesis. It claims that the idea of social rights played a role in the theory and ideology of bourgeois right from the beginning, even if the former only became institutionally operative later on, around 1900. Regarding Marshall's periodization of rights, Talcott Parsons writes that:

In one sense, the "social" component of citizenship is the most funda-mental of the three. Some form of equality of social condition as an aspect of "social justice" has been a primary theme of Western history since the French Revolution but one that did not become institutionally prominent until much later.[59]

As the Jacobin draft constitutions show in an exemplary manner, the opposition between the possessive-individualistic conception of property and the social-participatory one, as wealth of "means" necessary for life,[60] is governed not by the logic of historical sequence but by a logic governing the political struggle between simultaneous conceptions of law (which were successful to different degrees at different times).

In conceptual terms, this historical thesis entails that the right to social participation does not break, but is in conformity, with the bourgeois form of subjective rights. For the right to social participation *results* from the legal authorization of the subject's self-will (under the further premise that self-will is not merely a matter of choosing ends, but is evaluatively oriented to means [first step], and that means are social and hence must be appropriated through participation [second step]). This is why even social participatory rights are subjective rights, based on the subject's private self-will: *that, how, and to what end* the subject wants wealth through social participation is just as much a matter of her own self-will as is the free choice of her goals. Social participatory rights are rights to social participation *in one's own self-willed interest* – rights *to* private wealth *through* social participation. What is at stake in social participa-tion is the obtaining of private wealth through social participation. To have private wealth means nothing but ensuring that one is able to realize one's own interests (and interests are evaluatively oriented to means). The basis of property remains the same in wealth as a social participatory right as it is in right [*Recht*] as a private sphere controlled by choice. Even the private right to social participation is only a legalization of the *fact that the subject wants this*.

The theoretical and practical critique of possessive individualism gives rise to the concept of social participatory rights. In doing so, it also oper-ates on the basis of bourgeois law [*Recht*]: it is operative in the form of subjective rights. Possessive individualism is *only one possible ideological interpretation* of this form, but not its essential feature. Individualism of the will: the positivism of self-will – this alone is essential for the form of subjective rights. If the critique of possessive individualism understands itself as a critique of bourgeois law as such, then it thereby misunderstands itself. The critique of possessive individualism remains on the surface of

159

bourgeois law. It is only concerned with a transitory *ideology* of subjective rights. This ideology yielded an eighteenth- and nineteenth-century bourgeois liberalism defined by Locke's conception of natural law.[61] Bourgeois law can overcome this ideology (and in fact did overcome it in the twentieth century), without fundamentally changing itself in the process, since the fundamental basis of bourgeois law is – solely – the form of subjective rights. The goal of formulating a critique of bourgeois law that gets to the heart of the matter thus requires conceiving this form in a way that does not conflate it with one of its ideologies.

* * *

Our thesis is that bourgeois property, which is based on or legalizes subjective self-will, has *two irreducible, equiprimordial forms*:

(i) ensuring the exercise of choice (or the selection of goals) by means of *property as a private sphere of discretionary decisions*;
(ii) legalizing the realization of interests (or the evaluation of resources) by means of *property as private capacity* [*Vermögen*] *for social participation*.

These two forms of (bourgeois) property right are fundamentally distinct, because they are based on a likewise distinct conception of the will, namely as a capacity for discretionary choice and as a capacity for evaluation shaped by interests. A relation of opposition thus exists between the two conceptions of property, in both practical and political terms. These are the two parties in the "Struggle for Law" in civil society: in practical-legal terms, between private and social law; in political-legal terms, between liberalism and socialism (or between liberal and social democracy).[62] However, it is precisely because the two forms of bourgeois property are based on distinct conceptions of the will, as choice and as interest, as selecting and as evaluating, that they do not mutually exclude each other, and indeed that they do belong together, according to both the logic and theory of law. For both choice and interest belong to the subject's self-will. For this reason, the struggle between the two forms of bourgeois (property) right must not and *cannot* be decided. Bourgeois law *consists* in this struggle.

It consists in this struggle because both sides affirm the same thing – the legalization of self-will – though they do so on the basis of distinctive, even opposed interpretations. In other words, they are the same positivism in two different forms. In both of these opposed forms of bourgeois property, the same basic principle of bourgeois law is realized, namely the validity of self-will. With the form of subjective rights, law presupposes the fact *that the subject wants "this."*

160

— 10 —

THE PRIVATIZATION OF THE PUBLIC:
TWO EXAMPLES

In bourgeois law, property is fundamental because it is the primary form of authorization for the subject's self-will. At the same time, legal authorization in the form of property is merely an abstraction, since self-will and its legal validation are discrete here: self-will's validity *is established* in property. The self-will selects private goals or evaluates resources and means to realize its goals, but it owes its validity to what the juridical (lawmaking, political) will establishes through delimitation. In property, authorized self-will and authorizing political will stand opposed in a merely external manner, which here means "abstract."[1]

We have seen above that this contradicts the *meaning* of authorization by subjective rights. As Kelsen puts it, authorization by subjective rights is immanently political; subjective rights are participatory rights. In other words, the authorization of self-will always already or also authorizes the subject *itself* to *validate* its own will in the creation of law. This is evident, in the field of private law, with the institution of freedom of contract. Freedom of contract authorizes the subject's self-will to create valid law: bourgeois law authorizes the subject to dispose over law at her own discretion. At the same time, however, in doing so, the public relation between the individual subject and the legal system is transformed. The basic principle of bourgeois law, the authorization of self-will, is not limited to private law. The forms of public law themselves become media for the authorization of self-will.

This manifests itself in an exemplary manner in the reconceptualization of the right of action and the institution of basic rights.

161

Claiming One's Own

A legal system that determines the basis for a just division of something for each person, the *ius suum cuique*, thereby imposes an obligation to respect this division on every other person. Here, the legal rule consists precisely in defining the obligations that arise from just division. These obligations are usually expressed in order to determine what someone who has violated just division and taken another's share for her own must repay (if she has nothing else, she can even repay with her life). The other's right to the restoration of her fair share, even to her fair share itself, is here only mentioned afterwards. The right, or justified claim, comes after the obligation.

This is also the case when the legal system goes a step further and gives a person who has had her fair share taken by another the right to pursue its recovery herself. This is the right of action. When the legal system grants the right of action, the individual does not merely have a claim against others to her fair share, according to the legal system's definition of just division. Rather, she *also* has a *completely different* claim (in its logic and normativity): a claim on the legal system itself – that it actually enforce the other's obligation toward her, with its instruments of power. The right of action therefore concerns not a relation among equal individuals, but one between the individual and the legal system: *because and if she wants to*, the individual, by taking legal action, can mobilize the legal system to administer her right over against another person. Through her legal claim, the individual takes part in the operation of law. In other words, the right of action is political (since political rights are "defined as the power to influence the formation of the will of the state"[2]). What is the relation between these two rights, however? How are the individual's claim under private law and the individual's claim on the legal system (that it enforce his claim on others under private law) related?

Traditionally, these rights were not connected. As we have seen, the claim vis-à-vis another, under private law, is originally a secondary element of a legal system, which specifies, through its laws [*Gesetze*], the obligations by which a just division is restored in cases where it has been violated. In contrast, the right of action originally signifies a new legal system's recognition of the individual's power to avenge an injury to his own person or property by means of prosecution. If, in a system of justice prior to law, individual vengeance was required for the restoration of justice, even in cases where the individual was the executor of an anonymous order, then the introduction of the legal system does not completely result in his forfeiture of this power. Instead, his power to restore justice is recognized by law – and at the same time thereby tempered and restricted. The granting of this right is thus accompanied by very strong caution against its misuse. Taking legal action is simultaneously enabled and restricted. The first law in the *Code of Hammurabi* immediately declares: "If a man weave a spell and put a ban upon a man, and has not justified himself, he that wove the spell upon him shall be put to death."[3] This is why, even in Roman law, we find the strict formalization of acts, *actiones* that the individual must perform to be able to claim his right before the court. In repeating the requisite formulas verbatim, the individual mobilizes law on behalf of his "personal" goal to avenge himself, but only by paying a price, that of subjection, in ever-new symbolic manifestations, to law's new order and language.[4] Like all juridical entitlement, granting the right of action is simultaneously authorization and subjection of the individual.

This brief recapitulation suggests that, originally, the right of action is completely separate from the claim under private law. The granting of the right of action is a matter of the individual's relation to the legal system. It is a matter of politics (or of power), namely of regulating the relation between the individual's power to enforce justice, on the one hand, and the power of a legal system in which justice has been transformed through its juridification and is no longer a system of vengeance, on the other. The right of action preserves in law an aspect of pre-juridical power that must be surrendered by the individual when he becomes the member [*Bürger*] of a legal system. For this reason, the right of action is one of the oldest rights of all. Taking legal action was originally considered to be much more important for the operation of the legal system, because without such action by the offended party, there is no administration of justice at all.

Bourgeois legal theory, as a theory of the subjective right, defines the relation between the claim under private law and the political right of action in opposite ways. Hans Kelsen has most clearly formulated this opposition to tradition, when he inscribes the individual's public law claim on the legal system in the definition of the individual's private law claim over against another, as a subjective right: "a 'right' . . . is the legal power conferred for the purpose of bringing about by a law suit the execution of a sanction as a reaction against the nonfulfillment of an obligation."[5] The right of action therefore defines the "essence" of the subjective right:

the essence of the right characteristic for private law consists in this: the legal order confers a specific legal power upon an individual (not an "organ" of the community, but an individual traditionally designated as a "private person"), and usually upon the individual toward whom another individual is obligated to behave in a certain way – namely the legal power to start the procedure that leads to a court decision in which a concrete sanction is ordered as reaction against the violation of the obligation.[6]

A legal theorist such as Karl Larenz, who is concerned with the objective system of values (which he defines very differently at various times, depending on what is politically convenient: initially, he means the value-system of the German *Volk* and later that of human dignity), views this as a denial of the "autonomy of legal allowance," which he substantializes, thereby simultaneously removing its public legal significance.[7] The connection between subjective rights and the right of action is thus "thinking about actions."[8] However, Larenz thereby conflates two things that ought to be distinguished: whether Kelsen reduces the subjective right to the right of action or whether he derives the right of action from the subjective right. Insofar as he does the latter, Kelsen only expresses a general consensus of the bourgeois theory of subjective rights (which Kelsen otherwise subjects to sharp critique, because he objects to its naturalization). The right of action is therefore already contained in the claim under private law, understood as subjective right – it is a *consequence* of this claim. Rudolf von Ihering writes: "According to Roman law, the criterion [C.M. – for "rights under private law"] consists in taking legal action."[9] Likewise, we find the following passage in Georg Jellinek: "Formal positive legal claims come about . . . by recognizing an individualized claim to legal protection for what is at issue between the individual and state."[10] This approach assumes that the *same thing is at stake* in the right of action as in the claim under private law. Accordingly, the individual who takes legal action with the aid of the legal system only validates the private right that she already had over against another party. The political right of action *serves* the claim under private law.

Excursus: Taking Legal Action as the "Result" of the Legal Claim (Windscheid)

The assertion (from Ihering to Kelsen) that private law [*Privatrecht*] and the right of action [*Klagerecht*] have a standard of judgment in common thus encapsulates the redefinition of their relation in bourgeois law. This shared standard of judgment between private law and the right of action is not universally valid, but a specific iteration of the bourgeois form of subjective rights. This thesis allowed Bernhard Windscheid to radicalize the original historicization of Roman civil law that Savigny began, but did not himself pursue far enough. For if Savigny understands the "right of action to mean the right to legal protection that is produced by the violation of a right, the kind of right in which a right is transformed by its violation," he thereby only reflects the "modern understanding of law," according to Windscheid.[11] "The modern understanding of law views the right as primary, and legal action as secondary, the right as productive, while legal action is viewed as produced."[12] Conversely, in the Roman understanding of law, "*actio supplanted* the right":

> The legal system (in Rome) does not tell the individual: you have this or that right, but: you have this or that *actio*. It does not say: in this relationship, your will is law for another individual, but: in this relationship, you can make your will legally valid over against another individual. The legal system is not a system of rights, but of claims that are legally actionable. It bestows rights by granting them legal actionability. *Actio* is not something derivative, but something original that stands on its own.[13]

"The legal system [in Rome] is not a system of rights, but of claims that are legally actionable": it is hardly surprising that this pointed assertion should have met with crass misunderstanding – it seems to turn legal action into something groundless.[14] This, however, is exactly the – false – alternative that Windscheid's entire argument is devoted to rejecting and resolving. For the Roman example teaches us that the claim under private law is not the only possible, or even self-evident, basis for the right of action. In Rome, the right of action was based on something entirely different:

> I thus repeat: *actio takes the place* of the right; it does not result from the right. One can have an *actio* without having a right, and there can be no *actio* without a right to one. Thus where *actio* and right converge, where *actio* amounts to simply recognizing a right, one may not say, if one wishes to speak precisely, that the *actio* exists because of the right; it exists because of the magistrate's activity, which could have also denied it. But if the *actio* is not the *result* of the right, neither is it the *expression* of the right. The magistrate who grants or refuses it does not do so arbitrarily. If he does not thereby simply follow legal precedent, he nevertheless negotiates it in recognizing an order of things, which is, to be sure, not the legal system, but which his activity constitutes as the legal system.[15]

Just as Windscheid distinguishes between the Roman legal understanding and the modern legal understanding, one can understand the right of action as the "expression" or, in a completely different manner, as the "result" of the legal claim under private law. To understand it as *expression* means that the legal system grants the right of action because it understands such action to be part of the – political, public – process in which a just order of things, just division, is restored and in which each receives what belongs to her. The court's juridical activity, in which a just order of things is determined, is primary here. This is where individuals receive their right, and the legal system grants them the right of action for this purpose. Conversely, if the right of action is understood as *result*, then the claim under private law must precede it, as source or basis; it is logically prior. When the right of action is understood to be "the result of the [private] right," the latter exists in advance: the legal system must grant the individual's right of action, *because* she has a claim under private law; because this *results from* the fact that she has a claim under private law. Here – and here alone, in bourgeois law – "the material subjective right is understood as the cause (*causa*) of *action*."[16]

The right of action is a public right: it secures the public or political power to participate in the creation of law. And if court proceedings, above all, exemplify the legal system for its subjects, then taking legal action – whether one does this oneself or astutely understands the legal action taken by others – is also the primary way in which those who are subject to a legal system actively participate in it.

We can understand the conferral of this public right, the legal authority to take action, in two entirely different ways.

On the traditional understanding, taking legal action means contributing to the restoration of the just order through which each receives what belongs to him. This obviously holds just as much for the person who takes legal action; he too receives what belongs to him through the restoration of justice. However, his power to participate in the determination of justice by taking legal action is neither based on nor oriented by such participation: as plaintiff, he is anyone at all. He speaks only on behalf of justice that has been violated. The fact that the fair share that is restored is *his* lost share is irrelevant for his right to participate in legal proceedings by taking action. This is the case, but has no legal significance. The plaintiff speaks not for himself, but for law.

On the bourgeois understanding, in contrast, the individual has the right of action so that she can secure or claim her own. With the right of action, law [*Recht*] gives her the power to prove, in a legal proceeding, that what she claims as her own, her private sphere, or her private

166

wealth, belongs to her according to the law [*Gesetz*] of equality. A legal proceeding is conducive to proof and the enforcement of her legal claim. Law [*Recht*] bestows the right of action on her *not* to enable her to participate in the process of justice, *but rather* to give her the opportunity to validate her claim, to prove it valid and to enforce its fulfillment on the basis of such proof.

In the step from the traditional to the bourgeois right of action, the system of public legal authority and the system of the claim under private law reverse their positions: the traditional right of action is the right to participate in a proceeding that yields just division and thereby gives each what belongs to him, including the *plaintiff*. The bourgeois right of action is the right to prove and enforce one's own claim against another person by participating in a proceeding. Traditionally, the individual has the right of action in order to participate in a process of justice, but on the bourgeois understanding, in contrast, the individual has this right in order to prove the legality of what is her own.

This has nothing to do with "bourgeois egoism" (which unquestionably defines the bourgeois practice of taking legal action). We are concerned here not with morality, and thus with motives, but with the form of legal practice. The way in which the bourgeois form of subjective rights redefines the conception of the legal claim accounts for why the bourgeois right of action fundamentally redefines the relation between the claim under private law and public legal authority. Subjective rights are legal claims to what exists prior to law – the subject's self-will. Under this fundamental formal stipulation, the right of action only guarantees the individual's (public) participation in the legal process in such a way that it simultaneously realizes the individual's right to validate what is (privately) her own. And it only does the one by way of the other: the plaintiff, in her official role, by participating in the process of determining the law, must indeed thereby always also will *equality*, the equality of all, and thus universal equality, since validating what is one's own in particular means asserting the validity of one's own willing and acting according to a universal law [*Gesetz*] of equality.[17] To will equality here, under the sway of the form of subjective rights, *amounts to* nothing but willing it as the equality of the subjective self-will's private spheres and wealth. To will equality here is to will what is one's own. And to will the equality of what is everyone's own signifies authorizing each individual to will what is *her* own in particular. The bourgeois right of action therefore can only grant the individual the public or political power to participate in a legal process in such a way that it simultaneously grants her the power to validate her private self-will, which exists prior to law.

Public right becomes the medium of private authorization. The bourgeois right of action links the legal system to the individual's private will, which is prior to law. Law "only wants to will, if and insofar as the individual wills, and does not will, if the individual is unwilling. It revokes its own will in favor of the private will."[18]

The Declaration of Basic Rights

An upheaval occurred in the shift from the traditional to the bourgeois right of action, revealing that the form of subjective rights under private law is the basis for a radical change in how the legal system refers to the individual. In the bourgeois right of action, the legal system is no longer the individual's ultimate goal, as in Savigny's (and Hegel's) traditional moral definition.[19] On the contrary, the legal system *is now concerned with* the self-will of individuals – it is concerned with securing their private spheres and safeguarding their private wealth. Savigny's dichotomous modernization of law, its restriction to private law, without consequences for the public relation between law and individual, does not work (that is, it does not work *conceptually*; in practical terms, this dichotomy was and remains able to sustain itself temporarily). For law's presupposition of the subject's self-will is the *condition* for the *meaning* of the bourgeois form of subjective rights.

The declaration of basic rights is the way in which this presupposition is manifested in the legal system itself. The meaning of this declaration is not to be found in the immediate affirmation of the subjective rights that individuals can have against each other, on the basis of which they can take legal action against each other. Rather, basic rights affirm, for different social domains, *that there should be subjective rights*. Basic rights declare the right to subjective rights (and they specify what this means for each different social sphere). The declaration of basic rights is the act by which the legal system commits itself to the form of subjective rights.

Carl Schmitt described this as a fundamental redefinition of the relation between law and subject, between the general order and the individual:

> For the systematic treatment of the modern Rechtsstaat, the important thing is that the idea of basic rights contains the fundamental *principle of distribution*, on which rests the free bourgeois Rechtsstaat that is implemented with logical consistency. That means that the liberty sphere of the individual is *unlimited* in principle, while the powers of the state are *limited* in principle. The state during antiquity knew no liberty rights, because a private sphere with an independent right

against the political community appeared inconceivable and the idea [that] freedom of the individual would be independent of the political freedom of his people and of the state would have been considered absurd, immoral, and unworthy of a free man.[20]

According to Schmitt, the recognition of individual freedom as presupposition for the legal system is crucial for the modern conception of basic rights. Individual freedom is here the freedom to will at one's own discretion – the freedom of one's self-will. To say that "subjects have basic rights" means that their self-will is given, something on the basis of which the legal system has to proceed. It is something that the legal system has to recognize as fact, consider valid, or legalize. Self-will is defined by the fact that its decisions, the acts of selecting and evaluating by subjects, are negatively free: a willing that abstracts from the moral and appropriates the social. Subjective self-will is a field of *"unlimited"* freedom.[21] Basic rights assert that this freedom "exists." In other words, they claim that it is a given and valid for law, and they say what this means for the different social domains in which subjects exercise their self-will.

For this reason, there are different basic rights. According to Luhmann, the plurality of basic rights has a social significance: "Their diversification into individual basic rights reflects . . . social differentiation into several relatively autonomous spheres of the social formation of meaning."[22] Different basic rights *designate* the freedom of self-will in different social spheres. In each case, they provide the key element – opinion, movement, belief, property, contract, vote, conscience, and so forth – for a particular manifestation of subjects' self-will in the legal regulation of their relations between each other in different social spheres – economy, religion, politics, education, and so forth. And just as the securing of self-will necessarily emerges in two fundamental forms – negatively, as the securing of a private sphere (against other individuals), and positively, as securing of private wealth (through social participation) – so too basic rights have the double meaning of simultaneously ensuring "individual self-representation" *and* "social opportunities for communication" between subjects.[23] According to the double logic of bourgeois property, basic rights secure "Both the inclusion of the entire population in all function systems [C.M. – of society] and the exclusion of individual and institutional areas of autonomy from these function systems."[24]

The declaration of basic rights proclaims that the subject's self-will is a given for the legal system. The declaration of basic rights is the establishment of the form of subjective rights. Its primary subject matter is the relation of individuals to each other. Basic rights therefore determine the form of the system of private law: they determine which claims

169

made by individuals against each other are a general consequence of the validity of their self-will. "Private law's precedence determines . . . the function of basic rights" (in other words, basic rights are "accessories to private law");[25] they are concerned with establishing the form of subjective rights as (private) law's basic form. This is why, on Kelsen's view, "These constitutional guarantees do not in themselves compose subjective rights."[26] Basic rights are – primarily or "in themselves" – *principles of government*, of the bourgeois form of politics. "The declaration of human rights in society is unquestionably only the explication of a few general principles."[27] To declare basic rights means to determine the legal system's elementary formal definition. This determination applies to politics itself. It politically specifies the form for the political governance of the community. To say that "subjects have basic rights" means that they govern in the form of subjective rights.

The form of subjective rights thus obtains a public or political significance through the declaration of basic rights, since the declaration of basic rights makes it clear that the form of subjective rights implies nothing less than a form of government: it concerns the (private) relation of individuals with each other, but it thereby at the same time defines the relation between the individual and the public, legal order – the way in which this order addresses the individual. This is why the declaration of basic rights can also (but must not) include leaving open the further possibility of legally contesting how the legal system addresses the individual. (This is not a question that could be decided by legal theory – the *concept* of basic rights does not *entail* a corresponding right of action. Rather, it is a political and thereby practical question that is to be decided according to the maxim that "we should always look at both sides of any legal advantage."[28]) At the same time and above all, however, the declaration of basic rights confers a public and political power on the legal subject – because, as declaration of form, it produces the bourgeois structure of government. According to Schmitt, this results from the new distribution between the state's legal system and self-willed subjects that is expressed or created by the declaration of basic rights [*Grundrechten*]. For the constitutional [*grundrechtliche*] recognition of the freedom of self-will means "that 'its use against the state does not need to be justified' [Bernhard Schlink], while any state restriction of the general freedom of action requires justification."[29] The individual's argumentative position (her normative power) is transformed by this constitutional recognition of her self-will. According to Ingeborg Maus, this is why the asymmetric "schema for the distribution of freedom," which basic rights establish (in Schmitt's view), has the immediate political implication

170

"that it is not the powerful, but the powerless, who decide on how they will use their freedom."[30] With the declaration of basic rights, law turns the freedom of self-will into its pre-juridical presupposition. Because it concerns *their* freedom, their choice and interests, however, only subjects themselves can say what their basic rights are supposed to consist in: "They have a monopoly on the interpretation of these rights."[31] The authorization of subjects' self-will by basic rights (and thereby the act of defining their relation to each other by the form of subjective rights) simultaneously gives them the official or political power to participate in the process of creating law [*Rechtserzeugung*]. It does this not only in their own particular case, as in the right of action, but in general, through the "democratic 'positivization and amendment' of basic rights."[32] It therefore not only validates their self-will when they take action against others, but validates it in shaping the legal system.

In the declaration of basic rights, the form of subjective rights at the same time turns out to be the form of government – according to the thesis we have been considering. This has two aspects: the claim that (in this sense bourgeois) government takes place through subjective rights and the claim that legal subjects must simultaneously govern together. The second aspect is a consequence of the first. *Because* bourgeois government consists in securing self-will (and because this means selecting goals and evaluating means at one's discretion), the very persons whose authorization is at issue must be able to decide on it together. Their private authorization must include their political (co-)authorization.

This, however, immediately entails a third aspect: the claim that the political co-governance shared by legal subjects is here *bound to the form of subjective rights*. It is – solely, nothing but – participation in government by subjective rights. For the participation of individuals in government here necessarily takes on the form of exercising a subjective right, because the declaration of basic rights binds bourgeois government to the form of subjective rights (only in this form is government possible here), and because the individual's participation in government that is here implied must itself be governed – enabled, organized, structured, and managed. It thus includes the authorization of their subjective self-will. This is why, in taking legal action, the question of whether and how and to what end she participates in determining what would be justified for everyone to will and to do at their discretion is left up to the individual to decide. And, as with the right of action, so too legal subjects' constitutionally established participation in their own government is thus permeated by an irresolvable tension.

To validate the individual's self-will means to legalize it, and its legalization consists in establishing that an individual's self-will can coexist with everyone else's according to a law [*Gesetz*] of equality that externally limits all. Participation in this act of legalization therefore always simultaneously signifies validating *this particular* self-will – whether one's own or another's (either a self-will that one identifies with or advocates for) – *and* incorporating the perspective of *everyone*, as externally restrictive equality. The participation in government made possible by basic rights thus endlessly vacillates, back and forth, between particularism and generalism, between expressivism (the particular self-will) and legalism (the standpoint of abstract, formal equality). This vacillation, this swaying back and forth, is the law [*Gesetz*] of bourgeois democracy's movement. It results from the fact that, here, the determination of subjective rights occurs by exercising a subjective right. The mere expression of a particular self-will thereby becomes political. At the same time, however, and conversely, the law [*Gesetz*] of equality becomes merely a matter of private opinion.

Excursus: Freedom of Opinion, for Example (Spinoza, Habermas)

At the inception of the bourgeois revolution of rights, René Descartes begins his autobiographical "fable" of the "paths that have led me to considerations and maxims from which I have formed a method" by declaring that all are equal as beings capable of judgment:

> Good sense is the best distributed thing in the world, for everyone thinks himself to be so well endowed with it that even those who are the most difficult to please in everything else are not at all wont to desire more of it than they have. It is not likely that everyone is mistaken in this. Rather, it provides evidence that the power of judging well and of distinguishing the true from the false (which is, properly speaking, what people call "good sense" or "reason") is naturally equal in all men, and that the diversity of our opinions does not arise from the fact that some people are more reasonable than others, but solely from the fact that we lead our thoughts along different paths and do not take the same things into consideration. For it is not enough to have a good mind; the main thing is to apply it well.[33]

Hobbes endows this equality of the capacity for judgment with a political significance, because he considers it the key element of natural equality, the epitome of the "equal . . . faculties" that belong to the human being by nature.[34] However, if this equality, and thus the faculty that consti-

172

tutes it, is supposed to be natural – a "faculty" that "is naturally planted in him" (Hobbes) – then it does not only depend on exercise and is thereby not unequally distributed, as is everything that can be exercised, but is particularly incompatible with any normativity, since normativity is unnatural. Spinoza thus radicalizes the argument of Descartes and Hobbes as follows:

> as long as people are deemed to live under the government of nature alone, the person who does not yet know reason or does not yet have a habit of virtue, lives by the laws of appetite alone with the same supreme right as he who directs his life by the laws of reason. That is, just as a wise man has a sovereign right to do all things that reason dictates, i.e., [he has] the right of living by the laws of reason, so also the ignorant or intemperate person possesses the sovereign right to [do] everything that desire suggests, i.e., he has the right of living by the laws of appetite.[35]

There is thus "no [natural] difference between . . . human beings who are endowed with reason and others who do not know true reason."[36] Natural equality cannot be equality of judgment, since judgment is normatively defined – it always already means judging what is true *or* false, wise *or* foolish – and hence does not exist by nature and is not equally distributed. It is therefore impossible for there to be a natural right to judgment. Rather, there can only be a natural right to follow one's nature. However, this means following what one believes to be one's nature, *regardless* of whether this is true or false, wise or foolish. Natural right is the right to one's own opinion. And since the form of subjective rights consists in legalizing the natural (in society, rights are nothing but natural rights, which are limited by a law [*Gesetz*] of equality),[37] the freedom to have one's own opinion, without normative evaluation of that opinion, is also a legally guaranteed right. A subjective right to one's own judgment is impossible, since only the right to wise, true judgment (which contradicts the subject's self-will and the form of subjective rights) is possible. There is only an equal right to one's own "opinion."

At the same time, however, the basic right to one's own opinion (or freedom of opinion) is the citizen's basic political right: "Regarding the freedom of expression of opinion, it is, in fact, a matter of the principle of free discussion, which for the liberal idea is the actual means of integration of a social unity."[38] In order to be political, freedom of opinion must therefore be more than freedom of opinion – it must be freedom for public discussion, and public discussion does not allow any opinions, but only judgments. The political meaning of freedom of opinion presupposes that we are concerned with judgments that can be right or wrong, wise or foolish, and therefore themselves able to be judged. Freedom of opinion can only be a political right if the *legal* authorization of opinion is *de facto* the authorization of judgment. It can therefore only be a political right if the legally authorized expression of one's own opinion is *practiced* as judgment by the subject of this right.

This assumption is the (non-juridical, namely social or cultural) presupposition underlying the basic political right of freedom of opinion. It is therefore a presupposition that is unable to secure such a right itself. As a result, "the flipside of the 'publification' of private law [*Recht*]" is "the privatization of public law."[39] This reversal of publification into privatization is not a later, contingent decline of the original idea, but is inscribed in the conception of bourgeois basic rights. The declaration of basic rights, and thereby the establishment of the form of subjective rights, is the mechanism "of a progressive 'societalization' of the state simultaneously with an increasing 'stateification' of society."[40] The "dialectic" (Habermas) of bourgeois basic rights consists in the fact that they are political – since they involve the subjects of law in the governmental establishment of law. At the same time, they are private – since they authorize a normatively indifferent self-will, that of one's own opinion. Basic rights privatize politics precisely through politicization (by involving subjects).

The Government of Subjects

The new principle of distribution established by basic rights means that the political community's normative power over subjects is "*limited* in principle" (Schmitt). One consequence of this distribution of the power to make law is that the political community has only used its governing power to secure and enable self-will. For the fact *that* subjects will something forms the irreducible "foundation" (Locke) for all the activities of the bourgeois *Rechtsstaat*. The declaration of basic rights is thus the beginning of "government" – and the end of traditional "pastoral" rule, which had the power to pervade internality in order to guide the thinking and willing of subjects to their own good.[41]

Schmitt infers from this that "the powers of the state are *limited* in principle" by the new constitutional [*grundrechtliche*] principle of the distribution of power.[42] He thus infers that a restriction on the state's capacities to effectively influence subjects, to control them, and to normalize them also results from the self-limitation of the state's *normative* power – by how it presupposes the willing of legal subjects when it

174

declares basic rights. This inference from normative self-limitation to political self-disempowerment, however, is merely a liberal ideology that Schmitt here repeats uncritically and simply assesses in the opposite way. For the declaration of basic rights, in presupposing the self-will of subjects as something given for law, permits, indeed even compels, the empowerment and proliferation of state action to an unprecedented degree. The self-will of subjects is the foundation of validity for the modern state. In such a state, however, subjects here are not deprived of its power, but are – on the contrary – the object and goal of its incessant governmental activity.

In similar terms, Durkheim has described the strict, logical simultaneity of the subjectification of law and the growth of state power, which indeed defines liberalism's political practice, but must seem paradoxical to its theory. According to Durkheim, liberalism does not understand why governmental power is not limited at all by declaring the individual's rights, but is in fact extended further in all directions.

> We can only overcome these difficulties if we abandon the postulate that the individual's rights are given along with the individual, and instead proceed from the fact that these rights are first introduced by the state. We see that state functions are extended without the individual experiencing a restriction, and that the individual develops, without the state's significance diminishing, since the individual, in a certain sense, would be the product of the state . . . .The stronger the state, the greater its respect for the individual.[43]

With the declaration of basic rights, and the redistribution of normative power between the state and the individual, "state action is essentially oriented to individual liberty":[44] the securing of self-will now itself becomes the state's goal, and can only be achieved by declaring rights. For without legalization through subjective rights, subjective self-will *would not exist at all*. By declaring rights, the state must create the very thing that it then considers valid as its presupposition [*Voraussetzung*]. The state must itself establish [*setzen*] self-will as that which precedes it [*sein Voraus*]. Furthermore, this requires an ever-further *expansion* of government by rights, something which can be attributed to the fact that the securing of self-will fragments into two different forms: the securing of choice (or the selecting of goals through the ensuring of a private sphere), and the securing of interest as the evaluation of opportunities or means by ensuring private wealth from social participation. For each of these legal security regimes necessarily impedes the other in practice. The legal securing of a dimension of self-will jeopardizes that of interest, and thus provokes increased efforts to legally secure this other dimension, which in turn jeopardizes the first, with the result that the first dimension must now be firmly secured, and so on. The intensification of the government of subjects results from the struggle between the two basic forms of its (property) rights.[45]

Durkheim emphatically demonstrated the mutual jeopardization, and thereby the intensification, which defines the legal securing of self-will in both of its dimensions. He did so from the perspective of the second dimension, viewing it in terms of safeguarding the realization of interests. Such safeguarding occurs by providing "means" for subjects, and this in turn is facilitated by their social participation. Because subjects can only realize their interests in a social manner, they require a kind of government that safeguards the opportunity to participate from the rights of private choice: government by so-called social rights, and therefore the individual's rights to private participation in the social, to develop private wealth by participating in social wealth. The logic and form (in other words, the norm and normality) of social participation is thereby given in advance. According to Luhmann,[46] the plurality of basic rights reflects the social sphere's own normativity, namely the normative orders of the economy, religion, politics, education, and so forth, as they have developed over the course of their autonomous evolution. These orders thus underlie a particular social dynamic that is withdrawn from legal rules and thus governance. For this reason, government by rights can only be operative in an external manner. It must secure opportunities for social participation by continually adjusting to social developments. The legal securing of social participation affirmatively complies with the social order. It is a medium of adjustment, namely the adjustment of subjects, whose self-will it entitles, to the normativity of social spheres (or a medium of the "normalization" of subjects).[47]

Such a medium of adjustment threatens subjects' choice – the ability to freely select their goals. This ability is at issue in the securing of their private sphere. Because the legal guarantee of social participation constantly entails social adjustment, the subject's freedom of choice must therefore not only be protected from infringements by others. According to Durkheim, it must be secured as well, above all, from the "despotism" that all social groups, organizations, and powers exercise over individuals:

> Every group wields coercive power over its members, and accordingly strives to form them in its image, to consider how they should be shaped, as well as to compel them to act and to prevent any deviation. Every society is despotic, unless something from outside comes into play that keeps its despotism in check.[48]

176

To this end, rights that aim for the "freedom of individual personality" are needed, such as rights of choice that are directed against the tendency of the social "to completely absorb its members."[49] Rights that are directed against the tendency to promote rights of social participation are therefore needed. For while these rights open up the individual's opportunity to participate in the social (in the social, *just as it is*), they bind the individual to its normativity.

This is why the "rights of the individual . . . are thought to be in continual development." And this is precisely why it is "impossible to set a limit to rights that may not be exceeded,"[50] since they are themselves their own limits: one form of subjective rights is directed against the other, draws a limit for the other that the latter must continually – and increasingly – exceed. "The state's task is thus unlimited."[51] Its governmental task is unlimited, because the form of subjective rights is directed against itself: one form of subjective rights, in turn, dissolves what the other creates, on behalf of the *same* principle: subjective self-will. The subject of self-will thereby becomes the object of an endless governmental activity, in which ever-new rights must be devised to offset the effects, harmful to freedom, of other older rights. This is the logic of bourgeois "governmentality" (Foucault): because it is government by rights, it governs subjects "by enforcing [their] freedom." It is precisely the freedom of her own self-will that makes the subject "eminently governable."[52] The subject of self-will is not withdrawn from government, but eminently exposed to it, namely as a subject that only exists through government – the governable subject.

— 11 —

CONCLUSION:
THE BOURGEOIS SUBJECT –
LOSS OF NEGATIVITY

Let us recapitulate: the right to property is the paradigm of the "allowance" (Georg Jellinek) that private law grants to and secures for the individual. As bourgeois property, it is the allowance to not only exclusively dispose over something (as was already the case in traditional private property in Athens and Rome), but to also do so without limit. Since Jellinek, legal theory has distinguished "ability" [*Können*] or "competence" [*Kompetenz*] from the "permission" [*Erlaubnis*] that the legal system grants the individual. Jellinek and his followers define such ability as *inner*-legal or constituted by law. It is the power to change legal positions. They derive from this the thesis that, in distinction to the power to change legal positions, legal permission does not grant *any* ability, *any* power. "A permission itself has no effect on the capacity to act, which is fully independent."[1] In antithesis to this, Weber argued that allowance itself is to be conceived as authorization: legal allowance alone already authorizes, because it creates a new ability to will and to act and thereby a new subject – a capacity for willing and acting that, admittedly, is not legal, but which at the same time is only created *by* legal allowance: legally established ("interpellated"), but not legally constituted.

The subjective rights of bourgeois law grant and secure an allowance that is defined as each subject's equal entitlement to realize her own will [*eigenen Willens*] (or her "self-will" [*"Eigenwillens"*]). Since the subject's self-will has two dimensions, selection (of goals) and evaluation (of means and resources), her legal security must also take on two fundamentally different forms: securing a private sphere where choice can reign supreme and safeguarding the acquisition of private wealth through social participation. Both are forms of bourgeois law, but can only be put into effect in such a way that they conflict with each other. We can thus

178

define the unity of bourgeois law as the struggle between its two basic forms.[2] This struggle, which constitutes bourgeois law, is interminable, precisely because both sides presuppose the same thing: self-will. This presupposition is the defining feature of bourgeois law. *Bourgeois law is law that presupposes the subject's self-will.*

We can summarize the way in which bourgeois law presupposes self-will as follows: *the subject's willing is valid.* According to Foucault, the claim that the subject has her own self-will means that she "is a subject ... who appears in the form of a subject of individual choices which are both irreducible and non-transferable."[3] In allowance, law thus refers to the subject's will: her decisions are a fact for law. This fact – *that a subject wills this* – forms the "foundation" (Locke) on which law is constructed: legal rules can only be determined by proceeding without questioning these facts. The claim that subjective rights authorize the subject therefore means that they confer on her decisions the status, the authority of a fact. This is the empiricism (or positivism) of the form of subjective rights.

Bourgeois law is positivist because it proceeds from the subject's willing, considered to be fact – this is the basic tenet for the critique of subjective rights. Why, however, is it a basic tenet for *critique*? How is it different from the tenet formulated by liberalism to justify bourgeois law? This liberal justificatory tenet holds that bourgeois law *recognizes* subjects' wills. It holds that such law is based on (or justified in light of) what those subjected to it themselves think and will. According to its liberal justification, the authorization of self-will by the form of subjective rights entails the legal emancipation of the subject.

The critique of subjective rights objects to this liberal interpretation that liberalism misunderstands – more precisely: it disguises and conceals – the *positivism* of bourgeois law. To allow self-will to count as valid fact is the opposite of the subject's emancipation. This is evident when we consider the dialectic of the public in bourgeois law: by formulating political participation in the creation of law as subjective rights, it becomes a sheer medium for privately asserting one's own will. This dismantles the liberal equation (legal authorization as equivalent to subjective emancipation): emancipation does not simply mean being able to validate one's own self-will. Authorization by subjective rights, however, is unable to do anything more than validate self-will. This is also the reason why authorization by subjective rights results in an unprecedented intensification of governmental power: in the form of subjective rights, the subject can only validate her own self-will by doing so in *one* of its two basic forms – as choice *or* interest, as the right to a private sphere

179

for the realization of discretionary goals *or* as the right to private wealth through social participation – thereby diminishing or infringing its *other* form. Continual, endlessly recurring, and increasing governmental action is therefore needed to secure one form of self-will from the other. Legal authorization can only ever secure one form of self-will at the expense of the other. It is unable to realize the *unity* of its will, however.

We have now summarized the argument to this point. We must proceed one step further to discover the reason why the authorization by the form of subjective rights is non-emancipatory, even anti-emancipatory. This reason is found in how subjects are addressed by bourgeois law. Law forms subjects by how it addresses them, namely by positivistically proceeding on the basis of subjects' decisions as "the ultimate court of appeals" (Sellars), law transforms them into self-will. In validating the decisions of subjects as fact, their willing has the form of self-will *for law*. Subjective-legal authorization creates a new type of willing. This initially holds true in law: subjects *are* what they appear to be in law, that is to say – authorities of self-will. If (or since) law alone officially establishes what is obligatory for all, however, legal authorization has social effects. The legal creation of self-will produces a new social subject.

As we have seen, the subject's self-will only exists by, indeed *in*, disregarding the morality of the will's contents and whether it is independently carried out – and thereby appropriating the common, which is the only site for moral contents and for freely carrying out the will. Self-will is created by abstracting from normativity and by appropriating the social. The subject's self-will is its own power – the power of abstraction and appropriation. And the exercise of this subjective power is allowed or permitted in the form of subjective rights. "Wrong-doing is thereby *tacitly accepted* (insofar as it is not *legally* prohibited),"[4] since all that matters for law is *that* the subject's *own* will is thereby exerted, and externally limited by a law of equality.

The way in which law evaluates the subject's willing is fundamentally transformed by the unmooring of the will's legal validity from its virtue or reason (on which traditional law was based). And, at the same time, the way in which law understands the subject's willing – what it *is* or its mode of *being* – is thereby transformed. In traditional law, to abstract from morality means to be immoral or vicious. To abstract from autonomy means to be unfree or slavish. To appropriate the common means to be unjust or egotistic. For this reason, all of these things are prohibited in traditional law. Such a prohibition is indicative of how traditional law understands the subjective power to abstract from the moral or to appropriate the social, namely that it understands this ability to be an inability, as the privation of morality and freedom, and thereby of the will itself. For a striving that is unfree and puts itself before the common, instead of forming and performing itself in a common sphere, is not really willing at all, but mere desire. The traditional legal prohibition of immoral, unfree, and egotistic willing has an ontological basis. It is a consequence of the concept or being of willing. Immoral, unfree, and egotistic willing is not willing at all and therefore cannot claim any right.

If this is why bourgeois law legalizes subjects' self-will through the form of subjective rights, then it signifies not merely a fundamentally different kind of evaluation, but the creation of a new conception and thereby a new reality of willing. The permitting of self-will by the form of subjective rights is an ontological innovation. It proclaims what was a sheer paradox, even monstrous, on the traditional understanding, to be a conceivable, even fundamental possibility: the *non*-normative, *un*-free, *a*-social will as a *positive* capacity. To will non-morally, unfreely, and asocially becomes a non-privative, original possibility through the form of subjective rights. The (positive) definition of capacity comes from the lack of capacity. Permission through subjective rights is thus productive. It creates the possibility to will in a whole new way – a way that has never yet existed: a willing that has no standard, that has not been through an educational process, that recognizes no commonality, but merely establishes its own. It is willing as determining the fact of willing.

"Authorization through allowance" means that, through its permission, law creates a subject whose willing is indifferent to normative distinction, whose willing makes no claim to independence, and whose willing is carried out without any reference to a common sphere. To will therefore means to will one's own. The positivization of normative indifference and asocial privacy consists in a self-positivization. The subject itself becomes positive – becomes a fact. The subject's relation to itself becomes theoretical (or "contemplative")[5] – becomes a relation of registering, of determining.

This abstraction of willing seems to be a tranquil state of indifference at rest in itself – the "negative freedom" that the subject has by nature – to the subject of self-will. The abstraction of self-will only exists, however, by being created. The negative freedom of willing one's own only *exists* on the basis of – as the ontological effect of – a radical transformation of normativity: bourgeois law transforms the traditional prohibition of the immoral into permission for the non-moral and thereby (this is its ontological innovation) changes the private lapse of moral difference into the positive capacity for moral indifference. This capacity or power is unprecedented. Bourgeois law produces a new subject.

181

Excursus: The Pathology of Rights:
Critique of Liberalism (Dworkin)

Authorization by subjective rights creates a new type of willing by yielding a subject that is indifferent to morality and freedom and thereby only able to will for itself. Due to their form, subjective rights come to oppose the motives and intentions that served to create them (and thus to which they can *also* be applied). The bourgeois form of subjective rights emerges in connection with various types of subjectification in religion, morality, pedagogy, art, and so forth, which define bourgeois society. These various types of subjectification shape the "cultural framework" of bourgeois law, which is indispensable for explaining the development of the form of subjective rights.[6] This cultural framework, however, does not determine the inner meaning, the way in which legal form functions. Juridical subjectification consists in creating the subject of self-will. The fact that subjects can *also* use this new power to attain a purer faith, an autonomous way of life, an original work, a deeper education, is incidental, when viewed in legal terms. In a law book, pure faith, an autonomous way of life, the original work, and sound education are merely arbitrary contents that a subject may select as it will, without any priority over their opposites, namely conventional faith, a way of life that is heteronomously determined, boring work, or a superficial education.

A formulation by Jürgen Habermas (once given a twist) expresses this concisely:

> Because the options available to legal subjects should be restricted by prohibitions or commands as little as possible, the principle of legal freedom [C.M. – as defined by bourgeois private law] directly guarantees the negatively defined latitude for the pursuit of one's own interests. At the same time, however, it *enables* an autonomous conduct of life in the ethical sense of pursuing one's own conception of the good, which is the sense associated with "independence," "self-responsibility," and the "free development" of one's personality.[7]

We must therefore clearly distinguish between everything that law subsequently "enables" and what it guarantees through its form and thus alone creates. The decisive motivation for claiming (and perhaps even creating) subjective rights may be the desire to autonomously shape one's life. This form of subjective rights, however, does not yield such autonomy. "[T]he principle flaw of all legal freedom" is that "it secures a form of private autonomy that can only be sensibly exercised once we go beyond

182

the sphere of law."[8] This legal securing thus turns ethical autonomy into a mere possibility, a choice of how to use subjective rights, and thereby (in other words, as imposed by this form) turns it into an incidental content of permitted willing. Subjective rights "only make certain options available. One may choose to exercise the option or not. If, however, the option is exercised, then one is bound by its conditions."[9] Anyone who uses her rights to live in an autonomous manner has already, in so doing, turned them into a mere option, into the discretionary content of her own (morally indifferent and thus *non*-autonomous, *neither* autonomous *nor* heteronomous) self-will, and thereby devalued them: such a person is deprived of her autonomy. The "paradox of rights" (Wendy Brown) lies in the fact that, by virtue of their form, they *must* invert their own basis and goal.

This paradox can no longer be resolved by an art of drawing distinctions – for instance, by viewing the legal subject of self-will as a merely external "shell" in which the genuinely autonomous "ethical person" lies concealed as inner, true core.[10] Instead, there is a contradiction between possible (but contingent) moral justifications or ways of using subjective rights and the willing and acting that such rights necessarily authorize by their form. This contradiction defines bourgeois law but is misconstrued, indeed repressed and concealed, in every version of liberalism: liberalism *is* the repression or concealment of the contradiction of bourgeois law – the contradiction between the form of subjective rights and the moral reasons for establishing them.

This is not only obviously true for nineteenth-century classical liberalism, which understood itself to be a moral theory of progress, personal autonomy, self-responsibility, and education – and as a result always had to leave unanswered the question of how these liberal "values" are supposed to be realized by rights that, due to their form, are indifferent to *all* moral goods, reducing them to merely possible contents of subjective self-will (and thereby depriving them of their moral truth). Contemporary "political" liberalism also similarly continues to repress and conceal the contradiction of bourgeois law. On Rawls' definition, this is a version of liberalism that considers reference to "comprehensive moral ideals," such as "autonomy and individuality" in the theories of Kant and Mill, for example, to be "extended too far when presented as the only appropriate foundation for a constitutional regime." For "[s]o understood, liberalism becomes but another sectarian doctrine."[11] To avoid this, liberalism should no longer merely be formulated as a "political morality."[12] As Ronald Dworkin puts it, the demand that "government must be neutral on what might be called the question of the good life" is therefore central to "political" liberalism.[13] This basic liberal principle of neutrality is not supposed to be neutral itself, however. It includes a "positive commitment to egalitarian morality," since it "requires that the government treat all those in its charge *as equals*, that is, as entitled to its equal concern and respect."[14] In other words, it requires the government "to treat all citizens as free, or as independent, or with equal dignity."[15] Dworkin views this as the moral content of the individual rights that a liberal government must secure and safeguard: "The ultimate justification for these rights is that they are necessary to protect equal concern and respect."[16]

According to Dworkin, one consequence of this moral rationale is that individual rights cannot be understood as mere permission, the permitting of "negative freedom" – that is, in the discussion above: allowance for subjective self-will.[17] For this understanding of individual rights as mere permission cannot explain *why* we have rights, in the strong sense of claims against others. There can only be rights to something that is *valued*, taken into consideration, or respected – such as individual dignity. Dworkin's argument is thus that rights cannot be merely permissive, because they cannot be justified in such a manner, since legal permission is merely a matter of negative freedom, of the subject's self-will. Rights can only be justified in reference to the dignity of the person. Dignity alone has the power to ground the normative basis of rights.

Dworkin's argument, according to which dignity is the ground and goal of rights, completely ignores the determination of its *form*, as did classical nineteenth-century liberalism, which demanded rights in the name of progress, personal autonomy, self-responsibility, and education. This determination of form is the presupposition of self-will or the positivism of subjective rights. Due to the form of subjective rights, respect for the dignity of the person – which is supposed to ground a person's rights – always already thereby turns into the legalization of self-will. Dworkin is correct in claiming the permitting of negative freedom cannot ground the idea of subjective rights. However, he also ignores (or represses) the reciprocal context, namely that the form of subjective rights, however one might ground them, necessarily includes the permitting of negative freedom. Subjective rights *must* cede not only the "whether" but also the "how" of their exercise to self-will, to choice, and to the subject's interest.

Dworkin's liberalism, like every other version hitherto, suppresses the contradiction in which it is caught by declaring dignity or autonomy to be the moral ground and goal while wishing at the same time to establish the form of subjective rights. Dworkin's liberalism, like every other version hitherto, wants to have its cake and eat it too. This alone constitutes its ideological character: it moralizes subjective rights; it claims that they are rights due to dignity or rights to autonomy and thus leaves out of sight how this form *actually functions* – how and to what end it authorizes subjects (and how it thereby produces bourgeois society's forms of domination).[18] Raymond Geuss insightfully points out that the "essentially conservative bias" of liberalism is constituted by its simultaneously "easygoing, but narrow-minded, moralization": liberalism identifies rights with their moral motives and goals so that it can hide the social effects of their form. In other words, "the theoretical imagination is employed not to think about *alternatives* to the *status quo*, but in order to reproduce it schematically in thought."[19] In connection with an observation by Hegel in *Elements of the Philosophy of Right*, Axel Honneth has described the "pathological effects" of civil law.[20] Hegel defines abstract right as a "mere possibility" because it is a "determination of right" that "gives me a warrant, but it is not absolutely necessary that I should pursue my rights, because this is only one aspect of the whole relationship. For possibility is being, which also has the significance of not being."[21] This is also precisely why it, and it alone, *can* always be taken up, however. Legal authorization then becomes pathological: "If someone is interested only in his formal right, this [C.M. – sc. the subject's interest or willing, in its "particularity"] may be pure stubbornness, such as is often encountered in emotionally limited people."[22] "Taking legal freedom for the whole," "the over-generalisation of right itself" belongs to my right, which *cannot* be denied me.[23] Law's authorization of subjective self-will entails the deauthorization of every – moral or political – authority that wishes to limit self-will. For every limitation of self-will that does not occur in accordance with the – *sole* – legal principle of the equal validity of each self-will is now an infringement of a right. The self-will of the subject hence becomes potentially total due to the form of subjective rights. It can be validated anywhere – if it wants to do so. This results in a new version of the social that Hegel calls "civil society" [*bürgerliche Gesellschaft*]. For civil society "gives ... *particularity* ... the right to develop and express itself in all directions," by validating universality, the other side of the context of particularity, "only as the *relative totality* and *inner necessity* of this external *appearance*."[24] The autonomization [*Verselbstständigung*] of the social into a fateful power over individuals corresponds to the authorization of individual self-will. The pathology of rights is thus not to be found – that is, not merely or primarily – on the level of individual "behavioural symptoms."[25] It consists in nothing less than the creation of civil society.

Foucault's Diagnosis: The Regression of the Juridical

The basic definition of bourgeois law is that it authorizes subjects' self-will. This is bourgeois law's positivism, since legal authorization of self-will *makes* subjects' willing into a "fact," on the basis of which law must proceed.

The basic definition of self-will is that it is the capacity to author decisions as facts that found law. Self-will is the power of positivizing one's own, since it is the power to be normatively indifferent and to privatize the social.

Bourgeois law is therefore a normative order that produces normative indifference. It is a social order that permits the privatization of the social – *the normative and social authorization of an a-normative and asocial positivization of one's own.*

Foucault elaborates the consequences of these insights in his account of law in bourgeois society [*bürgerliche Gesellschaft*]. He writes that "we should not be deceived by all the Constitutions framed throughout the world since the French Revolution, the Codes written and revised, a whole continual and clamorous legislative activity." For despite – or, more precisely, *because of* – this ubiquitous juridification, it appears that "We have entered a phase of juridical regression in comparison with the pre-seventeenth-century societies we are acquainted with."[26] The "regression" of the "juridical" diagnosed by Foucault obviously cannot consist in the claim that the institution of law and its authorizing role in bourgeois society have become meaningless, since it is accompanied by a "continual and clamorous legislative activity." Foucault's diagnosis – the diagnosis that the juridical is regressing in bourgeois society – does not intend to suggest a qualitative or gradual sense for this regression at all. Rather, it aims at a fundamental, indeed revolutionary, *transformation* of law. Bourgeois law is itself the scene of juridical regression. As legalization and thus as warrant for the power of private self-will, it is de-juridified law: law that de-juridifies itself.

Foucault's argument for this is that bourgeois law – which authorizes the self-will of subjects – is a *law without subject*, or more precisely, law without a legal subject. How does this argument bear on the analysis of subjectivizing authorization by the bourgeois form of rights? The answer to this question hinges on how Foucault understands the legal subject:

What characterizes the subject of right? Of course, at the outset he has natural rights. But he becomes a subject of right in a positive system only when he has agreed at least to the principle of ceding these rights, of relinquishing them, when he has subscribed to their [C.M. – natural and thus pre-juridical] limitation and has accepted the principle of the transfer. That is to say, the subject of right is, by definition, a subject who accepts negativity, who agrees to a self-renunciation and splits himself, as it were, to be, at one level, the possessor of a number of natural and immediate rights, and, at another level, someone who agrees to the principle of relinquishing them and who is thereby constituted as a different subject of right superimposed on the first. The dialectic or mechanism of the subject of right is characterized by the division of the subject, the existence of a transcendence of the second subject in relation to the first, and a relationship of negativity, renunciation, and limitation between them, and it is in this movement that law and the prohibition emerge.[27]

The legal subject is defined by a split, namely it is split into nature and norm. As Pierre Legendre explains, this is what constitutes "the vital link between the subject and the space of the third, in which the juridical framework of prohibition is established."[28] The legal subject is constituted by its reference to law [Gesetz] and thus to its other – that which it is not (on the basis of nature), the "third." The legal subject is the scene of negativity. To put this more precisely: the legal subject is the *authority* [Instanz] of negativity, since it splits norm and nature, and thereby renounces nature, itself. The legal subject is the power of the norm's negativity over against nature.

Foucault's diagnosis of a juridical regression refers us to Legendre's thesis. The diagnosis thus indicates that the legal subject – as presently defined – *is deauthorized* in bourgeois law [Recht]. It claims that the legal subject loses its power of negativity. The subject of bourgeois law, the subject of subjective rights, is (as in another of Foucault's descriptions of the same transformation) the "living being," the subject that "formulates" life "through affirmations concerning rights."[29] This is the moment

when, breaking all the bonds of obedience, the population will really have the right, not in juridical terms, but in terms of essential and fundamental rights, to break any bonds of obedience it has with the state and, rising up against it, to say: My law, the law of my own requirements, the law of my very nature as population, the law of my basic needs, must replace the rules of obedience.[30]

The subject that reclaims its fundamental rights thinks and is no longer "juridical." For fundamental rights validate the "law of nature" – while the norm's power of negativity is juridically or legally directed against nature (according to Foucault's historical diagnosis). Explaining this diagnosis helps to comprehensively identify the inner contradiction of bourgeois law – which the work of critique aims to reveal, explicate, and intensify.

The background required to interpret Foucault's diagnosis of the regression of the juridical is the definition of classical law. Classical law conceives the power of negativity, which defines the subject, as the subject's autonomous reproduction [*Nachvollzug*] of juridical education (Athens) or dominion (Rome). Here we find that, "all things considered, law is the subject's first secure authority."[31] Normativity, as negativity, thus signifies enforcement against nature, whether this is temporary, to be sublated in the second nature of virtue (Athens), or permanent, contending with the always menacing corruption of nature (Rome). This is where we find the violence of law, which the legal subject perpetrates on himself. Law *curses* the individual with subjectivity, in order to turn him against himself as nature, as "mere life" (Benjamin).[32]

The self-reflection constitutive of *modern law* is directed against this. Classical law is the law of autonomy, because in it the difference of norm and nature is subjective, which is to say that it is carried out by the subject herself. In contrast, modern law begins by reflecting on the difference of norm and nature itself. In other words, the difference of norm and nature becomes the determination of and the way to perform the norm itself. The – external – difference of norm and nature becomes the – inner – form of the law and thereby yields the modern form of rights. What does this mean for the power of negativity that defines the subject of classical law?

As yet, we can only answer this question for the form of bourgeois law – the only actual form of modern law that has existed up to now. Bourgeois law carries out law's self-reflection, in its difference from the natural, in such a way that the natural, the non-normative, *is presupposed as fact*. Bourgeois law therefore understands the self-reflective reproduction of the difference of norm and nature in law in such a way that it requires reifying the natural into the given, into law's foundation. This occurs through the authorization of self-will, since the authorization of self-will signifies that the subject's willing – for and by law – is a valid fact. This is bourgeois law's empiricism or positivism.

This thesis is reciprocally elucidated by drawing on the basic positivistic definition of bourgeois law and on Foucault's diagnosis of juridical regression in bourgeois society. Foucault's diagnosis indicates that bourgeois law is law without a legal subject. The thesis offered by the basic positivistic definition of bourgeois law understands this to mean that in its authorization of the subject's self-will, bourgeois law simultaneously undermines its power of negativity. "The regression of the juridical" signifies that bourgeois law's positivism or empiricism relinquishes the negativity in the legal subject's self-reference.

Hegel, in his (above-cited) critique of the "empirical natural law" of bourgeois theory and practice, has formulated this crucial point as follows: "Since multiplex being is the principle of empiricism, empiricism is precluded from pressing on to the absolute nullity of its qualities which for it are absolute."[33] In other words, to put this more explicitly, we might say that empiricism consists in making multiplex being, in the positive givenness of its qualities, into a "principle" (or, as Locke would put it, into a "foundation"). Qualities are thereby established as "absolute." Juridical empiricism hence strips away the "absolute nullity" of qualities, their negation as qualities, and therefore their reference to the non- or trans-qualitative, to law [Gesetz] as third (or, as Hegel says, "the unity, which is the essential one").[34] This is the sense in which, on Foucault's diagnosis, the subject of bourgeois law as subject of self-will is no longer a "subject of right": the authorization of the subject's own self-will signifies its deauthorization as subject of negativity.

Did we not already see, however, that the subject's legal authorization can never merely mean that it exercises its rights, the right to its own self-will, against others?[35] Is it not true instead that the subject must always define what rights consist in by thinking – and must therefore think politically? And thinking politically means not merely thinking from one's own perspective, the perspective of one's self-will, but thinking from the perspective of each subject. The subject of bourgeois rights must therefore also "transcend" the perspective of her own self-will (as Foucault says the subject of classical law must).

Indeed, the subject must do so. It must "relinquish" or "renounce" (as Foucault puts it above) the realization of its own will, but in doing so the subject does not need to change it. In taking legal action against another person, for instance, the subject of bourgeois rights must always adopt a political perspective that heeds the external limitation of self-wills – it must consider each person's self-will and therefore what is one's own. If it does not do this, there will be no law [Recht] at all. However, in doing so, political legislation and interpretation presuppose the self-will's givenness. The bourgeois politics of law consists in providing validity to this givenness. The participation of the subject of bourgeois rights in a legal case signifies its participation in the legalization (in other words, external limitation, according to a law [Gesetz] of equality) of private self-will, and the limitation of private self-will entails its presupposition as given or as foundation of law [Recht]. Self-will is viewed as a "quality" that is "absolute" (Hegel) in the political process of bourgeois law, that is indeed "absolute" *through* this very process. This means that the bourgeois subject's self-will is relativized in terms of quantity, but absolute in terms of quality. It can be limited in scope, but the positive givenness of its definition and being remains unchanged. This signifies and entails the loss of negativity through the regression of the juridical. In particular, it signifies that the relation of norm and nature in bourgeois law is conceived in a more quantitative sense, as (self-)limitation, instead of being conceived qualitatively, as (self-)transformation.

The power that creates the form of subjective rights is the subject's power to participate in the legalization of self-will. The bourgeois subject is itself powerless in the face of its own self-will – in the face of *what* and *how* the subjective will *is*. The subject of bourgeois rights pays a price for its political authorization by being deauthorized from politics. For in losing its power of negativity, the subject simultaneously loses the power to "materially permeat[e] the content of the remaining, non-political spheres."[36]

— 12 —

SUBJECTIVE RIGHTS AND SOCIAL DOMINATION: AN OUTLINE

Legal authorization subjectivizes: it creates the subject of self-will. To be self-willed means to be a subject who selects (goals) and evaluates (means or resources). Law validates self-will in the form of subjective rights by securing private spheres for the will and by ensuring private wealth from social participation. This, however, is precisely why legal subjectification is simultaneously the mechanism that creates a new form of the social, namely bourgeois society.

Bourgeois society is negatively defined as a form of the social that is composed of morally indifferent subjects who appropriate what is common, or, in other words, as a society whose cohesion [*Zusammenhang*] must function *without morality*. Bourgeois society is the "loss of morality."[1] Of course, however, this does not mean that bourgeois society is a social context [*Zusammenhang*] without normativity – with no normativity within it or outside of it. (And, *a fortiori*, the loss of morality does not mean that it is a society of egoists; egoism is not a social category at all, but a moral one.)[2] For the authorization of morally indifferent self-will is a juridical operation, and therefore normatively created. To be a bourgeois subject of self-will means to be legally authorized (or "taken into consideration").[3] The fact of morally indifferent self-will is an effect of legal validation. The morally indifferent self-will that privately appropriates the social only *exists* through law's normative order and, in particular, through the bourgeois form of rights. Bourgeois society as the social context for morally indifferent subjects is a juridical creation.

As we have seen, the bourgeois subject's self-will has two components: the will as selection of individual goals and the will as evaluation of socially available opportunities. For this reason, legal authorization of

191

self-will also has two forms: the right to one's own private sphere of free choice and the right to private wealth through social participation. This thesis is directed against the narrow possessive-individualist interpretation of subjective rights (and the narrowing of criticism of the form of subjective rights to criticism of possessive individualism: such criticism has yet to accomplish anything). For the subject's private self-will, authorized by the form of subjective rights, does not – merely – *consist* in choice as the selection of goals. The form of subjective rights (which authorize self-will) must also safeguard private participation in the social, since self-will is oriented to the evaluation of opportunities and since opportunities are socially available. Because legal authorization is defined in two ways, the social context that is thereby generated also has two different definitions: on the one hand, bourgeois society is an interrelation between subjects, who exercise the right to their private sphere of free choice, and, on the other hand, it is an interrelation between subjects who exercise the right to their own wealth from social participation. What type or form of the social is constituted by this twofold exercising of a right? In other words, what constitutes the basic structure of bourgeois society as – or, insofar as it is – created by the form of bourgeois law?[4]

The first answer to this question is that bourgeois society is a free society. For it is a society solely based on the authorization of subjective self-will. It is a society that exists *through* willing for oneself. This answer, the liberal one, is correct: bourgeois society is a social context that is constituted by what subjects themselves will. To put this more precisely, it is a social context that is constituted by the fact that subjects will *as* they are legally authorized to will (that is, their willing has *this form*). This juridical determination of the form of willing precedes the freedom of the social context and is a hidden premise of the liberal response – the answer that bourgeois society is a free society.

A second answer is based on understanding the juridical formation of the will as authorization of private self-will: bourgeois society, which is formed by the legal authorization of subjects, is an unfree society – a society in which domination is exerted through the juridical formation or authorization of the subject. The thesis of this second answer is that the subject of free self-will is simultaneously the subject of social domination. This holds true in a double sense: such a subject dominates and is dominated. The subject of free self-will can be on both sides of different structures of domination that are formed in the social (and thus not merely political) relations of bourgeois society.[5] And this occurs (on either side) through law [*Recht*]: the subject dominates and is dominated by exercising the right [*Recht*] to her own self-will. Social domination

192

in bourgeois society has a juridical [*rechtliche*] form. It is domination produced by legal [*rechtliche*] authorization.

For this reason, both answers – bourgeois society is a society of freedom and it is a society of domination – are only true together, in contradictory unity: bourgeois society is a society of domination only *because* and *through its being* a society of freedom. *By being* a society of freedom, it is therefore a society of domination *at the same time.*

This double answer is the fundamental insight of the critical theory of bourgeois society first developed by Marx (and reformulated by Max Weber in a central argument of his sociology of law). Marx's insight is that domination in bourgeois society is the *content* of legal freedom, or that legal freedom is the *form* of social domination. If bourgeois political economy speaks of the "natural" laws [*Gesetze*] of production and thereby also speaks of the necessity to legally "safeguard . . . acquisitions," the "trivialities" that it produces in doing so "say more than their preachers know":

> Namely, that every form of production creates its own legal relations, form of government, etc. [. . . .] The bourgeois economists only see that production is carried on better with modern police than, e.g., under the law of the cudgel. They only forget that the law of the cudgel too is law, and that the right of the stronger still survives in a different form even in their "constitutional state" [*Rechtsstaat*].⁶

The bourgeois *Rechtsstaat* is only "the right of the stronger . . . in a different form." The bourgeois *Rechtsstaat* is not merely "different" in a historical sense, that is, different from the earlier legal form of *Faustrecht*, in which violence or domination and law are immediately equated. (*Faustrecht* literally means "law of the fist": the law of strength or law *as* strength.) Rather, the bourgeois *Rechtsstaat* is "different" in a structural sense: it differs from its own content. This is why bourgeois law *is* a "different form" of the law of the stronger. In other words, legal relations of equal recognition *are* social relations of domination, oppression, exploitation, and violence *in a different form* – changed into the form of equality. As Marx repeatedly notes,⁷ law's form and content stand opposed to each other. They contradict each other in how they are correlated. Law contradicts itself; not because it has normative content that is not yet (entirely) realized, but because it has a material basis or content that consists in social domination, while also having a different form that stands opposed to this. The logic of law is a double logic. It is a logic by which its own social content reverses into a different form.

For Marx, bourgeois law is therefore not mere ideology at all (false consciousness: "the darkening of the factual by law" [Claude Lefort]), but the "condition of existence" (Nicos Poulantzas) for precisely those social relations of domination that can appear to be relations of legal equality; the reversal of social domination into a different form of law performs a "necessary function" *for* social domination.[8] Social domination does not only require and create law's different form because it wishes to conceal itself. Rather, it only *functions through* the realization of juridical form: in bourgeois society, domination is *constituted* by law. Social domination thus requires not merely ideology, but the practical, normative *existence* of legal relations of equal recognition, so that it can exist in bourgeois society.

The central theorem of the Marxist theory of law – that legal equality is "a different form" of social domination – does not therefore entail any reductionism. For it does not dispute law's normative content. It does not simply equate law's normativity with domination. Law's normativity is irreducible to *and* functional in, indeed constitutive of, domination: the normativity of legal relations must be believed *for its own sake* to thereby make social domination possible. Legal relations therefore have a normative content, but not one that could be turned against social domination: it is a normativity without excess. Bourgeois law constitutes domination *through its normative content*. Marx's formulation of law as "a different form" conceives bourgeois society as an internal fusing of domination and law, or as domination through law.

Marx, however, carried out this program of conceiving bourgeois society from the unity-in-contradiction of law and domination in a one-sided and incomplete manner. For Marx conceived the subjective right, viewed in terms of bourgeois liberalism, as only the right to a private sphere of individual selection, as a right to choice. This is connected to the fact that he was only able to understand domination in bourgeois society in *one* form, as domination created by the legal authorization of private choice. In other words, he only conceived domination in the sphere of production, domination as *exploitation and coercion*. The legal authorization of the subject safeguards not only its own private sphere of choice, however, but also its participation in the social, namely the private appropriation of social wealth. Like the traditional, bourgeois-liberal ideology of civil liberties that he criticizes, Marx misunderstood the constitutive role increasingly played by this second, social form of subjective rights in bourgeois society.[9] Yet his general thesis that legal freedom and equality are a different form of social domination holds for these rights, too. This is a *fundamentally different* type of social domination (the *sine non qua* for bourgeois society – contra Marx's view, which

194

he shares with the traditional liberal ideology that he criticizes), however, namely social domination *as normalization*. In what follows, I will initially outline how the two basic types of the bourgeois form of rights, property as private sphere and property as private wealth, yield two types of social domination.[10] Next, I will outline how both types of bourgeois rights and both types of bourgeois domination are bound up with each other, come into conflict, and intersect ("Bourgeois Domination: A Tableau"). The intention behind the following reflections is thus limited in a twofold manner: it is a matter of understanding bourgeois society's forms of domination solely from the perspective of their legal constitution, and therefore a matter of understanding how the equality of rights leads to domination. Here I can only sketch an argument that will need to be gone through in a much more precise and sophisticated manner later on.

Private Law and Capitalism

Marx formulates his thesis that law is a different form of social domination in order to understand the constitutive interrelation between bourgeois private law and specific capitalist forms of domination – in other words, relations of domination between socioeconomically defined classes.

This means that Marx's critique of law only holds for this type of law: bourgeois private law is *the only* type of law that Marx critically analyzed, since he thought that it was bourgeois society's only structurally necessary form of law. The only law that Marx, a student of Savigny and Hegel,[11] therefore considers is "Modern" Roman Law [*Recht*] or "abstract right" [*Recht*]. Marx is also convinced that traditional Roman law formed the model for the modern development of this type of law by defining the juridical person through its capacity for acquisition through exchange. Roman law was thereby able "to develop the *attributes of the juridical person, precisely of the individual engaged in exchange*, and thus anticipate (in its basic aspects) the legal relations of industrial society, and in particular the right which rising bourgeois society had necessarily to assert against medieval society."[12] Drawing further on his teachers Savigny and Hegel, Marx argues that bourgeois private law reformulates the Roman conception of the legal person, though in such a way that it expresses "precisely the opposite" of ancient thought on law, which is based not only on the inequality of the free and unfree,[13] but on the presupposition that a shared ethos regulates the claiming of rights. In

195

bourgeois private law, however, the Roman models of law, centered on the person as party to a contract, are reinterpreted as media for the equal freedom of acquiring and disposing over things at one's discretion, and therefore as authorization of subjective self-will. This equal freedom of choice for all citizens, guaranteed by private law, is reclaimed in the revolution as an inalienable human or basic right over against the politically constituted commonwealth (the "state"). Law, as bourgeois private law, declares the person's equal right to freely dispose over the use of things (property), to which corresponds an equal right to the free exchange of such things with other persons (contract).

> With that, then, the complete freedom of the individual is posited: voluntary transaction; no force on either side; positing of the self as means, or as serving, only as means, in order to posit the self as end in itself, as dominant and primary [*übergreifend*]; finally, the self-seeking interest which brings nothing of a higher order to realization.[14]

Reference to bourgeois private law's break with the first principle of Roman persona law, the inequality of the free and unfree (and thus reference to the substantive human rights of bourgeois private law, which Savigny and Hegel emphasized),[15] makes clear that each individual is a legal person in bourgeois society. It also makes clear that any social relation which does not satisfy this condition is null and void. (Except in the relationship between parents and children, and formerly between husbands and wives, and between the normal and the insane, and so forth.) As conceived by private law, bourgeois society *is* in fact the realm of freedom and equality – "a very Eden of the innate rights of man":

> There alone rule Freedom, Equality, Property and Bentham. Freedom, because both buyer and seller of a commodity, say of labour power, are constrained only by their own free will. They contract as free agents, and the agreement they come to, is but the form in which they give legal expression to their common will. Equality, because each enters into relation with the other, as with a simple owner of commodities, and they exchange equivalent for equivalent. Property, because each disposes only of what is his own. And Bentham, because each looks only to himself.[16]

The normativity of freedom and equality (and that of property and Bentham) is also considered self-evidently valid for an economic transaction which, according to Marx's analysis, is the immediate expression of the structurally formative basic operation of capitalism: buying and selling of labor power as a commodity. In terms of private law, the selling of labor power as a commodity is nothing special:

The exchange between capital and labour at first presents itself to the mind in the same guise as the buying and selling of all other commodities. The buyer gives a certain sum of money, the seller an article of a nature different from money. The jurist's consciousness recognizes in this, at most, a material difference, expressed in the juridically equivalent formulae: "Do ut des, do ut facias, facio ut des, facio ut facias."[17] The equally free here exchange their commodities with others who are equally free, or they exchange the value of those commodities expressed in terms of money. As in any act of exchange that forms a contract, they thereby abstract from what use value the exchanged commodities will have for each of them. The "indifference" of use value is the condition for the realization of equal freedom in exchange.[18]

What the contractual exchange between capital and labor thereby abstracts from is not only the sphere of the qualitative and the particular, which defines use value in general, but also the fact that the use value of commodities is a specific kind of labor power. It is crucial to note that, as with the acquisition of any commodity, the capitalist, in legally acquiring labor power as a commodity, can only acquire an externally limited, and therefore internally unlimited right to its use.[19] This is an essential feature of the contractual acquisition of property, as defined by private law. Yet the use of labor power as a commodity is qualitatively different from the use of other commodities. The use of labor power consists in the exercise of labor power, and thus in labor. If the acquisition of labor power as a commodity includes the right to its use, then it therefore signifies the right to use the worker's use of that commodity: the right of one party to exercise the other's labor power. The right to use and the performance of use are here divided: the worker uses her labor power, by working, and the capitalist, who has purchased this labor power, has a right to this use (or more precisely: a right to use this use). The acquisition of labor power as a commodity is the acquisition of a particular commodity, because it involves obtaining a right *over* the only thing that can exercise this labor power: *the acquisition of labor power as a commodity entails the right to dominate the worker.* The two sides' equal freedom in exchanging labor power as a commodity, which is safeguarded by bourgeois private law, turns out to be merely "the surface process, beneath which, however, in the depths, entirely different processes go on, in which this apparent individual equality and liberty disappear":[20] processes in which one side controls and exploits the other. To put this more precisely, legal freedom and equality and social domination here exist *simultaneously* – and the latter, social domination, only exists *through* the former, legal freedom and equality. When labor power becomes a commodity that, like any

197

other commodity, is exchanged according to the rules of private law, and can then be used freely, at one's discretion, the bourgeois private law of a normative order of equal freedom changes into a mechanism for the simultaneous concealment *and* enabling of social domination.

Critique exposes this dialectical inversion – that of legal equality and freedom into social domination – at the heart of bourgeois law:

> we see that, by a peculiar logic, the right of property undergoes a dialectical inversion, so that on the side of capital it becomes the right to an alien product, or the right of property over alien labour, the right to appropriate alien labour without an equivalent, and, on the side of labour capacity, it becomes the duty to relate to one's own labour or one's own product as to *alien property*. The right of property is inverted, to become, on the one side, the right to appropriate alien labour, and, on the other, the duty of respecting the product of one's own labour, and one's own labour itself, as values belonging to others.[21]

The juridical realization of each market participant's equal freedom through the contractually formative exchange of labor power establishes "a power for lasting social domination" in the sphere where it is used, in production.[22] "In substance, law essentially amounts to the state-sanctioned violent disposal over alien labor."[23]

Marx describes the critical insight into law's constitutive role in domination as its diminishment into mere semblance [*Schein*]:

> The exchange of equivalents, however, which appeared as the original operation, an operation to which the right of property gave legal expression, has become turned around in such a way that the exchange by one side is now only illusory, since the part of capital which is exchanged for living labour capacity, firstly, is itself *alien labour*, appropriate without equivalent, and, secondly, *has to be replaced with a surplus by living labour capacity*, is thus in fact not consigned away, but merely changed from one form into another. The relation of exchange has thus dropped away entirely, or is a *mere semblance* [*Schein*].[24]

This has led to an interpretation which claims that, in capitalism, social domination over living labor power could exist even without legally constituted exchange and that the (self-)description of transactions between capitalists and workers in legal terms is merely an expression of false consciousness. This interpretation is wrong. In Marx (as in both Hegel and Nietzsche), the concept of appearance [*Schein*] does not mean a false view. Appearance is not an epistemological concept, but an ontological one. "Appearance" designates a mode of being that, first, is a result of what has been established and is thus dependent on presuppositions and that, second, isolates what has been established and what has been pre-supposed from each other so that they take on the character of something naturally given or even self-explanatory – which thus *appear* to have this character. Law is appearance because it turns out that the content and therefore the basis of its equality is – nothing but – social domination. At the same time, however, this means that law is appearance insofar as it results from social domination, in a process of reversal. For the social domination of capitalists over workers rests on the fact that labor power has become a "thing" over which one can legally dispose (and this means that it has become a commodity, has taken on the form of a commod-ity),[25] which was exchanged according to the contract's rules of equality. The fact that law (according to Marx) is appearance in capitalism *signi-fies* that law is necessary for the specifically capitalist form of domination to be able to exist – a form that is different from traditional types such as slavery and serfdom as well as from totalitarian forms of the command economy. Belief in legal equality and freedom is not an ideology, but the *necessary condition* for capitalist domination. Belief in law is not an opinion, but a practical belief: without it, no contracts could be agreed to – therefore no contract *would exist*. Without the formation of contracts, the exchange of labor power for wages would not exist. Capitalists would be unable to appropriate and control alien labor without such exchange. The fact that legal equality and freedom is appearance in capi-talism does not deny, but rather describes, their reality: the realization of legal equality and freedom in exchange is appearance, because it enables social domination in the production process.

Excursus:
Realization of Freedom as "Increase of Coercion" (Weber)

Max Weber concludes his examination of the "Forms of Creation of Rights" in *Economy and Society* with a critical demonstration of the inner reversal – in Marx's terms: the logic of inversion – that is inscribed in bourgeois private law. One side of this contradictory unity is the radical extension of the scope of free disposal:

> The development of legally regulated relationships toward contractual association and of the law itself toward freedom of contract, especially toward a system of free disposition within stipulated forms of transac-tion, is usually regarded as signifying a decrease of constraint and an increase of individual freedom. . . . The possibility of entering with others into contractual relations the content of which is entirely determined

199

by individual agreement, and likewise the possibility of making use in accordance with one's desires of an increasingly large number of type forms rendered available by the law for purposes of consociation in the widest sense of the word, has been immensely extended in modern law, at least in the spheres of exchange of goods and of personal work and services.[26]

The other side of bourgeois private law – which is thereby necessarily related to the first – begins when the question arises as to whether "this trend has brought about an actual increase of the individual's freedom to shape the conditions of his own life or the extent to which, on the contrary, life has become more stereotyped in spite, or, perhaps, just because of this trend."[27] Weber is in agreement with Marx here in arguing that this is only true if we abandon the view that we could answer this question "by studying the development of law's form alone."[28] Disclosure of the contradiction of bourgeois private law (thus the critique of this legal form) signifies, in methodological terms, a *step beyond* the immanent consideration of "law's form alone." In other words, it signifies moving beyond a perspective that merely focuses on their normative content, and therefore, according to Marx, requires analyzing the social content enabled and produced by law's form. Social content is not externally opposed to legal form – as the formalist critique supposes[29] – but constitutes its internal other. As with Marx, the methodological thesis of Weber's sociology of law is that the social content of law's form is the facticity of domination, which it produces itself and therefore through its own normativity. As Marx puts it, this occurs through its dialectical "inversion" into domination.

In the brief, prognostic sketch at the conclusion of his sociology of law, Weber discusses the dialectical inversion of legal equality into social domination, in connection with Marx's account of the radically asymmetrical relations between capitalists and dispossessed workers. At the same time, however, Weber advances decisively beyond Marx. Economic exploitation is central to Marx, particularly appropriation of the surplus value produced by workers, accompanied by the legal threat of violence. To be sure, for Marx too, what is crucial here is not the unequal distribution of (monetary) means, but the unequally distributed *disposal over* these means. It is Weber, however, who first draws the systematic consequence of this, namely that economic exploitation is to be conceptually analyzed *as a power relation* – or, more precisely, it is to be conceptually analyzed as an institutionalized, consolidated asymmetry of power; in other words, as domination.

Weber demonstrates this in two respects for "the differences in the distribution of property as guaranteed by law."[30] First, it holds for the relationship between two contracting parties in the sphere of circulation, of exchange:

> The formal right of a worker to enter into any contract whatsoever with any employer whatsoever does not in practice represent for the employment seeker even the slightest freedom in the determination of his own conditions of work, and it does not guarantee him any influence on this process. It rather means, at least primarily, that the more powerful party in the market, i.e., normally the employer, has the possibility to set the terms, to offer the job "take it or leave it," and, given the normally more pressing economic need of the worker, to impose his terms upon him. The result of contractual freedom, then, is in the first place the opening of the opportunity to use, by the clever utilization of property ownership in the market, these resources without legal restraints as a means for the achievement of power over others. The parties interested in power in the market thus are also interested in such a legal order.[31]

The "differences in the distribution of property," however, produce a radical asymmetry of opportunities to assert claims not only in the contractual relationship between capitalists and workers, but also in the production processes that are thereby established – in labor. Indeed, the "personal and authoritarian-hierarchical relations which actually exist in the capitalistic enterprise," the "authoritarian relationships," because they emerge from (free) "labor market transactions," are increasingly "drained of all normal sentimental content," which traditionally defined such relations. However, this

> not only continues but, at least under certain circumstances, even increases. The more comprehensive the realm of structures whose existence depends in a specific way on "discipline" – that of capitalist commercial establishments – the more relentlessly can authoritarian constraint be exercised within them, and the smaller will be the circle of those in whose hands the power to use this type of constraint is concentrated and who also hold the power to have such authority guaranteed to them by the legal order.[32]

Weber therefore concludes from this that:

> A legal order which contains ever so few mandatory and prohibitory norms and ever so many "freedoms" and "empowerments" can nonetheless in its practical effects facilitate a quantitative and qualitative increase not only of coercion in general but quite specifically of authoritarian coercion.[33]

This holds for the juridically produced social relations between groups or classes (and the individual as member of such collectives). They are defined by radically asymmetrical positions of power, which permit one class to (broadly) dictate conditions to the other, under which the latter have to work and thereby exist. The coercion exercised by members of one class on the other, however, is ultimately realized in the anonymous, fateful coercion that constitutes this social order's being, organized by private law, *for each person* who lives in it. To be sure, "the market community does not recognize direct coercion on the basis of personal authority" (but only qua a legally secured position). And yet:

> It produces in its stead a special kind of coercive situation which, as a general principle, applies without any discrimination to workers, enterprisers, producers and consumers, viz., in the impersonal form of the inevitability of adaptation to the purely economic "laws" of the market. The sanctions consist in the loss or decrease of economic power and, under certain conditions, in the very loss of one's economic existence.[34]

Like Marx, Weber defines bourgeois law through its interrelation of freedom and coercion. And like Marx, Weber conceives this interrelation dialectically: as a unity in contradiction (or as a contradiction in unity). Marx and Weber demonstrate that bourgeois law results in social coercion. This does not mean that bourgeois law *fails* to realize the equality of freedom. It means, rather, that bourgeois law results in social coercion *by* realizing the equality of freedom. The reason for this lies in the formal definition of freedom, and therefore in the formal definition of the subjectivity inscribed in bourgeois law by its basic model of subjective rights.

Social Law and Normalization

Bourgeois [*bürgerliche*] private law was the only form of law considered by Marx when he developed his thesis on law's constitutive logic of domination in civil [*bürgerlichen*] society. The central argument of Marxist theory offers a basis for this exclusivity, and Marx, looking back on his work, describes it as follows:

> My inquiry led to the conclusion that neither legal relations nor forms of state could be grasped whether by themselves or on the basis of a so-called general development of the human mind, but on the contrary they have their origin in the material conditions of existence, the totality of which Hegel, following the example of the Englishmen and Frenchmen of the eighteenth century, embraces within the term "civil

202

society" [*bürgerliche Gesellschaft*]; that the anatomy of this civil society, however, has to be sought in political economy.[35]

Marx's argument is that: (i) civil society is defined as politico-economic class domination; and (ii) the form of bourgeois [*bürgerlichen*] private law is constitutive for this class domination. Therefore, (iii) civil [*bürgerliche*] society only has *one* necessary form of law, bourgeois [*bürgerlichen*] private law.

This line of reasoning is rigorous, on its own terms, but empirically false: law in civil society, or civil law [*bürgerliche Recht*], is not merely private law (it necessarily includes public law for the regulation of its own creation and preservation). Law in civil society is simultaneously and irreducibly defined by a second conception of law: social rights, or, even better, *social law*. This term designates not only a further class of rights besides those of bourgeois private law, but another conception of law in comparison with (and *contrary to*) bourgeois private law: a "new type of law."[36] The two forms of law in civil society, private and social law, define the equality of freedom in opposite ways: as equality of private use and disposal, and as equality of social participation.

The institutional realization of social law is primarily understood as an achievement of the labor movement's political struggles (and of the developments in legal theory that accompanied this movement) in the second half of the nineteenth century.[37] Marx's ignoring of this legal form would accordingly only be due to the (legal-)historical conditions with which he was familiar. However, this interpretation misconstrues the fundamental systematic role played by social law in civil society's forms of domination. Social law is not the result of a political struggle against domination (supposedly constituted by private law in the first place) in civil society; it is constitutive *of* this domination. Nor is it the belated creation of a politics opposed to civil society, but emerged *simultaneously* with it.[38] The *conceptual* explanation of this is provided by an analysis of the dual performance in the character of modern rights (as permitting of choice and as authorization of interests), which results in civil law's dual conception of property – as sphere of discretionary decisions and as capacity for social participation.[39] Social law manifests itself *politically* as a central part of "the *state of necessity* and *of the understanding*"[40] that is required not only for the preservation of private law, but also for the securing of opportunities to participate in the "universal resources" of civil society.[41] This is not merely a revolutionary demand (and an article of the Constitution), but was even self-evident to anti-revolutionary liberals such as Benjamin Constant.[42] Social law as such is therefore not opposed to civil society at all in any critically substantive way. On the contrary, its inception is authoritarian – paternalistic.[43] This "authoritarian" conception of social law is only transformed into a critical concept when socialists from Babeuf through Proudhon and Lassalle all the way to the German Social Democrats take up the idea of human rights and reformulate them as "socialist 'basic rights'" (as Engels and Kautsky write in their critique of Anton Menger).[44] The twentieth-century social welfare state eventually realizes a portion of these socialist legal demands.

Marx has explicitly criticized one of the different forms in which social law emerged in civil society. He faulted the attempt by socialists to develop a conception of social law that is opposed to existing civil society, noting that, as he critically reformulates their intention, they want to simultaneously depict socialism "as the realization of the ideals of *bourgeois society* articulated by the French revolution."[45] Marx calls this "foolishness" – "the foolishness of those socialists."[46] This is initially a hermeneutic, diagnostic claim: the socialist idea of social law is foolishness, empty, absurd chatter, because it does not refer at all to the legal concepts that define class relations in capitalism – *nor* to the legal claims that workers assert against capitalists. Marx thus describes the struggle that is waged "between collective capital, i.e., the class of capitalists, and collective labour, i.e., the working class," over "the determination of what is a working day" as follows:

> The capitalist maintains his rights as a purchaser when he tries to make the working day as long as possible, and to make, whenever possible, two working days out of one. On the other hand, the peculiar nature of the commodity sold implies a limit to its consumption by the purchaser, and the labourer maintains his right as seller when he wishes to reduce the working day to one of definite normal duration. There is here, therefore, an antinomy, right against right, both equally bearing the seal of the law of exchanges. Between equal rights force decides.[47]

The fact that "right" here stands "against right" and that "both" equally bear "the seal of the law of exchanges" means that both claims, even those of workers, are of a private legal nature: under private law, the property owner's claim to labor power as a commodity stands opposed to the property owner's claim to the means of production. Marx therefore denies that workers are making another kind of legal claim in their struggle for an eight-hour day, since on his view there is no other kind of legal claim in civil society at all: claims under private law are the only legal claims there are.

The socialist strategy of criticizing civil society in the name of a legal claim, in the name of socialist basic rights or human rights, is therefore foolishness, for Marx, because it makes no reference to the struggles that are specific to capitalist class relations. The socialist conception of social law (in the strict sense, according to Marx's conception of law as a different form of social content) is vacuous: it does not refer to law's social content, social relations of domination. For in civil society, these relations are nothing but political-economic class relations, and the socialist conception of social law does not refer to them – neither in constituting rights (since, in civil society, according to Marx, relations of domination require private law alone), nor in criticizing them (since, according to Marx, the rights proclaimed by socialists only refer to the "distribution of the means of consumption").[48] Both points are wrong, however. And, indeed, they are wrong for the same reason: Marx misconstrues the critical content of the socialist conception of social law for the very same reason that he must also at the same time misconstrue why social law, even on the socialist understanding of it, is constitutive of the social relations of domination in civil society.

As regards the first point, the critical content of the socialist conception of social law, Marx (and Engels) interpret the demands for social rights made by socialists to only refer to a just distribution of the means of consumption. They reduce these claims to what is normatively significant in them. For the claim at issue here is not only much more extensive, but is also of a *different nature*, than the justice of distribution. In other words, the socialist conception of social law understands the justice of distribution as not only justice in the allocation of means, but as justice that enables participation in social life. This helps explain law's significance for education or for the legal regulation of work (also alluded to by Marx), such as a time limit for the working day. Social law proclaims the equal right to social life, indeed (as expressed in the programmatic text of "Juridical Socialism") it proclaims the "right of existence,"[49] the right to life.

This is accompanied by the claim to be able to *intervene*, for the sake of equality under social law, in the right of the capitalist buyer of labor power, under private law, to dispose over her thus acquired property, and it forms the critical content of the socialist understanding of social law.[50] At the same time, however, these claims are constitutive of domination precisely through their normative content, which establishes the critical force of social law claims against the capitalist domination by one class over another that is secured by private law. The critique of social domination and the constitution of social domination converge.

205

Like (liberal) private law, (socialist) social law is also constitutive for the relations of social domination in civil society. However, it constitutes a different kind of relations of domination: not the domination that, in its most fundamental sense, is exercised in production by one class over another, and therefore not domination in relations of production, but domination in *relations of communication or participation*. To put this more precisely, the socialist conception of social law is constitutive of the domination implicit in all social communication and participation, since social communication and participation always involve disciplining, forming, and normalizing. The socialist demand for rights to social participation, existence, or life enables and creates this form of social domination – normalizing domination carried out through social communication and participation. Just as capitalist domination over workers only exists through claims to their free choice under private law, so social domination over individuals only exists through claims to wealth from participation under social law. For this reason, claims under social law to wealth from participation are at the same time (*incontrovertibly*, or without entailing a contradiction) precisely the normative mechanisms that lead to the second form of social domination in civil society, social domination over individuals.

What is new in "the great struggles that have challenged the general system of power" in civil society, according to Michel Foucault, is that:

> what was demanded and what served as an objective was life, understood as the basic needs, man's concrete essence, the realization of his potential, a plenitude of the possible. ... The "right" to life, to one's body, to health, to happiness, to the satisfaction of needs, and beyond all the oppressions or "alienations," the "right" to rediscover what one is and all that one can be, this "right" – which the classical juridical system was utterly incapable of comprehending – was the political response to all these new procedures of power which did not derive, either, from the traditional right of sovereignty.[51]

The struggle against civil society's forms of domination is articulated in legal claims whose content (*and form*) is life: it is articulated in the name of the right to life, to life in society or social life. This holds in an exemplary way for socialist ideas of social law. Foucault's crucial insight here, however, is that such ideas appeal to *the very same thing* that forms the foundation of civil society's power, against which socialists believed themselves to be struggling; "against this power that was still new in the nineteenth century, the forces that resisted relied for support on the very thing it invested, that is, on life and man as a living being."[52] New "procedures of power," which Foucault characterizes as normalization, were developed (beginning in the eighteenth century) that were concerned with safeguarding and improving opportunities for social life. They were concerned with establishing, organizing, and developing participation in social processes. This normalizing form of social domination is structurally different (among other things) from the capitalist domination of one class over another, insofar as it is governmental [*staatlich*]: it concerns the relation of state and population, not the socioeconomic relation of classes mediated by private law. Normalizing domination is the form of government for a new state that safeguards "subjective public rights" (Jellinek). Normalizing domination, however, is primarily directed toward something other than capitalist domination: it is not a matter of exploitation and coercion, but of defining what social participation is and safeguarding and enforcing the conditions for its accomplishment, facilitating [*fördern*] and demanding [*fordern*] social participation. It thereby defines the identity of the subjects of these new rights as "living in the domain of value and utility."[53] The fact that the social rights claimed by socialists are a "political response" (Foucault) to this form of social domination does not mean that they contradict it from outside, on a conceptually and normatively independent basis. The social rights demanded by socialists (and, even more, their realization in a social welfare state) are simply a different form of this new type of social domination. Social rights *give* a legal type of equal recognition to social domination as normalization.

What Marx demonstrated in the relation of private law and capitalist class domination thus also holds for the relation between social law and normalization: namely that (normalizing) domination can only be performed *through* the "different form" of (social) rights. Just as private law is the "condition of existence" (Poulantzas) for capitalist domination, so social law conditions the existence of normalizing domination. And just as private law, in the course of its critical analysis, dialectically inverts into the social domination whose different form it is, so too does social law: the critique of social law – whether we consider social law that is paternalistically interpreted, that is enforced in an authoritarian manner, that is demanded by socialists, or that is realized by the social welfare state – reveals it to be the "mere semblance" of normalization.

Bourgeois Domination: A Tableau

The two basic forms of bourgeois domination are exploitation[54] and normalization. Both forms are carried out by law, something they have in common. Moreover, in both types of domination, ruling and being ruled are carried out in such a way that subjects exercise their rights. To be entitled means (includes) the ability to rule and be ruled. To be ruled therefore does not mean to be disenfranchised. In bourgeois society [bürgerlichen Gesellschaft], subjects can only be exploited through the – active, free – use of their right to decide over that which is their own at their discretion, and subjects can only be normalized through the – active, free – use of their right to obtain wealth through social partici-pation. Bourgeois domination is domination through legal authorization and, in particular, through subjectification and thus over subjects.

Control through entitlement is the basic structure shared by exploi-tation and normalization, which defines them as forms of bourgeois domination. At the same time, however, exploitation and normalization are different in two fundamental respects: in how they determine the author and in how they determine the addressee of domination. For in the first place, exploitation and normalization are distinguished by identifying who is being dominated: exploitation is domination through entitlement to a private sphere of discretionary decisions and thus over subjects with choice. Normalization, in contrast, is domination through entitlement to social participation and thus over subjects with interests. And, second, exploitation and normalization are distinguished by who gets to exercise domination. Exploitation is the domination of equal and free subjects over other equal and free subjects: domination through con-tracts. Normalization, in contrast, is an institution's domination over its members: domination through participation. Both forms of domination signify institutionalized (Popitz) or consolidated (Foucault) superiority or dominance, the hierarchical difference between positions of power. This occurs, however, in two fundamentally different dimensions of the social: Domination through contracts is exerted between individuals who are legally classified as equal to each other. Their legal equality is the medium through which their inequality in property, and thereby the unequal power they have in the marketplace, is translated into one party's domination over another. Domination through contracts is domination-between – intersegmental domination.

Domination through participation is exerted in the asymmetric rela-tion of membership between individuals and the public [Allgemeinen]. By socially instituting the entitlement of individuals to participate, a power to define the conditions for their participation is obtained. Domination through participation is domination-*in* – *institutional* [*institutionelle*] *domination*.

The two forms of bourgeois domination, exploitation and normalization, are therefore different in *two* respects:

First, they differ by the kind of entitlement exercised: by entitling private choice or by entitling interests in wealth. The forms of bourgeois domination are distinguished by *whom they juridically address*.

Second, they differ depending on which social dimension they are exerted in: intersegmental, as domination between social parts or members; or institutional, as domination through social membership. The forms of bourgeois domination operate in the two basic dimensions of the social, namely the horizontal and the vertical. They differ in their *social logic*.

How are these two differences related? Are they linked to each other – in such a way that only one of the two modes of juridical address can occur in one of the two basic dimensions of the social? This seems to be the case, so far: exploitation as a power relation between social classes takes place through the entitlement of choice *and* in the horizontal dimension of the social. Normalization as a power relation in social membership takes place through the entitlement to participate *and* in the vertical dimensions of the social. Exploitation, so it seems, *is* intersegmental domination, and normalization *is* institutional domination.

So it seems, but appearances can be deceiving. The links between juridical address and social logic are not fixed in place: differences in the two dimensions of domination intersect. Each of the two forms of bourgeois domination gives rise to the other. And they do this precisely because (and insofar as) they are enabled by law, particularly through their legal form. Coercion enabled by private law is simultaneously (i) a regime of – institutional – normalization, while normalization enabled by social law is simultaneously (ii) a regime of – intersegmental – coercion. To further clarify this, I would like to offer a few brief, concise remarks:

(i) The authorization of choice occurs by securing a private sphere in which subjects can decide on their goals at their own discretion. They thereby (also) obtain the power to "absorb" [*einzusagen*] (Preuß) other subjects into their sphere of domination through the free exercise of their rights – that is, through the free exercise of equal rights on both sides, among the ruling and the ruled. For this to happen, however, both sides must also equally submit to the conditions imposed on them by the legal safeguarding of their choice, since the freedom that is safeguarded, as

choice, is indeed amorphous and indefinite. It is the freedom of indifference. The legal safeguarding of indefiniteness, however, is not itself
indefinite. It always occurs under conditions. This is evident in the limits,
or more precisely, in the *kind* of delimitation by which legal safeguarding
circumscribes freedom of choice.

All rights limit what they permit. In their modern form, this delimitation occurs through the principle of equality, the compresence or
coexistence of rights for all. John Rawls formulates the obligation to
(self-)delimitation which results from this principle as follows:

> Very roughly, the idea is that, given just background institutions and
> given for each person a fair index of primary goods (as required by
> the principles of justice), citizens are thought to be capable of adjust-
> ing their aims and aspirations in the light of what they can reasonably
> expect to provide for. Moreover, they are regarded as capable of restrict-
> ing their claims in matters of justice to the kinds of things the principles
> of justice allow.[55]

The legal authorization of choice does not merely signify release from the
demands of moral normativity. It also requires the subject's willingness
to continually, flexibly adapt to the limits of equality, within which the
subject is entitled to exercise its choice. The legal authorization of choice
is simultaneously the creation of a subject that is willing and able to
adapt. To select goals *by choosing* simultaneously means being able to
make *other choices* at any time – when the delimitation of legal equality
demands it. For as long as this delimitation is guided by the principle
that "each person is [C.M. – supposed] to have an equal right to the
most extensive scheme of equal basic liberties compatible with a similar
scheme of liberties for others" or "that each person is owed a right to
the greatest possible measure of equal liberties that are mutually compatible,"[56] then any adjustment, exacted by the government, of rights on the
subject does not entail a loss of its freedom. The losses suffered by the
subject of choice due to legal limitations can only be quantitative ones
– hindrance from making its choice beyond the specified limit or dimension. If the subject of choice must select one thing rather than another,
however, it cannot suffer any qualitative losses: one freely chosen goal
is as good as another (since, for the subject of choice, only what is freely
selected *is* good). Whatever the subject selects is her free choice. From
a legal perspective in which subjective rights govern, there can be no
limitation in the name of equality. Such limitation is simply unacceptable
or unbearable for the subject as such. From a legal perspective in which
equal rights govern, anything subjects might say contrary to this is merely

a matter of "the strength and psychological intensity of their wants and desires,"[57] which can and indeed must be ignored.

We thus see that – intersegmental – domination, which subjects can exert over each other through the legal authorization of their own choice, presupposes – institutional – domination, which the legal system exerts over its members by standardizing (and thereby normalizing) their participation in law. For subjects are only entitled to their actions when they meet the formal requirement that such actions involve the exercise of choice. This formal requirement is the condition for the legal validity of the actions taken by subjects. This condition, however, remains latent as long as individual willing, either of its own accord or by chance, stays within the limits drawn by the new basic principle of equality. It is revealed to be domination, normalization through standardization, when conflict occurs. The domination of law then becomes manifest in an elementary and clear way: in the assertion (see Rawls) *that there is really no conflict at all.* The condition that law imposes when it authorizes subjects to choose is that subjects must recognize, precisely because their freedom is choice, that they no longer have power *against* legal limitation. They must therefore recognize that they cannot come into conflict with the law at all (otherwise, they misunderstand what they are). The authorization of choice normalizes, since it makes subjects into members of law with an unlimited ability, indeed willingness, to adapt.

(ii) Social law secures subjects' private capacity [*Vermögen*] to realize their interests by authorizing them to participate in the social. Participation in the social only exists under certain conditions: the subject's social authorization entails the social normalization of the individual; "every society is despotic" (Durkheim). As the vertical form of domination between the social public [*Allgemeinen*] and the individual, normalization is ubiquitous, indeed egalitarian; *everyone* is normalized. At the same time, however, normalization's domination under social law is closely connected with the intersegmental domination between elements of the social that are distinguished from each other by property and power. Such domination (re)produces exploitation and coercion between these elements.

This interrelation between the two basic forms of bourgeois domination can be conceived, initially, in functional terms. It determines the function of social politics for capitalist relations of domination. Jürgen Habermas has characterized this function as a compensatory service whose necessity begins to arise the moment that the "basic bourgeois ideology of fair exchange collapses."[58] This creates "an increased need for legitimation" that – supposing the inherent danger of politicization it is caught up in is averted – can only be met through displacement, culminating in a "welfare-state substitute program" that "elicits ... mass loyalty – but avoids participation." Social participation compensates for nonexistent political participation. It does this by facilitating consumption.

The social participation secured by social law, however, has a still more fundamental, productive function for capitalist relations of domination. It first reveals why social law is equiprimordial with their emergence (and does not merely compensate for their deficits of legitimacy afterwards). For after the dissolution of all moral forms of communalization (the *Great Transformation* [Polanyi] created by bourgeois society), specific artificial or technical mechanisms are required for the new state authority to safeguard social participation, to produce the labor power that capitalism exploits and coerces in generating its prosperity. The productive achievement of social policy consists in "proletariatization" (Claus Offe). "Social policy is the state's manner of effecting the lasting transformation of non-wage labourers into wage labourers";[59] it produces proletarians. To be proletarian, a wage-laborer, thus means not only being able to work, but being ready to sell one's own labor. Social policy serves "to contain workers within the wage-labour function." The goal – or norm – of social normalization is the production of the commodified subject.

It is clear that an irresolvable contradiction lurks within this double function of social policy, which is supposed to be simultaneously compensatory *and* productive: the securing of consumption *and* commodification.[60] This immanent contradiction – and thus bourgeois social policy's logic of domination – cannot be correctly understood as long as it is conceived as only one of its programmatic goals. This then also makes the interrelation between one form of bourgeois domination – social normalization – and the other form – exploitation and coercion – seem merely external, functional: exploitation and coercion (to be dealt with in a compensatory manner) as presupposition or as goal of social normalization (to be productively enabled). However, legal form – the form of social law – is crucial for bourgeois social policy. Social policy can only fulfill its compensatory-productive double function *through* this form. Social policy must serve not only to compensate but also to commodify in a legal form that secures self-will: social participation is enabled as a subjective right and hence appears in the form of privately appropriated wealth (for the realization of one's own interests).[61] This poses a fundamental problem for the social welfare state that enforces social law. The problem is that this state can indeed determine what constitutes social participation and can exert the institutional domination of normalization so that it then transfers wealth acquired or developed in it to a private disposal that it can no longer directly influence in a normalizing way. Its normalizing domination is evaded: through its legal form, normalizing social policy itself opens up the possibility of "withdrawing" from not only the "labor process" but also the sphere in which such social policy's programmatic goals can be effective.[62] In order to ensure that "only 'appropriate' use is made of [its] benefits,"[63] the only option that remains for the social welfare state is to then shift from institutional, normalizing domination to a different form of intersegmental domination that exerts coercion through contracts. This is the systemic site for "integration agreements" through which the German social code attempts to render the radical asymmetry in power and property between the state and the individual into a "different form" (Marx) of voluntary self-obligation – in precisely the same way that bourgeois private law turns the asymmetries of "market power" (Weber) into an expression of free agreements.

The Struggle for Law: Critique in Bourgeois Law

If both private law and social law are the different form of domination (and if all social domination is contested), then these two forms of law are also a field of social struggles. To be sure, here these struggles are waged in the form of contending legal claims between parties – in the form of litigation. Their social content, however, is not resolved in this legal form. Instead, conversely, every legal decision arrived at in a juridical proceeding also intervenes and hence remains inscribed in struggles in which social relations of domination are both established and always called into question again. Deciding a legal dispute between a buyer and a seller of labor power over its utilization (however rigorous its immanently legal foundation may be) is therefore simultaneously a tactical move in the social struggle between capitalists and workers for or against exploitation and coercion. And the same holds true for the legal dispute between social welfare state institutions and their individual members: here, every legal decision is at the same time the partisan adoption of a position in the struggle for or against a normalizing domination through social participation. Since legal form and social content overlap in a legal dispute, the legal decision can never put an end to social struggle: on the contrary, it propels it forward. As the adoption of a position in the struggle of social factions, it is at the same time non-juridical; it "would wrong at least one of them."[64] Social struggles (which are always struggles

213

within asymmetrical relations of domination) are not merely the content of the legal dispute; the legal dispute is itself a part of, an episode in, social struggles.

This not only holds, however, *within* the two basic forms of bourgeois law, in which fundamentally similar legal claims contend with one another – as, according to Marx, the conflicting claims of the buyer and seller of labor power are "both equal" (Marx) under private law.[65] The struggle of "right against right [*Recht wider Recht*]" (Marx) can also become a "struggle for law [*Kampf um's Recht*]" (Ihering): it can become a struggle over what should be understood by "right" or "law" [*Recht*]. The two definitions are opposed to one another insofar as bourgeois law's basic normative content here diverges: on the one side, claims to a private sphere in a subject's discretionary decisions about its goals – in other words, the fundamental decision of bourgeois private law; on the other side, claims to private wealth (or opportunities) through social participation – in other words, the fundamental decision of bourgeois social law. The reality of law in bourgeois society is defined by the opposition between these two fundamental decisions. For this reason, law in bourgeois society *is* the continual, endless struggle of social law with private law, and of private law with social law. In its ideological-political form, it is the struggle between liberalism and socialism (or social democracy).

This thesis has three aspects: (i) the social critique of law outlined to this point, which reveals law's logic of domination, must be supplemented and redoubled by a political critique that targets its logic of power or struggle. These two types of critique are linked by a dialectic of blindness and insight. (ii) Political critique demonstrates that social critique is a strategy that bourgeois forms of law use in their political struggle with each other. The critique of law is a strategy of legitimation in the bourgeois struggle for law. (iii) This indicates the structural limitation of the two kinds of critique that the forms of bourgeois law direct at each other. The limit of such critique is located precisely where the *unity* of bourgeois law must be conceived in both of its forms. The presupposition for overcoming bourgeois law, however, is to conceive its unity.

(i) Both forms of bourgeois law enable a basic type of social domination. Law is a different form of social domination. This constitutes law's social logic. At the same time, however, both forms of law are engaged in a struggle with one another. They struggle for power, in particular, for the power to define how, in essence, the bourgeois legal system should be constituted. This is a struggle over how to understand the basic idea of the bourgeois legal system, the idea that each person's self-will is equally valid. It is therefore a struggle for the power of normative interpretation.[66] This struggle between the two forms of bourgeois law is a matter not of social domination, but of political power. For this reason, the forms and histories of bourgeois law cannot solely be explained by its social logic – a logic that enables domination. They are equally defined by its political logic: the logic of the struggle for power between the two forms of law – the logic of political hegemony.

Law's social logic defines law in the singular. Social logic defines the constitutive interrelation between *one* form of law – private law *or* social law – and *one* type of social domination. Political logic, in contrast, defines the relation between the two forms of law, namely the relation between private law *and* social law. This is not simply a numerical difference, however. Instead, it concerns law's mode of being, that is, the way in which law exists.

To consider law's political logic involves understanding that its forms have been made – it is to understand law as making itself, as self-made or self-established. Viewed in political terms, each form of law not only is engaged in a struggle with its other form, but *emerges from* this struggle. The fact that law has a political logic defines its being as becoming. It defines its becoming as its self-establishment, and it defines law's self-establishment as an establishing of itself *against* different law. Law, as private law or as social law, only exists by acting to assert itself in a struggle for the hegemonic interpretation of the basic idea of bourgeois law.

As with the demonstration of law's social logic or its logic of domination, the demonstration of its political logic or its logic of power is also an act of critique. The political critique of law thereby complements its social critique. In this sense, critique signifies the dissolution of appearance [*Schein*]: accordingly, social critique is directed against the semblance [*Anschein*] of law's normative independence. Insight into law's social logic responds to this semblance by objecting that every form of law plays a constitutive role in the reproduction of social domination. In distinction to this approach, political critique is directed against the appearance that a given legal form has a settled definition. The critical demonstration of law's political logic reveals that every form of law is first formed in political struggle against different and opposed forms of law. It reveals that every form of law simultaneously abstracts from the political act of its self-creation and establishes itself as settled, justified in its own terms, and an independently existing normative order. The political critique of law dispels the appearance of law's finality, of law as enclosed within itself and thus concluded, by pointing out that law's framework can always be changed, due to its political logic of struggle.

It is immediately clear that the social critique of law and its political critique, the demonstration of its logic of domination and its logic of power or struggle, are neither smoothly related as supplementary to each other, nor so as corresponding with each other. Rather, they are in tension with one another, since what one presupposes is called into question by the other: social critique presupposes the givenness of a specific legal form, whose domination-enabling logic it demonstrates, and thereby necessarily disregards the political logic according to which a form of law, in its struggle against a different form, is perpetually recreated and hence continually transformed. Political critique, in contrast, dissolves every specific normative legal content into the processes of its creation and transformation in struggle with a different form of law – and thereby undermines precisely the unambiguousness and finality through which law is constitutive for relations of social domination. *Both* forms of critique thereby succumb to an irresolvable entanglement of insight and blindness: their critical insight *causes* their blindness. Furthermore, each form of critique, blinded by its insight, cannot see what the other form of critique's insight reveals.

Social critique's blind spot is to be found precisely where it recognizes law as a different form of social domination. For social critique does not understand, indeed it never questions, the formation of the process through which law's – categorically different – normative logic is created *from* relations of social domination. How and in what way does a form of law *arise* that enables domination? Admittedly, on Marx's view, "this juridical relation . . . is a relation between two wills, and is but the reflex of the real economic relation between the two."[67] The (juridical, normative) form of this relation, however, is not provided by its economic content. Instead, it must be created, and political critique's insight is that this occurs in the struggle to define and enforce the correct understanding of law. For this reason, however, conversely, it sees all law as only ever coming into being, transforming itself, and remaining contingent. Political critique follows Nietzsche's motto: "The form is fluid, but the 'meaning' is even more so" (and "The 'evolution' of a thing . . . is . . . a succession of more or less profound, more or less mutually independent processes of subduing, plus the resistances they encounter, the attempts at transformation for the purpose of defense and reaction, and the results of successful counteractions").[68] Just as the social critique of law is therefore unable to conceive its own emergence, so political critique cannot conceive how it exists: it cannot conceive how *specific* forms of law are established. Political critique's blind spot, which social critique targets, is that while the solidification of a meaning that is fluid (in itself) into a fixed form, the inversion of the – original – contingency of what has

216

been established into the necessity of second nature, must remain forever a mystery to it,[69] social critique recognizes the *meaning* of law in this act of establishment – law's social logic consists precisely in establishing a specific normative order that also enables specific relations of social domination.

(ii) The insight offered by the political critique of law is that the struggle between the two forms of bourgeois law is a struggle for power, namely a struggle for hegemony in interpreting the basic idea of bourgeois law. The insight offered by the social critique of law is that each of these two interpretations simultaneously serves to enable a basic type of social domination. This critical demonstration of the social logic of law is not a free-floating, theoretical insight, however. Instead, it is located *in* the political struggle of its two basic forms. Private law and social law do not merely justify themselves in this struggle by arguing that each respectively represents the correct interpretation and realization of the idea of bourgeois law – the idea that each person's self-will is equally valid. Rather, they justify themselves by claiming to demonstrate to their respectively opposed form of law how its normative content inverts into the enablement of social domination, namely because it is only a different normative form of a social content that signifies domination. The (liberal) party of private law criticizes social law as a different form of normalizing domination, and the (socialist or social democratic) party of social law criticizes private law as a different form of capitalist domination. Social critique is part of the political struggle in bourgeois law. In bourgeois society, critique of law is a strategy to justify law: bourgeois law is essentially law that is critical of domination.

The struggle between capitalists and workers over the length of the working day reveals this in an exemplary manner. As we have seen, Marx describes this as a struggle of "right against right, both equally bearing the seal of the law of exchanges."[70] He thus describes it as a struggle between two claims, in terms of bourgeois private law. In fact, however, it is a struggle between two different conceptions of law whose demands are opposed to each other. When capitalists assert their right to freely dispose over workers' labor power and time, they appeal to the fact that they acquired this legal claim in a contract that was freely entered into by both sides. In contrast, if workers demand a shorter working day, they do not do so (at least not merely and primarily) by appealing to their own right to dispose over their labor power. They therefore do not make this demand in the name of their freedom to form a completely different contract with capitalists in which they would exchange their labor for wages. Rather, according to Durkheim's theoretical reformulation of their argument, they oppose the legal conception of "contractual solidarity" under social law to the legal conception of freedom of contract under private law.[71] For they claim that a labor contract with capitalists is valid not merely (in terms of private law) because both sides have freely entered into it, but only because *or when* it is a "matter of doing justice."[72] To be legitimate, it must not only validate the freedom to dispose, but must also equally validate the "ideal . . . to maintain social life" and social "existence" for both sides.

In the struggle over the length of the working day, classes and their parties contend by portraying their own respective conception of bourgeois law as the correct interpretation of its basic normative idea. The strategy of leveling social criticism against the other conception of law that they dispute is just as important, however. By contending in this way, they convincingly prove to each other that their normative idea of law is merely, in fact, the different form of a type of social domination. The party of social law thus disputes liberal private law by arguing that the latter serves to render distinctions in property, and hence in market power, normatively invisible and to thereby establish relations of capitalist exploitation and coercion. Durkheim, for instance, argues that "[i]f one class of society is obliged, in order to live, to secure the acceptance by others of its services, whilst another class can do without them, because of the resources already at its disposal, resources that, however, are not necessarily the result of some social superiority, the latter group can lord it over the former."[73] Liberal private law, however, also proceeds in a critical manner: it supports its rejection of the demand for social justice by arguing that this demand is only a different form of normalizing domination, which the modern state exerts over its subjects so that it can organize and realize their claims to social participation. The argument here is always that social law, whether instituted in an authoritarian manner or as a result of socialist demands, is "the greatest conceivable *despotism*," since it proceeds on the model of a *"paternal government"* under which "the subjects, as immature children who cannot distinguish what is truly useful or harmful to themselves, would be obliged to behave purely passively and to rely upon the judgement of the head of state as to how they *ought* to be happy, and upon his kindness in willing their happiness at all."[74] Both of bourgeois society's forms of law enumerate the consequences of their social realization to each other. Both sides equally criticize law's social logic of domination – as it manifests itself on the other side.

Just as one side's critique only holds for its respective other side's logic of domination, however, so each of the two forms of bourgeois law, in

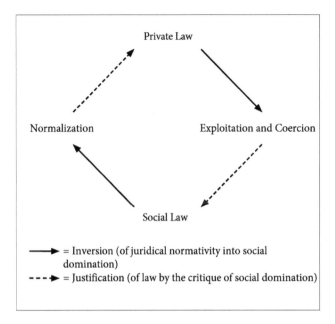

Private Law

Normalization   Exploitation and Coercion

Social Law

━━━━▶ = Inversion (of juridical normativity into social domination)

- - - ▶ = Justification (of law by the critique of social domination)

The Struggle for Law in Bourgeois Society

The Struggle for Law in Bourgeois Society, themselves revert to enabling domination. The critique *of* the legal enablement of social domination and inversion *into* the legal enablement of social domination are two sides of the same idling dynamic of bourgeois law. Social critique is merely one element in the cycle [*Kreislauf*] of bourgeois law. Indeed, it is the motor that drives this cycle onward.

(iii) The cycling back and forth, around and around, of private law and social law is the basic model of bourgeois law's politics: the politics of bourgeois law (and therefore bourgeois politics, which *is* nothing but a politics of law) consists in the struggle for hegemony between its two basic forms. Critique is an essential strategy of justification in this struggle. As we have seen, this holds, first and foremost, for social critique that dispels the appearance of law's normative independence and deciphers it as a "different form" (Marx) of social domination. However, it also holds for political critique directed against the appearance of law's settled determination, exposing the processes of overpowering and "transformation" (Nietzsche) that give rise to this appearance. Bourgeois law is essentially law that is critical (of law): critique of law is immanent in bourgeois law.

219

The immanent critique of bourgeois law is also limited, however. Yet this is not merely, and indeed never primarily, because it is for the most part only a critique of its respectively different type of law. Critique and justification are usually considered to be two separate positions: critique of the other side is conducive to the justification of one's own side. It makes sense, however, to anticipate and forestall the other side's critique. Critique then becomes autocritique: both types of law are able to see through and perceive their own appearance (their appearance of settled definition and normative independence). They are able to see through and perceive how they emerge through a preponderance of political power and enable social domination. Both then establish mechanisms for correcting themselves. This is characteristic of the constitution of bourgeois private law and social law in reflexive modernity (from around the 1960s onward).[75] This internalization of critique, however, does not change anything in the cycle of bourgeois law, since it does not change anything in the *structural* limitation of critique in bourgeois law.

The bourgeois critique (or autocritique) of law is structurally limited because it obeys a logic of external opposition. Either (in political critique) it confronts one normative conception of law with another: the claims to a private sphere of discretionary decisions are confronted by claims to private wealth through social participation. Or (in social critique) it confronts a normative conception of law with its effects of social domination: claims to a private sphere of discretionary decisions are confronted by their enablement of exploitation and coercion, while claims to private wealth through social participation are confronted by their enablement of conformity and normalization. In bourgeois law, critique consists of confronting one side with its other; it consists in demonstrating contradictions. Such critique is limited precisely insofar as it does not conceive the *unity* of these oppositions – and therefore cannot understand why they *must* arise. It cannot understand the basis and necessity of the contradictions that it demonstrates.

In bourgeois law, political critique cannot understand why claims to a private sphere of discretionary decisions are opposed to claims to private wealth through social participation. Why are *these* two conceptions – and only these two – constitutive of the fundamental types of bourgeois law that contend with each other?

In bourgeois law, social critique cannot understand why both forms of law invert (unwittingly, in its view) into the enabling of social domination. Why *must* these normative conceptions of equal freedom result in relations of coercion and normalization?

Both questions require us to move beyond the type of critique [*Kritik*] practiced by bourgeois law itself. As we have already seen, Marx describes this as a step from "dogmatic" to "true" criticism [*Kritik*]. "Dogmatic" (or "vulgar") criticism is criticism that "*fights* with its subject-matter . . . True criticism, by contrast, shows . . . not only . . . contradictions as existing; it *explains* them, it comprehends their genesis, their necessity. It considers them in their *specific* significance."[76] Dogmatic criticism shows that both of the two forms of bourgeois law are entangled in oppositions. It confronts law's appearance of normative independence with this insight. In contrast, "true" criticism (or "truly philosophical criticism") examines the basis for these oppositions. It is regression to the basis. This basis, however, is nothing but form: the basis for all oppositions and contradictions that arise in bourgeois law is such law's – *one* – form. This is the form of subjective rights. It explains why bourgeois law duplicates itself into precisely two forms that politically contend with each other. And it explains why bourgeois law continually remains the enablement of social domination. The two forms share the same basis, insofar as the form of subjective rights validates, and therefore authorizes, the subject's self-will. The consequence of bourgeois law's establishment of juridical positivism is that political struggle between its two types of law remains undecidable and its social logic of domination cannot be broken.

When ("true criticism's") regression to the form of subjective rights is able to conceive the unity of bourgeois law, it will then be able to pose, from this point forward, the question of what lies beyond bourgeois law.

Part IV

Revolution: The Dialectic of Judgment

> The conception of unfettered activity, of uninterrupted procrea-
> tion, of chubby insatiability, of freedom as frantic bustle, feeds
> on the bourgeois concept of nature that has always served solely
> to proclaim social violence as unchangeable, as a piece of healthy
> eternity. It was in this, and not in their alleged levelling-down, that
> the positive blue-prints of socialism, resisted by Marx, were rooted
> in barbarism . . . "being, nothing else, without any further definition
> and fulfillment," might take the place of process, act, satisfaction,
> and so truly keep the promise of dialectical logic that it would
> culminate in its origin.[1]

The development of the form of subjective rights – and thus the authorization of the subject as well as its submission to new types of domination
(part III of this volume) – is part of a historical process in which bourgeois society emerges through the de-moralization [*Entsittlichung*] of the
public normative order, the legal system. The development of the form
of subjective rights is an element in a complex evolutionary occurrence,
in which the economy, politics, law, education, art, religion, and so
forth are systematically transformed at the same time. Causal relations
between the transformations that occur in these different fields can only
be discerned in an ad hoc and provisional manner. Law does not precede
other historical spheres, but *without* a fundamental transformation of
its structure, without radically reformulating rights as subjective rights,
radical upheavals in the economy, politics, education, art, religion, and
so forth cannot take root. This is why capitalism cannot exist without the
form of subjective rights.

One way to understand the form of subjective rights is to view them as
an evolutionary effect, a social (or relative) necessity, whose "elucidation

is part of a *functional* explanation and not a normative justification of law."[2] At the same time, however, the form of subjective rights only exists by being reproduced in actions. These are precisely the actions that define the contents of subjective rights – by general rules or specific decisions, in institutionalized roles or in the unregulated formation of opinions. This defining of content is the reproduction of form, collaboration in the continual re-creation of the form of subjective rights. Every substantive definition of *what* a right is and *to what end* subjects should be legally authorized simultaneously adopts a position on *how* law should govern: it affirms, knowingly or unwittingly, *that* this should happen in the form of subjective rights. Every substantive definition comes with a definition before the definition, a (pre- or founding) act of formation. In other words, the form of subjective rights has not only an evolutionary, historical existence, but also a political one. It is not only a functional necessity, but a political goal. The form of subjective rights is political because it only exists *as formation* and because politics is concerned with the question of form. Politics is form as formative activity.

If every substantive definition of rights as an act of (re)producing their form is political, this is nevertheless only the case surreptitiously – concealed from itself. In contrast, *to pose* the question of form is, as such, a revolutionary act. Revolution asks about form, since it is not primarily and fundamentally an upheaval in the order of things, but an upheaval in our "way of thinking" (Kant), or an upheaval in which formation emerges from under contents. (Revolution is therefore precisely the beginning, the irruption of thinking, since thinking is the self-consciousness of form.)[3] For this reason, political revolution often (perhaps always) comes after things have already changed. Political revolution is not the origin, and never the beginning of a new order, but order in a different, new form, namely as act or deed. It is defined not by the fact that it *changes* things, namely their form, but by the fact that it allows form to become manifest as *one* way of formation and thereby able to be changed. Revolution makes form changeable: at the moment of revolution, form is *not* "given in advance" (as Habermas says of the form of subjective rights) any longer in a language "not at its disposal," whose "choice" can no longer be "free."[4] At the moment of revolution, form is no longer the medium of our action, but our creation – which we can thus create in an entirely different way or not at all.

The bourgeois revolution is the political act in which the form of subjective rights is performed as formation. The bourgeois revolution is both a re-enactment and a new enactment: It is a re-enactment because the creation of the form of subjective rights has already begun the moment when political domination is no longer understood to be already present and legitimated by existing morality or natural reason, but is understood to have to produce and justify itself by proceeding from "natural" strivings that are simply given. The modern name for this new "legal" form of domination is sovereignty or the state:[5] the bourgeois revolution re-enacts a modern upheaval in domination and law that has already occurred. At the same time, however, the bourgeois revolution *newly* carries out this upheaval because it only recognizes its normative principle in the form of subjective rights and declares this principle entirely valid as such. The bourgeois revolution thereby politicizes the form of rights by making their mode of formation into a deliberate and intentional political action. Precisely in doing so, in the fact that it does this and in how it does this, however, the bourgeois revolution simultaneously *depoliticizes* the society that it has itself created by establishing this form of law. Bourgeois society thereby becomes a field with entirely new forms of domination. The paradox of the form of subjective rights (in which the authorization of the subject turns into the enabling of social domination [*Herrschaft*]) *is rooted in* the aporias of bourgeois politics, in which politicization and depoliticization go hand in hand, because the politicization of rights is the depoliticization of society. This aporia, which is inscribed in bourgeois politics from the beginning, currently manifests itself as a crisis in the constitution of the social welfare state, since this crisis results from a self-straining that is not external to it. It does not, for instance, come from excessively "making claims,"[6] but is rooted in the essence of bourgeois politics (see chapter 13).

This crisis can be harnessed to pose the question of the relation between politics and society in a new way. A division is created between politics and society when the bourgeois revolution makes the form of subjective rights into its basic form: on the one side, a society presupposed by politics and, on the other, a politics subordinate to society. If, however, this division is politically created, it can also *not* be created politically, as well. If, at the moment of the bourgeois revolution, legal form becomes the political act of formation, this revolutionary moment occurs in the time and place of a politics *before* rights. It is a politics that will have created the form of rights, but has not yet done so. Revolutionary politics can only solve Marx's puzzle – the puzzle of why bourgeois politicization turns into juridical depoliticization – by analyzing this moment. For only after this has been done can we pose the decisive question: *why* do rights in their modern form, as law's self-reflection, *exist at all*, and therefore legalize the natural? In (or *before*) the struggle for rights, as the bourgeois revolution understands itself, we suddenly perceive a

225

struggle over *whether there should be a form of rights at all*. The slave or servant who dares to revolt does not demand her rights – as though this form already existed – but demands, if anything, *rights themselves*; she demands the form of rights. Her revolt is a politics of form. The form of rights can only be understood on the basis of revolutionary insurrection, by answering the question of why the servant who revolts demands rights at all. Critical analysis of Nietzsche's interpretation of the slave revolt will show that there are two radically different answers to this question (see chapter 14).

The prospect thus arises of a *new right*: a right that radically reflects itself, without also thereby creating bourgeois society as a space whose forms of subjectivity and rule [*Herrschaft*] are deprived of political power. This new right is based on the negative dialectic of political judgment: it is the right of political judgment. To this end, it must simultaneously safeguard the power of participation while securing the powerlessness of non-participation. This new right reconceives rights as counter-rights in the political process (see chapter 15). Marx's puzzle – which was discussed at the beginning of this book – is as follows: why does the bourgeois revolution declare the equality of rights and thereby reduce politics to the police administration of bourgeois society? The new right solves this puzzle. It clears up the puzzle of the bourgeois revolution. New right declares equal rights against politics in politics. In doing so, it *realizes* politics.

226

— 13 —

THE APORIA OF THE BOURGEOIS CONSTITUTION

The substantive determination of individual subjective rights is a legislative act, while the *form* of subjective rights, in contrast, is established by a constitution. The bourgeois constitution does this by declaring basic rights. Basic rights are rights to (subjective) rights. The declaration of basic rights establishes the form of subjective rights, since all basic rights only essentially express one thing in respectively different substantive ways: "the systematic decision in favor of freedom as such"[1] – which here means: in favor of the subject's freedom to decide according to her own self-will. The declaration of basic rights states that self-will is valid regardless of whether its contents are moral or it has been formed in a moral manner – that is, regardless of whether it is normatively justified. (Accordingly, the different pamphlets of basic rights are "historical concretions" [Dieter Grimm] of this basic systematic decision, and are therefore changing substantive definitions of which private spheres and capacities are required for a subject in a given social situation to realize her self-will.) More precisely, this systematic decision in favor of the freedom of the subjective self-will is the specific new significance of "bourgeois" constitutions, which fundamentally break with tradition. It is the *normative* significance of bourgeois constitutions, which is realized not by a substantive prescription of specific modes of action and judgment, but by a decision on form that now signifies "the renunciation of a materially defined ideal of virtue that is determined in advance":[2] a decision in favor of the form of subjective rights.

The bourgeois constitution does two things at once by declaring basic rights. Its first achievement consists in a new order and regulation of politics: the constitution defines procedures and authorities for the exercise of political power. A prerequisite for this is that the modern state

227

not only monopolizes political power and excludes all other agents (for instance, the church and those with landed property) from such power, and is therefore termed "sovereign," but at the same time, and above all, releases political power from being conditioned by virtue or reason, which traditionally grounded the morality of politics. The bourgeois constitution presupposes the de-moralization of monopolized political power. This happens when the ruler's traditional right is fundamentally reconceived as a (subjective) right for the modern sovereign's exercise of power. Sovereignty here signifies the subjectification of the ruler's right.[3] It was only this that "enabled ... regulated access to a constitution" to "thus be retained,"[4] when the bourgeois constitution proceeded to not only reorganize political power but also redefine it by redistributing the right to the political exercise of power to all, thereby democratizing it. The modern state thus begins with the systematic and consistent codification of political power. To this end, it defines who wields a specific power and grasps such power as the *right*, the entitlement that someone *has*, to exercise a particular kind of violence. The bourgeois constitution adopts this juridical reconception of political power as an order of rights, but connects it to the right to participation, to co-governance, which belongs (in principle) to everyone. The modern state is not abolished by the bourgeois constitution, but transformed in an egalitarian manner. The bourgeois constitution accomplishes this by attributing to every individual an equal right to participate in the political exercise of power.

In the bourgeois constitution, political participation is thus the exercise of a subjective right: it ensures political participation as a possibility or option, and therefore releases us from having to exercise it. "If we disregard the different modalities in the use of these rights, then we must be able to interpret political rights, too, as subjective liberties."[5] The same thing that holds for all rights with a subjective form thereby holds for political participation: the subject is authorized to do or not do something according to its own will, one way or another, and this is guaranteed or otherwise safeguarded. (The bourgeois constitution thus defines voting, as an act of political participation, to be the expression of an "opinion.") In this way, precisely by declaring basic political rights, the bourgeois (self-) constitution of politics in the form of subjective rights is "a new kind of foundation for *and* limitation of ruling."[6] It is a new kind of foundation for ruling [*Herrschaft*], because politics is now founded in each individual's basic right to participate in political power. This, however, is also precisely why it is a new kind of limitation on ruling, since if all rights are now subjective in their form or are freedoms [*Freiheitsrechte*], they entitle the freedom of subjective self-will "as such" (Grimm). They do so not merely in politics, but also toward politics. The basic right *to* politics already contains the declaration of basic rights *toward* politics – "the independence of basic rights from the democratic process."[7] By its mere form, the right to participate in political power implies the existence of other rights that limit the exercise of political power.

The bourgeois constitution of politics has an external side because political power externalizes itself through its inner structure or produces an externality that is outside of it. For if the bourgeois constitution of politics consists in changing political participation so that it takes on the form of a subjective right, it implies the authorization of subjective self-will in general and thereby the creation of a social sphere prior to or beyond politics:

> If mediated by the freedom of individual decision, different social realms such as the economy, science, religion, art, education, and family have to be emancipated from political control and must be subject to their own respective criteria of rationality.[8]

> [The] binding limitation of the scope of state activity . . . manifests itself in individual freedoms, in human and civil rights, which are simultaneously social freedoms and individual freedoms in their social context. The distinction between and contrast of state and society is here consolidated and distorted as a means for the individual to secure freedom.[9]

By declaring basic rights, the bourgeois constitution of politics creates bourgeois society (and again, it indeed already does this by declaring basic *political* rights). The autonomy of social relations and needs, their independence *toward* any political government, is an external consequence of the individual's political autonomy. The bourgeois constitution authorizes the subject's self-will, and it thereby depoliticizes social bonds and structures that self-willed subjects have established among themselves. It releases subjects from political rule and thereby first makes independent social relations (operating according to their own logic) possible at all.

In the constitutions of classical liberalism, this is the "internal relation" (Habermas) of basic political rights, subjective authorization, and the social independence of an intrinsic goal – which, however, cannot be expressly stated in these constitutions. Liberal constitutions are limited to the guarantee of basic rights. The fact that they thereby establish the form of subjective rights and release social relations from political government by authorizing subjects is the essential impetus of such constitutions, indeed it is their intrinsic meaning, though it never explicitly appears in them: constitutions speak of individual freedoms, but not of bourgeois society's independence, which they thereby create. This is no problem as long as the social is understood to be self-regulating. Classical liberalism assumed that "the desired harmony" would result *naturally* from the egoistic interplay of *immediate* interests."[10] The liberal assumption of natural harmony claims that only the constitutional authorization of the freedom of each individual's subjective self-will from political government yields social relations in which everyone can simultaneously (but not together) realize their self-will. It therefore claims that the freedom guaranteed by the bourgeois constitution through basic rights vis-à-vis political government is not threatened or restricted by the autonomous operation of social relations itself. The illusory character of this presupposition is nevertheless so obvious that few share it or adhere to it consistently for very long, even in the field of bourgeois thought. In opposition to this presupposition, bourgeois consciousness, from its inception, understands that "the liberation of a sphere of commodity exchange and social labor from state intervention [itself a political matter] must itself be realized and asserted ... within the framework of a total constitution which always embraces society itself."[11] The depoliticized "natural order" of bourgeois society is "*organized by the state.*"[12] Its distance from the state is dependent on the state: bourgeois society only exists through the state.

The awareness that the existence of bourgeois society as depoliticized context is due to political government characterizes the conception of natural law found in classical liberalism, which Habermas has demonstrated in French thought of the eighteenth century.[13] This awareness defines the French conception of revolution: the French Revolution *is aware* that it is creating a state whose constitution unleashes civil society. It is aware that the unleashing of the social by politics is a political achievement. It is also aware that this is an external effect of – more precisely, an effect of the external on – the internal upheaval of politics. In being aware of this, however, the bourgeois revolution is also aware that this cannot merely happen all at once: politics' unleashing of the social is a *perpetual* political task for the bourgeois constitution that is aware of its revolutionary origin. The insight that the social relations unleashed by the bourgeois constitution are essentially in crisis is part of its own revolutionary self-understanding.

The perpetually looming danger that bourgeois society is disintegrating from within, because it has generated radically asymmetric positions of power, is the state of crisis inscribed in the juridically depoliticized social sphere. This danger was seen from the beginning – from the emergence of bourgeois society. According to Franz Böhm, it is even a crucial motor of bourgeois revolutions, which are directed not only against traditional forms of domination [*Herrschaft*], but also against "*social* positions of power." They are therefore directed against positions of power constituted in the "social sphere" and, at the same time, call this sphere (as one of the subject's autonomy *and* the autonomy of the social) into question.[14] At present, which is what Böhm's diagnosis of a crisis aims to consider, this corresponds to the tendency toward the formation of monopolies, in which Böhm sees nothing less than a calling into question of the principle of bourgeois society's construction. For monopolies are social concentrations of power [*Macht*] that simultaneously obtain a quasi-political character through their dominance [Über*macht*]:

> The freedom that this private power uses against the *state* is not the freedom of its system of private rights, drawn from its own private relations in life, but the freedom of an authoritative order for general public matters. This private power does not oppose state power in the manner of a citizen, but in that of an autonomous bearer of powers for self-administration.[15]

The formation of monopolies signifies the achievement of political power through social mechanisms and as a social agent – it thereby signifies destroying the autonomy of the social from within. Admittedly, monopolies appeal to "an individual's right, granted and protected by the *private* legal order."[16] At the same time, however, in bourgeois society, they claim the quasi-political authority "of an autonomous bearer of powers for self-administration" (Böhm). Monopolies *blend* what the bourgeois revolution divided: the social and the political. They exercise a power *in* society that threatens to destroy the foundation of bourgeois society, the "freedom of its system of private rights." The "neoliberal" (because it is opposed to classical liberalism's illusion of harmony) – in Michel Foucault's sense of the term – diagnosis of this crisis is that the juridical release of the individual from political government yields autonomous social relations, which, however, have *in themselves* the tendency toward an authoritarian monopolization of social power. They therefore tend toward a perverted repoliticization that both threatens individual autonomy and undermines the autonomy of social relations.

This fundamental state of crisis confronts the bourgeois state with the task of protecting bourgeois society, as a realm released from political government, by continually intervening against itself and thereby preserving itself. The bourgeois state "does not intervene from strength, but from weakness."[17] In other words, the state continually intervenes in bourgeois society precisely to preserve it as a realm that it is *unable* to govern. The state does this by protecting the rights of the less powerful from attempts by social monopolists to gain an authoritative position for asserting their particular interests. Whether such monopolists attempt to defend their exclusive right to private spheres of free choice or to safeguard their exclusive right as their capacity [*Vermögen*] for social participation, the bourgeois state defends basic rights as "positive guarantees for participation with equal opportunity in the process of the production of social wealth, as well as that of the formation of public opinion."[18] And it does this to safeguard the autonomy of the social from its self-destructive tendencies, by securing subjective rights. "Accordingly, the state, in its preservative function for society, is thought to intervene in 'free social processes' as guarantor of a *free* society and of individual freedoms."[19]

It is therefore obvious that the ("neoliberal") step beyond the natural law found in classical liberalism – the step from deregulation to permanent intervention – simply results from the principles of the bourgeois politics of basic rights. Whenever this step may have really been politically taken, it is already present in the bourgeois constitution's revolutionary self-awareness in advance. The bourgeois revolution *is aware* that bourgeois society has been politically created – and that it is to be perpetually recreated, due to its state of crisis. The conception of basic rights as mechanisms for securing the social only appears *new* when set against the backdrop of the forgetting of politics or revolution by a natural law liberalism that misunderstands itself and considers such rights to be socialism, thereby ignoring the fact that even the demands for "socialist basic rights" only bring the revolutionary origin of the bourgeois constitution back to the fore in the present once more. To understand basic rights as not only rights of defense against the state, but comprehensive safeguards against authoritarian social domination, turns out to be a compelling consequence when the illusions of natural harmony have been dispelled from the social. It is therefore also a step in the social, even social-scientific, self-enlightenment of bourgeois politics.

If, however, the definition of basic rights as mechanisms of a comprehensive social safeguard – the safeguarding of the social through the securing of the subject's exclusive rights – does not break with the basic principle of the bourgeois constitution, but is its logical realization, then the contradiction irresolvably inscribed in the bourgeois politics of subjective rights becomes evident even in this definition's aporias.

Constitutional Crisis

The bourgeois politics of securing the social yields the following aporia: *On the one hand*, bourgeois politics must ensure society's independent existence. This results, in the first place, from its knowledge of the bourgeois constitution, and, second, from its knowledge of bourgeois society. For it thereby knows that bourgeois society only exists *through* politics. In other words, and more explicitly, it knows that, due to its essential state of crisis, bourgeois society (depoliticized, removed from politics) only *exists* as long as politics intervenes in it by safeguarding subjective rights. This was the only way to limit attempts at an "authoritative order" (Böhm), a de-socialization of society by the quasi-political monopolization of social, economic, or cultural power. Bourgeois society is politically produced, and only reproduces itself through political interventions, too.

On the other hand, however, bourgeois politics is utterly unable to command the power and the means to ensure the independent functioning of society. Bourgeois politics is powerless against its own social effects. This is obvious when politics attempts to guide and *administer* bourgeois society. Bourgeois society cannot be entirely managed without thereby dissolving it. The fact that bourgeois politics is powerless against its own effects only becomes clear, however, when it attempts to preserve bourgeois society by means of a constitution [*Verfassung*], by declaring and enforcing basic rights [*Grundrechten*]. For any attempt to constitutionally [*grundrechtliche*] authorize subjects as a political response to the social threat of monopolistic power again reproduces precisely that crisis of social relations created by the formation of monopolies themselves, and thereby necessitates a renewed attempt at securing subjective private rights (and so on). The bourgeois constitution's systematic extension is precisely what causes it "to wither into a partial order."[20] Its power is only partial because it generates its own countervailing power. It always comes too late, since it runs ahead of itself.

The aporia of the bourgeois constitution is as follows:

(i)   The constitutional establishment of the form of subjective rights produces bourgeois society as an autonomous relation toward political governance. Yet this relation, due to its immanent state of crisis, can only be preserved by continual political interventions.

(ii) Because political intervention in bourgeois society takes place by constitutionally securing the form of subjective rights, it once again gives rise to bourgeois society precisely as an autonomous relation toward political government, but one which requires continual political interventions to preserve it, due to its immanent state of crisis.

The bourgeois politics of basic rights is as necessary as it is powerless. It creates the very problem that it wishes to solve.

Social Constitutionalization: A Different Politics

The argument outlined above rests on a crucial assumption. It presupposes that bourgeois society is politically created, or, to put this more precisely, that bourgeois society is created by a politics of depoliticization. Modern politics begins to depoliticize itself by defining itself as the state and by defining the state through its goal of legalizing the natural. Bourgeois constitutional revolutions carry out this operation in a foundational manner by declaring the basic or human right to subjective rights. Bourgeois society cannot exist without this politics of depoliticization through subjective rights. Bourgeois society is made political – by a turning of politics against itself that becomes legal form. This is the thesis presupposed in the diagnosis of a bourgeois constitutional politics structurally in crisis due to its aporetic structure.

This prompts an objection whose discussion allows for a sharper conception of the diagnosis of crisis. The objection is that this thesis only reproduces the social blindness of its subject matter, the centrality of politics and the state in the bourgeois constitution, with its declaration of basic rights. This blindness is evident in the fact that bourgeois constitutions "contain the tacit premise that a compulsory order of formal and general norms would be translated directly into the organizing conditions of social life."[21] Bourgeois constitutions assume that their rules immediately – by themselves – give rise to an autonomous society. In other words, they share a "legal prejudice," since they fail to recognize, indeed completely deny, that the structuring of society through constitutional rules systematically depends on prior processes of social *self*-structuring:

> Fundamental rights are seen as areas of freedom for individuals, who are defended by protective rights against state intervention. Activities in civil society are not ascribed to social institutions but rather to the individuals themselves, who order their areas of freedom under private law but without reference to the state constitution.[22]

Constitutions with fundamental rights [*Die grundrechtlichen Verfassungen*] leave their social presuppositions and effects in "a strange twilight." They stand "in the shadow of constitutionally-protected individual freedoms" cast by the "light of the enormous draw of the state constitution."[23] Bourgeois constitutions are also unable to under-

234

stand what they are really supposed to be doing: according to Teubner, they exist to *serve* the "self-constitution" of different functional social relations. The constitution and the rights enabled by it play a "merely supporting role": "The primary aspect of constitutionalization is always to self-constitute a social system."[24] The bourgeois constitution, with its politics of declaring and enforcing fundamental rights, belongs not at the beginning, but all the way at the end, in the logical order of things: the self-constitution of differentiated social systems comes *first*. "Social constitutions" are formed *next*, the constitution of the economy, science, media, public health, and so forth, which "generate their own autonomy . . . by formalizing their own communicative medium."[25] And *only then* are these acts of social constitutionalization "supported by the law," whose basic principles constitutions, in turn, stipulate:

> Law comes into the self-foundation processes of social systems when they cannot fully accomplish their autonomy. This happens either when the social system cannot be adequately closed by its own first-order and second-order operations, or when reflexive social processes are unable to stabilize themselves or, especially, when they are becoming paralysed by their paradoxes. In such cases, additional closure mechanisms come in to support the self-foundation of social autonomy.[26]

Legal norms, even constitutional ones, always therefore operate by presupposing the "constitutive norms" that are developed *within* system-specific or function-specific social communications in order to unleash their own "dynamics."[27]

This sequence of steps, which is Teubner's response to the forgetting of society by bourgeois constitutions (a sequence of steps *from* the self-constitution of autonomous systems *through* their constitutionalization *to* rights whose basic form is declared by the constitution) can nevertheless be interpreted in two different ways: as a relation of conditions or one of meanings. On the first interpretation, the self-constitution of autonomous social spheres precedes, of its own accord, the constitution with basic rights. This is why the bourgeois constitution only safeguards a process of social self-constitution against external dangers (according to Luhmann: the dangers that arise from wrong politics). It therefore safeguards a process that can only be carried out in a purely immanent manner and on its own. The bourgeois constitution only comes into play externally. "Basic rights presuppose a social state of development in which they exist and serve only to prevent their corruption [C.M. – that is, the corruption of the autonomy of social spheres] by the political system."[28] On the second interpretation, in contrast, the three levels in

Teubner's sequence of steps do not designate separate processes. The fact that the self-constitution of autonomous social spheres precedes the declaration of rights in the bourgeois constitution does not here mean that it is independent of them, but that the bourgeois constitution is *a matter of* the self-constitution of autonomous social spheres. This is the *social meaning* of the constitution with basic rights, though it is unable to speak of this in its own legal language. In this case, however, the bourgeois constitution is much more than a safeguard that is merely added from outside: it is the political enabling of social relations that are autonomous from politics.

Both readings of Teubner's argument interpret the bourgeois constitution on the basis of its constitutive reference to the autonomy of social relations. However, they understand this autonomy and hence that reference in a completely different way. On the first interpretation, the difference and autonomy of social spheres is their natural state, which operates of its own accord, if things develop according to their own laws [*Gesetzen*] – autonomy as given, social autonomy as an evolutionary effect.[29] The second interpretation, in contrast, brings a completely different understanding of social autonomy into play. The autonomy of the social from politics and its normativity has only been created *by* a fundamental political transformation in the normative (which the bourgeois revolution foundationally re-enacts). It is therefore an autonomy that has been made: the autonomy of the social from politics is a political effect. The difference and independence of social relations from politics only *exists* through the difference of politics in itself and thereby from itself.[30]

By distinguishing these two interpretations, Teubner's socio-theoretical conception of the constitution helps us obtain a more precise understanding of the presupposition that forms the basis for the diagnosis of the bourgeois constitution's aporia, namely the thesis that bourgeois society is politically made. It also gives us a more complex picture of *how* bourgeois politics creates bourgeois society. Until now, the answer has been that it does so by constitutionally establishing the form of subjective rights. Teubner demonstrates that this answer is inadequate. It merely reproduces the immanent self-understanding of bourgeois constitutions and overlooks how they represent levels of "social constitutionalization" *between* the self-constitution of social systems and the bourgeois constitution's politics of law. Processes of social constitutionalization are necessary precisely because the self-constitution of the social does not happen of its own accord, because its autonomy is not automatic. Rather, it must be *made* by establishing and enforcing "social constitutions." The social is *constituted* by establishing "constitutive norms" that create respectively specific modes of communication – economic, familial, political, pedagogical, etc. The *constitutionalization* of the social advances beyond this, since it knows that the existence of constitutive norms is indefinite and uncertain as long as there are no processes and no norms for these processes, for creating and applying them. The constitutionalization of the social is nothing but the self-reflection of its act of constitution – the act of constituting the social in a reflective form.[31] Self-reflection, in practical terms, here means self-government: the process of constituting the social is a political act. "Here social systems are dealing with their own founding and decision-making paradoxes – a process that is always problematic and can never be determined 'technocratically.' And in this respect the independent constitutions of society beyond the state are highly political."[32] The social act of constitution is a politics *in* the social: the "'internal' politicization" of the social,[33] which it constitutes and *thereby* first creates.

This distinguishes the politics of social constitutionalization from the politics of a constitution with basic rights. One operates within the social, while the other externally enables it. It is precisely here that they are connected to each other, however. They are directed toward the same thing. Indeed, Teubner's argument against the social blindness of bourgeois constitutions is precisely that they do not see that, and *especially how*, they enable autonomous social relations. They are only able to speak of this by talking about something else, namely authorizing self-will, setting subjects free. Teubner's theory of social constitutionalization fills the gap between knowing and doing that bourgeois constitutions and their associated theories cannot close. The question of how bourgeois constitutions enable the formation of autonomous social relations by declaring basic rights can now be answered: by declaring basic rights, bourgeois constitutions enable processes of social constitutionalization, and the autonomous self-constitution of social relations only happens through them.

The theory of social constitutionalization does not merely not dispute the thesis that civil society is politically made. Rather, it further strengthens this thesis, since it doubles bourgeois politics. Bourgeois politics exists in a dual form: its generally visible form is the constitutional politics of authorizing subjects with basic rights, and its shadow is a politics of the inner constitutionalization of the social. This is the uniquely modern form of politics as "micro-power" that Foucault called "governmentality": politics that operates in the social and thereby creates it. This leads Foucault to say that "[c]ivil society is . . . a concept of government technology."[34] In Teubner's terms, it is an effect of government through social constitutionalization. This governmental constitutionalization of the social, however, is enabled in turn by the bourgeois politics of basic rights. A more precise definition of the social meaning of a constitution with basic rights is that it is the legal authorization to participate in social constitution. It creates subjects of governmentality. The constitution with basic rights is the "juridical structure (*economie juridique*) of a governmentality pegged to the economic [C.M. – or, more generally, "social"] structure (*economie economique*)."[35]

* * *

The politics of the creation of civil society is a double politics: concerned with basic rights and governmental, a constitutional state and social constitution. Both forms are interconnected, and their duality forms the unity of bourgeois politics. At the same time, however, they are contradictory. This contradiction does not merely pertain to their means (basic rights as norms versus the social power of self-direction), but is mainly to be found in their understanding of when social relations function according to their own laws (or are autonomous). The politics of basic rights designates social relations autonomous if they are formed by the equal authorization of all subjects and reflect them. Governmental politics, in contrast, speaks of the autonomy of the social when functional modes of self-direction have been developed and stabilized. These two politics are not identical. However, their difference entails that both types of bourgeois politics, which are connected to each other, can come into contradiction with one another. This becomes evident in the crisis of bourgeois politics.

Above, we defined the aporia of bourgeois constitutional politics, showing that, in it, the effect turns against its cause, the product against its producers: with the equal legal authorization of subjects, bourgeois politics creates social relations (bourgeois society) that are independent of political normativity. These social relations, as they autonomously develop, lead to authoritarian, quasi-political attempts to impose order (through a monopoly of social power). Conversely, bourgeois politics then validates the equal legal authorization of subjects, which in turn results in the creation of social relations that are independent of politics, and the cycle begins once again through these social relations. The aporia of the politics of the bourgeois constitution is its systematic self-undermining and thus its self-overextension – its self-overextension due to its self-undermining.

If bourgeois politics is more accurately described by the governmental stage of social constitutionalization, it becomes possible to more accurately describe how its aporia becomes evident at the moment of crisis. The contradiction here, in the concept of bourgeois politics, manifests itself as the opposition of its two forms. And, indeed, they are opposed because the danger of the social, due to authoritarian monopolizations of power, recurs within governmental politics. For in obtaining a "relative independence" from "state policies," social constitutionalization succumbs to "a new dependence on . . . specific power and interest constellations" that prevail in respective social relations:

> Not only will the various partial rationalities exert their influence, which is, in principle, unavoidable and which should result in a greater responsiveness to social needs than the constitutional law laid down by state authorities. But there is also the risk that "corrupt" constitutional norms may develop from an excessively close coupling of sub-constitutions to partial interests.[36]

As immanent politicization, social constitutionalization can do what is inconceivable, and hence impossible, for a constitution with basic rights: it can constitute social processes. However, it pays for its immanence – and thereby its effectiveness – in the social by having to face the perpetually looming danger of corruption via social dominance. It is powerless against this. In fact, to respond to this danger, an external politicization, which is asserted *against* "legal autonomy" and which asserts "the civilizing achievements of the nation-state constitutions" in constituting social domains, is in turn necessary.[37] In short, just as the bourgeois constitution, to be effective in the social, requires a different immanent politics of social constitutionalization, so social constitutionalization, in order to not be corrupted by social power relations, requires the external normativity of a constitution with basic rights. The constitution with basic rights and social constitutionalization require each other without referring to each other, indeed, while remaining invisible to each other.

The aporia of bourgeois politics, which exercises its power in such a way that it renders itself impotent, is reflected in the constitution's self-splitting into (legal) normativity and (social) effectiveness or power. We only find one where the other is absent. The aporia of bourgeois politics consists in the fact that its normativity and its power can never be united and therefore *must* – eventually – disintegrate. Crisis is the moment when this happens. In a crisis, one of these two moments is validated at the other's expense. The power of governmentality assumes an independent existence over and against the constitution with basic rights, which first made it possible, and becomes *mere governmentality*: the mere ensuring that social systems function. The normativity of the constitution with basic rights is validated in opposition to the autonomy of social relations, which give the former their meaning, and becomes *pure normativity*: the realm of pure demands for the equal entitlement of subjects. In a crisis, the contradiction of bourgeois politics intensifies into the self-contradiction of both of its moments, which are set against each other in seeming independence. What remains are governmental prose and constitutional lyrics.

Excursus: Proceduralization (Wiethölter)

The most ambitious attempt to abide by the promise of bourgeois constitutions, despite or in light of their aporias, is the model of the proceduralization of law:

> "Proceduralization of law" might be the contemporary manifestation of a bourgeois society which, while it does not (yet?) give up its institutional hopes (synthesis of individual and societal needs, reconciliation of achieved "culture" and realizable "interests"), does start to follow different paths to that institutionalization.[38]

The model of proceduralization thereby proceeds by grasping the perpetual danger of the "corruption" (Teubner) of social relations released from politics. Rudolf Wiethölter describes this as the danger "of simply pursuing the assessment of 'the good' instead of the 'assessment' of goods." In other words, "an interest advances – as general (or at least relatively general) interest – to simultaneously become the arbiter of itself and its rivals."[39] The traditional strategy for dealing with this was to establish an impartial authority over various powerful interests by means of state-sanctioned law. The concept of proceduralization wishes to deal with the "collisions of incompatible bodies of law," which form the bourgeois struggle for law, in a different way.[40] It conceives a model of legal procedure that neither relies on the externality of state-guaranteed impartiality nor signifies surrender to social power relations.

A new understanding of basic rights is required to achieve this. Proceduralization means reconceiving the bourgeois constitution's basic rights as "legal conflict rules."[41] In other words, it means reconceiving them as (meta-)rules for how opposed collisions of legally established interests, which occur in social constitutionalization, can *run their course* [*durchgespielt*] and be struggled through. The concept of proceduralization is therefore supposed to internally link the two levels of bourgeois politics. For it no longer understands basic rights, by authorizing subjects,

240

as merely enabling autonomous processes of social constitutionalization, in normatively releasing them, but understands them as *norming* such processes *from within*. "Norming" here means ensuring the equality of subjects, while "from within" here means to understand subjects – whose equality is at issue – as participants in processes of social constitutionalization (and social struggle). Law becomes the "law of society" through proceduralization.[42]

This remains an ambiguous program, however, even in the concept of proceduralization. Law's reference to the social, its "production of law" (Wiethölter) from the social, is exposed to the same ambiguity that was elaborated by the two interpretations of Teubner's conception of the constitution. This becomes evident in how proceduralized law refers to social relations in which (and no longer to which) its conflict rules are supposed to be applied. Wiethölter imposes an imperative on this reference, namely that it be directed toward the social matter at issue – to keep to the subject matter.[43] What, however, are the social matters and their autonomous relations (and, above all, *how do they exist*), toward which procedural conflict rules are supposed to be directed?

One option is to understand the autonomy of the social in terms of systems theory. In that case, it is given of its own accord (in other words, evolutionarily), and the "internal regulation" (Teubner) of the social, which the concept of proceduralization wishes to norm with egalitarian conflict rules, reaches its limits at the level of social evolution – indeed, it finds its proper task to be securing and preserving the autonomous functioning of the social. Another option is to understand egalitarian proceduralization in such a way that the constitutionalization of the social becomes its true *inner* politicization. This constitutionalization or politicization neither merely enables the autonomous constitution of social relations nor merely secures and reinforces them, but traces them forward or backward. It therefore not only regulates conflicts over which interests are realized in which ways, but decides whether social relations in general should be understood as effects of the legal authorization of subjects. To carry out the constitutionalization of the social in this way means to turn the mode of the being of the social itself (*whether the social is an autonomous system* that ought to be secured and preserved) into a political question.

Habermas objected to Wiethölter's concept of proceduralization, arguing that his "concept of social autonomy ... reduces private and public autonomy to a common denominator too quickly."[44] If we remove the "too quickly," then Habermas is right. For if we pursue the second option for understanding Wiethölter, then he in fact aims at an inner politicization of the social that considers the distinction between private and public autonomy to be not merely given, but up for decision: he aims at politicization as "democratization of social subsystems."[45] Because, however, this decision (and therefore the decision between bourgeois society and state politics) is precisely what the constitutional declaration of the form of subjective rights gives rise to, the form of subjective rights themselves comes into question with the proceduralization of law. If we think it through, the concept of proceduralization *resolves* the aporias of bourgeois politics. For it resolves the mechanism of subjective rights, which is the basis for these aporias.

— 14 —

SLAVE REVOLT: CRITIQUE AND AFFIRMATION

The demand for equality is a revolutionary demand. The bourgeois constitutional revolution realizes this demand by declaring equal rights: in the bourgeois constitution, the declaration of equality coincides with the declaration of rights, the establishment of the form of subjective rights. As we have seen, this results in politics' self-disempowerment over against the sphere of bourgeois society, which is in principle exempt from political governance and in which politics must at the same time perpetually intervene to preserve bourgeois society's autonomous operation.

What, however, is the *reason* for the bourgeois identification of equality and rights? It is not enough to identify the self-destructive consequences of the bourgeois politics of rights. We must explain this politics. We must explain why it emerged, by returning to the "act of its birth" (Marx). This act is that of the bourgeois revolution, which Nietzsche characterized as the beginning of "the last great slave revolt."[1] In this revolt, equality is defined *as* equality of rights, and therefore by demanding equality, this revolt at the same time demands the form of rights. Why is this form demanded here? And how is the form of rights understood at the moment of its revolutionary demand? Is the form of rights demanded in this revolution identical to the type of rights established after the revolution, subjective rights? Or does returning to the bourgeois constitution's revolutionary act of birth reveal a contradiction? Does this act of birth have an antithetical meaning that can intensify and be turned against its result?

Nietzsche's examination of the slave revolt in morality provides an illuminating answer to the question of why the revolution demands rights. This answer has the form of a genealogical analysis: it explains a given structure of normativity – that of equal rights – by examining the structure of a subject who demands and requires this particular normative order. We know that the subject authorized by rights is defined as the subject of self-will.[2] But who is the subject that demands rights, and how does this subject make such a demand? Do the demand for rights and the subject authorized by rights amount to the same thing? Why this is not the case will be shown with, and against, Nietzsche – with Nietzsche's genealogical analysis, and against his own interpretation of this analysis. Genealogical insight into the constitution of the slave in revolt, who demands rights, reveals something in the revolutionary basis of such rights that contradicts their bourgeois form. For it demonstrates that this revolt or revolution gives birth to a "new man."

Before we can understand Nietzsche's insight into the basis of rights, we need to take an intermediate step. We have to show why the customary declaration of rights is false. This customary declaration states that the basis of rights is equality. The demand for equality *is* – nothing but – the demand for rights. This is the identity-thesis of liberalism. Liberalism considers this identification of equality and rights to be self-evident, since it believes that the demand for rights is the only demand that can be justified. Marx opposes this liberal self-evidence with his insight that equality can be conceived *without rights* – indeed, that it must be conceived in this way if it is supposed to be understood as true *political* equality: not as the equality of subjects of self-will, but an equality in which "'All' are to participate 'individually' in 'deliberating and deciding on the general affairs of the state'; that means then: *All* shall not thus participate as all but as 'individuals.'"[3] Marx calls this "true democracy."[4] It defines the individual as a part whose existence is social or communal. Equality without rights, which true democracy realizes, is communism.[5]

Communist equality without rights is therefore a radical alternative to the liberal identification of equality and rights. We must keep this alternative in mind to deprive the liberal identity-thesis of its self-evidence, and thus to grasp why the step *from* equality *to* rights raises a question and why this question requires a genealogical examination of the revolutionary subject, the slave or servant in revolt, for its answer. Communism opposes the idea of equality without rights to the liberal identification of equality and rights, thereby making it possible to analyze revolution as slave revolt.

Without Rights: True Democracy

The true democracy of communism achieves equality without rights. At the same time, it also thereby overcomes the bourgeois [*bürgerliche*] separation of the political state and civil [*bürgerlicher*] society. "The French have recently interpreted this as meaning that in true democracy the *political state is annihilated.*"[6] For true democracy dissolves "the accommodation between the political state and what falls outside such a state," which was the root of the bourgeois constitution's aporias. In achieving equality without rights, true democracy realizes "[t]he striving of *civil society* to turn itself into *political* society, or to turn *political* society into *actual* society."[7] Both belong together. To achieve equality without rights means to redefine the relation of society and politics. This happens when society is conceived *as practice* and politics is conceived as the *self-government of practice.*

Practices are basic units of the social: they are contexts for action whose unity is provided by the good "at which human beings characteristically aim" in doing them.[8] For this reason, all particular elements of practices realize the same good that is common to them. This occurs through the mediation of rules that constitute respective practices. Rules constitutive of practice determine what something (and someone) is in such a practice. They define things, actions, persons, and so forth, that are present in a practice – that practice's respective ontology. The totality of constitutive rules specifies a practice as the realization of some respective, intrinsic good. Education is therefore a practice because (in other words, if and *insofar as*) it determines persons or roles, actions and inactions, intentions and wishes, and so forth, in such a way that they realize the same good together, a good that constitutes the respective practice of education in a given society. On the traditional understanding, this is habituation to virtue. On the modern understanding, this is education for freedom. The economy is likewise a practice because (which, again, means if and *insofar as*) it arranges the production and circulation of commodities (and thereby also the corresponding modes of willing, judging, calculating, and thinking) in such a way that the good is realized in it. This is traditionally defined as the common good. We can therefore already see that not every social context for action forms a practice. Social contexts can cease to be formally defined as practice and can thereby lose the organizing power of an intrinsic good. Hegel refers to this state of affairs in civil society as a "loss of ethical life" (Hegel) – or the loss of "unity," namely the form of unity specific to practice, which the young Marx calls "alienation."[9] Practice is therefore simultaneously a social-ontological category and a social-critical category. Social practices always already exist. A society without such practices cannot exist, since capacities and thus subjects capable of judgment and action can only be developed in practices, in orientation to their good. Societies, however, can constitute increasingly larger domains that lack the form of practices, but must instead be described as "social systems" – as "a system of complete interdependence," as a "system of ethical life, split into its extremes and lost."[10]

Social practices are normatively constituted by intrinsic goods and by the constitutive rules through which these goods are expressed. Both goods and rules only exist in being performed. They are present when they are performed. The existence of intrinsic goods and constitutive rules, and thus of social practice, is something that is performed, and the logic of its performance is the realization of the general in the particular. Every particular realization of something general, however, is the resumption or repetition of an – earlier – particular realization of something general. This is the *historical life* of practice. In other words, a social practice only exists, only lives, by further determining itself, namely by rendering its general form – intrinsic goods through constitutive rules – particular in ever-new ways. Practice is performed by being determined. For this reason, anyone who participates in a practice, anyone whose willing and doing are part of a practice that is constituted by its rules and is a realization of its good, at the same time participates in a process by further determining the practice in question. *Every* participant in practice and *only* participants in practice are determiners of practice. The goods and rules of a practice "demand judgment and the exercise of the virtues requires therefore a capacity to judge and to do the right thing in the right place at the right time in the right way. The exercise of such judgment is not a routinizable application of rules."[11]

The *self*-determination [Selbst*bestimmung*] of a practice is to be distinguished from how it is determined [*Sichbestimmen*] in its performance. The self-determination of a practice is its being determined in a different form, namely by performing its determination knowingly and voluntarily. The self-determination of practice is its determination in a self-aware manner. In other words, it is the *politics* of practice: practice is political to the extent that it is self-determinative, since politics means self-government, and government's basic feature is thought, the conscious articulation and guidance of the performance of practice. Politics *is* social practice, insofar as it "thinks and knows itself and implements what it knows in so far as it knows it."[12]

The step from being determined to self-determination – from partici-pation to government is the – inner – politicization of practice. The form of practice is thereby changed and generates a new category of subjectiv-ity. Each participant who is constituted by the rules of a practice is also a participant in the determination of that practice. Each participant in a practice is a subject who determines practice. This is what it means to be a practical or social subject. Participants in a practice cannot be merely passive and fail to use their own judgment in reproducing it without thereby dissolving it as a practice – perverting its intrinsic good into a merely external goal and turning its constitutive rules into rules that merely govern externally.

In contrast, the political self-determination of practice, through which it governs itself, creates a new category of subjectivity. This subjectivity is defined by the capacity to not merely participate, but also to think participation – to articulate and shape it. "To be a conscious part of something means consciously to acquire a part of it, to take a conscious interest in it. Without this consciousness the member of the state would be an *animal*."[13] Political practice is different from social practice, but this is a difference of social practice in social practice. It is internal to social practice, since what constitutes a social practice can only be articu-lated and decided within a practice – what its goods are and how its rules express them. At the same time, self-government, as the thinking of social practice, is a free act or the act of freedom. It is not determined by that to which it refers. For this reason, the political self-government of the social is able to do what was impossible for bourgeois politics to do with the form of subjective rights: it can change social practice from within.

The communist definition of the political is that it is freedom in the social over against the social. As a result, the basic formal definition of communist equality is equality without rights.

Marx understands traditional, pre-bourgeois forms of politics as the realization of self-government *in the social* that thereby entails the loss of self-government's *freedom*. Such forms of politics constitute "the democ-racy of unfreedom."[14] They therefore repeat and reinforce, in political practice, precisely the inequalities that already define social practice. In particular, the distribution of political subjectivity in government here reproduces the unequal distribution of social subjectivity in practice. "Democracy of unfreedom" thus simultaneously means a democracy of inequality. In opposition to this, the bourgeois constitutional state establishes "universal reason" – government as the free thinking of the social – "over against the other spheres, as ulterior to them."[15] Through this freedom over against the social, the bourgeois state is able to think

247

equality, but it can only realize it "in the heaven of its generality over against the *earthly existence* of its actuality."[16] To put this more precisely, the bourgeois state is only able to realize equality in an abstract form (that is, the form of subjective rights), as the legalization of natural acts by externally limiting them. The bourgeois constitution realizes equality by not realizing it: it realizes the equal validity of subjects, but does not *convert* this into an egalitarian form.

The true democracy of communism, in contrast, is the inner politicization of the social: true democracy is the self-government of social practices. It realizes equality *in* the social. And it establishes equality *on the basis of* the social. Both amount to the same thing: they signify defining equality – which is established by true democracy – as equality of social participation. The definition of equality as equality of social participation is the communist response to the question of both equality's *basis* and its *content*, and therefore also its form.

The politics of the bourgeois constitution defines the basis of equality as external to the social: in contrast to our always unequal social appearance (as rich or poor, capable or incapable, clever or stupid, and so forth), we are equal in a deeper or higher sense, possessing a pre- or supra-social quality – as creators, rational beings, human beings, or the like. Communism, in contrast, bases equality on the fact that we are all equally social participants. *How* we participate in social practices makes us unequal; *that* we do it (more precisely: that this activity is essential to our being) makes us equal. The basis of equality is social being.

This also holds for equality's content. The politics of the bourgeois constitution defines equality as equality of rights. Rights (in the modern sense) legalize the capacity for subjective self-will, which is thereby positivized and effectively removed from normative regulation. Rights therefore create bourgeois society (or they transform social practice into bourgeois society). In the form of subjective rights, equality's content is self-will. Communist equality, in contrast, is equality of social participation. It is equality of participation in practice or equality of the "part" (Marx). Equality can *only* exist in participation in a practice, and therefore in orientation to a good intrinsic to that practice, not in the subject's self-will.

True democracy defines politics as the self-government of social practice: it realizes freedom, which politics defines, in the social. As a result, politics is here the politicization of the social. It revolutionizes the social – not, however, by directing an external demand at it, but by turning it against itself. It realizes equality by confronting an unequal social situation with itself, with its own concept. It does this by showing that each person, in a completely different way, *is* nevertheless equally a social participant. The political power that likewise belongs to each person in equal measure is rooted in this social being. The argument for true democracy is that everyone can co-govern equally because all participate in social practice. "[T]heir social *being* is already *their real participation*" in political self-government.[17] True democracy therefore infers the equality of political power from the equality of social being. And by realizing the equality of political participation, it transforms social practice in turn. The democratic self-government of social practice arranges relations within it so that they correspond to the fact that each person is equally a social participant. The political self-government of social practice yields an egalitarian form through the equality *of its participants.*

There is no conceptual room here for rights – in the modern sense, as equal claims to private spheres of and capacities for self-will. Equality of social relations is nothing but the political realization of the social being of individuals. The basis and content of equality is "social being" (Marx). Politics lies between the two.[18] It is movement that bases its power of political (co-)government on each individual's equal social existence and that realizes equality of the social in the social through each individual's political self-government.

The Right to Passivity

Marx has clarified what the bourgeois revolution amounts to from the perspective of "true democracy" – it is simply a failed revolution or, more precisely, a revolution in the mode of its self-caused, indeed, paradoxically, its self-willed failure. For according to Marx, the "political emancipation" pursued by the bourgeois revolution is at the same time society's emancipation *from* the political, namely politics that has deprived itself of power. The communist counter-concept of "true democracy" is supposed to show that this self-deprivation of political power is *unnecessary*, since it is not a consequence of the idea of equality, which is what liberalism wishes to base it on in defining equality as an equal claim to subjective rights. If, however, equality without rights exists (or if such equality is possible), then we have *another option* besides the bourgeois deprivation of political power vis-à-vis a civil society that has thereby been unleashed.

At the same time, however, Marx's dismantling of the normative foundation for the bourgeois constitutional revolution – the idea of equality – leaves completely unclear how politics' self-deprivation of its power can be *explained*. Marx believes that the "puzzle" of this self-deprivation of power is "easily solved."[19] He thought that it could be found in bourgeois society, in the capitalist economy created by the bourgeois revolution. The consequence is supposed to be the cause. This is teleological – or circular: it is an explanation that proceeds from the end or from outside. We are seeking an explanation from within, namely an explanation proceeding *from* the act of revolution.

This is the systematic locus where Nietzsche's genealogical analysis of the slave revolt is relevant for the critique of rights. Along with Marx, Nietzsche is the other great critic of bourgeois [*bürgerlichen*] society. And, like Marx, Nietzsche too describes the bourgeois revolution as a puzzling event in which the self-deprivation of power is actively pursued. In contrast to Marx, however, Nietzsche explains this self-deprivation of power in the form of a genealogical analysis. Genealogical analyses are analyses of forms of subjectivity. (Critical theory links Marx to Nietzsche because the latter teaches us to examine the forms of subjectivity through which social orders are reproduced.) One such analysis is that of the subject of bourgeois revolution, namely analysis of the slave or servant in revolt as a form of subjectivity. The particular relevance of Nietzsche's analysis for the critique of rights is that it describes this type of subject as the slave in revolt, indeed thereby defining it as a subject *who wants rights*, who demands the form of rights and thereby creates this form. This is the *only* feature of Nietzsche's analysis of slave revolt, his analysis of slave revolt as a revolution of rights, which is significant here, although it is frequently overlooked. At the same time, he thereby traces a path that leads to a different interpretation of the slave revolt, an anti-liberal or anti-bourgeois one, and thus to the modern form of rights.

Nietzsche rarely uses the term "right" [*Recht*] in the subjective sense of the term – as the right *of someone* (to something).[20] It is all the more significant that he uses the term in the first essay of *On the Genealogy of Morals* in two opposed senses: he initially uses it to designate the central feature of master morality and then proceeds to use it to designate slave morality. Both master and slave morality have a conception of right, but they define it in opposed ways. The struggle between master and servant is a struggle for law [*Recht*]. The slave revolt is a revolution (in the conception) of rights.

Masters understand their right [*Recht*] as the right to create values:

the judgment "good" did *not* originate with those to whom "goodness" was shown! Rather it was "the good" themselves, that is to say, the noble, powerful, high-stationed and high-minded, who felt and established themselves and their actions as good, that is, of the first rank, in contradistinction to all the low, low-minded, common and plebeian. It was out of this *pathos of distance* that they first seized the right to create values and to coin names for values.[21]

The master's right is the right to create values: the right to judge what is good and bad (for themselves); what good and bad are supposed *to mean* for themselves, and, by means of this act of definition itself, to lead themselves. It is the right to judge for oneself concerning the good. It is their right to govern on the basis of their judgment concerning the good itself. Masters have this right by taking it for themselves. And they take this right for themselves by exercising it. Masters are allowed to create values because they are able to create values. Their ability, their power, gives rise to their right: the power of masters to create values is simultaneously their right to create values. The master's power is both the content and basis of his right. The right of masters is simply an expression of their power: anyone with the ability to define something as her good, and thereby to lead herself, also has the right to do so.

The slave in revolt opposes *her* right to that of the master. Indeed, her revolt is simply the assertion of a new right. Against the master's right to create values and to judge for himself concerning what is good or bad, the slave proclaims a completely different right of holding another responsible for what he does, namely "the right to make the bird of prey *accountable* for being a bird of prey."[22] This is characterized by Nietzsche as the right of lambs, the weak or slaves, to hold the master accountable for what he does in performing his self-created values, to regard this as his free self-chosen activity for which he must take responsibility and which he must justify, and which therefore can even lead to condemning him as "evil." The initial, surprising observation about the slave revolt is that the slave, in revolting, does not claim to become the master herself. The slave does not claim to *also* create values *as* the master does and to judge what is good for the latter. Rather, the slave devises a completely new right. In revolting, the slave asserts the right of the weak, allowance to obligate the strong to take responsibility for what they do to the weak; the duty of the strong to show consideration for the weak while willing and acting.

The talk of the master's "right" to exercise his power of judgment has the same merely negative meaning that, according to Spinoza, defines right as "Nature's . . . established order": no one else has the right to impede the master, because there is no normative relation, no relation of right and duty, between the master and anyone else.[23] In contrast, the new right asserted by the slave in revolt is a right *in relation* to – *over and against* – another. Right is thereby understood as "subjective" and "relative,"[24] and thus as intersubjective and relational. At the same time, however, this relation takes on a specific form. Nietzsche describes it as the "inversion of the value-positing eye": "While every noble morality develops from a triumphant affirmation of itself, slave morality from the outset says No to what is 'outside', what is 'different', what is 'not itself.'"[25] The new right is a right *against the other*, since it is one person's right to be taken into consideration by another, even against the other person's own wishes and contrary to her goals. It *demands* from the other that "each one also ought to take into consideration the interest of the other,"[26] or limiting one's own willing and doing by considering another's willing and doing. It demands that the other limit herself. The slave revolt defines *each person's right to be considered by the other insofar as the other limits herself* as a basic right.

The establishment of this new right is an act of authorization: by revolting, slaves win power over others, initially masters. They obtain the normative "authority" to present another person with their own situation, which this other person has caused, as a "*reason* for acting."[27] This new normative power provided by the insurrectionary slave's declaration of a right nevertheless comes at a cost, namely the fact that they still define themselves as slaves (*in their being*, in what they are and how they are), as the weak and powerless who suffer from a strong and powerful person's actions and therefore must demand their consideration. "[T]he slave who has not stopped being a slave prevails over the master who has stopped being one."[28] Instead of asserting herself as strong and powerful, as someone who is able to guide herself to her good through her own judgment, the slave in revolt, on the contrary, establishes a right that presupposes a position of weakness and thereby eternalizes it. Nietzsche's central thesis on the new right asserted by the slave revolt is therefore that the subject of this right *is* (and hence remains) a slave. By using and exercising such a right, this subject *defines* itself as a servant: as someone who *needs* consideration. The new power won by slaves through their revolt only perpetuates their powerlessness; it *fixes* this powerlessness in place. The slave's being, her weakness, is not transformed but universalized through each person's right to consideration.

* * *

This thesis requires closer analysis. It includes an insight into the basis for the modern form of rights, which Nietzsche obscured more than elucidated, concealing it beneath a number of similar motifs – such as the critique of religion and the psychology of ressentiment. This insight indicates that the insurrectionary slave's demand for a right to consideration is conceived from the perspective of "suffering,"[29] and that it therefore implies the right to *be* a sufferer. The right to consideration is the right of the sufferer: a right for and by the sufferer. The sufferer is object and subject of the right to consideration.

We only grasp the significance of this thesis if we do understand Nietzsche to be using the concept of suffering not in a psychological or moral sense at all, but in terms of action theory. Aristotle defines suffering as being affected (*paschein, passio*) in contradistinction to action (*poiein, actio*):[30] to be a sufferer means to be affected by an action – for instance, by being moved away or held close, increased or decreased, created or transformed or dismantled. Acting and suffering thus reciprocally refer to each other. Acting and suffering reciprocally make each other possible: the effect of one party's action on another is only possible where the latter can take it in. The reciprocal reference of acting and suffering is an interaction between two "potentialities": potentiality "is partly in the patient (for it is because it contains a certain principle, and because even the latter is a kind of principle, that the patient is acted upon; i.e., one thing is acted upon by another) . . . and partly in the agent; e.g. heat and the art of building: the former in that which produces heat and the latter in that which builds."[31] Whatever suffers is not itself active. Its capacity is the passive capacity of taking in another's activity.

To be a sufferer means to be passive. It thereby stands opposed to activity as agency. At the same time, however (and this is a crucial point regarding Aristotle's model of capacity), the passivity of suffering and the activity of agency have a relation of correspondence. They form two correlated moments of *one* relation. Kant emphasized this when he characterized the "reciprocity between agent and patient" as "community" [*Gemeinschaft*].[32] The person who acts and the person who suffers an action – passively receiving it, taking it in – form a community that Kant calls "dynamical":

> The word "community" is ambiguous in our language, and can mean either communio or commercium. We use it here in the latter sense, as a dynamical community. . . . Through this commerce the appearances, insofar as they stand outside one another and yet in connection, constitute a composite.[33]

The sufferer and the agent form a community, because they are what they respectively are – taking in effects or creating effects – only in relation to the other. At the same time, however, this community is only a "composite" – *commercium*, not *communio* – because its elements "stand outside one another": they stand in a relation of "reciprocal causality" (Kant).

We can now articulate what it means when the slave in revolt demands consideration for the position of the "sufferer" and does not nullify this position by demanding consideration, but perpetuates it. To be a sufferer means to be exposed to the effects of another's action. And, according to Kant, this means standing with another in the external community of the *commercium*. The demand for consideration is a demand that the other limit her activity, recognizing its effects; consideration means self-limitation. The demand for consideration, however, is therefore not directed against the *only* type of community (of external "reciprocity") *in which* acting – producing effects[34] – and suffering – taking effects in – *exist*. Rather, the demand for consideration presupposes this community as *commercium*, and thereby presupposes the existence of agents and sufferers: the ontological presupposition of the demand for consideration, as a right won in revolt, is *commercium* between agent and sufferer.

Excursus: Causal and Legal Relation (Kant)

In his doctrine of right, Kant again returns to this model of community, which he developed in the *Critique of Pure Reason* into a definition of the causal interaction between acting and suffering, and which defines the social ontology of bourgeois law. We therefore only have subjective rights against each other where we stand together in the community of *commercium*. For Kant, to have a right means to be able to obligate another to show consideration for my choice. For Kant, a right is a subjective right. This conception of right, however, can only be concerned "with the external and indeed practical relation of one person to another, insofar as their actions, as facts, can have (direct or indirect) influence on each other."[35] This means that we must view the legal relation "by analogy with presenting the possibility of bodies moving freely under the law of the *equality of action and reaction*."[36] Legal claims by one party to another party's consideration (and thereby to the latter's self-limitation) can only exist where the effect of one (the agent) on the other (the sufferer) remains external. If they are able to internally affect one another, because they exist in the community of *communio*, there is also no longer a relation of subjective rights between them.

The demand to be shown consideration says no to suffering. It does not say no, however, to *being* a sufferer. The sufferer's position is one

254

of passivity. This position does not wish to give up the demand for consideration, but acquiesces to it, indeed presupposes it and thereby reinforces it. It accepts passivity. The demand for consideration therefore also affirms the only relation in which acting and suffering from action is possible: it affirms the *form* of the social relation as *commercium*. The no to suffering is a yes to the social form in which suffering and acting exist merely "as facts" that "can have (direct or indirect) influence on each other" (Kant). In other words, in the slave revolt's assertion of each person's right to have consideration shown for the suffering they have experienced at the hand of agents, we simultaneously find an assertion of the right to be a mere sufferer in relation to another within the community of *commercium*, namely the right to passivity. The basis of the right to consideration – the right at the basis of all rights – is the right to passivity.

This thesis forms the conclusion for Nietzsche's insight that existing conditions are reinforced by the slave revolt – in every act of saying no to a master. In revolting, the slave reinforces her being. She does not want to change what she is. She does not want to become anyone else. Nietzsche views the slave, who expresses a demand for consideration and does not question it, as essentially a sufferer. This stands in contrast to being or becoming an agent. On Nietzsche's view, the slave affirms her position as sufferer and does not want to become someone whose actions cause others to suffer. Since, however (as Aristotle and Kant show), the positions of agent and sufferer stand in one and the same social relation, are elements of the same form, the affirmation of the sufferer's position is simultaneously the affirmation of this form. The significance of affirming this form is revealed by the other form that is thereby dismissed.

Kant calls this other social form community as *communio*. In this community, there are no agents and sufferers, since here there is no relation of mere interaction – in which actions "as facts, can have (direct or indirect) influence on each other." As a result, *communio* eliminates the static positions of agent *and* sufferer who "stand outside one another" (Kant). *Communio* is a social practice that forms the basis for the communist conception of true democracy. Its unity has a form that is different from the *commercium*'s composite form: the *communio*'s unity is endowed by its inherent good. Its parts do not "stand outside one another" and operate on each other, but are internally connected: they are realizations of the same good, constituted by the same rules. *Communio* is a community that exists not through the interaction of its elements, but through the participation of all in the same good, as equals.

This is the alternative dismissed by the slave in revolt when she

255

demands the right to be shown consideration. The demand for consideration is directed against the agent: it demands her self-limitation. This is the sufferer's claim to a right vis-à-vis the agent. However, this demand for consideration – as has been shown – always already presupposes another demand: the insurrectionary slave's demand for the right to be shown consideration is simultaneously a demand for the right to stand in a relation of non-participation to another, the agent, or to be a sufferer in relation to another. The basic right to passivity (the right at the basis of the right to consideration) is nothing but the right to not be a participant, to be a non-participant.[37] If, however, only social participants can be political (because politics is the self-government of the social), then the non-participant's right to passivity is simultaneously a right without politics: a non-political right, indeed a right *against* politics.

The New Man

Nietzsche's conception of the slave revolt depicts a revolution that creates the modern form of rights, a revolution that raises the demand for equality *as* a demand for equal rights – for rights to the pre-legal or natural. This interpretation of revolutionary equality stands in contrast to communist equality, since communism wants to create equality in the social through its political self-governance. It understands equality as equality of participation in the same practice, in the same good. Communism makes the "effort to unite people around a positive idea of the Good; even more than this, it identifies Man with projects of this kind."[38] The slave revolt described by Nietzsche and the communist revolution of equality are therefore opposed to each other.

(i)   The communist revolution demands that everyone have equal power to politically govern. The slave revolt, in contrast, demands everyone's equal right to consideration.

(ii) The communist revolution wants equal participation in social practice – community as *communio*. The slave revolt, in contrast, reproduces the interaction of acting and suffering – community as *commercium*.

The crucial feature in the revolution of rights emerges in this opposition to the communist revolution: it does not want to give each person equal power to participate in social practice and its political self-governance. It wants to give each person the equal right to consideration *regardless* of a practice, not as a part of it. In other words, it does not view each person as someone who can participate, who has the capacity or power to participate. The bourgeois revolution wants to show consideration for non-participation, for passivity, but not to overcome it. It affirms passivity.

A glance at the communist alternative reveals that the revolution of rights cannot be defined by the demand for equality. Equality does not *mean* rights. The (modern) *form* of rights is not based on equality. It is based on an unwillingness to *compensate* the sufferer's position by providing her with the equal power to participate. It is based on the demand to be shown consideration *as* sufferer, and therefore based on the demand to be able *to be* a sufferer, to be passive. The modern form of rights is based on the active affirmation of passivity: its basis is a paradox.[39] How can this paradox be resolved?

The solution seems simple. It is the view that the slave in revolt wants to be passive because she *cannot* be active or, in other words, because she lacks the power or strength to be active. The willing of passivity is an expression of inability. Nietzsche does not view the slave revolt to be directed against the sufferer's position, because this would mean becoming, *like* masters, "rounded men replete with energy and therefore *necessarily* active."[40] Because the slave is too weak for this, however, she forgoes it, and is thereby content to remain what she is ("Weakness is being lied into something *meritorious,* no doubt of it,"[41] as Nietzsche remarks).

By establishing that this unwillingness is rooted in inability, Nietzsche reconstructs the very same argument for the equality of rights that was raised by the bourgeois revolution from its inception, and which was thereby directed against its communist radicalization into "true democracy" (which Marx observed in the "French ... recently").[42] This bourgeois argument against the communist version of revolution was formulated with exemplary clarity by Benjamin Constant. According to Constant, the radicals of the French Revolution have forgotten what (and, above all, *how*) we actually will:

The aim of the ancients was the sharing of social power among the citizens of the same fatherland: this is what they called liberty. The aim of the moderns is the enjoyment of security in private pleasures; and they call liberties the guarantees accorded by institutions to these pleasures.[43]

The French radicals are in agreement with the ancients here. They conceive the human being politically and therefore socially, as a participant. In other words, they define human existence as participation. To participate means to actualize capabilities. The participant is thus someone who is capable, the embodiment of social and political power. Constant contrasts this understanding with the striving of moderns for "pleasures," since pleasure is private. In pleasure, the human being is not a part of practice. Someone feeling pleasure does not strive for social goods. Her feeling of pleasure is not participation: it is not an achievement that has the form of social participation, and this is why it also cannot be something that can be politically self-governed. Private pleasure is the bourgeois argument against true democracy: such pleasure presents an insurmountable limit to its idea of political self-governance. Private pleasure cannot be politically governed (in other words, it can only be governed externally, "by the state"),[44] because it does not have the form of participation in social practice and because self-government is only possible in (and from) a social practice. This is why the equality of pleasure, too, cannot be realized by equal participation in political self-government. Equality in pleasure must be secured by "guarantees" (Constant).

The bourgeois argument against the communist radicalization of the revolution, as true democracy, is that private pleasure is not *and can never become* social participation. The bourgeois argument against communism takes the form of pointing out a fact. It points out the fact that the human being is "thus-and-thus":[45] the fact that the human being *exists in such a way* that she cannot – entirely – become a participant and thus a sufferer (or an enjoyer of pleasure, which structurally amounts to the same thing). It points out the fact that the human being must remain exposed to another's action and therefore must be shown consideration. Constant still thinks of this as a historical fact (or a fact in the history of philosophy): he views it as a fact about modern human beings. Whether it is historical or not, however, the bourgeois argument against communism – against the idea that the sufferer's *existence* can be superseded if she *receives* her "share" – is an anthropological claim. This anthropological claim is structured in the way Nietzsche indicated: it asserts an essential non-ability (the modern human's unwillingness is not based on her own wish to rule, as with the ancients). Human beings *are* also enjoyers of pleasure or sufferers, and are therefore unable to (completely) transform themselves into active, self-governing participants.

The basic bourgeois argument is that the communist demand for an equality without rights is a demand that overburdens the human being. The radical attempt to turn the individual into a participant in a self-governing practice rests on a category mistake. It is an "overtribunalizing" that mistakes "that which, in humankind itself, is *nature*" and "thus also marks out the human qualities in relation to which questions

258

of legitimation are meaningless."[46] Because the human being, in private pleasures, does not follow her own judgment, but only expresses what she is, she is therefore also unable to justify her private pleasures. They *cannot* become the object of political self-governance. Only actions that have the form of social participation are able to do this. This is why the bourgeois revolution is concerned with proclaiming fundamental and human rights "which are meant to protect (to the extent that this can be done by means of law) freedom from the demand that persons should justify their existence and their being the way they are."[47] Bourgeois rights are "fundamental rights, which ward off the legitimation-compulsion."[48] Bourgeois rights are thus rights against participation in political self-governance (in which "the legitimation-compulsion" prevails: here one cannot experience and say whatever one believes, since in this case we are concerned not with "beliefs" but with judgments, and with thinking, in particular). Bourgeois rights are rights against politics.

On this thesis, the bourgeois revolution's demand for rights to consideration of the natural is a demand for rights against participation in the political. The fact that the bourgeois revolution – additionally – *also* demands participation in political self-governance changes nothing in this regard. For in the first place, political self-governance is thereby partialized or halved. It is accompanied by the emergence of the sphere of the "*human being*" who is by nature "the *citizen* [*Bürger*] (in the sense of *bourgeois*)": the sphere of civil [*bürgerlichen*] society.[49] Second, political self-governance is thereby simultaneously defined as self-limitation and therefore as the self-deprivation of the political – in the name of the human being's apolitical nature. And third (as well as fundamentally), political self-government is here itself necessarily an additional content of subjective rights and thereby privatized. It is merely one more option for the self-will.

Excursus: The Fact of Pluralism (Lefort and Gauchet, Rawls)

The bourgeois revolution does not merely demand equal power to participate, but (in addition and in contrast) also demands each person's right to consideration as a non-participant. This demand is central to liberalism. The liberal justification for this demand examined to this point is a claim about the definition of the human being's nature: the human being is by nature – as an enjoyer of pleasure – a non-participant. However, this seems to be only one way, and not the most important, in which liberalism justifies the demand for consideration.

259

Another way to justify this demand is to do so not from the human being's natural existence, but from her individual existence. This form of justification proposes that the human being requires the right to consideration, not because she is a non-participant, but because each human being – at least potentially – participates in a completely different way than others, and this is because each human being is different, is distinctive as a social participant. The individuality of each individual is manifested in (the possibility of) her difference from others; individuality entails plurality. Every attempt to realize the equality of all must proceed on this basis, according to the liberal credo. The claim that equality must be the form of individual difference determines the form in which alone this can occur. This, in turn, according to the liberal conclusion, requires that equality be realized as equality of rights, namely as each individual's equal right to be considered.

This inference from individuality to consideration is overhasty, however. For the political self-government of the social that is realized by true democracy also involves each individual participating distinctively and as an individual. Indeed, Marx (in his critique of Hegel's critique of democracy) says that "*All* shall not thus participate as all but as 'individuals'" in political self-government.[50] The liberal critique of communism has understood this to mean the assertion of an always already given "imaginary" identity of each with all, of the particular and the general. According to Claude Lefort and Marcel Gauchet, this imaginary identity marks the "moment when power is convinced to *be* what it is supposed to represent [C.M. – and, therefore, is supposed to be universal]." It is thereby simply "reduced to the status of the particular."[51] However, Marx's basic definition of political judgment – that "individuals as All" exercise political judgment – cannot be understood this way. It defines not a universal condition (or being-universal), but a process that universalizes the particular. In true democracy, political participation therefore begins with the individual (with her particular experiences, needs, deliberations) who *makes* herself a part of the universal, in the process of political self-government. Communist democracy does not obliterate individuality. It realizes individuality *in* political participation. The liberal demand – that individuality requires consideration and thus subjective rights – must therefore be understood as directed against the communist thesis – that individuality is realized in the power of participation. The argument for this position (without which liberalism cannot justify its conclusion at all) is that the political transformation of the particular into the universal must necessarily remain incomplete. The universal is not universal. Rather, it is particular, an always respectively particular universal. It thus always stands in a relation of exclusion toward another particular, since the field of the particular is the field of many different determinations that cannot all be valid at the same time. John Rawls suggests this when he speaks of the "'fact of oppression'" that holds true for any political order which is based on a "comprehensive philosophical and moral doctrine" (and which is thereby something particular).[52] Lefort and Gauchet grasp it more fundamentally and define it as the unavoidable reinscription of "conflict," and therefore of plurality, of the particular, *in* the political: in the moment of decision, and therefore in the moment in which the political universal takes on a specific content, this universal loses its "autonomy" vis-à-vis the field of the diverse particular and its conflicts, and turns into its "continuation."[53] In the moment of decision, the political universal, as something specific, is a particular universal, and as a result, like anything particular, comes into conflict with another particular: it overpowers or oppresses a particular or individual. In the decision, it becomes manifest that the political universal remains in power or follows a hegemonic logic.

The liberal objection is directed against the communist idea of realizing individuality in political participation. The more extreme version of this objection, by Lefort and Gauchet, has two implications: the fact that the political universal is always something specific and therefore something particular, and the fact that the political universal – at certain moments and on certain points – is thereby reinscribed into the field of the particular and its conflicts, from which it attempts to extricate itself. The fundamental asymmetry that (even on Lefort and Gauchet's interpretation) exists between one particular and another, however, is not resolved in this way: the political, in each case particular, and the individual, in each case particular, are logically different. Their asymmetry has the following form: the political is a process of universalization in which all individuals have the power of participation, but through which some – the "majority" (Lenin)[54] – obtain a hegemonic position. This process is only political as long as it is a process of universalization: hegemonic particularity is that particularity which triumphed in political universalization. The obtainment of universality, however, is nothing but a process of reason. Particular individuality, overwhelmed by each particular political decision, can only be non-rational individuality: individuality *against* political reason.

This stands in contrast to how Rawls understands the irreducible variety of the particular or of individualities, which he views as the foundation of the right to consideration. Rawls speaks here of "the fact of reasonable pluralism," which he distinguishes from "the fact of pluralism as such."⁵⁵ Pluralism "as such" is "a variety of doctrines and views" that gives rise to "peoples' various interests and their tendency to focus on narrow points of view." He distinguishes this from "a diversity of reasonable comprehensive doctrines" that are due political consideration:

> They are not simply the upshot of self- and class interests, or of peoples' understandable tendency to view the political world from a limited standpoint. Instead, they are in part the work of free practical reason within the framework of free institutions.⁵⁶

According to Rawls, in addition to ordinary beliefs, there is thus an irreducible variety of equally rational belief or an *inner*-rational plurality, which results from "the work of free practical reason." This can only hold, however, in the realm of the ethical, in which individuals form their beliefs about the good independently of and without regard for each other. Reason and pluralism are mutually exclusive *in* the political process, since the only political process is one in which "individuals" judge "*as* all." It is therefore a process in which they overcome the merely particular or individual and judge in the name of the universal. For this reason, one cannot simultaneously judge politically *and* assert the divergent rationality of others. The divergence of others necessarily manifests itself politically as the *merely* particular. Pluralism is always apolitical, a pluralism of mere opinions and therefore irrational.⁵⁷ The political process, in contrast, is a rational process of universality, which is why it is not plural.

If liberalism claims that the political universal, due to its hegemonic logic, is necessarily opposed to the individual particular; and if, in making this assessment, liberalism justifies the demand that divergent and marginalized individuality has a right to consideration – then this cannot be established, as Rawls claims, on the basis of the rationality of individual diversity. As long as Rawls wishes to conceive the individual as rational, he has always already eliminated the difference that alone can justify the right to consideration. Instead, the individual must be conceived as that which is non-rational, extra-social or natural; "the (individual!) human being is always part of the [social] system's environment."⁵⁸ The divergence of the particular from the political universal is irrational, and the divergent individual's right to consideration from the hegemonic universal *can only be the right to unreason*: it can only "[be] the 'right' *not* to be rational."⁵⁹

There are thus not two forms of liberalism, namely a justification of the right to consideration on the basis of the human being's apolitical and therefore irrational nature, and a second justification on the basis of her individuality and particularity. The second justification is only another version of the first: only the individual's difference *from* political reason can rebut the communist thesis that individuality is realized by participation in the political.

The crucial question is therefore something else entirely. It does not apply to the source of the difference (this question is answered: it is the difference of the non-rational as merely natural), but questions its structure and its locus. Is liberalism right that this difference can only be conceived as a separate sphere, the sphere of civil society constituted by subjective rights? Or does the difference of the natural *from* politics have to be conceived as a difference *in* politics?

The slave revolt that establishes equality of consideration instead of equality of participation comprises a paradox: the active willing of passivity. The bourgeois revolution resolves this paradox into human nature. The insurrectionary slave also demands consideration, instead of simply demanding involvement, because it is human nature to be a citizen, as bourgeois, who pursues personal pleasure, without being able to govern it (and therefore herself). The bourgeois revolution establishes the right to consideration with resigned acceptance of the human being's weaknesses. Its response to the communist idea of true democracy is a pessimistic anthropology.

There is a second way to understand the paradox at the basis of the modern form of rights, however, which is completely different from the first. This different conception does not resolve the paradox, but intensifies it. The bourgeois understanding describes the slave revolt from the perspective of its ending, namely a condition in which the right to private pleasure is legally secured. It seems natural to this understanding to will the securing of such a right. This is in contrast to how the revolt appears initially, when it is first carried out. For Nietzsche, the world-historical significance of the Jews lies in the fact that they dare to revolt, which is why he calls them a people "of the first rank."[60] While fifth-rate people such as "the Chinese or the Germans" have settled comfortably into their weaknesses and rights, the Jews are *subjects* of revolt. In their case, the paradox of the slave revolt is intensified into irresolvability since, for them, weaknesses are not given by nature, not facts that they accept with resignation. In the moment of revolt, "it is precisely facts that do not exist, only *interpretations*."[61] What matters here for the insurrectionary slave is not what she is, but what she *wills*. The insurrectionary slave demands consideration instead of realizing her equality by participating in collective self-government. She demands this not because she *is* a sufferer, passive, but because she *wants* to be a passive sufferer. The

263

insurrectionary slave affirms that she wants to be able to not participate. This is the "dark riddle" that the Jews in revolt posed to their Roman masters, something for the latter to think over.[62] They do not appeal to the human being's natural weaknesses. Instead, their revolt is an act of affirmation: *the affirmation of passivity, the willing of inability.*

If we interpret the slave revolt by starting from its Jewish origins and not from its bourgeois end, then the position of passivity, the existence of suffering, the incapacity of non-participation is not a fact of human nature that is to be accepted. Instead, it is affirmed, a goal that is willed in revolt and directed against domination: the servant who frees herself *wants* to be this way. For her, therefore, passivity is not a mere fact, but something good (since the good is the will's object). To put this more precisely, passivity, non-participation, for her, is a *moment* of the good. The servant who frees herself wills passivity for the sake of the good.

The bourgeois understanding of weakness and passivity in need of consideration is resigned: the human being is bourgeois because she is by nature incapable of changing into a participant in the (political) determination and (social) realization of the good. The affirmation of passivity stands opposed to this understanding at the moment of revolt, since passivity is understood here not as the good's natural other, but as a condition for the good – an other *in* the good. The weakness of passivity first makes the good possible. Looking back on the beginning of the Jewish slave revolt reveals that the insurrectionary slave is not a bourgeois pessimist. She believes in the good. The slave in revolt is an optimist: an optimist of weakness.

* * *

If we understand the insurrectionary slave in this way (and therefore as anti-bourgeois), then she simultaneously stands in contrast to the way in which communism conceives the revolution of equality. For if the slave revolt affirms passivity, because it understands passivity as a moment of, indeed a condition for, the good, it thereby not only has a conception of passivity that is completely different from that of the bourgeois revolution (i.e., as the good's immanent other), but also has a conception of the good that is different from that of the communist revolution, namely one in which the political determination and social realization of the good *require* passivity, and therefore non-participation. The insurrectionary slave's optimism of weakness opposes bourgeois *and* communist revolution.

The bourgeois revolution bases the right to passivity on human nature: on the fact that the human being is natural. For to be natural means not

264

to be social – things that are naturally accomplished (such as private pleasures) do not have the form of participation in a social practice. For this reason, equality cannot be realized by political self-government in the realm of nature. In natural accomplishments, the human being can only be equally considered.

This is opposed to the way in which communist democracy conceives the human being. For communist democracy, the subject of political self-government is not the natural, finite human being, but the human being as "immortal." Alain Badiou's communist critique of bourgeois pessimism reaches this conclusion. He argues that we may think of the human being as "*something other than a mortal being*," since as long as the human being is a subject and therefore "thinks" her social being, carries it out knowingly and deliberately, or politically, she obtains "rights of the Infinite, exercised over the contingency of suffering and death."[63] Participation in the political self-determination of the common good, the good of social practice, signifies the overcoming of weakness. It is activity without passivity.

The same thing holds for the communist revolution as for the bourgeois one, though conversely: neither moves beyond the conceptual opposition of masters and servants. In naturalizing passivity, in declaring the bourgeois to be the human being's natural form of existence, the bourgeois revolution only reinforces and thereby strengthens servile existence, namely the subject's existence as a sufferer who is exposed to another's actions, because she merely exists along with the latter in the commercium's external interaction. The bourgeois revolution does not abolish the position of passivity, but safeguards and reinforces it with the right to consideration. While the bourgeois revolution thus fails to overcome servitude, instead universalizing it, the communist revolution wishes to turn slaves into masters: *everyone* is supposed to become a master. As we have seen, Nietzsche defines the master's right as the right to create values and thereby to govern the self. True democracy dissolves this right of status and privilege and distributes it to all social participants – simply because they are members of social practice. Just as the bourgeois revolution does not therefore overcome servitude, but declares it to be the human being's (as bourgeois) anthropological truth, so the communist revolution does not overcome mastery, because it does not overcome the *concept* of the master.

In their opposition, the bourgeois and communist revolutions are two sides of the same coin. That is, they are two sides of the same conceptual opposition of servant and master. On the one side, we have a passivity that must be considered mere fact, and on the other, we have an activity consisting in the politically self-aware exercise of social capacities. The alternative interpretation of the slave revolt, which begins with its Jewish origins, rejects this opposition. Understood in this way, the slave revolt wishes neither to legally safeguard weaknesses nor to distribute the master's right to all equally. Rather, it wants to do away with masters and slaves at the same time. It wishes to end their existence. The slave revolt is thus an anthropological revolution: "human emancipation,"[64] or the human being's emancipation from both the concept of the master and that of the slave. As anthropological revolution, the slave revolt wants to create a human being who does not correspond to either category, neither that of the master nor to that of the servant or slave. The slave revolt – the same one that is opposed to bourgeois pessimism – is concerned with creating a new human being.

The slave revolt, which creates a new human being (a human being who actively wills her passivity, who has the power to affirm her weakness), also creates a new right. This simply means, however, that it creates the modern form of rights in a new way. It renews or revolutionizes the modern form of rights. The slave revolt as human emancipation gives it a new form that radically breaks with its existing old form, the bourgeois form of subjective rights.

— 15 —

A NEW RIGHT

The modern revolution of equality has two opposed forms: the bourgeois and communist revolutions. The bourgeois revolution declares equality of consideration, the communist revolution creates equality of participation. Bourgeois and communist revolutions realize equality in opposed forms, since they understand the subject in conflicting ways. The bourgeois revolution declares the right to equal consideration because the human being is weak by nature and in the position of a sufferer. The communist revolution creates the power of equal participation, since the individual is a social member and is capable of self-government.

This opposition of sufferer and participant shows that the bourgeois and communist revolutions do not go deep enough. They wish to establish equality in opposition to the distinction between masters and servants. They do so, however, in such a way that they continue to rely on this distinction: the bourgeois revolution universalizes the servant because it naturalizes her weakness, while the communist revolution universalizes the master because it distributes his power. The revolution of equality must proceed more radically, getting to the root. In addition to doing away with the distinction between masters and servants, it must also do away with the concept of the master and that of the servant. It must conceive a subject that is neither master nor servant, namely a subject whose passivity is not servile since it is freely willed, and whose activity is not that of a master since it is not a free creation.

This is the goal of the slave revolt on its affirmative interpretation. This interpretation understands the insurrectionary slave to affirm her weakness and to will her passivity. The affirmative slave revolt thereby de-naturalizes the sufferer's existence. As we have seen, to be a sufferer means to stand in an external relation of mere interaction with another,

267

since one is not a participant in collective social practice and thus does not participate in its self-government. To be a sufferer therefore means not exercising judgment. The bourgeois interpretation of the slave revolt understands this to mean that the human being is too weak by nature, which is why she is incapable of – consistently – guiding herself through judgments. Instead, on this interpretation, it is "human" to obey one's nature. In *wanting to be* a sufferer, however, the insurrectionary slave declares that her incapacity to determine the good by exercising judgment is a moment in the good itself. She thereby transforms the concept of the good and its definition. The good and the activity of determining it are the master's prerogative. The insurrectionary slave does not merely want this right to be distributed to all. Rather, she targets the master's *conception* of the creation of values, of self-determination, judgment, and governing. The slave revolt's radicality lies in its willing of passivity: *it revolutionizes the concept of judgment.*

This conceptual revolution consists in reconceiving the relation of activity and passivity. On its affirmative interpretation, the slave revolt calls their external opposition into question. It declares passivity to be the *internal condition* for the successful activity of judgment. The sufferer's existence is that of the non-participant. The activity of judgment, in contrast, is carried out by participating in social practice and its political self-government. The insurrectionary slave therefore wants non-participation – the incapacity to participate – as a condition for the success of social and political participation. The affirmative slave revolt demands a form of participation that includes its opposite in itself. It demands *the right to non-participation on the basis and for the sake of the good of participation.* The non-participant's right is the right [*Recht*] to consideration. The affirmative slave revolt's radical idea is therefore that the sufferer's basic right to consideration is created by active participation in political self-government. The anti-political basic right to consideration has a political basis: it is based on a new, radical conception of politics created by the affirmative slave revolt in opposition to both bourgeois *and* communist revolutions.

The affirmative slave revolt thereby creates the basic ontological definition of modern law [*Rechts*]. The thesis of part II of this volume was that modern law's ontology is defined by its self-reflection. This definition has two aspects. First, it indicates that modern law is materialist. The basic definition of modern self-reflective law is the materialism of form. The second aspect of the definition of self-reflective law indicates that its materialism conceals a contradiction, namely the contradiction between a positivist and a dialectical materialism. The argument of part

III was that the positivist (or empiricist) understanding of materialism forms the basis of bourgeois [*bürgerlichen*] law. It determines the form of subjective rights. For subjective rights authorize the subject's self-will, which they presuppose as given. Dialectical materialism criticizes this as a myth (and thus as false authority). Law's matter cannot be operative as something given *in* law – as a power or force of normalization. According to Adorno, matter is something "mediated" in normalization: in law's self-reflection, matter as form's other is a "moment" in its dialectical mediation with form. The self-reflection of law means the *justification* of the norm's other. Positivist materialism conceives this as its justification in the face of the norm, to which dialectical materialism opposes the justification of matter as the norm's other *in* normalization. The dialectical materialism of self-reflective law thus creates a new, anti-bourgeois conception of rights, namely rights not as subjective rights or private rights, but as *counter-rights*.

The program of the affirmative slave revolt is the optimism of weakness, the affirmation of passivity as condition for the success of the activity of judgment – a new conception of politics.

The program of the dialectical materialism of law is matter as force, the setting free of form's other in form – a new conception of rights.

The two programs are identical. The affirmation of passivity is, in politics, what dialectical materialism is, in law.

The slave revolt's affirmative concept explains why revolutionary politics creates the basic right [*Grundrecht*] to consideration: there is no politics without counter-*rights* (contra the communist revolution).

The dialectical materialism of law [*Rechts*] explains why matter is only operative in normalization: there are no *counter*-rights without politics (contra the bourgeois revolution).

The affirmative slave revolt in politics and law's dialectical self-reflection are two parts of the same conception. This is the conception of a new right: the insurrectionary right [*Rechts*] to counter-rights.

The double program for this new right can also be characterized as follows: the new right [*Recht*] is *a form of modern law* [*Rechts*], since it is self-reflectively constituted. At the same time, the new right *stands opposed to bourgeois law*, since it is dialectical or anti-positivist.

Modern law is self-reflective by applying matter that is foreign to norms in law – in the process of its normalization or formation. Modern law has a broken form. It is the form of the difference between form and non-form, or matter. Modern law's basic operation is the legalization of the non-legal as "natural."

Bourgeois law is empiricist (or positivist), because it allows private self-will to count as fact. In bourgeois law, *the fact that* a subject wants something is the starting point from which its normalization proceeds – which it considers valid in its normalization. Force is interpreted as validity. The bourgeois revolution demands this as the right [*Recht*] to consideration: as the subject's right to be considered without having to involve herself in political self-government. It is the right to passivity vis-à-vis politics.

This demonstrates that the juridical positivism of private self-will – deemed a fact in bourgeois law [*Recht*] – and the anti-political passivity of its consideration are two definitions of bourgeois law that amount to the same thing.

As a result, overcoming bourgeois positivism through the dialectical materialism of self-reflection is only possible by politicizing consideration – by politicizing passivity.

The Dialectic of Judgment

To conceive law politically means to examine the acts of normalization (and formation) that result from law. These are acts of judgment, and the way in which politics and law are drafted decides how a judgment that is politically performed and juridically realized is understood. If, therefore, the slave revolt is affirmatively understood, then we are dealing with a revolution in judgment.

According to the opening definition of Aristotle's *Politics*, judgment is the human being's specific capacity:

> man alone of the animals possesses speech [*logos*]. The mere voice [*phonē*], it is true, can indicate pain and pleasure, and therefore is possessed by the other animals as well (for their nature has been developed so far as to have sensations [*aisthēsin*] of what is painful and pleasant and to signify those sensations to one another), but speech is designed to indicate the advantageous and the harmful, and therefore also the right and the wrong; for it is the special property of man in distinction from the other animals that he alone has perception of good and bad and right and wrong and the other moral qualities.[1]

The basic condition for judgment is freedom from feeling – from desire and pain, to which non-human living things are bound. This occurs through speech. To put this more precisely, it occurs when the particular and the universal are simultaneously distinguished and linked in the predicative structure to which judgment [*Urteil*] owes its name. The act

270

of judging thereby obtains "situation-independence" and thus "the possibility of answering 'No' . . . [to] a stimulus."² Judgment differentiates between the particular, between an object identified with singular terms, and the universal, the concept that we attribute to an object or deny with respect to an object. The basic definition of judgment, which, on Aristotle's view, categorically distinguishes it from the mere indication of feelings of pain and pleasure, is that judgment is *conceptual*: to be able to judge means being able to apply concepts.

By distinguishing and linking the particular and universal, judgment makes it possible to react to a stimulus, and therefore to an object and a situation "by abstaining, or by questioning, and based on this questioning, also by expressing doubt or deliberation" – it makes thought and deliberation possible as "inquiry . . . into *reasons*."³ In silencing the voice of "pain and pleasure," which is shackled to the object, judgment is the condition for thought, reason, and freedom. In the act of judgment, an original act that distinguishes judging from the object, and therefore distinguishes judging from feelings, must have been carried out in or prior to any distinction of particular and universal: an act of distinguishing prior to distinguishing, freedom from the power of feelings – an act which first makes it possible for judgment to be rational.

Hannah Arendt conceives this liberating distance as an achievement of imagination, since it replaces sensuous feelings with self-constructed representations:

> Only what touches, affects, one in representation, when one can no longer be affected by immediate presence . . . can be judged to be right or wrong, important or irrelevant, beautiful or ugly, or something in between. One then speaks of judgment and no longer of taste because, though it still affects one like a matter of taste, one now has, by means of representation, established the proper distance. . . . By removing the object, one has established the conditions for impartiality.⁴

One is only able to judge by "removing" the object – by *representing it to ourselves* through the (aesthetic) operation of the imagination, since only in this way is an object no longer a stimulus that one must react to in a certain way, but something *about which* one speaks, namely a thing with properties, whose determination in judgment can play the role of reasons in rational deliberation.

It is precisely this conception of judgment as capacity for a distanced and free application of concepts that forms the basis for Aristotle's claim that "natural" slaves exist. We therefore find such a conception of judgment at the beginning of Aristotle's *Politics*. It is the criterion for

271

distinguishing the free from the unfree. This distinction is only legitimate if it differentiates their respective capacities. Aristotle notoriously defines a natural slave as a human being who only "participates in reason so far as to apprehend it but not to possess it."[5] He defines natural slaves in terms of lack: they have the capacity for judgment, but only in a passive, deficient way. They can understand judgments, but cannot themselves judge. Without guidance from others, natural slaves, like non-human living things, have only "sensuous desire":[6] "for the animals other than man are subservient not to reason, by apprehending it, but to feelings."[7] On his own, without a master, the slave can only indicate his feelings, but cannot use concepts. He only has a voice, not language. The definition of judgment as a capacity to use concepts is political. It establishes a "symbolic distribution of bodies that divides them into two categories": "those who really speak and those whose voice merely mimics the articulate voice to express pleasure and pain."[8] The logos of judgment is political, not only because it articulates the common good, but also because it differs at every moment from another kind of speech, namely from the "voice" as a kind of speech that merely expresses feelings of pleasure and pain.

This is the "order" or "partition of the perceptible" (Rancière) that constitutes politics: not order *in* the perceptible, but an order that distinguishes *between* the perceptible, which is only a matter of taste, and the conceptual, which can judge, and "organizes ... domination" by means of this distinction.[9] This is why it is not merely the content of judgment that is political. Rather, the concept of judgment itself is political, because the original distinction between judging and non-judging, in which language frees itself from the perceptible voice, is the criterion for distinguishing between classes, which is a political concern, namely the difference between masters and servants.

What does the insurrectionary servant demand when she rises up against this "partition of the perceptible"? The bourgeois revolution's answer to this question is one response: the servant demands consideration for her perceptible willing, since it is simply part of the human being's weak nature. All human beings are – *also* – servants. The communist answer is another response: servants demand to become masters – to *also* be recognized as "speaking beings sharing the same properties as those who deny them these." Indeed, servants already *demonstrate* that they can judge just as well as masters and are "human beings" just as the latter are, by making their demand.[10]

Both answers thereby misconstrue the slave revolt's true radicality, since this revolt does not merely transform the separation of social classes

272

into one of two sides of the distinction between *phonē* and *logos*. Rather, it overturns this fundamental distinction itself – which both interpretations, the bourgeois and communist, leave intact. The true slave revolt goes much further than asserting the equal capacity of all to judge, formerly reserved for masters. It revolutionizes the conception and thus the practice of judgment itself.[11] And it thereby first makes true equality in judgment possible.

The revolution of judgment consists in an act of affirmation. The insurrectionary slave affirms her weakness. This weakness, which according to Aristotle necessitates rule over her, consists in the fact that she cannot exercise judgment because, on Aristotle's explanation, she does not possess reason in the full sense. She only possesses reason in such a way that her perceptible "voice," with which she indicates her feelings, remains audible in her judgment. The insurrectionary slave affirms this: she does not want to remove reason from the voice, she does not want to remove her exercise of conceptual judgment from sense-impressions. In the master's judgment, which has been freed from the power of the perceptible voice, such feelings merely form the material to which the conceptual distinction of good and bad is applied. The insurrectionary slave, in contrast, wants a judgment that proceeds from feelings and perpetually refers back to them. For the perceptible is not merely the material to which concepts are applied, but the medium of a preconceptual evidence that forms the basis for conceptually articulated judgment and is operative in such judgment. For this reason, the new judgment that the insurrectionary slave opposes to the master's old judgment is essentially (and thus nothing but) the process of reflectively transforming perceptible, affective evidence. It cannot be separated from the perceptible. "The somatic moment as the not purely cognitive part of cognition is irreducible."[12] Perceptible feeling is irreducible in judgment, because judgment proceeds *in a manner different* from feeling, and yet at the same time there can be no judgment *without* feeling. The other judgment created by the revolution against its master-concept is the effect of judgment's other in judgment: judgment *as* the work of judgment's other.

Perceptible feeling is at work in judgment as force: it drives judgment. As force, it drives conceptual definitions of good and bad forward and moves beyond them. This is why the insurrectionary slave affirms her passivity, her being-driven. She thereby affirms the perceptible force, which, as the other of the capacity for conceptual judgment, is the condition for her success. Aristotle's master-theory of judgment establishes the rule of one class over another. In opposition to this, the servant's revolt first draws the consequences of the insight formulated by Aristotle

273

himself in the *Metaphysics*: the fact that "the potentiality for acting and being acted upon is one";[13] the fact that there is no conceptual judgment that does not include its other, perceptible affection, in itself.

The affirmation of passivity, of the perceptible drive in reflective judgment, is the opposite of the pessimism of natural weaknesses accepted as given, by means of which the bourgeois revolution staved off the master's practice of self-government. Bourgeois politics binds judgment – the judgment of what is legal and illegal – to the fact of private self-will, which it validates in law's normalizations. In this regard, private self-will is something given for judgment, on the basis of which it is to proceed. This is the positivism of bourgeois law. Its positivism is its pessimism.

This ruptures the revolution of judgment by the insurrectionary slave. For indeed, it is opposed to the communist "wishful image of an uninhibited, vital, creative man,"[14] because it remains bound to the master-concept of judgment: the insurrectionary slave's new judgment, which affirms her passivity, is materialist because it understands perceptible feeling not as "raw material" for conceptual operations, but as "a driving force."[15] At the same time, however, this new judgment's materialism is dialectical, not positivist, because, in performing it, the "driving force" of the perceptible is not something given, its external presupposition, but a moment. "The affirmation of value-formative passions does not represent a final decision that first makes possible all acts of evaluation"; "Instead of becoming the ground, it becomes a moment."[16] The driving force of the perceptible is a moment in judgment because it is mediated. Feeling is only at work in judgment through the – dialectical – mediation with its counterpart, the conceptual.

The positivism of bourgeois law consists in its inability to conceive the mediation of the perceptible and the conceptual in judgment. However, "mediation makes no claim whatsoever to exhaust all things; it postulates, rather, that what it transmits is not thereby exhausted"; it is "to make progressive qualitative distinctions between things which are mediated in themselves."[17] The radical difference between the perceptible and the conceptual is only conceivable through insight into their mediation. The positivism of bourgeois law conceals the mediation between the perceptible and the conceptual, thus simultaneously distorting the difference between the two: it makes the perceptible into a fact, into something given – "the obverse form, as it were, of the precedence of objectivity."[18] The perceptible, which stands immediately opposed to the conceptual, simply becomes its mere reflection. That which is heterogeneous to it has been "bewitched . . . by tailoring its categories."[19] The perceptible can only properly be conceived in an anti-positivist,

274

and therefore dialectical, manner, namely as the conceptual's immanent other. It can only be conceived as its own other, or what is its own *as* its other. The mediation of the perceptible with the conceptual transforms the perceptible. It frees it to be what it is. In its mediation with the conceptual, the perceptible first becomes the conceptual's other – it becomes the non-conceptual, or a conceptual void. It is thus the force that drives judgment's conceptual determination forward and at the same time always moves beyond it. It "survives . . . as the unrest that makes knowledge move, the unassuaged unrest that reproduces itself in the advancement of knowledge"[20] – the "unrest of the passive."[21] While the empiricism of bourgeois law binds the subject to the positivity of the latter's own self-will, in the insurrectionary slave's new judgment, the perceptible obtains the power to create and therefore transform the conceptual – the power of negativity.

The insurrectionary slave thus governs herself by her own judgment. In governing herself, she creates the norms of law, by thinking through the evidence of her feelings:

In opposition to the master's logos, she does not have a source of normativity at her disposal that frees her from – makes her independent of – the perceptible voice of her affective certainty. The insurrectionary slave governs by allowing herself to be driven onward and forward by her own perceptible willing, namely by thinking this perceptible will and creating conceptual determinations from it.

In opposition to bourgeois positivism, she thus declares perceptible willing to not be something given. In the political process of self-government established by the slave revolt, there are no facts of willing that are "valid" and "shown consideration" as such. In self-government, everything must be mediated through and through. There is no basis; everything becomes a moment. The insurrectionary slave refuses the positivism of facts and breaks through this positivism with reflection, through mediation with the conceptual. She breaks through it with politics (since the political process is the negative process of mediation). That which is merely given does not merit our consideration. As merely given, the perceptible is the private sphere of the bourgeois self-will, *against* which the perceptible as force of unrest and of negativity – as the other of the conceptual *in* the conceptual – is politically generated.

The insurrectionary slave's political self-government is a dialectic that is put into practice. It *transforms* the perceptible that it considers – in opposition to bourgeois positivism. And it *considers* the perceptible that it transforms – in opposition to the master's logos. The insurrectionary slave's new judgment breaks through the alternative that holds modernity

275

in thrall. Instead of the master's activist logos *or* pessimistic bourgeois positivism, it offers the negative, dialectical affirmation of passivity.

Counter-rights

The revolution of judgment constitutes a revolution of law [*Rechts*]. It is a new foundation for the right [*Rechts*] to consideration. The revolution of judgment is therefore a new foundation for the modern form of rights, since rights in the modern sense are rights to something non- or extra-legal, which they permit and enable. They are rights without a moral basis; rights that someone has even if she is not in the right. Modern rights are rights to consideration. To have a right to be considered means having a binding claim on another. It means limiting the other's will by my will, without having to justify my will in a judgment (which can only be done in common with others).

In the modern form of rights, the bourgeois revolution establishes consideration for the other on the basis of a fact, namely one's own self-will. The revolution of judgment is directed against this. It is anti-positivist. Instead of understanding the passivity of the perceptible as – positively – given, it understands this passivity as force, unrest, or negativity. The revolution of judgment is an anti-bourgeois declaration of the basic right to consideration: consideration not of what is one's own but of the perceptible as counter-force. The bourgeois revolution declares the right to subjective rights: the right of private rights. The revolution of judgment declares a new right: the right of counter-rights. – This thesis has three aspects:

(i) The first aspect concerns the basis for counter-rights.

The central ("genealogical") insight of Nietzsche's analysis of the slave revolt is that the conception of right is determined by the subject's position in the framework of doing and suffering, activity and passivity. Masters and servants have opposed understandings of that to which they have a right, indeed, of what a right is, because the former are active and the latter are passive. Masters are able to judge and to act, because they have the power to assume the right to do so. Slaves suffer the judgments and actions of others and therefore demand the right to their consideration. The demand to be considered expresses the passivity of making demands.

This can be understood in two opposed ways. The – bourgeois – pessimism of weakness is one way to understand passivity. To be passive or a sufferer means being exposed to another's action. According to

Kant, this is rooted in the fact that those who act and those who suffer do not form a community as *communio*. The sufferer does not participate in practice and its self-government. Because, however, a definition of the good is only possible in such practice and self-government, the passive person is someone who does not judge, and in particular someone who *cannot* judge because she is bound to the "voice," *phonē*, to her perceptible feelings. Exposed to their – natural – power, she demands consideration for her feelings – her suffering and her pleasure. Her pessimism is a positivism: the bourgeois positivism of one's own as given.

To claim that passivity is an internal condition for judgment is another, opposed way to understand it. The insurrectionary slave who affirms her passivity carries out this revolution of judgment, since she thereby no longer understands such passivity to be an external incapacity with respect to judgment. The bourgeois revolution thus established the right to consideration, and communism condemned it, because it identifies the human being as merely "*a mortal being*" (Badiou). The insurrectionary slave opposes her optimism of weakness to this right: her passivity is not mere incapacity, and incapacity is not merely the lack of capacity. Instead, incapacity forms the necessary precondition for the existence of capacity. There is incapacity *in* capacity.[22] There are perceptible feelings operative in judgment that must run counter to conceptual determination. It is only for this reason that passivity must be given consideration: its right to consideration vis-à-vis the activity of judgment is based on that activity's success.

This is the first aspect of the declaration of counter-rights. Like bourgeois private rights, counter-rights are rights to the consideration of passivity. They are rights against the activity of judgment. At the same time, counter-rights stand in contrast to bourgeois private rights, since they are based on what they are directed against. They are not rights to one's own nature over against judgment, but rights to consideration of the natural, perceptible forces *in* judgment. The basis of rights is the good: the basis of rights over against judgment is the good of judgment.

(ii) The second aspect concerns the content of counter-rights.

The content of counter-rights is passivity: they consider the existence of the sufferer. The theory of judgment defines passivity as a moment of perceptible affection that is required for any act of judgment to be successful. Through its perceptible affection, the subject is exposed to stimuli and thereby to a situation. Perceptible affection is operative of its own accord in the subject, but the subject does not operate of her own accord in it: the subject *suffers* her own perceptible affection.[23] The subject therefore has to suffer even the activity of her own conceptual determination as something that, at the same time, is perceptibly passive. To be sure, the perceptible only exists in judgment as a moment in its mediation with the conceptual. This mediation, however, is asymmetric. The perceptible or immediate is "a moment that does not require cognition – or mediation – in the same sense in which cognition necessitates immediacy."[24] Conceptual determination is as necessary for, as it remains external to, perceptible affection. Conceptual determination proceeds from perceptible affection, but a conceptual determination that grasps perceptible affection as such – as it is on its own – is impossible, since the determination of perceptible affection is its indeterminacy, its unrest as negativity. This is why the interplay [*Zusammenspiel*] of conceptual determination with perceptible affection remains a contrast [*Widerspiel*], indeed a conflict [*Widerstreit*].

The ontology of the subject of counter-rights holds that the subject who demands the counter-right of consideration is the subject of judgment. It is the subject as scene in which the opposition between conceptual determination and perceptible affection plays out. This opposition in the subject is identical to the opposition in her participation, namely to the way in which she is social. In the conceptual determination of the good, the subject of judgment participates in a practice. She tells us how the good of a social practice is supposed to be understood – correctly, differently, better, in a new way, and so forth. In contrast, the subject does not participate in her perceptible affection. Since she is not herself active in her perceptible affection, the subject does not exercise any capacity and is therefore not self-consciously directed toward the good of a practice. Perceptible affection signifies social non-participation. At the same time, however, just as conceptual participation in social practice is only a moment in mediation with perceptible non-participation, so too perceptible non-participation in social practice is only a moment in mediation with conceptual participation. Neither participation nor non-participation is intact. Both are split in different, indeed opposed, ways: conceptual participation, because it depends on perceptible affection but can never catch up with it; perceptible non-participation, because it requires conceptual determination and, at the same time, is exposed to and must suffer it. Perceptible non-participation is the counter-moment in social participation.

This is the second aspect of the declaration of counter-rights. Counter-rights are similar to bourgeois private rights insofar as they are the expression of a subject's rights to her social non-participation, rights opposed to her social participation. At the same time, counter-rights stand in contrast to bourgeois private rights, since they do not authorize the private self-will's indifference toward moral normativity. Rather, they enable non-participation *in* participation. The content of counter-rights is the disruption of social participation.

(iii) The third aspect concerns the government of counter-rights. Nietzsche describes two radically different ways to speak of a right: the master's right to judge for and rule himself, and the servant's right to be considered. The first right is an expression of power. Anyone who can rule themselves should not be ruled. If everyone is capable of this (as communism claims), then everyone should also do it. The second right, in contrast, is an expression of powerlessness. This right is removed from power, since the right to consideration is a right based on, and a right to, passivity.

The declaration of the basic right of the passive, the right to be considered, is therefore simultaneously the disenfranchisement of the powerful or active. *The powerful have no rights* if rights, in their modern form, are rights to consideration. Anyone with the power to judge, anyone who can participate in the practice of self-government, does not need to be considered. And he is also not *able* to be considered – above or beyond his participation. Anyone who can participate in the practice of self-government has already spoken, deliberated, judged, and decided with others. A person who governs with others has transformed the "voice" of her perceptible willing into the logos of conceptual determinations, which she cites as reasons. She has thereby made her deliberations part of a common deliberation. She has co-governed: she has co-governed *herself* and can therefore never be considered by government. To have power – to participate in government – entails not having any rights to consideration. A powerful person is right [*hat recht*] (since he decides what is legal and illegal by participating in government), but *has no rights*. Rights, in their modern form, are – *only* – rights of the powerless. All rights are rights of the powerless. They are rights of those who are unable to participate, of passivity. In other words, they are rights against having to participate, namely rights against becoming, completely or in general, a participant in government.

Anyone who cannot participate in government requires consideration and therefore rights. To be able to participate in government means to articulate one's own experiences and thoughts as part of a universal determination of the good. It means being able to participate in language and not merely having a voice that emits signs of feelings. Anyone who cannot do this is powerless, requiring consideration and therefore rights. The traditional legitimation of domination understood this as what defines a class, the class of servants. Servants are those who cannot govern themselves and must therefore be governed. While the communist revolution of equality denies that this powerlessness really exists, the slave revolt that affirms passivity asserts, on the contrary, that the subject is structurally powerless. This powerlessness, however, is not a lack, not the mere absence of power, but its internal condition: it is the subject of government – the subject of governmental power – who wants to be powerless. Need – to be in need of consideration – is rooted in willing. It is rooted in the insight that whoever wishes to have the power of government must simultaneously will her powerlessness and consideration for it, since this is the only way to satisfy the concept of government. Government must consider the suffering that its activity of judgment inflicts on the passive, because the passive is its unavoidable point of departure, because government requires the passive. Government would destroy itself if it did not consider the passive. It would become totalitarian were it not to consider the passive: it would completely turn the subject of government into a participant in government – and thereby destroy itself. For totalitarian government is not a logically consistent form of government, but rather a kind of government that turns against itself by attempting to sublate its turning of itself against itself (turning against itself in judgment), a condition for its success, into a whole. Good government is government that does not form a whole: repugnant [*wider Willen*] government.

This is the third aspect of the declaration of counter-rights. Like bourgeois private rights, counter-rights take political powerlessness, the subject's non-participation in government, into consideration. At the same time, counter-rights stand in contrast to bourgeois private rights, since they do not naturalize powerlessness. They do not reify it and make it into the principle of a depoliticized sphere – the sphere of bourgeois society. Counter-rights consider the incapacity for language, for logos, *in* government, as a condition for its success. The government of counter-rights is a repugnant government.

This argument leads *from* the dialectic of judgment *to* the counter-right of the powerless. Its three steps are as follows:

(i)   Counter-rights are based on the good of judgment.
(ii) Counter-rights enable non-participation.
(iii) Counter-rights take powerlessness into consideration.

The new right [*Recht*] – the right of counter-rights – is rooted in the revolution of equality, in the revolt against masters who claim to alone judge for all. This also holds for the two other types of revolution, namely the bourgeois and the communist. All three types of revolution overthrow the old domination of judgment and thereby create a new right. They do this in ways that are mutually opposed, however.

The *communist revolution* distributes the master's power of judgment to all and thereby turns each person into a participant in the social practice of self-government – "true democracy." In communism, law [*Recht*] secures the equal power of all to govern together.

The *bourgeois revolution* relieves the subject from judging, from living according to her master's judgment as well as according to her own. For judgment is conceptual and thereby common. Bourgeois law is law that validates private self-will.

The *revolution to come* must dissolve the master-concept of judgment presupposed in equal measure by the communist and bourgeois revolutions. It establishes a practice of judgment that develops the – negative – dialectic of perceptible affection and conceptual activity. It thereby establishes a new right [*Recht*], namely one that realizes the power of co-governance against suffering and the right of the powerless in government.

* * *

Modern rights are rights to the natural. In this respect, they are the form of self-reflection. Law's [*Rechts*] self-reflection – which draws the distinction between law and non-law in law – transforms law. It creates a new form of law. This is the thesis of the first and second parts of this book.

The third part has shown that this both applies and does not apply to bourgeois law. Critique reveals the contradiction in bourgeois law: such law *carries out* and *denies* the modern self-reflection of law. Bourgeois law is self-reflective – it opens law up to the non-juridical. Bourgeois law is positivist (and a denial of self-reflection) – since it validates the non-juridical as given. This contradiction defines the fundamental bourgeois model of subjective rights.

The new right of counter-rights ends this contradiction. It achieves self-reflection without denying it. Because, however, law's self-reflection only consists in developing judgment's process of turning against itself, the new right must be *the form of this process* and *the unity of turning-against-itself*. This establishes the formal – or ontological – difference between the new right's counter-rights and bourgeois law's private rights. Private rights are claims to something given, something that is positively present prior to law and its process: the subject's self-will, her choice and her interests. Counter-rights are claims to a – transitory *and* recurring – moment in the political process of law, namely the moment of perceptible affection in its dialectical mediation with the other moment of conceptual determination. Private rights suspend the political process that they create. Counter-rights rehearse the political process that they enable – precisely by interrupting it.

Excursus: Politics and Police – The Possibility of the New (Badiou, Rancière)

The relation of form and process or act is central to Jacques Rancière's theory of politics. According to Rancière, this – ontological – relation defines politics' mode of being. Politics therefore exists in two mutually opposed forms. On one side, there is, in each case, an existing order, which Rancière, in connection with Aristotle, describes as an order of "division" or "distribution." In other words, "Politics is generally seen as the set of procedures whereby the aggregation and consent of collectivities is achieved, the organization of powers, the distribution of places and roles, and the systems for legitimizing this distribution."[25] Rancière calls this the "police." "The police is, essentially, the law, generally implicit" (what the law is, as implicit).[26] Politics as politics or politics as such is opposed to this. According to Rancière, however, politics as terminologically distinguished from the police is not the other opposed to order. In contrast to order as police, politics is instead an act or process, precisely because it is the resolution of the opposition between order and its other. "Politics occurs when there is a place and a way for two heterogenous processes to meet."[27]

Each existing order (or police) is unequal as a specific order. It establishes criteria for distribution that form hierarchies. This "counting" – in which distinctions are made – is experienced by politics as a "wrong." Conversely, according to the prevailing standards in a given case, politics is always a "*miscount*," since it validates the "principle" of the unconditioned and therefore indeterminate equality of each person – which "is nothing political in itself"[28] – against the respective police order. The "form"[29] of politics is thus the confrontation of order with equality. The form of politics – the form that makes something politics, which makes it political – is form's confrontation with the formless (in other words, as Étienne Balibar puts it, politics is "a 'bad infinity'" of "the negation of the inequalities which are always still present in the principle of equality": the paradox of revolt as "the permanent state of the republic").[30] The opposition of police and politics is asymmetric: the police is the order against – *over and against* – the indeterminacy of equality. Politics is the act or process of confrontation *between* order and equality.

Each police order is thus like any other. To be sure, according to Rancière, this "is not to say that we can draw from this the nihilistic conclusion that the one example is the same as the other," since "[t]here is a worse and a better police."[31] For Rancière, there are conceptual reasons why, however, there is no such thing as good police – that is, there is no such thing as a *different* police, there is no police order that is different in its mode of being from all those that have preceded it, which have opposed their unequal distribution to the principle of equality.

In this regard, Rancière's thinking of politics echoes the basic tragic structure described by Badiou when the latter alludes to Hölderlin's interpretation of *Antigone*, attributing a paradigmatic significance to it for the modern thinking of revolution: it can only conceive "[t]he effect (the course) of insurrection" as "a reversal by which the road of the new is barred."[32] For the effect of revolt is always the same: the existing order's confrontation with unconditional equality, which exposes that order's injustice, thereby – perhaps – undermining it. At best, the existing order is replaced by a better one, which, however, is *again* an unequal distribution and must for this reason *again* be undermined in confrontation with unconditional equality, and so on. Badiou contrasts this with the experience of the *Oresteia*, in which "the dispute must be settled by instituting the new [rule]": the advent of a "new right."[33] In contrast to Sophocles, for Aeschylus: "[t]here is never a return to order in his theatre, but rather the recomposition of a different order."[34] Badiou calls this different order "nonlaw as law," or, better, "the law of nonlaw."[35]

This is the idea of an order that is no longer only better in terms of its content (as Rancière puts it: "a better police"), but is "new" because it has a *different composition* and mode of being. It is an order where what is systematically excluded by Rancière prevails, namely an order that is *just as* reflectively doubled in itself as he claims politics is. It is therefore an order where order and equality "meet" *within* order itself. Because this meeting, however, is the act or process that constitutes politics, this different, new order has to be an order *of* the process. In particular, it must be an order that will never be undermined by the political process again (as all previous ones have been), because it is an order that makes this process itself possible.

* * *

In a more recent text, Jacques Rancière himself has suggested defining the structure of this different kind of police or legal order by reinterpreting the rights of man.[36] In making this suggestion, he is drawing on Étienne Balibar's reflections on "a politics of the Rights of Man," developed years ago.[37] The basic idea can be understood as a way to interpret Badiou's formulation of "the law of nonlaw." The idea here is that law *enables* non-law by entitling it: it is the idea of an order that entitles us to politics – an order of the right to politics. If, however, politics consists in validating equality as unconditional, but every order carries out a particular and thereby unequal division, then an order cannot entitle us to politics by distributing participation in politics according to a particular established rule. Regulated or ordered politics is depoliticized politics. An order that enables politics has to be an order that does not order what it enables. It has to be a non-ordering order.

According to Balibar and Rancière, the – true, political – meaning of the rights of man is precisely that they are rights whose revolutionary declaration marks the transition from one legal order to another, new order. For such rights move "between two forms of existence": "*First, they are written rights.*" As such, they are "part of the configuration of the given,"[38] part of a police order.

> Second, the Rights of Man are the rights of those who make something of that inscription. ... Man and citizen do not designate collections of individuals. Man and citizen are political subjects. Political subjects are not definite collectivities. They are surplus names, names that set out a question or a dispute (*litige*) about who is included in their count. Correspondingly, freedom and equality are not predicates belonging to definite subjects. Political predicates are open predicates: they open up a dispute about what they exactly entail and whom they concern in which cases.[39]

The rights of man can therefore be understood as the "law of nonlaw" because, on the one hand, they are codified as rights and in this regard are part of an order, and, on the other hand, however, they simultaneously call every given determination into question and exceed it. They do this in the name of "man without determination": "The rights of man reduce right to a basis which, despite its name, is without shape."[40] They are the right of anyone at all to determine right without further qualifications and conditions. In Balibar's formulation, the rights of man are the right to "*extend* the rights of man and eventually *invent* them as rights of the citizen."[41] The declaration of the rights of man creates a *new kind* of legal order, namely an order in which insurrection against this order is inscribed *in the form of a (human) right*.

This attempted solution, however, does not go far enough, since Rancière and Balibar do not thereby call the form of rights itself into question.[42] This is why their attempt to overcome the "indefinite oscillation" between constitution and revolt,[43] police and politics, always ends up reverting to it. In the Declaration of the Rights of Man, according to

Balibar and Rancière, indeterminate rights or rights of the indeterminate are declared. By declaring the rights of man, right is thereby opened up to the political process of definition. What does it mean, however, to determine rights? And *how are* rights politically determined – how do such rights function? Balibar and Rancière say that if such rights are understood as realizations of the rights of man, they exist in a different way, since they exist as determinable in a different way, as transformable. Balibar and Rancière therefore understand the indeterminacy of the rights of man as simply the ability to redetermine rights or to determine them *differently*. The indeterminacy opened up by the rights of man is thus the past or future of legal determinacy, but never exists in the present. Rights here and now always exist and function in the same old way: they enable by authorizing and determining. Factoring in the rights of man does not therefore change the basic problem at all. It remains stuck in the paradox of rights described by Wendy Brown, namely the (endless) changing of political enabling into an authorization that is definitive – that is disciplinary or normalizing.[44] For it remains stuck in the "indefinite oscillation" (Balibar) between determination and indeterminacy, police and politics, constitution and revolt.

If Balibar and Rancière are correct in their hypothesis that the idea of a different order, of the "law of nonlaw" (Badiou), is the idea of an order that entitles its other (an order of the right to politics), then the form of entitlement must be understood differently from how Balibar and Rancière understand it in their reinterpretation of the rights of man. Balibar and Rancière describe the form of entitlement, under the rights of man, by opposing determination and indeterminacy. The political process enabled by the order of human rights leads from a given (positive-legal) determination through the indeterminacy of the rights of man to a different (positive-legal) determination. Badiou claims that a new right is necessary, which must have a different structure: its *determinations*, and thus its entitlements, must have a different structure. There cannot be only *one* given determination and merely the possibility of a different one. The determinations of right must be different *in themselves*: both one and another. The determinations of new right must *respectively* be two determinations that are *opposed* to each other. New right thus includes indeterminacy – it is the "law of nonlaw": it includes indeterminacy in the contrast, in the *between* of determinations.

Only because new right regulates in such a way that it conflicts with itself in its regulation is such right able to be regulation of the political process as regulation of the other and as foundation for all regulation. New right [*Recht*] enables a political process that simultaneously secures

285

participation and non-participation in it. Each person for him- or herself makes politics impossible: the authorization to participate is invariably a police distribution of power that contradicts its radical indeterminacy and equality. Consideration for non-participation is a – likewise police – distribution of power and powerlessness that creates private or social spheres of ungovernability. An order can only enable politics with both together and in opposition to each other – by enabling participation as opposed to non-participation *and* by enabling non-participation as opposed to participation. Order must turn against itself *in itself* to be able to be an order of politics as order's other.

The Justice of Splitting

Rights are counter-rights. Counter-rights are an anti-positivist, anti-bourgeois type of the modern form of rights. They consider the non-legal *in* law [*Recht*], without thereby turning it into something given *before* law. For they take it into consideration as a moment in the process of law, namely in the process of judgment that creates legal regulations, and therefore in the political process. Counter-rights – as we have argued so far – are rights in the political. They secure consideration for the passivity of perceptible affection in judgment. Government must declare this right for its own sake. It must declare this right for the sake of being a good government – for the sake of the good as government.

Government, however, does not act "for its own sake." Government is the self-aware accomplishment of self-determination, which occurs in every social practice. Government is a reflective practice or the self-reflection of social practice. The political practice of government, *through* its own success, wants to ensure the success of the social practice toward which it is directed, or more precisely, in which it takes place. Good government is hence concerned with the good of social practice. From the perspective of its participant, the good state of a practice is "just." The state of a social practice is just if it "promotes adequate treatment – in terms of the role assigned to each different social sphere in the context of the 'ethical division of labour' in a given society."[45] It is therefore just if it achieves the goal that forms its *raison d'être for* members of society. The political self-government of social practice is therefore concerned with establishing or maintaining its just state. Government does this with the right, since "*Droit* [Tr. – right] is nothing other than the application of the idea of justice to social interactions."[46] Government orders social practice by means of the right, so that it is just.

286

Good government is thus good in two senses: it is good as government, in its own performance, and good for social practice, or just. As we have seen, to be good as government means showing consideration for each person's counter-right to passivity, in achieving the equal power of all to govern together. This is a result of the new dialectical conception of judgment created by the slave revolt, on its affirmative interpretation. At the same time, however, it also results from the fact that, as the self-aware performance of government *in social practice*, it must introduce the *same antagonism* between participation and consideration, between power and counter-right. The only good political government of a social practice is one that takes the counter-right of passivity into consideration *in itself*, and the only just political government of a social practice is one that takes the powerlessness of passivity into consideration *within it*. The declaration of political counter-rights simultaneously signifies the declaration of social counter-rights, namely of counter-rights in the social.

The reason for this is simple: political government and social practice are two different modalities of judgment. Judgments are the mode of being of social practices. Practices only exist in the self-determination of their good and of rules that delineate this good. The formal determination of the good of a social practice therefore consists in *how* it carries out its judgments. The how of judgment is the form of practice. At the same time, however, the how of judgment – as we have seen – is the decisive engagement of political struggle: the slave revolt revolutionizes judgment. It thus initially revolutionizes the mode of government *and thereby* the form of practice. Because revolutionary government is the self-government of a social practice, it must realize the same negative dialectic of perceptible affection and conceptual determination in this practice that it carries out in its own performance. In doing so, good government is just. In other words, by ensuring that the dialectic of judgment can unfold in social practice, it creates a just order of the social.

The universal definition of social justice is therefore that a social practice is just when everyone has the power to participate *and* each has the counter-right of the powerless. For this social order is one that is just to the subject. To be a subject means to be a participant and non-participant at once. To be a subject means to be split. The justice of new right consists in securing the subject's split, in giving rise to the split of the social in itself – and thereby *from* itself: the splitting of the social in the social.

This universal definition of new right's [*Rechts*] justice must be more precisely grasped. This can only happen through a critique of bourgeois law [*Recht*], namely in the bourgeois interpretation of the modern form of rights as subjective rights. For this is the only form of modern rights

287

that we know. By critiquing them, we can learn how new right [*Recht*] must proceed differently to realize the justice of splitting.

The critique of bourgeois law [*Recht*] indicates that it is unjust. It is not unjust, however, because it is an order of inequality: subjective rights are by definition equal rights.[47] Nor is bourgeois law unjust because it only recognizes rights to participation or rights to powerlessness: subjective rights have a dual performance. They enable social participation *and* they permit private choice.[48] Bourgeois law is unjust, however, in *how* subjective rights do this. It (i) *separates* participation and non-participation because (ii), with the form of subjective rights, it bases *both* on the subject's self-will and thereby understands both apolitically.

(i) The justice of splitting, into participation and non-participation, contends with a dual injustice. One injustice is the identification of the subject as a participant, and the other injustice is the identification of the subject as a non-participant. The injustice consists in identifying the subject as participant *or* as non-participant. Bourgeois law, however, carries out the justice of splitting while simultaneously committing the injustice of identification. For it carries out the split into participation and non-participation by developing rights with two performances that differ from each other, namely rights that enable and rights that permit. The first kind of rights identifies the subject by her social interests, the second kind identifies the subject by her private choice. Both *together* carry out the subject's split. Each respectively defines the subject as the one *or* the other, however, and both are thereby unjust: identifying the social subject, a subject with interests, normalizes her. This identification subordinates the subject to a socially established form. Identification of the subject as a subject of private choice authorizes it for exploitation and command. It creates a depoliticized sphere of social domination.

Bourgeois law carries out the splitting of justice, yet it does this not in a process, through its negative mediation, but by separating two identifications. It carries out the splitting of justice *as* injustice. Bourgeois law is a travesty of justice.

(ii) The reason for this has to do with how bourgeois law construes the modern form of rights. Bourgeois law carries out the injustice of its identificatory splitting by declaring subjective rights. Subjective rights authorize by defining the subject through claims (claims to the private capacity for participation or to private spheres of disposal) that the subject *has* of its own accord because it *wants* them. This authorization occurs in the form of laws [*Gesetzen*]. Laws declare subjective rights in two ways: they determine that these claims exist prior to law or by nature, and they limit them against each other according to a rule of equality. Bourgeois law [*Gesetz*] determines which given claims to a right (made by private self-will) are justified, and under what limits. In bourgeois law [*Recht*], general law [*Gesetz*] and private claim reciprocally define each other. Law is the private claim's (general) form, and the private claim is law's (natural, given) content.

Two sovereigns are connected – or combined – with each other in bourgeois law: the "sovereign rights of the individual,"[49] in whose name the social is evaluated and shaped, and the sovereign rights of the legislator to establish which natural claims are legal, and under what limits. The individual and the legislator are both sovereign, because neither takes part in a social practice. The private claim exists prior to social practice – it is directed from outside to a social practice and thereby dissolves it – and general law stands over social practice – it governs it from outside, on behalf of the pre-social subject of self-will. Law's content is pre-social and its status is extra- or supra-social. As a result, bourgeois law [*Recht*] dissolves political self-government through its laws [*Gesetze*], since the acts of political self-government only exist in social practice.

The reason for the unjust justice of bourgeois law [*Recht*] is that the two entitlements which are opposed to each other in political self-government – the power to participate and consideration for powerlessness – can only be mediated as antagonistic moments. By transforming these entitlements into private claims that are given prior to practice and determined from outside or from above by laws [*Gesetze*], bourgeois law [*Recht*] at the same time fixes them in opposition to each other. Bourgeois law becomes the travesty of justice because it wants to establish justice apolitically.

The critique of bourgeois law thereby indicates how new right must proceed in a different way, in order to be just. The legal determination of private claims in bourgeois law turns the justice of splitting into its opposite. It creates the injustice of a dual identification. To be just, new right must therefore engage with the form of the law [*Gesetz*] itself, since law is identificatory. It is the expression of a false generality, the semblance of a knowledge of what is justified, which is the price of its positivism. To be sure, in new right, we know, in general and beforehand, that social practice for the sake of the good requires the authorization of participation *and* consideration for non-participation. We therefore know that – from the subject's perspective – the demand of justice is to safeguard both at the same time. Yet we do not know in general and in advance *how* this can be safeguarded. It would presuppose a (sovereign) standpoint outside of social practice and its self-government, from which individuals can be identified by general laws in their private claims. If we do not have such an external standpoint (or we do not want to have such a standpoint), because we are concerned with "a new right that is both antidisciplinary and emancipated from the principle of sovereignty,"[50] new right cannot therefore use laws to safeguard the justice of splitting.

To be sure, in new right, the political self-government of social practices is subordinated to *one* strict, unconditioned, prevailing basic law [*Grundgesetz*]: the law that such practices must simultaneously involve all as persons capable of judgment and must take each person into consideration as powerless. Government is subordinate to this law, since this *is* its law – the law that constitutes government and for this reason makes government good. The basic law of new right is the (external) version of the (inner) law of a government opposed to government.

Furthermore, in new right, the political self-government of social practices itself issues laws. These laws formulate its insight into how the justice of splitting is to be understood for the sake of the good of practice, as a general rule, namely that it is to be understood in the form of a rule, and not merely a measure. The fact that it must express this insight in a general form is based on government's claim to make a rational decision concerning the just. Its "decision of the just . . . must follow a law or a prescription, a rule."[51] Every generalization thereby signifies a self-externalization. In giving its insight into justice the form of generality, government divides itself from itself and confronts itself. Since, however, *this* self-externalization has no basis in what is (pre-) given outside of practice (the subject's private self-will) and thus cannot be stabilized, since the laws of new right are therefore not, like those of bourgeois law, sovereign, supra-social, and supra-political laws, and since their externality is hence an inner externality, the laws of new right have a paradoxical status: they are valid – and invalid. They formulate political government's reasons for a decision, but they do not determine its further decisions in the future. New right's decisions are always new decisions.

This is the only way that a decision of political self-government can be just. In order to be just, "it must . . . be both regulated and without regulation: it must conserve the law and also destroy it or suspend it enough to have to reinvent it in each case, rejustify it."[52] The justice of splitting requires a break in – not with – the form of law. Since nothing that is limited by laws and can thereby be fixed in place is positively given for new right, its laws are unable to achieve any independence over against the political self-government that is immanent in practice. While each of its decisions is based on a law, none of them obeys a law. New right is simultaneously formative of and a betrayal of law.

* * *

290

The critical distinction between new right [*Rechts*] and bourgeois law [*Recht*] is unstable. It is not given, since it is an impure or indirect distinction. New right is simultaneously like bourgeois law and opposed to it. It breaks from bourgeois law and reverts to it. New right is not distinct from bourgeois law, but is the continual reiteration of its self-distinction from bourgeois law. New right's difference from bourgeois law is therefore uncertain. Yet its difference from bourgeois law consists precisely in this uncertainty.

LAW AND VIOLENCE

Law's [*Rechts*] task is to limit violence. Violence is a specific way in which one person has an effect on another, namely an effect in which one injures another. In contrast, law governs the reciprocal effects of persons on each other according to the principle of equality. Violence between persons is not thereby excluded. It is limited, however, to the kinds of effects whose injuries do not compromise equality – status as a legal subject or as citizen (such violence therefore cannot "wrong" me).[1]

Law is violent, however, through its limitations. This is initially true of its means: without the ability to threaten violence (and to use it in "case of emergency"),[2] law cannot enforce its limitation of violence. Violence is one of the "symbiotic mechanisms" of law's normative order, which "mediates the relationship of the symbolic to the organic level."[3] As a *normative* order, law must claim to articulate a consensus. As a normative *order*, it must be able to confront the always looming "risks of dissension."[4] It thereby includes the possibility of violence. In judging for itself and punitively turning against the injurer, law is itself violent: it (counter-)injures the injurer.

Law, however, is unable to limit its violence to this instrumental role: it has no power over its violence. The real violence of law – the violence of violence – lies in its inability to limit and control legal violence.[5] For its violence succumbs to the repetition compulsion, which law is unable to stop, since this compulsion comprises its essence. As we have seen,[6] law is a form of normativity that is opposed to the non-normative (or natural) and thereby perpetually re-creates it as normativity's other. Law must therefore be violently enforced against its other, in perpetuity (since, in establishing itself, it simultaneously opposes its other). All "lawmaking is power making," since "law ... does not dismiss violence ... at the moment of instatement; rather, at this very moment of lawmaking, it specifically establishes as law not an end unalloyed by violence, but one necessarily and intimately bound to it."[7] Every act of preserving the law "repeats" the original establishment of law. In doing so, it is concerned never merely with formulating or applying this or that law, but with confirming "law itself." This is due to the logic that already governs the instatement of law, namely that the instatement of law is its opposition to the extra-juridical or to non-law. Law remains stuck in the opposition of law and non-law because it never establishes this opposition itself. Law can therefore never merely be a matter of preservation, proceeding according to its normative logic, but must, within each normativity, continually oppose its power to the extra-legal. Law cannot get past the act of its instatement. Its fate is to have to endlessly repeat its instatement. In this regard, the violence of law is "[m]ythical violence."[8]

Modern law wants to break this violence by *carrying out* the opposition of law and non-law *in a different way*. Modern law does not get past its opposition to non-law (since it would thereby simultaneously lose the capacity to limit the violence of an injury one person inflicts on another), but carries it out in the mode of self-reflection.[9] Law's self-reflection consists in examining itself in opposition to non-law and thereby bringing this opposition inside law itself. Law's self-reflection thereby creates the modern form of rights. Rights in their modern form apply the basic definition of law, the limitation of violence, to the violence that law [*Recht*] itself is. *Rights are the right* [*Recht*] *of rights*. They limit law's violence by legalizing the non-legal (or natural).

This self-reflective operation is also the basis for bourgeois law – its "genesis" (Marx). Bourgeois law realizes modern law's double limitation of violence – limitation of the violence of one person toward another and limitation of legal limitation's violence – by determining each person's private claims, which may be infringed neither by another person nor by law [*Recht*] itself. This occurs through bourgeois law [*Gesetz*]. The "material sense" of the bourgeois rule of law[10] is the securing of the private. To secure means to secure against violence. And violence here means any infringement of the private sphere (of choice) and private capacity (for participation) that is not justified by a law of equality. The basic program of bourgeois law [*Recht*] is the securing of private claims against violent injury. Bourgeois law wants to accomplish law's modern self-reflection in this way.

At the same time, however, the injustice of bourgeois law is rooted precisely in its program of security. The injustice of bourgeois law lies in its legal authorization of private claims that it presupposes as given. This is the positivist sense in which it understands the modern self-reflection of law. If new right [*Recht*] wants to put an end to the injustice of bourgeois law [*Rechts*] (and, as we have seen, if this requires calling the form of bourgeois law into question), then it must itself engage the basic bourgeois program. New right denies the presupposition – the basic equation – from which the bourgeois form of law [*Gesetzes*] obtains its "material sense" (Franz Neumann). This presupposition is that law's [*Rechts*] modern self-reflection – the self-reflection that constitutes modern law – *signifies*, or is identical to, the securing of private claims against its violence.

In bourgeois law, however, security from violence is irresolvably ambiguous: it is security from violent injuries and, at the same time (due to the way in which bourgeois law carries it out), security from the violence of change. It is security from the violence with which change intervenes in existing conditions and the given. The security of bourgeois law is the *abstract* objection to violence. It abstracts from the difference between violence and violence, between the violence of injury and the violence of change. Because it rules out changing what it legalizes, the legal securing of one's own is indistinguishable from the preservation of existing conditions. In this regard, the basic bourgeois program of security turns out to be the anti-political program as such. The legal securing of one's own deprives it of change. Bourgeois law is "what rules, without really ruling," since it relinquishes the power "[to] materially permeat[e] the content of the remaining, non-political spheres," to "*revolutionis[e]* these components themselves or subject them to criticism."[11]

In contrast, new right *wants* the power to politically permeate and revolutionize the non-political. Because new right's counter-rights are forms of performing its dialectical self-reflection, they dissolve the semblance of the given conferred by the bourgeois securing of one's own. New right intervenes in the entitlement of the given; counter-rights transform by showing consideration. Counter-rights split that which they consider in itself: they free its true form from its "existing caricature."[12] They exercise violence because they change things. Only a right that exercises violence is capable of changing things.

New right therefore abandons the bourgeois program of security from violence – from violence *in general*. New right, however, breaks the (mythic) repetition compulsion that underlies all of law's violence hitherto, precisely by exerting the violence of change. Violence, as what changes things, is always renounced when it achieves its goal. New right [*Recht*] is therefore law [*Recht*] whose violence consists in dissolving itself: violence that with its exercise "will begin to wither away immediately."[13] The violence of new right is the violence of liberation.

NOTES

Marx's Puzzle

1 [Tr. – The adjective *bürgerlich* will generally be translated in what follows as "bourgeois," though in some contexts it will be rendered as "civil," e.g., when modifying *Gesellschaft* ("civil society"), since there is precedent for this in Menke's citations of Hegel and Marx. The German word *Recht* can mean either "law" or "right." In what follows, it will generally be translated as "law" except where "right" seems necessary due to context. The plural of *Recht* – *Rechte* – will generally be translated as "rights." "Rights" or "*a right*" (*ein Recht*) refer to the subjective dimension in which rights are individual claims, while "law" or "right" without a definite or indefinite article [*Recht*] denotes the objective dimension in which "right" is a system of laws. The former involves the imposition of an obligation by one person upon another, while the latter is an "objective rule of law." *Gesetz* will also generally be translated as "law" with the German in brackets.]

2 Karl Marx, "On the Jewish Question," in: *Marx and Engels Collected Works*, vol. 3 (London: Lawrence & Wishart, 2010), 146–74, here 164.

3 And in which the "destiny" of human beings "to lead a universal life" is fulfilled (G.F.W. Hegel, *Elements of the Philosophy of Right*, trans. by H.B. Nisbet [Cambridge: Cambridge University Press, 1991, 276 [§ 258]).

4 Marx, "On the Jewish Question," 165.

5 Marx, "On the Jewish Question," 165.

6 Marx, "On the Jewish Question," 166.

7 Marx, "On the Jewish Question," 166 and 153 [Tr. – translation modified].

8 In Hegel's sense of the word: as the "authority [*Macht*] of the universal that guarantees security" in civil society (Hegel, *Elements of the Philosophy of Right*, 260 [§ 231]). For Hegel, "police" means politics that maintain and secure civil society – thus the police are no longer "sovereign," as they were in the (late-absolutist) "police state," which claimed to rule society as a whole (Michel Foucault, *The Birth of Biopolitics: Lectures at the Collège de France*, trans. by Graham Burchell [London: Palgrave Macmillan, 2008], 7).

9 This thesis stands in strict contrast to a critique of rights that only recognizes content. Contra Marx, Duncan Kennedy formulates its basic thesis as follows: "[T]here is no more a legal logic to Liberal rights than there is an economic logic to capitalism" (Duncan Kennedy, "The Critique of Rights in Critical Legal Studies," in: Wendy Brown and Janet Halley [eds.], *Left Legalism/ Left Critique* [Durham/London: Duke University Press, 2002], 178–227, here 216). The only thing then left to say is that "Rights just means rules in force to protect particular interests" (210). What Marx writes in his critique of bourgeois economy holds for critical legal studies: "it has never once asked the question why this content takes on that form" [Tr. – translation modified] (Karl Marx, *Capital*, vol. 1, in: *Marx and Engels Collected Works*, vol. 35 [London: Lawrence & Wishart, 1996], 91f.). Sonja Buckel argues along these lines in *Subjektivierung und Kohäsion: Zur Rekonstruktion einer materialischen Theorie des Rechts* (Weilerswist: Velbrück, 2007), 226.

10 Marx, "On the Jewish Question," 153.

11 The legitimate objection to the contrary is that, with the critique of the egoism of rights, Marx merely reproduced a specific historical ideology of rights that is unnecessary for its (bourgeois) form. Cf. Jürgen Habermas, "Natural Law and Revolution," in his *Theory and Practice*, trans. by John Viertel (Boston: Beacon, 1973), 82–120. See also Claude Lefort, "Human Rights and Politics," in: *The Political Forms of Modern Society: Bureaucracy, Democracy, Totalitarianism*, trans. by Alan Sheridan (Cambridge: MIT Press, 1986), 239–72.

12 For preliminary thoughts on this, see Christoph Menke, *Reflections of Equality*, trans. by Howard Rouse and Andrei Denejkine (Stanford: Stanford University Press, 2006). In my earlier studies of the critique of law I did not make the necessary break with liberalism clearly enough; cf. Christoph Menke, "From the Dignity of Man to Human Dignity: The Subject of Rights," in: *Values and Norms in the Age of Globalization*, ed. by Ewa Czerwińska-Schupp (Bern: Peter Lang, 2007), 83–94. For a first step in this direction, see "Subjektive Rechte: Zur Paradoxie der Form," in: *Nach Jacques Derrida und Niklas Luhmann: Zur (Un-)Möglichkeit einer Gesellschaftstheorie der Gerechtigkeit* (Stuttgart: Lucius & Lucius, 2008), 81–108.

13 Karl Marx, "Contribution to the Critique of Hegel's Philosophy of Law," in: *Marx and Engels Collected Works*, vol. 3, 3–129, here 91.

14 Karl Marx, "On the Jewish Question," 167 [Tr. – translation modified].

Part I History: The Legalization of the Natural

1 Michel Villey, *La formation de la pensée juridique moderne*, ed. by Stéphane Rials (Paris: Quadrige/PUF, 2006), 267.

1 A Philosophical History of Right's Form

1 William of Ockham, *A Letter to the Friars Minor and Other Writings*, trans. by John Kilcullen (Cambridge: Cambridge University Press, 1995), 24. Above all, one should consult Michel Villey's classic essay "La genèse

du droit subjectif chez Guillaume d'Occam," *Archives de philosophie du droit*, IX (1964), 97–127. Part of this text appeared in a posthumously published book that gathered his lectures from the 1960s, *La formation de la pensée juridique moderne*, ed. by Stéphane Rials (Paris: Quadrige/PUF, 2006), 220–68.

2 Ockham, *Letter to the Friars Minor*, 29.

3 Richard Tuck refers to Jean Gerson as the first person who provided "an account of *ius* as a *facultas*" (Richard Tuck, *Natural Rights Theories: Their Origin and Development* [Cambridge: Cambridge University Press, 1979], 25 f.). The central figure in his history of natural rights is Grotius.

4 Tuck, *Natural Rights Theories*, 13. On the role of glossators and the reception of Roman law see also Michel Villey, "Le 'jus in re' du droit romain classique au droit moderne," in: *Conférences faites à l'Institut de Droit Romain en 1947* (Paris: Sirey, 1950), 185–227, here 189; Helmut Coing, *Zur Geschichte des Privatrechtssystems* (Frankfurt: Klostermann, 1962), 38–41. In addition, Brian Tierney emphasizes the disruptive moments in the formation of canonical law; Brian Tierney, *The Idea of Natural Rights: Studies on Natural Rights, Natural Law, and Church Law 1150–1625* (Grand Rapids/ Cambridge: Eerdmans, 2001), esp. ch. 2.

5 Hugo Grotius, *The Rights of War and Peace*, book I, ed. by Richard Tuck (Indianapolis: Liberty Fund, 2005), 136–8.

6 Francisco Suárez, *Tractatus de Legibus ac de Deo Legislatore: Abhandlung über die Gesetze und Gott als Gesetzgeber*, 2.17.2, in: *Opera omnia*, ed. by M. André and C. Berton, vol. 5 (Paris: Ludovicus Vivès, 1856–78), 159–62.

7 [Tr. – "law" and "right" are in English in the original here, following Hobbes' usage.]

8 Thomas Hobbes, *Leviathan or The Matter, Forme, & Power of a Commonwealth, Ecclesiasticall and Civil*, ed. by Richard Tuck (Cambridge: Cambridge University Press, 1996), 91.

9 Hobbes, *Leviathan*, 200.

10 [Tr. – "right" is in English in the original here, equated with *ius*, and thus the subjective sense of right that is otherwise consistently rendered throughout "a right," "rights," "claim," or "subjective right" and must be distinguished from "law" or "right" as prevalent system of laws, which Menke immediately goes on to do in the very next lines.]

11 Friedrich Carl von Savigny, *System of the Modern Roman Law*, trans. by William Holloway (Madras: J. Higginbotham, 1867), 6. For the historical background of this terminological suggestion, see Alejandro Guzmán Brito, "Historia de la denominación del derecho-facultad como 'subjetivo'," *Revista de Estudios Histórico-Jurídicos*, XXV (2003), 407–33.

12 Immanuel Kant, *The Metaphysics of Morals* (Cambridge: Cambridge University Press, 1996), 63 [Tr. – translation modified]. In what follows, I am using the term "claim" in a manner different from its juridical usage. I take it to mean a legitimate claim and thus to be *coextensive* with the capacity to put others under obligations.

13 [Tr. – "law" and "right" are in English in the original here.]

14 [Tr. – "law" and "right" are in English in the original, following Hobbes' usage. In keeping with Hobbes' distinction, *Gesetz* is translated as "law" here and *Recht* is translated as "right." I switch back to translating *Recht* as

"law," as noted below, where Menke draws a parallel between *Gesetz* and *Recht* in his discussion of Strauss' interpretation of Hobbes.]

15 Leo Strauss, *The Political Philosophy of Hobbes* (Chicago: University of Chicago Press, 1952), 156.

16 Strauss, *Political Philosophy of Hobbes*, 156.

17 In the passage omitted with ellipses we find: "in other words, because Hobbes's political philosophy, as the harshest critic which that philosophy has recently found . . . is itself based . . . on assumptions representing an extreme form of individualism: an individualism more uncompromising than that of Locke himself" (Strauss, *Political Philosophy of Hobbes*, 157). Strauss here refers to Charles Edwyn Vaughan, *Studies in the History of Political Philosophy before and after Rousseau* (Manchester: Manchester University Press, 1925), 25. For Strauss' argument, see Leander Scholz, *Der Tod der Gemeinschaft: Ein Topos der politischen Philosophie* (Berlin: Akademie Verlag, 2012), 32–7.

18 [Tr. – Here and elsewhere *Anspruch*, which I generally translate as "claim," is equated by Menke with *Recht* in the "subjective" sense of "a right."]

19 Strauss, *Political Philosophy of Hobbes*, 160.

20 Leo Strauss, *Natural Right and History* (Chicago: University of Chicago Press, 1953), 181.

21 Strauss, *Natural Right and History*, 182.

22 [Tr. – I now return to translating *Recht* as "law," due to Menke's parallel here of *Recht* and, in the Hobbesian context, *Gesetz*.]

23 "If we may call liberalism that political doctrine which regards as the fundamental political fact the rights, as distinguished from the duties, of man and which identifies the function of the state with the protection or the safeguarding of those rights, we must say that the founder of liberalism was Hobbes" (Strauss, *Natural Right and History*, 181–2). Hannah Arendt sees the fundamental assumption of the French Revolution, which for this reason can or must be called "liberal" in comparison to the republicanism of the American Revolution, as rooted in the view that "these rights [Tr. – i.e., the Declaration of the Rights of Man and the Citizen] indeed were assumed not to indicate the limitations of all lawful government, but on the contrary to be its very foundation" (Arendt, *On Revolution* [London: Penguin, 1963], 148).

24 [Tr. – "separates . . . from" and "*set apart*" are translations of *trennt . . . von* and *getrennt*, respectively, which Menke is repeating for emphasis but which I've had to vary in their rendering to avoid awkwardness in English. Readers should here note that Menke intends "*set apart*" to refer back to "separates" for emphasis.]

25 [Tr. – "law" and "right" are in English in the original. See note 15.]

26 Jeremy Bentham, *Anarchical Fallacies*, in: *Nonsense upon Stilts: Bentham, Burke and Marx on the Rights of Man*, ed. by J. Waldron (London: Methuen, 1987), 46–76, here 53.

27 Raymond Geuss, *History and Illusion in Politics* (Cambridge: Cambridge University Press, 2001), 144.

28 [Tr. – Menke cites two editions of this work by Kelsen at various points throughout. There is an English translation, but it does not contain everything that Menke cites. I have therefore followed Menke in citing both German editions as he does, and on occasion provide the pagination for the

English translation, where possible.] Hans Kelsen, *Reine Rechtslehre*, ed. by Matthias Jestaedt (Tübingen: Mohr Siebeck, 2008), 53.

29 Kelsen, *Reine Rechtslehre*, 57.
30 Benedict de Spinoza, *The Complete Works*, trans. by Samuel Shirley (Indianapolis: Hackett, 2002), 685 (ch. 2, § 8 of *A Political Treatise*).
31 Manfred Walther, "Grundzüge der politischen Philosophie Spinozas," in: Michael Hampe and Robert Schnepf (eds.), *Baruch de Spinoza: Ethik* (Berlin: Akademie Verlag, 2006), 215–36, here 222.
32 Kant, *Metaphysics of Morals*, 45.
33 Kant, *Metaphysics of Morals*, 45.
34 Kant, *Metaphysics of Morals*, 90. In "Toward Perpetual Peace," Kant speaks about the fact that "in the state of nature, there can be nothing other than private right" (*Toward Perpetual Peace and Other Writings on Politics, Peace, and History*, trans. by David L. Colclasure [New Haven: Yale University Press, 2006], 106). The state of nature is thus without right in the sense that no "public right" exists in it, as a *legally secured process* established by legislation (*Toward Perpetual Peace*, 109). According to Kant, it is not a state without law, since it would then also be one without private law.
35 Kant, *Metaphysics of Morals*, 44.
36 Kelsen, *Reine Rechtslehre*, 71. Also, see 56–8.
37 For an analysis of rights as elements in legal relationships see Wesley Newcomb Hohfeld, *Fundamental Legal Conceptions as Applied in Judicial Reasoning* (Dartmouth: Ashgate, 2001). Hohfeld shows that rights can be respectively defined in four distinct ways through their opposite and correlative (*Fundamental Legal Conceptions*, 12ff.).
38 Alexandre Kojève, *Outline of a Phenomenology of Right*, trans. by Bryan-Paul Frost and Robert Howse (Lanham: Rowman & Littlefield, 2000), 40.
39 [Tr. – "right" and "law" are in English in the original here.]
40 Kelsen, *Reine Rechtslehre*, 58 and 61, respectively. On the problematic of the concept of reflex, see p. 64, as well as note 6, and pp. 125–7 in this volume.
41 [Tr. – "right" and "law" are in English in the original here.]
42 Cf. Rolf Göschner, "Dialogik der Rechtsverhältnisse," in: *Rechtsphilosophie im 21. Jahrhundert*, ed. by Winifred Brugger, Ulfrid Neumann, and Stephan Kirste (Frankfurt: Suhrkamp, 2008), 90–110, here 93 and 97. Yves Charles Zarka has shown that – in contrast to a reductive critique of subjectivism and atomism in the bourgeois theory of rights – Pufendorf and Leibniz already understood rights in the context of intersubjective legal relationships; see Yves Charles Zarka, "L'invention du sujet de droit," in: *L'autre voie de la subjectivité: Six études sur le sujet et le droit naturel au XVIIe siècle* (Paris: Beauchesne, 2000), 3–32. However, at the same time, rights in bourgeois law are authoritative instances of subjectification. For more on this, see part III of this book.
43 Savigny, *System of the Modern Roman Law*, 18. This does not mean *separating* them from each other: private law only obtains the "reality of its existence" (19) *through* public law. For a more explicit treatment of this issue, see Savigny's excursus on the political presupposition of private law in this same work.
44 Savigny, *System of the Modern Roman Law*, 271.

45 Savigny, *System of the Modern Roman Law*, 18.
46 This already holds true for the first basic definition of the modern character of rights: that they are supposed to assure or secure self-preservation and are thus *enabling* [*ermöglichend*]; see pp. 49–60 in this volume.
47 Franz Böhm, "Privatrechtsgesellschaft und Marktwirtschaft," *Ordo*, 17 (1966), 75–151, here 76. Marx formulates the same thesis as follows: "In Roman law, the servus is therefore correctly defined as one who may not enter into exchange for the purpose of acquiring anything for himself (see the *Institutes*). It is, consequently, equally clear that although this legal system corresponds to a social state in which exchange was by no means developed, nevertheless, in so far as it was developed in a limited sphere, it was able to develop the attributes of the juridical person, precisely of the individual engaged in exchange, and thus anticipate (in its basic aspects) the legal relations of industrial society, and in particular the right which rising bourgeois society had necessarily to assert against medieval society. But the development of this right itself coincides completely with the dissolution of the Roman community" (Karl Marx, *Grundrisse: Foundations of the Critique of Political Economy* [London: Penguin, 1973], 245–6).
48 As Richard Tuck explains, we should also note why Grotius was in a position "to treat the law of nature as totally to do with the maintenance of people's rights": "Rights have come to usurp the whole of natural law theory, for the law of nature is simply, respect one another's rights" (Tuck, *Natural Rights Theories*, 67).
49 Niklas Luhmann, "Subjektive Rechte: Zum Umbau des Rechtsbewußtseins für die moderne Gesellschaft," in: *Gesellschaftsstruktur und Semantik*, vol. 2 (Frankfurt: Suhrkamp, 1981), 45–104, here 47. This is directed against the theory of subjective right's self-conception: according to Michel Villey (to whom Luhmann refers), rights are necessarily subjective because they are grounded in the subject: it is "a right which emanates from the person, which is inherent in the person, which is its *attribute* [. . .]. To be precise: subjective right is a *quality* of the subject, one of its *faculties*, more precisely a franchise, a liberty, the possibility of acting" (Villey, "La genèse du droit subjectif chez Guillaume d'Occam," 101).
50 Luhmann, "Subjektive Rechte: Zum Umbau," 46.
51 See chapter 5 in this volume.
52 Ernest J. Weinrib, *The Idea of Private Law* (Cambridge: Harvard University Press, 1995), esp. ch. 2: "Legal Formalism." For the quotes that follow, see the overview in Weinrib, *Idea of Private Law*, 10f., and ch. 5, "Correlativity," in particular.
53 Friedrich Nietzsche, *On the Genealogy of Morals and Ecce Homo*, trans. by Walter Kaufmann and R.J. Hollingdale (New York: Vintage, 1989), 64.
54 It is only for this reason that the exchange relationships between these two persons can be binding for a third party. Every third party is obligated to recognize the new arrangement reached between the two persons in question (instead of saying, for example, that an item has been abandoned and can thus be appropriated by anyone the moment a person *relinquishes* his item – which occurs in every act of exchange).
55 And thereby ultimately on a difference of power, according to Nietzsche, since the demand for "equivalence" (which breeds a creature capable of

promises) succeeds exogenously through "a stronger power" (Nietzsche, *On the Genealogy of Morals*, 75).

56 Savigny, *System of the Modern Roman Law*, 8. This methodologically corresponds to the argumentative flow in Hegel's theory of abstract right: from the (property) claim of the individual person to the (contractual) relationship between two persons with each referring to the corrective authority of the third; see G.F.W. Hegel, *Elements of the Philosophy of Right*, trans. by H.B. Nisbet (Cambridge: Cambridge University Press, 1991), 73f., 10 f., 130f. (§§ 41f., 71f., and 103f.).

57 Regarding Cicero's definition of *ius civile*, Villey writes: "What is to be defined is civil law, *ius civile*. According to Aristotle, the nature of law in the strict sense is *political*. [. . .] The actualization of law presupposes a judge (*dikastēs*). A procedure is necessary, institutions which can only exist in a city. True law was only exercised within the same actual city, and Aristotle called it *dikaion politikon*, which was translated into Latin as *ius civile*" (Michel Villey, *Le droit et les droits de l'homme* [Paris: Quadrige/PUF, 2008; 1st edn 1983], 57f.).

58 Following Weinrib, Florian Rödl discusses the "a-historical" character of private law, in "Normativität und Kritik des Zivilrechts," *Archiv für Rechts- und Sozialphilosophie*, Supplement 114 (2007), 167–78, here 174. For a critique of this thesis see the discussion of Weinrib's interpretation of Aristotle in the next chapter, note 9.

59 Weinrib, *Idea of Private Law*, 23ff. According to Weinrib, private law is free of any "political aspect" because it has no extrinsic purpose (*Idea of Private Law*, 212).

60 Tuck, *Natural Rights Theories*, 2.

61 Niklas Luhmann, "Zur Funktion der 'subjektiven Rechte'," in: *Ausdifferenzierung des Rechts. Beiträge zur Rechtssoziologie und Rechtstheorie* (Frankfurt: Suhrkamp 1999), 360–73, here 361. At a – systematically – later point, the category of the subject will nevertheless become indispensable for the analysis of the understanding of rights in *bourgeois* law.

62 Luhmann, "Subjektive Rechte: Zum Umbau," 46.

63 Luhmann, "Subjektive Rechte: Zum Umbau," 49.

64 Luhmann, "Subjektive Rechte: Zum Umbau," 51.

65 Luhmann, "Subjektive Rechte: Zum Umbau," 73.

66 Luhmann, "Subjektive Rechte: Zum Umbau," 54.

67 "De iustitia et iure," (I.I) in: *The Institutes of Justinian*, trans. by Thomas Collett Sandar (London: Longmans, Green, 1878), 5.

68 Villey, *Le droit et les droits de l'homme*, esp. chs. 1 and 9. For a critique of the "German" critique of Roman law, see *Le droit et les droits de l'homme*, 55.

2 Interest in Self-Preservation

1 Aristotle, *Nicomachean Ethics*, trans. by H. Rackham (Cambridge: Harvard University Press, 1934), 267 (1131a).

2 Aristotle, *Nicomachean Ethics*, 281 (1132b).

3 Aristotle, *Nicomachean Ethics*, 275 (1132a).

4 [Tr. – translation modified] Aristotle, *Nicomachean Ethics*, 277 (1132a) [C.M. – my italics].
5 Aristotle, *Nicomachean Ethics*, 279 (1132b) [C.M. – my italics].
6 Aristotle, *Nicomachean Ethics*, 275 (1132a).
7 [Tr. – translation modified] Aristotle, *Nicomachean Ethics*, 285 (1133a–b) [C.M. – my italics].
8 Ernest J. Weinrib, *The Idea of Private Law* (Cambridge: Harvard University Press, 1995), 63.
9 "There would be no point [. . .] in concentrating on this quantitative equality unless the annulment vindicated equality in some sense. For if the initial sets of holdings embodied only an inequality, the subsequent gain by one party at the expense of another, to the extent that it mitigated the initial inequality, would itself be just" (Weinrib, *Idea of Private Law*, 63). In contrast to the interpretation outlined here, Weinrib does not want to understand this insight – "of course corrective justice presupposes the existence of entitlements" (80) – to mean that the justice of restitution and exchange presupposes the justice of equitable division. On the contrary, his argument is that this contradicts the "autonomy" (which he proclaims on 34–9 of his book) of private law (79f.). For one thing, however, that presupposes what remains to be demonstrated in the first place, and second, it is not evident why the formal difference of corrective and distributive justice is not supposed to be compatible with the substantive and normative dependence of corrective equality on the justice of distribution. Weinrib's interpretation of Aristotle's theory of private law subscribes to the maxim that nothing exists which ought not to. The price he has to pay for this consists in his having to deny that Aristotle has any understanding at all of the entitlements presupposed in private law: this is "a troubling lacuna in Aristotle's explication of corrective justice" (76), a missing piece that was later provided by Kant (81f.). Weinrib wants to contest the political presupposition, and nature, of private law in every possible way. He is therefore prepared to fault Aristotle for not thinking of something and, in a radical act of dehistoricization, to present Kant as the solution to Aristotle's supposed problems with providing a logical basis for his explication.
10 Cicero, *De Officiis*, trans. by Walter Miller (London: Heinemann, 1928), 255 (II.78).
11 Cicero, *De Officiis*, 263 (II.85). Nevertheless, this is only one part of justice: it further requires people "to use common possessions for the common interests, private property for their own" (*De Officiis*, 23 [I.7]).
12 Michel Villey, "Suum jus cuique tribuens," in: *Studi in onore di Pietro de Francisci* (Milan: Antonino Giuffre, 1956), vol. 1, 363–71, here 365.
13 Michel Villey, *La formation de la pensée juridique moderne*, ed. by Stéphane Rials (Paris: Quadrige/PUF, 2006), 247.
14 Cicero, *De Officiis*, 211 (II.41–2).
15 Michel Villey, *Le droit roman* (Paris: PUF, 1964), 20.
16 G.W.F. Hegel, *Phenomenology of Spirit*, trans. by A.V. Miller (Oxford: Oxford University Press, 1977), 290.
17 Villey, *La formation de la pensée juridique moderne*, 247.
18 Villey, *La formation de la pensée juridique moderne*, 249.
19 Villey, *La formation de la pensée juridique moderne*, 247. Roman law

"refrained from providing a definition of the content of the right of owner-ship" (Villey, *Le droit roman*, 84).

20 For the relation of private law and the commencement of action, see chapter 10, "Claiming One's Own," in this volume.

21 *Body of Civil Law*, in: *The Institutes of Justinian*, trans. by Thomas Collett Sandar (London: Longmans, Green, 1878), 13–17 [I.3.1].]

22 Michel Villey, "La genèse du droit subjectif chez Guillaume d'Occam," *Archives de philosophie du droit*, IX (1964), 97–127, here 104.

23 Cf. the critique of Villey in Richard Tuck, *Natural Rights Theories: Their Origin and Development* (Cambridge: Cambridge University Press, 1979), 22–4, and Brian Tierney, *The Idea of Natural Rights: Studies on Natural Rights, Natural Law, and Church Law 1150–1625* (Grand Rapids/Cambridge: Eerdmans, 2001), 13–42. Both criticize Villey's fixation on Ockham, and not merely on the grounds of historical fidelity. They also criticize his fixation by arguing that the idea of natural rights (in Ockham, and, for Villey, beyond) is rooted in philosophical nominalism. For this, see also the discussion of the relation between the logical and the legal-political category of the individual [*Individuums*] in Ockham by Arthur Stephen McGrade, "Ockham and the Birth of Individual Rights," in: Brian Tierney and Peter Linehan (eds.), *Authority and Power: Studies on Medieval Law and Government Presented to Walter Ullmann on his Seventieth Birthday* (Cambridge: Cambridge University Press, 1980), 149–65 esp. 149–51. Lastly, for an overview of the debate and a defense of Villey – both his interpreta-tion of Ockham and the critique of modernity that he based upon it – see John Milbank, "Against Human Rights: Liberty in the Western Tradition," *Oxford Journal of Law and Religion*, 1 (2012), 1–32. Villey's insight into the fundamental difference between the modern and traditional – Greek *and* Roman – idea of rights is not affected by the question of his interpretation of Ockham.

24 Villey, "La genèse du droit subjectif chez Guillaume d'Occam," 112.

25 Villey, "La genèse du droit subjectif chez Guillaume d'Occam," 114f.

26 William of Ockham, *A Letter to the Friars Minor and Other Writings*, trans. by John Kilcullen (Cambridge: Cambridge University Press, 1995), 21.

27 Villey, "La genèse du droit subjectif chez Guillaume d'Occam," 117.

28 Ockham, *Letter to the Friars Minor*, 24. See also, in this volume, p. 9.

29 Giorgio Agamben, *The Highest Poverty: Monastic Rules and Form-of-Life* (Stanford: Stanford University Press, 2011), 115. Agamben cites Villey (134), but misinterprets him as having overlooked Ockham's subtlety and attributes to him the *intention* of developing an affirmative concept of "subjective right." Villey's thesis, however, is precisely that Ockham unintentionally created this concept, and thus that his subtlety got him into trouble. One can speak of a systematic suppression of the modern character of rights in Agamben. For this, see chapter 6, "Excursus: The Biopolitical Context (Agamben)," in this volume.

30 Agamben, *Highest Poverty*, 138.

31 Agamben, *Highest Poverty*, 113.

32 Leo Strauss, *Natural Right and History* (Chicago: University of Chicago Press, 1953), 194. This initially holds true for the right (as power) of the sovereign: "only if *potentia* and *potestas* essentially belong together, can

there be a guaranty of the actualization of the right social order" (194). Yet it defines the concept of legal power in general, regardless of whether it is the power of the sovereign or of an individual.

33 Thomas Hobbes, *Leviathan or The Matter, Forme, & Power of a Commonwealth, Ecclesiasticall and Civil*, ed. by Richard Tuck (Cambridge: Cambridge University Press, 1996), 200.

34 Hobbes, *Leviathan*, 91.

35 Benedict de Spinoza, *A Theological-Political Treatise*, trans. by Michael Silverthorne and Jonathan Israel (Cambridge: Cambridge University Press, 2007), 195.

36 Spinoza, *Theological-Political Treatise*, 195–6.

37 Hobbes, *Leviathan*, 117. For the "final cause" or "end" of the state see Hobbes' discussion over the next few sections following this citation in *Leviathan*, passim. At a similar point, Spinoza speaks of "interest" in *Theological-Political Treatise*, 224. Leo Strauss (*The Political Philosophy of Hobbes* [Chicago: University of Chicago Press, 1952], 43) and Carl Schmitt (*The Leviathan in the State Theory of Thomas Hobbes*, trans. by George Schwab and Erna Hilfstein [Westport: Greenwood, 1996], 91, 96) refer to this goal-oriented character of the state, its advantageous character, when they call the concept of the state in the natural law tradition a "technical" concept.

38 [Tr. – Hobbes' conception of "the sovereign" does not require that it be a single person of a specific gender, and the pronoun "his" here is simply a matter of convenience rather than an indication of anything essential about the sovereign. Where possible, I will use the gender-neutral pronoun "its" in reference to "the Sovereign."]

39 Hobbes, *Leviathan*, 148.

40 Hobbes, *Leviathan*, 148. Cf. also ch. 40: "[T]he inward *thought* and *beleef* of men, which humane Governours can take no notice of" (323). In addition, see pp. 52–5 in this volume.

41 Spinoza, *Theological-Political Treatise*, 202. Martin Saar thus speaks of a "non-normative reformulation of the idea of a natural law" that connects the rules for living together back to the natural; Martin Saar, *Die Immanenz der Macht: Politische Theorie nach Spinoza* (Berlin: Suhrkamp, 2013), 35.

42 Hobbes, *Leviathan*, 100f. (ch. 15) and 170f. (ch. 24). For more on the modern conception of property, see chapter 9, "Property before Property," in this volume.

43 Talcott Parsons refers to law's new function as "mediating 'interface'" in the modern differentiation of politics and economy, state and society: "English legal developments contributed substantially to differentiating government from the societal community. Law became less an instrument of government and more a mediating 'interface' between the two. It had to serve the needs of government but was sufficiently independent to serve pluralistic private needs as well" (Talcott Parsons, *The System of Modern Societies* [Englewood Cliffs: Prentice Hall, 1971], 62). Law can only fulfill this social function with the mechanism of the modern character of rights.

44 Hobbes, *Leviathan*, 92 (ch. XIV).

45 Immanuel Kant, *The Metaphysics of Morals* (Cambridge: Cambridge University Press, 1996), 187–8.

46 Carl Schmitt opposes "the mere enactment of acts ... consistent with the manner of thinking of the positivistic legal system, translated with the word *law*" to "a spatially concrete, constitutive act" of law as distributive "act of spatial ordering" (Schmitt, *The Nomos of the Earth in the International Law of the Jus Publicum Europaeum*, trans. by G.L. Ulmen [New York: Telos, 2003], 78 and 81f.). According to Schmitt, law in its constitutive sense is external demarcation that nevertheless becomes substantial order. Schmitt therefore conceives constitutive law as the naturalized form of modern law. The real alternative, ethical or just law, breaks down in Schmitt (see also 113–19).

47 C.B. Macpherson, *The Political Theory of Possessive Individualism: Hobbes to Locke* (Oxford: Oxford University Press, 2011), 88.

48 Benedict de Spinoza, *Political Treatise*, in: *The Complete Works*, trans. by Samuel Shirley (Indianapolis: Hackett, 2002), 676–754, here 683 (ch. 2).

49 Hobbes speaks of "qualities" in relation to natural laws (*Leviathan*, 253 [ch. 26]). Spinoza speaks of being "determined" in his *Theological-Political Treatise*, 195 (ch. 16).

50 Rudolf von Ihering, *Geist des römischen Rechts auf den verschiedenen Stufen seiner Entwicklung* (1865), unaltered reprint of the 10th edn. (Aalen: Scientia, 1968), part 3, 339.

51 Ihering, *Geist des römischen Rechts*, 330.

52 Ihering, *Geist des römischen Rechts*, 350. For what follows, see chapter 4, "Excursus: The 'Formal' and the 'Material' Side (Ihering)," in this volume.

53 See Markus S. Stepanians, "Einleitung: 'Rights is a term that drips confusion'," in: Stepanians (ed.), *Individuelle Rechte* (Paderborn: mentis, 2007), 7–33, esp. 23ff., with reference to Donald Neil MacCormick, "Rechte in der Gesetzgebung," in: Stepanians, *Individuelle Rechte*, 164–83. For what follows, see also the overview in Jeremy Waldron, *The Right to Private Property* (Oxford: Oxford University Press, 1988), 79–94.

54 Joseph Raz, *The Morality of Freedom* (Oxford: Clarendon, 1986), 171; cf. Joel Feinberg, "The Nature and Value of Rights," in: *Rights, Justice, and the Bounds of Liberty* (Princeton: Princeton University Press 1980), 143–58, here 148f.

55 Raz, *Morality of Freedom*, 169.

56 Raz, *Morality of Freedom*, 181. To state this in greater detail: "Rights are the grounds of duties in the sense that one way of justifying holding a person to be subject to a duty is that this serves the interest on which another's right is based. Regarded from the opposite perspective the fact that rights are sufficient to ground duties limits the rights one has. Only where one's interest is a reason for another to behave in a way which protects or promotes it, and only when this reason has the peremptory character of a duty, and, finally, only when the duty is for conduct which makes a significant difference for the promotion or protection of that interest does the interest give rise to a right" (183).

57 Spinoza, *Theological-Political Treatise*, 196.

58 Villey, "La genèse du droit subjectif chez Guillaume d'Occam," 101 (with regard to property rights): "But such a law did not create property, it only authorized it."

59 Niklas Luhmann, *Law as a Social System*, trans. by Klaus A. Ziegert (Oxford: Oxford University Press, 2004), 111.

60 Luhmann, *Law as a Social System*, 86. This can also be seen as the point of Luhmann's own concept of the self-reflection of law; for more on this, see Part II in this volume.
61 Luhmann, *Law as a Social System*, 113.

3 Inner Choice

1 Aeschylus, "Eumenides," line 691, in: *Aeschylus*, vol. II (London: William Heinemann, 1926), 339. Cf. Christoph Menke, *Law and Violence: Christoph Menke in Dialogue*, trans. by Gerrit Jackson (Manchester: Manchester University Press, 2018), 17–22.
2 Aeschylus, "Eumenides," 321 (lines 522–7).
3 Aristotle, *Nicomachean Ethics*, trans. by H. Rackham (Cambridge: Harvard University Press, 1934), 263 (book V, 1130b) [C.M. – my italics].
4 Aristotle, *Nicomachean Ethics*, 259 (book V, 1129b).
5 Werner Jaeger, *Paideia: The Ideals of Greek Culture*, vol. I, trans. by Gilbert Highet (Oxford: Oxford University Press, 1945), 113.
6 Aristotle, *Nicomachean Ethics*, 259 (book V, 1129b).
7 Aristotle, *Nicomachean Ethics*, 259 (book V, 1129b).
8 Aristotle, *Nicomachean Ethics*, 259 (book V, 1129b).
9 Pierre Aubenque, "La loi selon Aristote," *Archives de philosophie du droit*, 25 (1980), 147–57, here 150.
10 Aristotle, *Nicomachean Ethics*, 259 (book V, 1129b).
11 Aristotle, *Nicomachean Ethics*, 261 (book V, 1130a). For this reason, Michel Villey speaks of Aristotle's distinction between law and "morality" and therefore of the "autonomy" of law (Villey, *La formation de la pensée juridique moderne*, ed. by Stéphane Rials [Paris: Quadrige/PUF, 2006], 84f.).
12 Aristotle, *Nicomachean Ethics*, 73 (book II, 1103a–b).
13 Aristotle, *Nicomachean Ethics*, 73 (book II, 1103a).
14 Aristotle, *Nicomachean Ethics*, 391 (book VII, 1147a).
15 Aristotle, *Nicomachean Ethics*, 391 (book VII, 1147a).
16 Aristotle, *Politics*, trans. by H. Rackham (Cambridge: Harvard University Press, 1944), 605 (book VII, 1333a). For more on education via law, see also *Nicomachean Ethics*, book V, 1130b, and book X, 1180a.
17 Jaeger, *Paideia*, vol. I, 118. According to Aristotle, only law provides the authority required for education: "Now paternal authority has not the power to compel obedience, nor indeed, speaking generally, has the authority of any individual unless he be a king or the like; but law on the other hand is a rule, emanating from a certain wisdom and intelligence, that has compulsory force. Men are hated when they thwart people's inclinations, even though they do so rightly, whereas law can enjoin virtuous conduct without being invidious" (Aristotle, *Nicomachean Ethics*, 635 [book X, 1180a]).
18 All members of the family – wife, children, slaves – are thus subject to the male head of the household. "They are not '*sui juris.*' That does not mean that they are actually unprotected by ethical rules or precepts of Roman religion" (Michel Villey, *Le droit roman* [Paris: PUF, 1964], 55). These ethical-religious rules are later adopted as law: "But at the present day no persons under our rule may use violence toward their slaves, without a reason

recognized by the law, or ever to an extreme extent. [. . .] as it concerns the public good, that no one should misuse his own property" (Justinian, *The Institutes of Justinian*, trans. by Thomas Collett Sandar [London: Longmans, Green, 1878], 28 [I.8.2]).

19 Cicero, *On the Commonwealth and On the Laws*, ed. and trans. by James E.G. Zetzel (Cambridge: Cambridge University Press, 1999), 111–12 (I.18–19) [Tr. – translation modified to reflect the German edition that Menke refers to here, which provided the Greek and Latin terms in brackets].

20 Cicero, *On the Commonwealth and On the Laws*, 134 (II.13).

21 Cicero, *On the Commonwealth and On the Laws*, 133 (II.11) [Tr. – translation modified to include the Latin in brackets, in keeping with Menke's German edition].

22 Martin Heidegger, *Parmenides*, trans. by André Schuwer and Richard Rojcewicz (Bloomington: Indiana University Press, 1992), 40. Without explicitly referring to Cicero, but with clear references to his formulations, Heidegger writes: "In the essential realm of the 'command' belongs the Roman 'law', *ius*" (40). Heidegger sees here a feature shared by the Roman and Jewish conception of laws. In contrast, "The gods of the Greeks are not commanding gods but, rather, ones that give signs, that point" (40). This recalls the young Hegel's thesis that Greek law is being, not something established. For more on this, see Christoph Menke, "Hegel's Theory of Liberation: Law, Freedom, History, Society," *Symposium*, 17.1 (2013), 10–30.

23 Cicero, *On the Commonwealth and On the Laws*, 111 (I.18).

24 Cicero, *On the Commonwealth and On the Laws*, 117 (I.33).

25 Cicero, *On the Commonwealth and On the Laws*, 115 (I.28).

26 Aubenque, "La loi selon Aristote," 149.

27 Cicero, *On the Commonwealth and On the Laws*, 126 and 134 (I.58 and II.14).

28 Cicero, *On the Commonwealth and On the Laws*, 127 (I.58). "Reason existed, derived from nature, directing people to good conduct and away from crime; it did not begin to be a law only at that moment when it was written down, but when it came into being; and it came into being at the same time as the divine mind. And therefore that true and original law, suitable for commands and prohibitions, is the right reason of Jupiter, the supreme god" (133 [II.10]).

29 Cicero, *On the Commonwealth and On the Laws*, 133 (II.11) [Tr. – translation modified].

30 Cicero, *On the Commonwealth and On the Laws*, 158 (III.3).

31 Cicero, *On the Commonwealth and On the Laws*, 117 (I.33).

32 Cicero, *On the Commonwealth and On the Laws*, 72 (I.31).

33 Cicero, *On the Commonwealth and On the Laws*, 122 (I.49).

34 Cicero, *On the Commonwealth and On the Laws*, 116 (I.31) (*error mentis*).

35 Thomas Hobbes, *Leviathan or The Matter, Forme, & Power of a Commonwealth, Ecclesiasticall and Civil*, ed. by Richard Tuck (Cambridge: Cambridge University Press, 1996), 144 (ch. 20). Hobbes explains the absoluteness of sovereignty (in ch. 20, cited here) by positively comparing political dominion with "both *Paternall* and *Despoticall* dominion" (which, traditionally, had been sharply distinguished from political dominion).

36 Hobbes, *Leviathan*, 144 (ch. 20). Just after this, we find the following: "Because every Subject is by this Institution Author of all the Actions, and Judgements of the Soveraigne Instituted; it follows, that whatsoever he doth, it can be no injury to any of his Subjects; nor ought he to be by any of them accused of Injustice" (*Leviathan*, 124 [ch. 20]).

37 Hobbes, *Leviathan*, 124 (ch. 18) and 153 (ch. 21).

38 The denial of this thought forms the basis for Spinoza's counter-thesis to Hobbes, that the democratic form of governance is the "most natural." "In a democracy no one transfers their natural right to another in such a way that they are not thereafter consulted but rather to the majority of the whole society of which they are a part" (Benedict de Spinoza, *A Theological-Political Treatise*, trans. by Michael Silverthorne and Jonathan Israel [Cambridge: Cambridge University Press, 2007], 202 [ch. 17]).

39 Hobbes, *Leviathan*, 151–2 (ch. 21). Cf. Spinoza, *Theological-Political Treatise*, 220–2 (ch. 17). Here too, according to Spinoza, a democracy is better; cf. 200 (ch. 16).

40 Hobbes, *Leviathan*, 151 (ch. 21).

41 Hobbes, *Leviathan*, 91 (ch. 14).

42 Spinoza, *Theological-Political Treatise*, 208.

43 Hobbes, *Leviathan*, 324 (ch. 40). Hobbes speaks of "inward *thought*, and *beleef* of men" (323): belief is by definition "inward."

44 For the theological foundation of Hobbes' liberalization of belief see Rainer Forst, *Toleration in Conflict: Past and Present* (Cambridge: Cambridge University Press, 2013), 193–6. Koselleck, in contrast, points out that Hobbes is talking not about faith (in a specifically religious sense), but about belief; Reinhart Koselleck, *Critique and Crisis: Enlightenment and the Pathogenesis of Modern Society* (Cambridge: MIT Press, 2000), 29 (n. 27) and 165f. At the same time, this implies that Hobbes' argument for tolerance – which despite all of its limitations has for precisely this reason a fundamental significance – is rooted in the bases for his conception of the state: "Whether I harbor anarchist, revolutionary, or atheistic thoughts is not the state's concern. That would have been inconceivable to Socrates or Cicero. Sovereignty, positive law and subjective rights are equiprimordial" (Hauke Brunkhorst, *Einführung in die Geschichte politischer Ideen* [Munich: Fink, 2000], 202).

45 Carl Schmitt, *The Leviathan in the State Theory of Thomas Hobbes*, trans. by George Schwab and Erna Hilfstein (Westport: Greenwood, 1996), 57. On the text's anti-Semitism and Schmitt's own later self-interpretation, see Raphael Gross, *Carl Schmitt and the Jews: The "Jewish Question," the Holocaust, and German Legal Theory*, trans. by Joel Golb (Madison: University of Wisconsin Press, 2007), 230–40.

46 Schmitt, *Leviathan in the State Theory of Thomas Hobbes*, 58.

47 Schmitt, *Leviathan in the State Theory of Thomas Hobbes*, 57. In *Roman Catholicism and Political Form* trans. by G. L. Ulmen, (Westport: Greenwood, 1996), Carl Schmitt takes up Georg Jellinek's historical explanation of the emergence of human rights from religious freedom or freedom of belief (Georg Jellinek, *The Declaration of the Rights of Man and of Citizens* [New York: Henry Holt, 1901], 59–77) and interprets it as a "privatization" of religion that had to end with economic liberalization, 28f.

48 "The absolute prince is also the sole representative of the political unity

of the people. He alone represents the state. As Hobbes puts it, the state has 'its unity in the person of a sovereign'; it is 'united in the person of one sovereign'" (Carl Schmitt, *Constitutional Theory*, trans. and ed. by Jeffrey Seitzer [Durham/London: Duke University Press, 2008], 247).

49 Ernst Kantorowicz, *The King's Two Bodies: A Study in Medieval Political Theology* (Princeton: Princeton University Press, 1957), 29.

50 Thus we find Hegel's definition in *Elements of the Philosophy of Right*, trans. by H.B. Nisbet (Cambridge: Cambridge University Press, 1991), 69 (§ 38), "The determination of right is therefore only a *permission* or *warrant*," and Savigny, *System of the Modern Roman Law*, trans. by William Holloway (Madras: J. Higginbotham, 1867) (right in "a subjective sense" is "synonymous with privilege" [7]).

51 See p. 53 in this volume.

52 Hobbes, *Leviathan*, 436–7 (ch. 37) [C.M. – my italics].

53 Hobbes, *Leviathan*, 253 (ch. 26). Cf. 147 (ch. 15). See p. 39 in this volume.

54 Spinoza, *Theological-Political Treatise*, 195 (ch. 16). For this radicalization of Hobbes by Spinoza, see Leo Strauss, *The Political Philosophy of Hobbes* (Chicago: University of Chicago Press, 1952), 169f.

55 [Tr. –Spinoza, *Theological-Political Treatise*, 196 (ch. 16).]

56 Benedict de Spinoza, *Political Treatise*, in: *The Complete Works*, trans. by Samuel Shirley (Indianapolis: Hackett, 2002), 676–754, here 683 (ch. 2).

57 "For *right* is *freedom*, namely that liberty which the civil law leaves us" (Hobbes, *Leviathan*, 276 [ch. 26]).

58 Immanuel Kant, *The Metaphysics of Morals* (Cambridge: Cambridge University Press, 1996), 46.

59 Kant, *Metaphysics of Morals*, 47.

60 Kant, *Metaphysics of Morals*, 56.

61 Kant, *Metaphysics of Morals*, 42.

62 Kant, *Metaphysics of Morals*, 56.

63 Kant, *Metaphysics of Morals*, 56.

64 Kant, *Metaphysics of Morals*, 56.

65 Kant, *Metaphysics of Morals*, 63.

66 Kant, *Metaphysics of Morals*, 63. This enabling sense is definitive for the type of right known as *liberties*: they establish that the bearer of a right is not stand under an obligation. Cf. H.L.A. Hart, "Are There Any Natural Rights?" in: Jeremy Waldron (ed.), *Theories of Rights* (Oxford: Oxford University Press, 1984), 77–90, here 80f.

67 In addition, the right to do something wrong belongs to law; Jeremy Waldron, "A Right To Do Wrong," in: *Liberal Rights: Collected Papers 1981–1991* (Cambridge: Cambridge University Press, 1993), 63–87.

68 Kant, *Metaphysics of Morals*, 56. See p. 52 in this volume. Also, see a more explicit treatment of this issue in chapter 14, "Excursus: Causal and Legal Relation."

69 Kant, *Metaphysics of Morals*, 64.

70 Once again, the reflections from part II of this volume are relevant here.

71 See chapter 4 in this volume.

72 See p. 39 in this volume. On the redefinition of the human being as the other side of the citizen, see Koselleck, *Critique and Crisis*, 36f.

73 In the precise sense of the term, as elaborated by Michel Foucault in

Discipline and Punish: The Birth of the Prison, trans. by Alan Sheridan (New York: Vintage, 1977), 170–94. The replacement of paideia with discipline means that the resistance of the natural remains impossible to resolve. Dieter Thomä has shown this pertinence of what lies outside of the law in Hobbes' figure of the *puer robustus* and outlined its modern history; see Dieter Thomä, "Der kräftige Knabe," *Zeitschrift für Ideengeschichte*, VI.2 (2012), 73–90. See also Christoph Menke, "Die Disziplin der Ästhetik ist die Ästhetik der Disziplin: Baumgarten in der Perspektive Foucaults," in: Rüdiger Campe, Anselm Haverkamp, and Christoph Menke, *Baumgarten-Studien: Zur Genealogie der Ästhetik* (Berlin: August Verlag, 2014), 233–47. For Foucault's analysis of juridical subjectivity, see chapter 11, "Foucault's Diagnosis: The Regression of the Juridical," in this volume.

4 Antagonism of Performance

1 Michel Foucault, *The History of Sexuality*, vol. 1: *An Introduction*, trans. by Robert Hurley (New York: Pantheon, 1978), part 5, 133–60.
2 For legal permission is the normative mechanism that brings about social domination and economic exploitation, and legal enablement is the mechanism by which social normalization is enforced. See chapter 12 in this volume.
3 For a more detailed treatment of this issue, see chapter 6, "The Naturalization of the World," in this volume.
4 Rudolf von Ihering, *Geist des römischen Rechts auf den verschiedenen Stufen seiner Entwicklung* (1865), unaltered reprint of the 10th edn. (Aalen: Scientia, 1968), part 3, 338 and 350. Cf. 60f. in that volume, where we find Ihering claiming that if a right were realized in the way that the will theory supposes, it would be a "right's spiritual pleasure," "delight in pure power as such, the satisfaction of carrying out our will" (*Geist des römischen Rechts*, 337). Ihering is obviously thinking of Shylock's answer: "You'll ask me why I rather choose to have / A weight of carrion flesh, than to receive / Three thousand ducats: I'll not answer that! / But say it is my humour, – is it answer'd?" (William Shakespeare, *The Merchant of Venice*, IV.1, 41–4). In *The Struggle for Law*, Ihering nevertheless defends Shylock: he speaks "the language which the wounded feeling of legal right will speak, at all times and in all places; the power, the firmness of the conviction, that law must remain law, the lofty feeling and pathos of a man who is conscious that, in what he claims, there is question not only of his person but of the law" (Rudolf von Ihering, *The Struggle for Law*, trans. by John J. Lalor [Chicago: Callaghan, 1915], 86f.).
5 Ronald Dworkin reformulates this interest-theory objection against will theory, independently of this controversy. His response to the question "What rights do we have?" is that there is no right to freedom – in other words, there is not "any general right to liberty at all," understood as general, indefinite "license" (Ronald Dworkin, "Which Rights Do We Have?" in: *Taking Rights Seriously* [Cambridge: Harvard University Press, 1977], 266–78, here 266–7). Instead, we only have a right to *specific* "basic liberties." And we thereby find ourselves in the field of interests: "If we have

a right to basic liberties . . . [this is] because an assault on basic liberties injures us or demeans us in some way that goes beyond its impact on liberty, then what we have a right to is not liberty at all, but to the values or interests or standing that this particular constraint defeats" (Dworkin, "Which Rights Do We Have?" 271).

6 [Tr. – translation modified; see the last sentence of the quote immediately following this parenthetical note for the unmodified version of this line.] "Not all interests *require* legal protection, and not all of them *are able* to be legally protected. Not every law that protects an interest grants a right (in the subjective sense) to an interested party – that is, there is not a legal right to being granted such protection. Law, which introduces protective duties into certain sectors of industry under the heading of 'interest', *benefits* manufacturers, it *promotes* and *protects* them as they engage in business, and yet it does not grant them any *rights*. How is this consistent with our earlier definition – that rights are legally protected interests?. . . . The answer is that we are here simply presented with a mere *reflex effect*, a relationship that is indeed very similar to law, but which must be distinguished from it all the more carefully as a result. The state really enacts law in *its own* interest, which here admittedly amounts to the interests of industrialists, as with a bequest in which someone leaves behind a dowry for their niece in the event of her marriage, to be distributed to the heiress and her husband. Manufacturers have as little of a legal claim to carrying out their lawful protective duties (the enforcement of which is completely independent of *their* will or what they do not will, ultimately just a matter for the authorities) as does the heiress to a payout of her inheritance" (Ihering, *Geist des römischen Rechts*, part 3, 351f.). Ihering's distinction between a legal claim and a reflex of the legal system is a fundamental one. It is ignored by the interest theory of right.

7 Ihering, *Geist des römischen Rechts*, 339.

8 [Tr. – my translation] Georg Jellinek, *System der subjektiven öffentlichen Rechte* (Darmstadt: Wissenschaftliche Buchgesellschaft, 1963; reprint of the 2nd edn. [Tübingen: 1905]), 44–5.

9 Niklas Luhmann, *Law as a Social System*, trans. by Klaus A. Ziegert (Oxford: Oxford University Press, 2004), 418.

10 For a more explicit treatment of this topic, see chapter 10, "Claiming One's Own," in this volume.

11 Ihering comes close to this when he speaks of the "*freedom of disposition*" as "*freedom* in *choosing at our pleasure*" (Ihering, *Geist des römischen Rechts*, part 3, 349).

12 For more on this, see chapter 12, "The Struggle for Law: Critique in Bourgeois Law," in this volume.

Part II Ontology: The Materialism of Form

1 Modification of an aphorism by Hegel from his Jena period (Hegel himself is speaking of self-consciousness, not of right); cited by Karl Rosenkranz, *G. W. F. Hegels Leben* (Berlin 1844; reprint Darmstadt: Wissenschaftliche Buchgesellschaft, 1977), 552. For an interpretation of its significance in this volume, see pp. 85–9.

2 François Ewald, following Foucault, characterizes his methodological program of a "radical positivism" in such terms in his examination of law: François Ewald, *L'etat providence* (Paris: Bernard Grasset, 1986), 40–3.

5 Legality's Gap

1 [Tr. – translation modified] Max Weber defines the juridical concept of the "legal" type of authority: it proceeds on the basis of the idea "That any given legal right may be established by agreement or by imposition, on grounds of expediency or value-rationality or both, with a claim to obedience" (Max Weber, *Economy and Society: An Outline of Interpretive Sociology*, ed. by Guenther Roth and Claus Wittich [Berkeley: University of California Press, 1978], 217).
2 In what follows, if "rights" or the "form of rights" are spoken of without qualification, it should be borne in mind that their specifically modern form is what is meant.
3 See part I.
4 Jürgen Habermas, *Between Facts and Norms: Contributions to a Discourse Theory of Law and Democracy* (Cambridge: MIT Press, 1996), 100.
5 Michel Foucault thus writes on the self-limitation of liberal governance: "[This approach] starts from government practice and tries to analyze it in terms of the de facto limits that can be set to this governmentality . . . .precisely in terms of the objectives of governmentality" (Michel Foucault, *The Birth of Biopolitics: Lectures at the Collège de France*, trans. by Graham Burchell [London: Palgrave Macmillan, 2008], 40). Yet Foucault believes that this structure of liberal governance has nothing (or little) to do with "the juridical question of rights" (*Birth of Biopolitics*, 42). For more on this, see chapter 11, "Foucault's Diagnosis: The Regression of the Juridical," in this volume.
6 Franz Neumann, "The Change in the Function of Law in Modern Society," 101–2f., in: *The Rule of Law under Siege: Selected Essays of Franz Neumann and Otto Kirchheimer* [(Berkeley: University of California Press, 1996), 101–41. (The text is an abridged version of the argument of Neumann's second, London dissertation: *The Rule of Law: Political Theory and the Legal System in Modern Society* [Oxford: Berg, 1986], originally published in *Zeitschrift für Sozialforschung*.) [Tr. – The last part of this excerpt, from the final ellipsis to the very end of the quotation, could not be found in either of the English translations listed above and so I have translated it myself here.]
7 Neumann, *Rule of Law: Political Theory and the Legal System in Modern Society*, 212.
8 Neumann, *Rule of Law: Political Theory and the Legal System in Modern Society*, 212.
9 Carl Schmitt, *Constitutional Theory*, trans. and ed. by Jeffrey Seitzer (Durham/London: Duke University Press, 2008), 181–96 (§ 13).
10 Neumann, *Rule of Law: Political Theory and the Legal System in Modern Society*, 212.
11 Schmitt, *Constitutional Theory*, 183–4.

12 Neumann, *Rule of Law*, 213–14. Even this interpretation reformulates one of Schmitt's theses: see chapter 10, "The Declaration of Basic Rights," in this volume.

13 Thus the definition of the state of exception: Carl Schmitt, *Political Theology: Four Chapters on the Concept of Sovereignty*, trans. by George Schwab (Cambridge: MIT Press, 1985), 12. The authoritarian state merely draws the structural consequence of the unavoidability of exception.

14 Schmitt, *Constitutional Theory*, 257.

15 Neumann, *Rule of Law: Political Theory and the Legal System in Modern Society*, 291.

16 Neumann, *Rule of Law: Political Theory and the Legal System in Modern Society*, 293.

17 Neumann, "Change in the Function of Law in Modern Society," 132–3.

18 Niklas Luhmann, "Paradox of Form," in: *Problems of Form*, ed. by Dirk Baecker, trans. by Michael Irmscher and Leah Edwards (Stanford: Stanford University Press, 1999), 15–26, here 16.

19 Niklas Luhmann, *Law as a Social System*, trans. by Klaus A. Ziegert (Oxford: Oxford University Press, 2004), 100. [C.M. – I have removed the italics from the original here.]

20 I have here modified an observation made by Niklas Luhmann regarding the "Sign as Form." Luhmann's original text reads: "Now we have to consider yet another outside, namely, the outside of the difference between signifier and signified, that is, the outside of the unity of this difference, the outside of the sign. This would then be the world" (Niklas Luhmann, "Sign as Form," in: *Problems of Form*, 46–63, here 57).

21 Luhmann, *Law as a Social System*, 105 [Tr. – translation modified].

22 H.L.A. Hart, *The Concept of Law*, 2nd edn. (Oxford: Clarendon, 1994), 94f. Upon recognizing a legal rule, a second step, the determination and formation of the rule, follows: secondary rules are thus additional rules for the regulation of rules. See Hart, *Concept of Law*, 95f.

23 Niklas Luhmann, *Social Systems*, trans. by John Bednarz, Jr. and Dirk Baecker (Stanford: Stanford University Press, 1995), 448 and 450.

24 Gunther Teubner, *Law as an Autopoietic System* (Oxford: Blackwell, 1993), 20. Teubner calls this level of basal self-reference "self-organization" and explains it with reference to Hart's theory of secondary rules.

25 Luhmann, "Paradox of Form," 17.

26 Luhmann, "Paradox of Form," 17.

27 Luhmann, "Sign as Form," 57 [Tr. – translation modified].

28 Luhmann, *Law as a Social System*, 180.

29 Luhmann, *Law as a Social System*, 181.

30 Luhmann, *Law as a Social System*, 73.

31 Luhmann, "Paradox of Form," 15.

32 Katrin Trüstedt, "*Nomos and Narrative*: Zu den Verfahren des Orestie," in: Ingo Augsberg and Sophie-Charlotte Lenski (eds.), *Die Innenwelt der Außenwelt der Innenwelt des Rechts: Annäherungen zwischen Rechts- und Literaturwissenschaft* (Munich: Fink, 2012), 59–78; see also Trüstedt's "Die Person als Stellvertreter," in: Jörg Dünne, Martin Jörg Schafer, Myriam Suchet, and Jessica Walker (eds.), *Les Intraduisibles/Unübersetzbarkeiten* (Paris: Éditions des Archives contemporaines, 2013), 321–30.

33 [Tr. – my retranslation] Martin Heidegger, *Parmenides*, trans. by André Schuwer and Richard Rojcewicz (Bloomington: Indiana University Press, 1992), 41. According to Heidegger, bringing to a fall is a dissembling (38) that is at the same time a "letting hold" [*geltenlassen*]. Heidegger considers this to have been a contrivance of Roman law and thus to be as "un-German" as the word "false," from which he derives *Fall*.

34 This is at issue in Kleist's *The Broken Jug*; see Christoph Menke, "Nach dem Gesetz: Zum Schluß des *Zerbrochnen Krugs*," in: Martina Groß and Patrick Primavesi (eds.), *Lücken sehen Beiträge zu Theorie, Literatur und Performance* (Heidelberg: Winter, 2010), 97–112.

35 Jacques Derrida, "Force of Law: The 'Mystical Foundation of Authority'," in: *Deconstruction and the Possibility of Justice*, ed. by Drucilla Cornell, Michael Rosenfeld, and David Gray Carlson (New York: Routledge, 1992), 3–67, here 23. Instead of "legitimate" [*rechtlich*], Derrida's translator uses the term "just" [*gerecht*]. It holds for both, however: for justice and for law.

36 [Tr. – my translation] Isabell Hensel, "Klangpotentiale: Eine Annäherung an das Rauschen des Rechts," in: Christian Joerges and Peer Zumbansen (eds.), *Politische Rechtstheorie Revisited: Rudolf Wiethölter zum 100. Semester* (Bremen: ZERP, 2013), 69–99, here 89 and 87, respectively.

37 [Tr. – "secondary rules" is in English in the original.]

38 Luhmann, "Paradox of Form," 18.

39 For what follows, see Christoph Menke, *Violence and Law* (Manchester: Manchester University Press, 2018), part I.

40 [Tr. – "Presupposition" in German is *Voraussetzung*, while *setzen* is "to establish," so that "to establish law's 'pre-'" (*Voraus*) is to *voraus-setzen*.]

41 Schmitt, *Political Theology*, 13f.

42 Giorgio Agamben, *State of Exception*, trans. by Kevin Attell (Chicago: University of Chicago Press, 2005), 60. See chapter 10, "Excursus: The Biopolitical Context (Agamben)," in this volume.

43 See p. 81 in this volume (Luhmann, "Paradox of Form," 15).

44 Dirk Baecker believes that the same view can also be found in Marx and Simmel, though simply with reversed hierarchies: for them, form "is still the extrinsic, the merely accidental in relation to the substance or content of something, in other words, that which can be distinguished from matter, which would have to inquire into what is really substantial, how so, and thus how the essential is constituted" (Baecker, *Form und Formen der Kommunikation* [Frankfurt: Suhrkamp, 2007], 55). Regardless of whether this is a good interpretation of Marx and Simmel, in what follows I hope to sketch the idea of a materialism that is not vulnerable to this objection.

45 Luhmann, "Paradox of Form," 15.

46 Luhmann, "Paradox of Form," 15f.

47 Luhmann, *Law as a Social System*, 181f.

48 See note 1 in part II above (p. 311).

49 See chapter 3 in this volume.

50 Thus Nietzsche's translation; cited by Martin Heidegger, "Anaximander's Saying," in: *Off the Beaten Track*, trans. and ed. by Julian Young and Kenneth Haynes (Cambridge: Cambridge University Press, 2002), 242–81, here 242. Heidegger himself translates the second part of the saying as

follows: "along the line of usage; for they let order and reck belong to one another (in the surmounting) of disorder" (280).

51 Sophocles, *Sophocles*, vol. 1 (*Oedipus the King, Antigone, Oedipus at Colonus*), trans. by Francis Schorr (London: Heinemann, 1912), 17 (verse 132).

52 In Luhmann's text, we have "reflection" here. Nevertheless, Gunther Teubner speaks of "self-reference" in this passage (Teubner, *Law as an Autopoietic System*, 10). The reason for this can be found in Luhmann's own discussion of the difference between "self-reference" and "reflection": "reflection" is that form of "concentrated self-reference" that refers to the "identity of the system"; see Niklas Luhmann, "Selbstreflexion des Rechtssystems: Rechtstheorie in Gesellschaftstheoretischer Perspektive," in: *Ausdifferenzierung des Rechts: Beiträge zur Rechtssoziologie und Rechtstheorie* (Frankfurt: Suhrkamp, 1999), 419–50, here 423.

53 Luhmann, *Social Systems*, 444.

54 This is how Spinoza radicalizes Paul's "For I was alive without the law once" (Romans 7:9, KJV); Benedict de Spinoza, *A Theological-Political Treatise*, trans. by Michael Silverthorne and Jonathan Israel (Cambridge: Cambridge University Press, 2007), 196 (ch. 16).

55 Blaise Pascal, *Pensées* (New York: E.P. Dutton, 1958), 18 and 20 (no. 72).

56 See p. 84 in this volume. For a more extensive treatment of what follows here, see Christoph Menke, *Reflections of Equality*, trans. by Howard Rouse and Andrei Denejkine (Stanford: Stanford University Press, 2006), ch. 6, "Mercy and Law: Carl Schmitt's Concept of Sovereignty," 177–98.

57 What Schmitt had previously said about dictatorship also holds true for sovereignty (as it is employed in *Political Theology*): its "goal" is to ensure the "realization of law," and thus to (re-)produce the "normal state" that the rule of law can only assume: Carl Schmitt, *Die Diktatur: Von den Anfängen des modernen Souveränitätsgedankens bis zum proletarischen Klassenkampf* (Berlin: Duncker & Humblot, 1994), 133f. Thus it is equally true of sovereignty and dictatorship that "A dictatorship that does not depend on a normative realization but is to be concretely brought about, which accordingly does not have a goal but makes itself superfluous, is an arbitrary despotism" (xvii).

58 Bettine Menke, *Das Trauerspiel-Buch* (Bielefeld: Transcript 2010, 94) (with a citation – "heavy with crowns" – from Walter Benjamin, *The Origin of German Tragic Drama* [London: Verso, 1998], 125).

59 Carl Schmitt, *The Leviathan in the State Theory of Thomas Hobbes*, trans. by George Schwab and Erna Hilfstein (Westport: Greenwood, 1996), 57. For more on this, see Schmitt, *Leviathan in the State Theory of Thomas Hobbes*, ch. 3, 31f.

60 Agamben, *State of Exception*, 64.

61 In Agamben's reflections on study, play, and the "deactivation" of law, Daniel Loick sees a reflection on the relation of law and life, which is similar to the self-reflection of law that I am about to sketch here. See Daniel Loick, "Von der Gesetzeskraft zum Gesetzeskraft: Studium, Spiel, Deaktivierung: Drei Strategien zur Entsetzung der Rechtsgewalt," in: Loick (ed.), *Der Nomos der Moderne: Die politische Philosophie Giorgio Agambens* (Baden-Baden: Nomos, 2011), 194–212. See also the preliminary sketch of a critical

theory of law "without sovereignty" in Daniel Loick, *Kritik der Souveränität* (Frankfurt: Campus, 2012), part III, 279–322.

62 Cf. Dieter Henrich, *Fichtes ursprüngliche Einsicht* (Frankfurt: Klostermann, 1967), 11ff.

63 [C.M. – My italics] Immanuel Kant, *Critique of Pure Reason*, trans. and ed. by Paul Guyer and Allen W. Wood (Cambridge: Cambridge University Press, 1998), 245 (B 130).

64 Jürgen Habermas, *The Philosophical Discourse of Modernity*, trans. by Frederick Lawrence (Cambridge: Polity, 1987), 31 and 136 respectively.

65 Kant, *Critique of Pure Reason*, 381 (B 345).

66 G.W.F. Hegel, *Science of Logic*, trans. and ed. by George Di Giovanni (Cambridge: Cambridge University Press, 2010), 323. The next stage ("but in itself") develops Hegel's theory of reflection: see *Science of Logic*, 347–53.

67 Rodolphe Gasché, *The Tain of the Mirror: Derrida and the Philosophy of Reflection* (Cambridge: Harvard University Press, 1988), 93.

68 [Tr. – "rites of passage" is in English in the original.] Arnold van Gennep, *Rites of Passage* (Chicago: University of Chicago Press, 1960).

69 Victor Turner, *The Ritual Process: Structure and Anti-Structure* (New Brunswick/London: Aldine, 2008), 94ff.

70 Mary Douglas, *Purity and Danger* (London: Routledge, 2002), 198.

71 Victor Turner, *The Anthropology of Performance* (New York: PAJ, 1987), 24. For the formulation which follows, see the same work, 25.

72 Victor Turner, *From Ritual to Theatre: The Human Seriousness of Play* (New York: PAJ, 1982), 41.

6 Materialization

1 Niklas Luhmann, "Sign as Form," in: *Problems of Form*, ed. by Dirk Baecker, trans. by Michael Irmscher and Leah Edwards (Stanford: Stanford University Press, 1999), 46–63, here 57 [Tr. – translation modified].

2 It is thus irrelevant whether what law considers to be matter or natural follows *a different* form or norm. For law, all form that is different, that is not legal, is *not* form. The positing of legal form is "jurispathic": "Judges are people of violence. Because of the violence they command, judges characteristically do not create the law, but kill it. Theirs is the jurispathic office. Confronting the luxuriant growth of a hundred legal traditions, they assert that this one is law and destroy or try to destroy the rest" (Robert Cover, "Nomos and Narrative," in: *Narrative, Violence, and the Law*, ed. by Martha Minow, Michael Ryan, and Austin Arat [Ann Arbor: University of Michigan Press 1992], 95–172, here 155).

3 Hannah Arendt, *The Human Condition* (Chicago: University of Chicago Press, 1998), 312.

4 Arendt explains as follows: "For the only tangible object that introspection yields, if it is to yield more than an entirely empty consciousness of itself, is indeed the biological process" (Arendt, *Human Condition*, 312). This explanation does not succeed in understanding non-law's naturalness in the self-reflection of law.

5 Andrzej Rapaczynski characterizes this as Hobbes' positivism or scientism: see his *Nature and Politics: Liberalism in the Philosophies of Hobbes, Locke, and Rousseau* (Ithaca/London: Cornell University Press, 1987), 61ff. Samantha Frost has developed a reading of Hobbes' materialism that disentangles it from modern dualism when she structurally links his concept of matter (matter as body) with that of self-consciousness; see Samantha Frost, *Lessons From a Materialist Thinker: Hobbesian Reflections on Ethics and Politics* (Stanford: Stanford University Press, 2008), ch. 1 (esp. 24ff.). As Frost emphasizes, against the equation of Hobbes' human being with the Cartesian subject, the concept of the subject thereby loses its foundational status at the same time.

6 Thomas Hobbes, *Leviathan or The Matter, Forme, & Power of a Commonwealth, Ecclesiasticall and Civil*, ed. by Richard Tuck (Cambridge: Cambridge University Press, 1996), 146 (§ 21).

7 Thomas Hobbes, *Of Liberty and Necessity*, cited by Samantha Frost, "Fear and the Illusion of Autonomy," in: Diane Coole and Samantha Frost (eds.), *New Materialisms: Ontology, Agency, and Politics* (Durham: Duke University Press, 2010), 158–77, here 161.

8 Hobbes, *Leviathan*, 70 (§ 11). Cf. the critique of the idea of "final causes" or "purposes" as perversion of nature in Benedict de Spinoza, *Ethics*, in: *The Complete Works*, trans. by Samuel Shirley (Indianapolis: Hackett, 2002), 238–43 (part I, appendix). For more, see the contributions of Hans Blumenberg (144–207), Günther Buck (208–302), and Dieter Henrich (303–13) in: *Subjektivität und Selbsterhaltung: Beiträge zur Diagnose der Moderne*, ed. by Hans Ebeling (Frankfurt: Suhrkamp, 1976. In this anti-teleological structure, Joseph Vogl sees the new "political anthropology" of "economic man"; see Joseph Vogl, *Kalkül und Leidenschaft: Poetik des ökonomischen Menschen* (Zurich: Diaphanes, 2004), ch. 5.

9 Hobbes, *Leviathan*, 70 (§ 11).

10 To this first line of the natural will's self-reflection there corresponds a second one, in which it again determines itself. The will that is self-reflectively aware that it will posit aims which it cannot know, reflectively turns to itself in its willing: to be sure, the natural will does not know what will be willed, but it does know *that* it will will, and hence must will its being-able-to-will (in other words, its being-able-to-realize-its-will). The natural will wills itself – not because it is egotistical (it is not a question of morality or immorality here), but because here it is concerned with the infinity of its (further-) willing, due to the indeterminacy of its aims. Its willing relates to the power of willing or striving: the capability to realize something. Instead of willing for the ultimate aim or greatest good, the natural will is a "will to power." See chapter 9, pp. 154–60, in this volume.

11 See part I.

12 According to Carl Schmitt's fitting interpretation, a first formulation of this understanding of modern law as resigned can already be found in Hobbes; see chapter 3, pp. 49–60, in this volume.

13 G.W.F. Hegel, *Natural Law: The Scientific Ways of Treating Natural Law, Its Place in Moral Philosophy, and Its Relation to the Positive Sciences of Law*, trans. by T.M. Knox (Philadelphia: University of Pennsylvania Press, 1975), 103. See the reconstruction in Christoph Menke, *Tragödie*

im Sittlichen: Gerechtigkeit und Freiheit nach Hegel (Frankfurt: Suhrkamp, 1996), 307–9.

14 Hegel, *Natural Law*, 104.

15 G.W.F. Hegel, *Science of Logic*, trans. and ed. by George Di Giovanni (Cambridge: Cambridge University Press, 2010), 106. This occurs in an incomplete way with the "ought": "The ought . . . is the transcending of restriction, but a *transcending* which is itself only *finite*" (107).

16 Max Weber, *Economy and Society: An Outline of Interpretive Sociology*, ed. by Guenther Roth and Claus Wittich (Berkeley: University of California Press, 1978), 884 [Tr. – translation modified]. In what follows, I will be here abstracting from the context and the particular, for the most part critical, intentions of Max Weber's definition of law's materialization and only reconstructing the new formal structure thus depicted. On the former's context, see Jürgen Habermas, *Between Facts and Norms: Contributions to a Discourse Theory of Law and Democracy* (Cambridge: MIT Press, 1996), 392–409, and Duncan Kennedy, "The Disenchantment of Logically Formal Legal Rationality, or Max Weber's Sociology in the Genealogy of the Contemporary Mode of Western Legal Thought," *Hastings Law Journal*, 55 (2004), 1031–76. Kennedy has analyzed sociological theory of law from the end of the nineteenth century (the proper context for Weber's reflections on materialization) in a series of studies. For a brief summary, see Kennedy, "Legal Formalism," in: *The International Encyclopedia of the Social and Behavioral Science* (Amsterdam: Elsevier, 2001), vol. 13, 8634–8.

17 [Tr. – translation modified] Weber, *Economy and Society*, 884.

18 [C.M. – my emphasis] Weber, *Economy and Society*, 885.

19 Weber, *Economy and Society*, 886.

20 [Tr. – translation modified] Weber, *Economy and Society*, 886.

21 [Tr. – translation modified] Weber, *Economy and Society*, 886.

22 Weber, *Economy and Society*, 884.

23 Gunther Teubner, "Substantive and Reflexive Elements in Modern Law," *Law & Society Review*, 17.2 (1983), 239–86. Teubner adopts the term from Philippe Nonet and Philip Selznik, *Law and Society in Transition: Toward Responsive Law* (New York: Harper, 1978). For the link between law's reflexivity and responsiveness (and thus its constitutive dependence "on something external"), see Francesca Raimondi's concise summary, *Die Zeit der Demokratie: Politische Freiheit nach Carl Schmitt und Hannah Arendt* (Konstanz: Konstanz University Press, 2014), 142–8.

24 Gunther Teubner, "Self-Subversive Justice: Contingency or Transcendence Formula of Law?" *Modern Law Review*, 72.1 (2009), 1–23, here 8–9.

25 However, see Petra Gehring, "Can the Legal Order Respond?" *Ethical Perspectives: Journal of the European Ethics Network*, 13.3 (2006), 469–96, here 493 and 473. Gehring's critique of law's responsivity is that: "It is not the claims of an Other that suddenly surface in the law – say when a judge has difficulties with his decision. Rather, it is claims that are quite familiar to the law that 'interrupt' the course of law: there are no dilemmas that the law does not already know. That is to say, even interruptions will be dealt with in legal categories, and if the order is disturbed by being reminded of the 'blind spot' of its work in the course of performing its business, then it will not feel the Other, but itself" (491). In a nutshell: "[I]t is not the Other *in* the law,

but rather the Other *to* law that marks the threshold of the legal order and thus its essence" (473). This is the alternative that is undermined by law's self-reflection.

26 The systems theory of law is formulated as follows: "In addition, system and environment always coexist and one side of the form of the system is never without the other side of its environment. However, by internalizing this distinction in the form of the distinction between self-reference and external reference, the system gains the freedom to change 'leadership' in what it refers to in guiding its own (and always only its own!) operations. It can shift from self-reference to external reference and back" (Niklas Luhmann, *Law as a Social System*, trans. by Klaus A. Ziegert [Oxford: Oxford University Press, 2004], 118). "For the neo-evolutionists, legal autonomy means that law changes in reaction only to its own impulses, for the legal order – doctrines, institutions, organizations – reproduces itself. But in doing so, the legal system is not insulated from its environment. The key idea, central to the neo-evolutionary theories, is the 'self-reference of legal structures.' Legal structures so conceived reinterpret themselves, but in the light of external needs and demands. This means that external changes are neither ignored nor directly reflected according to a 'stimulus-response scheme.' Rather, they are selectively filtered into legal structures and adapted in accordance with logic of normative development. Even the strongest social pressures influence legal development only insofar as they first shape 'legal constructions of social reality.' Thus, broader social developments serve to 'modulate' legal change as it obeys its own developmental logic" (Teubner, "Substantive and Reflexive Elements in Modern Law," 248–9).

27 Andreas Fischer-Lescano, *Rechtskraft* (Berlin: August Verlag, 2013), 57.

28 [Tr. – The German here is *materiale oder materielle*, the former meaning "material" in the sense of "important" or "germane," while the latter means "material" in the sense of "composed of matter" or "denoting physical objects."]

29 Thus the decisive insight in ch. 3 of Fischer-Lescano's *Rechtskraft*.

30 Luhmann, *Law as a Social System*, 213.

31 Luhmann, *Law as a Social System*, 216. Law's justice is its self-reflection, because it precisely consists in realizing what law is. As contingent positing, justice thereby realizes the general structure of meaning in law: "Meaning is processed via the selection of distinctions, of forms. Something specific is indicated (and nothing else): for example, 'This yew-tree is nothing but itself, and it is a yew tree and no other tree.' The two-sided form substitutes for the representation of the world. Instead of presenting the world as phenomenon, this form reminds us that there is always something else – whether this something is unspecified or specific, necessary or undeniable, only possible or dubitable, natural or artificial. ... This shows clearly that, and in what ways, one can speak of meaning (as we are doing right now) and that the actual infinity of the unreachable, intangible world of Nicholas of Cusa can be transformed into, and set in motion as, an infinite process. As a self-reproducing (autopoietic) process, meaning must always begin with the actual, a historically given situation in which it has placed itself. It follows that systems constructed in such a manner cannot observe their own beginning or end and that they experience whatever constrains them temporally or

factually from within a boundary they need to transcend. In the medium of meaning there is no finitude without infinity" (Niklas Luhmann, *Art as Social System*, trans. by Eva N. Knodt [Stanford: Stanford University Press, 2000], 108).

32 Teubner, "Self-Subversive Justice," 9–10.
33 Teubner, "Self-Subversive Justice," 14.
34 Gunther Teubner, *Law as an Autopoietic System* (Oxford: Blackwell, 1993), 33.
35 For more, see the texts in Christoph Menke and Francesca Raimondi (eds.), *Die Revolution der Menschenrechte* (Berlin: Suhrkamp, 2011), part II: "Deklaration;" esp. the introduction by Francesca Raimondi (95–101).
36 This is the theme of part IV.
37 I am here referring to Ernst Tugendhat's critique of moral contractualism in: *Vorlesungen über Ethik* (Frankfurt: Suhrkamp, 1993), 76 (*"Quasimoral"*).
38 G.W.F. Hegel, *Elements of the Philosophy of Right*, trans. by H.B. Nisbet (Cambridge: Cambridge University Press, 1991), 35 (§ 4).
39 Habermas, *Between Facts and Norms*, 85.
40 Habermas, *Between Facts and Norms*, 126.
41 Jürgen Habermas, "Rawls's Political Liberalism: Reply to the Resumption of a Discussion," in: *Postmetaphysical Thinking II*, trans. by Ciarin Cronin (Cambridge: Polity, 2017), 189–209, here 201.
42 Habermas, *Between Facts and Norms*, 111–12. For more detail, see Klaus Günther, "Diskurstheorie des Rechts oder liberales Naturrecht in diskurstheoretischem Gewande?" *Kritische Justiz*, 4 (1994), 470–87.
43 Albrecht Wellmer, "Models of Freedom in the Modern World," in: *Endgames: The Irreconcilable Nature of Modernity: Essays and Lectures*, trans. by David Midgley (Cambridge: MIT Press, 1998), 3–38, here 29.
44 Fischer-Lescano, *Rechtskraft*, 89.
45 Albrecht Wellmer formulates this in regard to Habermas as follows: "no communal freedom is conceivable in the modern world which is not based on the institutionalization of an equal negative freedom for all" (Wellmer, "Models of Freedom in the Modern World," 25). This corresponds to Klaus Günther's unsuccessful alternative to Habermasian establishment [*Begründung*]: establishment from the paradox that rationality implies irrationality (Günther, "Diskurstheorie des Rechts oder liberales Naturrecht in diskurstheoretischem Gewande?" 473).
46 Cf. Habermas, *Between Facts and Norms*, 287–328. For an explanation of the "proceduralist understanding of law" from the self-reflection of law, see 427–46.
47 Giorgio Agamben, *State of Exception*, trans. by Kevin Attell (Chicago: University of Chicago Press, 2005), 33 and 3. See pp. 84–92 in this volume.
48 Agamben, *State of Exception*, 73.
49 Agamben, *State of Exception*, 29.
50 [C.M. – My emphasis] Giorgio Agamben, *Homo Sacer: Sovereign Power and Bare Life*, trans. by Daniel Heller-Roazen (Stanford: Stanford University Press, 1998), 121–2.
51 Agamben, *Homo Sacer*. In the introduction, Agamben dates the biopolitical structure to Roman law's break with Greek morality law. This is the moment for the "entry of zoē into the sphere of the polis – the politicization of bare

life as such" (4). At another point, Agamben says that the inclusive exclusion of life "lies at the foundation of Western politics" (11). Thus it is *not* modern, contra Foucault (12). For more on this question of dating, see Eva Geulen, *Giorgio Agamben zur Einführung* (Hamburg: Junius, 2009), 93–8.

52 In this sense, the predicate "biopolitical" functions in Agamben in a manner similar to the term "mythical" in Benjamin (cf. Walter Benjamin, "The Critique of Violence," in: *Reflections: Essays, Aphorisms, Autobiographical Writings*, trans. by Edmund Jephcott [New York: Schocken, 1986], 277–300). It designates law as a time without history. History first begins after law.

53 Maria Muhle, *Eine Genealogie der Biopolitik: Zum Begriff des Lebens bei Foucault und Canguilhem* (Bielefeld: Transcript, 2008), 261.

54 Muhle, *Eine Genealogie der Biopolitik*, 263. The citation in parentheses is from Georges Canguilhem, *The Normal and the Pathological*, trans. by Carolyn R. Fawcett (New York: Zone, 1989), 139f.

7 The Critique of Rights

1 This is already heralded in Lenin's definition of the socialist state. At its core, we find (Engelsian) thoughts on the withering away of the state (V.I. Lenin, "The State and Revolution," in: *Collected Works*, vol. 25 [Moscow: Progress, 1964], 385–498, esp. 400–5). Lenin thus gives the modern idea of law's self-reflection its most radical expression. Benjamin's idea of *Entsetzung* [Tr. – suspension] is connected to this. With this text, however, at the same time, Lenin already reverts to the two basic operations of traditional law, which will become central after the revolution: empire (the organization of still-necessary "oppression" [392] and "an organ for the *oppression* of one class by another" [392]) and paideia (having human beings "*become accustomed*" so that they learn how to begin "observing the elementary conditions of social life *without violence* and *without subordination*" [461]).

2 Wellmer argues along these lines (with reference to "the anthropological premises of individualist theories"); Albrecht Wellmer, "Models of Freedom in the Modern World," in: *Endgames: The Irreconcilable Nature of Modernity: Essays and Lectures*, trans. by David Midgley (Cambridge: MIT Press, 1998), 3–38, here 29. The formulations in this paragraph come from a conversation with Jan Völker.

3 Jürgen Habermas, *Knowledge and Human Interest*, trans. by Jeremy J. Shapiro (Boston: Beacon, 1973), vii.

4 [C.M. – my italics] Wilfrid Sellars, *Empiricism and the Philosophy of Mind* (Cambridge: Harvard University Press, 1997), 68–9.

5 Sellars, *Empiricism and the Philosophy of Mind*, 69.

6 Theodor Adorno, *Negative Dialectics*, trans. by E.B. Ashton (New York: Continuum, 1973), 187.

7 Adorno, *Negative Dialectics*, 161.

8 See chapter 9 of this volume, pp. 149–52.

9 Adorno, *Negative Dialectics*, 192 [Tr. – translation modified] and 182.

10 Theodor Adorno, *Der Positivismusstreit in der deutschen Soziologie* (Darmstadt: Luchterhand, 1972), 66 and 90.

11 G.W.F. Hegel, *Natural Law: The Scientific Ways of Treating Natural Law, Its Place in Moral Philosophy, and Its Relation to the Positive Sciences of Law*, trans. by T.M. Knox (Philadelphia: University of Pennsylvania Press, 1975), 63.
12 Hegel, *Natural Law*, 63.
13 Cf. Christoph Menke, *Force: A Fundamental Concept of Aesthetic Anthropology*, trans. by Gerrit Jackson (New York: Fordham University Press, 2013), 41–4.
14 Rosa Luxemburg, "Fragment über Krieg, nationale Frage und Revolution," in: *Politische Schriften*, ed. by Ossip K. Flechtheim (Frankfurt: Europäische Verlagsanstalt, 1968), vol. III, 142–9, here 147. This is why the question of whether the contradiction in civil law between its essence and its appearance, between the act of self-reflection and the form of rights, can be resolved, or whether it should be carried through to its logical conclusion as paradox, remains open here; for more, see Christoph Menke, "Subjektive Rechte: Zur Paradoxie der Form," in: *Nach Jacques Derrida und Niklas Luhmann: Zur (Un-)Möglichkeit einer Gesellschaftstheorie der Gerechtigkeit* (Stuttgart: Lucius & Lucius, 2008), 81–108. I take this question up again in chapter 15 of this volume.

Part III Critique: The Authorization of One's Own

1 Richard Wagner, *The Ring of the Nibelung* (New York: E.P. Dutton, 1960), 110.
2 Elfriede Jelinek, *Rein Gold* (Reinbek bei Hamburg: Rowohlt, 2013), 8.
3 For a justification of this term, see p. 179 in this volume. Because (or insofar as) it adheres to a principle of legal subjectification, even present-day society can be called "bourgeois" [*bürgerlich*].
4 Niklas Luhmann, "Subjektive Rechte: Zum Umbau des Rechtsbewußtseins für die moderne Gesellschaft," in: *Gesellschaftsstruktur und Semantik*, vol. 2 (Frankfurt: Suhrkamp, 1981), 45–104, here 84. Cf. Niklas Luhmann, *Law as a Social System*, trans. by Klaus A. Ziegert (Oxford: Oxford University Press, 2004): "If the legal system has to deal with differentiated sub-systems such as money economy, privatized families, politically programmed state organizations, etc. and has to rely on corresponding structural couplings to do that, it must also reformulate its relations with systems of consciousness. . . . Modern legal development has done that by abstracting general, socially based norms of reciprocity from the legal figure of subjective rights" (413).
5 Roberto Esposito, *Immunitas*, trans. by Zakiya Hanafi (Cambridge: Polity, 2011), 21–8.
6 [Tr. – I translate *Ermächtigung* as "authorization," but it should be noted in what follows that this German term also signifies "empowerment" or "license."]

8 Authorization

1 Max Weber, *Economy and Society: An Outline of Interpretive Sociology*, ed. by Guenther Roth and Claus Wittich (Berkeley: University of California Press, 1978), 53; Immanuel Kant, *Metaphysics of Morals* (Cambridge: Cambridge University Press, 1996), 63 [Tr. – translation modified].

2 For the relation between *having* and *exercising* a right, see chapter 10, S "Claiming One's Own," in this volume.

3 Cf. the (Roman) metaphor of rights as reins in Ernst Tugendhat, *Vorlesungen über Ethik* (Frankfurt: Suhrkamp, 1993), 338f. For the concept of normative power, see Rainer Forst, *Normativity and Power: Analyzing Social Orders of Justification*, trans. by Ciaran Cronin (Oxford: Oxford University Press, 2018).

4 This is the subject of part I.

5 Weber, *Economy and Society*, 319. This distinction follows that of Rudolf von Ihering, *Geist des römischen Rechts auf den verschiedenen Stufen seiner Entwicklung* (1865), unaltered reprint of the 10th edn. (Aalen: Scientia, 1968), part III, 351f. (see part I, note 196, there); cf. Georg Jellinek, *System der subjektiven öffentlichen Rechte* (Darmstadt: Wissenschaftliche Buchgesellschaft, 1963; reprint of the 2nd edn. [Tübingen: 1905]), 67–81. Gerhard Wagner reconstructs Ihering's concept of reflex in: "Rudolf von Jherings Theorie des subjektiven Rechts und der berechtigenden Reflexwirkungen," *Archiv für civilistische Praxis*, 193 (1993), 319–47, esp. 331ff.

6 Weber, *Economy and Society*, 329 [Tr. – translation modified].

7 Weber, *Economy and Society*, 329–30 [Tr. – translation modified].

8 See chapter 1, pp. 9–16, in this volume.

9 Weber, who introduces this concept (see *Economy and Society*, 329–30 [Tr. – translation modified]), uses it in a special sense; for more on this, see pp. 126–39 of this volume. For the second meaning, according to which a subjective right is empowerment, in contrast to a reflex right, see Hans Kelsen, *Reine Rechtslehre*, 2nd edn. (1960); cited in excerpted passages in: Markus S. Stepanians (ed.), *Individuelle Rechte* (Paderborn: mentis, 2007), 96–112, here 104.

10 G.W.F. Hegel, *Elements of the Philosophy of Right*, trans. by H.B. Nisbet (Cambridge: Cambridge University Press, 1991), 69 (§ 38).

11 Hegel, *Elements of the Philosophy of Right*, 70 (§ 38).

12 Jellinek, *System der subjektiven öffentlichen Rechte*, 45.

13 Jellinek, *System der subjektiven öffentlichen Rechte*, 46.

14 Jellinek, *System der subjektiven öffentlichen Rechte*, 47.

15 Jellinek, *System der subjektiven öffentlichen Rechte*, 48.

16 Jellinek, *System der subjektiven öffentlichen Rechte*, 52 and 47.

17 Jellinek, *System der subjektiven öffentlichen Rechte*, 51.

18 Jellinek, *System der subjektiven öffentlichen Rechte*, 49.

19 Jellinek, *System der subjektiven öffentlichen Rechte*, 50.

20 Jellinek, *System der subjektiven öffentlichen Rechte*, 82f. The opposition of the two versions of liberalism, as theories (and justifications) of civil private law, revolves around this insight, which Jürgen Habermas has reconstructed; see Habermas, "Natural Law and Revolution," in: *Theory and*

Practice, trans. by John Viertel (Boston: Beacon, 1973), 82–120, esp. pages, 82–120.

21 For more, see chapter 1, "A New Form of Government: 'Modern Roman Law'," pp. 16–20, in this volume.

22 [Tr. – The English translation cited elsewhere is for volume 1 of Savigny's opus. Where Menke cites volume 2, I refer to the German.] Friedrich Carl von Savigny, *System des heutigen römischen Rechts* (Berlin: Veit, 1841), vol. II, 2. This is directed against the first clause of Roman personal law: "The principal division of the law of persons is the following, namely, that all men are either free or slaves" (*The Institutes of Justinian*, trans. by Thomas Collett Sandar [London: Longmans, Green, 1878], 13 [I.3]). Likewise Hegel: "Thank God that in our states one may put the definition of the human being – as a being who is capable of right – at the head of the legal code – without running the risk of coming upon definitions of human rights and duties that contradict the concept of the human being" (Hegel, *Elements of the Philosophy of Right*, § 2) [Tr. – apparently a note not included in the English translation, so I've translated the German here]. And: "It is to be regarded as a great development that now the human being, because he is a human being, must be viewed as having rights, so that his being human is more elevated than his status" (Hegel's *Lectures on Natural Right and Politics* of 1818–19, cited by Manfred Riedel, *System und Geschichte* [Frankfurt: Suhrkamp, 1973], 114).

23 Friedrich Carl von Savigny, *System of the Modern Roman Law*, trans. by William Holloway (Madras: J. Higginbotham, 1867), 18.

24 Savigny, *System des heutigen römischen Rechts*, vol. II, 333.

25 Savigny, *System of Modern Roman Law*, 18.

26 Ulrich K. Preuß, *Die Internalisierung des Subjekts: Zur Kritik der Funktionsweise des subjektiven Rechts* (Frankfurt: Suhrkamp, 1979), 127. Jellinek himself avoids this transference with his talk of "status" (*System der subjektiven öffentlichen Rechte*, 81ff.) – an example of the false equivalence of private and public law to be found in the contemporary discussion is Robert Alexy's *A Theory of Constitutional Rights*, trans. by Julian Rivers (Oxford: Oxford University Press, 2002), 196ff. Alexy here employs a Hohfeldian analysis of the private law form of subjective rights to classify constitutional rights.

27 Étienne Balibar, "Citizen Subject," in: Eduardo Cadava, Peter Connor, and Jean-Luc Nancy (eds.), *Who Comes after the Subject?* (New York: Routledge, 1991), 33–57, here 40–4. The person who has been subdued (*subditus*) is not a servant (*servus*), since "as *subditi*, the subjects *will* their own obedience": the prince rules them to realize their own best or highest end (41f.). Ingeborg Maus takes aim at this structure, in her critique of contemporary legal theory, when she speaks of a "refeudalization." The structure is here again the same as in Savigny: subjective entitlement without political authorization. See Ingeborg Maus, *Zur Aufklärung der Demokratietheorie: Rechts- und demokratietheoretische Überlegungen im Anschluß an Kant* (Frankfurt: Suhrkamp, 1992), 32–42.

28 Jellinek, *System der subjektiven öffentlichen Rechte*, 82.

29 Jellinek, *System der subjektiven öffentlichen Rechte*, 82.

30 Jellinek, *System der subjektiven öffentlichen Rechte*, 57.

31 Hans Kelsen, *Pure Theory of Law* (Berkeley: University of California Press, 1967), 138f.
32 Kelsen, *Pure Theory of Law*, 138f. [C.M. – my italics].
33 Jellinek, *System der subjektiven öffentlichen Rechte*, 55 [C.M. – my italics]; the term "power of disposition" comes from the first edition. I would like to thank Klaus Günther for his helpful suggestions on this point.
34 Wesley Newcomb Hohfeld, *Fundamental Legal Conceptions as Applied in Judicial Reasoning* (Dartmouth: Ashgate, 2001), 21 [Tr. – translation modified]. Alexy's conception of "competence" has this in mind: he calls the entire field of a person's capacities to change legal positions "institutional," regardless of whether it is a matter of private *or* of public law (Alexy, *Theory of Constitutional Rights*, 219ff.).
35 Klaus Günther, "Anerkennung, Verantwortung, Gerechtigkeit," in: Rainer Forst, Martin Hartmann, Rahel Jaeggi, and Martin Saar (eds.), *Sozialphilosophie und Kritik* (Frankfurt: Suhrkamp, 2009), 269–87, here 273.
36 Hans Kelsen, *The Essence and Value of Democracy*, trans. by Brian Graf (Lanham: Rowman & Littlefield, 2013), 31.
37 For this essential presupposition, see "The Ability to Exercise Discretion" in this chapter.
38 See "Excursus: The Political Presupposition of Private Law (Savigny)" in this chapter. For the legal person as authoritative judge, see Christoph Menke, "From the Dignity of Man to Human Dignity: The Subject of Rights," in: *Values and Norms in the Age of Globalization*, trans. by Birgit M. Kaiser and Katherine Thiele (Pieterlin/Bern: Peter Lang, 2007), 83–94.
39 Jeremy Waldron, "Participation: The Right of Rights," in: *Law and Disagreement* (Oxford: Oxford University Press, 1999), 232–54, here 250 ("rights-bearers" as "rights-*thinkers*"). For what follows, see Jürgen Habermas, *Between Facts and Norms: Contributions to a Discourse Theory of Law and Democracy* (Cambridge: MIT Press, 1996), 118f.
40 [Tr. – translation modified] Weber, *Economy and Society*, 668.
41 Weber, *Economy and Society*, 683–4.
42 Weber, *Economy and Society*, 683. Weber describes this change as a replacement of "status" with the "purposive" contract: 674.
43 Weber, *Economy and Society*, 682 [Tr. – translation modified]. This is primarily considered true in a negative sense: as limitation of responsibility for the consequences; cf. Karl-Heinz Ladeur, *Negative Freiheitsrechte und gesellschaftliche Selbstorganisation: Die Erzeugung von Sozialkapital durch Institutionen* (Tübingen: Mohr Siebeck, 2000), 60ff.
44 [Tr. – Kelsen, *Pure Theory of Law*, 296.]
45 For more on this, see chapter 10 in this volume. Catherine Colliot-Thélène (citing Kant and Weber) emphasizes the political character of subjective rights, but ignores the crisis of the political they engender; see Colliot-Thélène, *Democracy and Subjective Rights: Democracy without Demos* (Colchester: ECPR Press, 2018), 4–10 and 108–112.
46 See pp. 140–5 in this volume.
47 Louis Althusser, *On the Reproduction of Capitalism: Ideology and Ideological State Apparatuses*, trans. by G.M. Goshgarian (London: Verso, 2014), 232–72, here 269.

48 [Tr. – translation modified] Weber, in considering modern law, distinguishes three ways in which it can confer power on a person. It can be the power "to prescribe, or prohibit, or allow, an action vis-à-vis another person." These three forms of legal power correspond to different types of expectations: "that other persons will either engage in, or refrain from, certain conduct or that one may himself engage, or fail to engage, in certain conduct without interference from a third party: authorizations" (Weber, *Economy and Society*, 667).

49 Thomas Hobbes, *Leviathan or The Matter, Forme, & Power of a Commonwealth, Ecclesiasticall and Civil*, ed. by Richard Tuck (Cambridge: Cambridge University Press, 1996), 91.

50 Hobbes, *Leviathan*, 91.

9 Self-Will

1 Michel Foucault, *The Birth of Biopolitics: Lectures at the Collège de France*, trans. by Graham Burchell (New York: Palgrave Macmillan, 2010), 271–2. (We have here a transcript of the lecture, hence the unevenness of formulation.) Foucault calls this irreducible and non-transferable decision "interest." In the context of legal theory, this term has a technical meaning: it designates a "material" aspect of decision, understood in an empiricist manner; for more, see chapters 2 and 4 in this volume, as well as "Capacity" in this chapter.

2 Foucault, *Birth of Biopolitics*, 272.

3 Foucault, *Birth of Biopolitics*, 272.

4 Cf. Christoph Menke, "Autonomy and Liberation: The Historicity of Freedom," in: Rachel Zuckert and James Kreines (eds.), *Hegel on Philosophy in History* (Cambridge: Cambridge University Press, 2017), 159–76.

5 Hannah Arendt, *Denktagebuch*, ed. by Ursula Ludz and Ingeborg Nordmann (Munich: Piper, 2002), 327. While Arendt for the most part conceives this operation of individual appropriation as specific to the modern era (86f.), her critique here already refers to Aristotle, in whom she sees the beginning of a naturalism whose modern radicalization subsequently leads to politics as "the expansion of the individual" (335).

6 Arendt, *Denktagebuch*, 327.

7 Or to put this more precisely: that for which the subject actively and more strongly strives; self-will recognizes distinctions, but they are of a qualitative nature. For more on this, see the model of "weak" evaluation that defines "The utilitarian strand in our civilization" (21), in Charles Taylor, "What is Human Agency?" in: *Philosophical Papers: Vol. 1, Human Agency and Language* (Cambridge: Cambridge University Press, 1985), 15–45, esp. 15–27.

8 Foucault, *Birth of Biopolitics*, 272.

9 Martin Heidegger, *Nietzsche*, vols. 3 and 4, trans. by David Farrell Krell (San Francisco: Harper, 1991), 75; Martin Heidegger, *Logic: The Question of Truth*, trans. by Thomas Sheehan (Bloomington: Indiana University Press, 2016), 58.

10 Karl Marx, "On the Jewish Question," in: *Marx and Engels Collected Works*, vol. 3 (London: Lawrence & Wishart, 2010), 167.

11 Foucault, *Birth of Biopolitics*, 309.
12 Foucault, *Birth of Biopolitics*, 61.
13 Carl Schmitt, *Constitutional Theory*, trans. and ed. by Jeffrey Seitzer (Durham/London: Duke University Press, 2008), 170 and 204.
14 Hans Kelsen, *Reine Rechtslehre*, ed. by Matthias Jestaedt (Tübingen: Mohr Siebeck, 2008), 54.
15 Jürgen Habermas, "Natural Law and Revolution," in: *Theory and Practice*, trans. by John Viertel (Boston: Beacon, 1973), 82–120, here 94 and 97.
16 Kelsen, *Reine Rechtslehre* (1st edn.), 61.
17 Kelsen, *Reine Rechtslehre* (1st edn.), 61.
18 This is evident in Schmitt's claim that conceiving individual freedom as being simultaneously "conditioned" by law would exclude the legal recognition of individual freedom as given; for this reason, "essentially *socialistic* rights of the individual are dependent on the positive services of the state" in a completely different (and above all: not absolute) way than civil liberties [*Freiheitsrechte*]. See Schmitt, *Constitutional Theory*, 207.
19 We must "proceed from the fact that these (individual) rights are only instituted by the state," indeed the fact that "the individual" is "in a certain sense the product of the state" (Émile Durkheim, *Leçons de sociologie: physique des mœurs et du droit* [online edn., accessed at: https://unige.ch/sciences-societe/socio/files/1214/0533/6006/Durkheim_1950.pdf]), 59.
20 Durkheim, *Leçons de sociologie*, 110.
21 Durkheim, *Leçons de sociologie*, 107.
22 "Jurisprudence has long since reduced these powers to three in total: *jus utendi, jus fruendi*, and *jus abutendi*. The first is concerned with the right to use something as it is, to live in a house, to ride a horse, to walk in the forest. *Jus fruendi* is the right to the fruits of something, fruit from a tree and crops from the soil, to the interest income from an amount of money, to the rental income from a house, and so forth. As we can see, *jus utendi* and *jus fruendi* are distinguished by a nuance at best. Both involve the right to use something without materially or legally denaturing it, in other words, without changing its physical or legal constitution. The third power, *jus abutendi*, is understood as the right to change something or even to destroy it, either by using it up or selling it, thus changing its legal status" (Durkheim, *Leçons de sociologie*, 108).
23 Wesley Newcomb Hohfeld, *Fundamental Legal Conceptions as Applied in Judicial Reasoning* (Dartmouth: Ashgate, 2001), 56. Cf. the distinction between "special" and "general" rights in H.L.A. Hart, "Are There Any Natural Rights?" in: Jeremy Waldron (ed.), *Theories of Rights* (Oxford: Oxford University Press, 1984), 77–90, here 83–8; Jeremy Waldron, *The Right to Private Property* (Oxford: Oxford University Press, 1988), 106–24.
24 Aristotle, *Politics*, trans. by H. Rackham (Cambridge: Harvard University Press, 1944), 87 (II.2, 1263a). For the context of this Aristotelian argument, see John Finnis, "Natural Law: The Classical Tradition," in: *The Oxford Handbook of Jurisprudence and Philosophy of Law*, ed. by Jules L. Coleman (Oxford: Oxford University Press, 2002), 1–60, here 51f. At any rate, Finnis thinks that we can conceive the structure of bourgeois property in this way.
25 Aristotle, *Politics*, 89 (II.2, 1263b).
26 The way in which this relation of conditioning is practically realized can here

remain an open question. On Jan Szaif's interpretation, Aristotle "does not think that lack of generosity should be punished" (Jan Szaif, "Aristoteles: eine teleologische Konzeption von Besitz und Eigentum" [J.S. - "Aristotle: A Teleological Concept of Possession and Property"], in: *Was ist Eigentum? Philosophische Klassiker der Eigentumstheorie*, ed. by A. Eckl and B. Ludwig [Munich: Beck, 2005], 43–58). The link between the private right to decide and virtue must not be understood as a command or prohibition on a case-by-case basis, but can even be understood as law's condition for meaning altogether. This was the case for Roman property (Michel Villey, *Le droit roman* [Paris: PUF, 1964], 84). According to Max Kaser (*Roman Private Law*, trans. by Rolf Dannenbring [Durban: Butterworths, 1965], 96f.), in the "early times" of Roman law it was the task (and decision) of the censor to enforce a "restriction [C.M. – of property] in the interest of *society*."

27   John Locke, *Two Treatises of Government*, ed. by Peter Laslett (Cambridge: Cambridge University Press, 1988), 298.

28   "And this, I think, it is very easie to conceive without any difficulty, *how Labour could at first begin a title of Property* in the common things of Nature" (Locke, *Two Treatises of Government*, 302).

29   Locke's talk of the right of property's natural "foundation" is therefore *not* in contradiction to the distinction between "*possession*" and "*property*" (G.W.F. Hegel, *Elements of the Philosophy of Right*, 76–7) or between the "*sensual*," the "*physical*," or the "*intelligible*" as "*merely rightful*" possession (Immanuel Kant, *The Metaphysics of Morals* [Cambridge: Cambridge University Press, 1996], 68). In other words: Locke's talk of property's natural foundation must not be understood in a reductionist manner. Talk of the right of property's natural basis characterizes the *systematic context of categorical distinctions.*

30   Locke, *Two Treatises of Government*, 298 and 287.

31   John Locke, *An Essay Concerning Human Understanding*, ed. by Roger Woolhouse (London: Penguin, 1997), xxvii, § 26, 312: "forensic term," cf. Waldron, *Right to Private Property*, 179.

32   Locke, *Essay Concerning Human Understanding*, 312 [C.M. – my italics].

33   Locke, *Essay Concerning Human Understanding*, 308.

34   Locke, *Essay Concerning Human Understanding*, 312.

35   Werner Plumpe, "Eigentum – Eigentümlichkeit: Über den Zusammenhang ästhetischer und juristischer Begriffe im 18. Jahrhundert," *Archiv für Begriffsgeschichte*, 23 (1980), 175–96, here 191. Jeremy Waldron (*Right to Private Property*, part II; see the context on 127–36) distinguishes between two ways of understanding bourgeois property: as a "special" right that is based on the factual and thus contingent things a person does in connection with something, and a "general" right that is based on each person's ethically based need. Waldron sees the first mode as operative in Locke and the second as operative in Hegel. The idea that ownership of things is a matter of property in itself indirectly underpins this distinction; the two modes share this idea. It is true even for Hegel that only the human being who "takes possession of himself and becomes his own property and no one else's" can be a legal person and thus a property owner: the actual "is posited for the first time as one's own . . . thereby taking the form of the 'thing'" and thus becoming property by "taking possession of oneself" (Hegel, *Elements of the*

Philosophy of Right, 86 [§ 57]). The distinction between Locke and Hegel lies in the fact that Locke understands the *actualization* of self-property (in laboring on a thing) to be something we do, and hence contingent, while, for Hegel, self-appropriation is considered to be the *premise* of law: "the body . . . must first be *taken possession of* by spirit (see § 57). —But *for others*, I am essentially a free entity within my body while I am in immediate possession of it" (Hegel, *Elements of the Philosophy of Right*, 79 [§ 48]). However, Locke's and Hegel's shared definition of bourgeois property claims that self-property is the "*great Foundation*" of property "in himself."

36 Friedrich Carl von Savigny, *System of the Modern Roman Law*, trans. by William Holloway (Madras: J. Higginbotham, 1867), 270 [Tr. – translation modified]. "Something is considered private, if one can control access to this 'something' all by oneself" (Beate Rössler, *Der Wert des Privaten* [Frankfurt: Suhrkamp, 2001], 23). Private property is *one* way to legally ensure privacy.

37 Kant, *Metaphysics of Morals*, 68. The individualist premise of bourgeois property thus becomes evident: it forms the basis for the "idea of the will's sacredness" (Durkheim, *Leçons de sociologie*, 102; for more, see Hans Joas, *The Sacredness of the Person: A New Genealogy of Human Rights* [Washington, DC: Georgetown University Press, 2013], 69–97). According to Durkheim, this is the specifically modern way in which the "religious character" of all right of property becomes evident (Durkheim, *Leçons de sociologie*, 114). There are "religious reasons that lead to the fact that property becomes property" (Durkheim, *Leçons de sociologie*, 117), since property entails exclusion from use and disposal over a thing due to its sacred character. In modernity, according to Durkheim, the sacredness that establishes property is that of the individual.

38 Crawford Brough Macpherson, *The Political Theory of Possessive Individualism: From Hobbes to Locke* (Oxford: Oxford University Press, 2011), 199. Rolf Knieper argues for the thesis that bourgeois property is also normatively restrictive, since it has a normative foundation. He finds this borne out in the fact that in civil law codes "property rights are defined in positive terms as use, possession, and disposal over, and we do not find talk of negative powers such as misuse, non-use, or destruction" ("Die Freiheiten des Willens, der Person und des Eigentums in der Metaphysik des Zivilrechts," *Kritische Justiz*, 40 [2007], 156–66, here 165). In addition, bourgeois property has no "restrictions" because it is "embedded in and oriented to normatively defined reason" (166). Knieper thus misconstrues the categorical difference between traditional and bourgeois property (and civil law's authorization to neutralize the normative; see chapter 11 in this volume): property is restricted in traditional property – and indeed precisely by the virtue or reason that it establishes. In contrast, with bourgeois property, *individual* property, *each person's* property is restricted – and indeed only by someone else's property, or more precisely: by the general system for the simultaneous coexistence of each person's property. Bourgeois property only restricts property – not virtue or reason. (Or, as we find stated in a decision of the *Bundesverfassungsgericht* [Tr. – "Federal Constitutional Court"] on tenant–landlord relations: "The protection of the tenant's property is not structurally different from that of the landlord and property owner" [BVfG, Beschluß des 1. Senats vom 26. 5. 1993, 1 BvR 208/93] [Tr. – see the

official record at: http://www.servat.unibe.ch/dfr/bv089001.html].) Gerald A. Cohen concludes from this that a radically egalitarian (or Marxist, for him) conception is "therefore obliged to criticize the thesis of self-ownership itself" (*Self-Ownership, Freedom, and Equality* [Cambridge: Cambridge University Press, 1995], 229).

39 Karl Polanyi, *The Great Transformation* (Boston: Beacon, 2001), 116–35.

40 Ulrich K. Preuß, *Die Internalisierung des Subjekts: Zur Kritik der Funktionsweise des subjektiven Rechts* (Frankfurt: Suhrkamp, 1979), 43. "I am designating this process – of subsuming the sphere that establishes an individual's subjectivity in the subjective realm of another – 'internalization'" (Preuß, *Die Internalisierung des Subjekts*, 44).

41 Locke, *Two Treatises of Government*, 287–8 (II, § 27).

42 This is Waldron's view of Locke's concept of the person; Waldron, *Right to Private Property*, 401. "Personality, therefore, is constituted by the creative activity of a free and conscious agent" (179).

43 Cf. John Rawls, *Political Liberalism* (New York: Columbia University Press, 1996), 82f. Rawls is discussing the claim that the "fair value" of liberties must be guaranteed. This occurs by ensuring that "All . . . have the same basic rights, liberties, and opportunities" (79).

44 Immanuel Kant, *Religion within the Boundaries of Mere Reason and Other Writings*, trans. and ed. by Allen Wood and George di Giovanni (Cambridge: Cambridge University Press, 1998), 50 [Tr. – translation modified].

45 Martin Heidegger, "Nietzsche's Word: 'God is Dead'," in: *Off the Beaten Track*, trans. by Julian Young and Kenneth Haynes (Cambridge: Cambridge University Press, 2002), 157–99, here 170–1. With the help of Nietzsche's concept of the will (of willing as evaluating), Heidegger analyzes a model of the subject that has become predominant in "the European history of the last three centuries" (241): evaluation is a fundamental feature of bourgeois subjectivity.

46 Heidegger, "Nietzsche's Word," 173.

47 I am here following Albert O. Hirschman, who demonstrated the internal link between the categories of interest and utility: *The Passions and the Interests: Political Arguments for Capitalism Before Its Triumph* (Princeton: Princeton University Press, 1977), 128ff.; Albert O. Hirschman, "The Concept of Interest: From Euphemism to Tautology," in: *The Essential Hirschman*, ed. by Jeremy Adelman (Princeton: Princeton University Press, 2013), 195–213. Stephen Holmes' objection to Hirschman's analysis claims that he "leaves undeveloped . . . the egalitarian implications of the postulate of *universal* self-interest" (Holmes, "The Secret History of Self-Interest," in: *Passions & Constraints: On the Theory of Liberal Democracy* [Chicago: University of Chicago Press, 1995], 24–68, here 55). The opposite is in fact true: the modern concept of equality presupposes the concept of interest – and is thus only able to understand social generality (or universality) as the compatibility of externally restricted, but internally unrestricted individual interests.

48 Choice and interest are two terms that I have used to describe the dual form adopted by the natural in its legalization (part I of this volume: for an overview, see chapter 4). I have here interpreted choice and interest as two aspects of that which precedes the law: as, simultaneously, unfathomable indeterminacy and determinacy that can be identified. In the move from the

self-reflective structure of modern law (part II of this volume) to the form of subjective rights (part III), we again touch on free choice and interest, in their subjective configuration: as determinations of the subject's will.

49 Amartya Sen argues along these lines in his critique of Nozick: Sen, "Rights and Capabilities," in: *Resources, Values and Development* (Cambridge: Harvard University Press, 1984), 307–24, here 315.

50 Locke, *Two Treatises of Government*, 288 (II, § 27).

51 Robert Nozick, *Anarchy, State, and Utopia* (Oxford: Blackwell, 1974), 174–5. Obviously, Nozick's argument is directed not against the idea of *self-ownership* as such, but only against Locke's labor-theory explanation. This explanation, as will be shown in a moment, can be turned against possessive individualism – and this was also true of the Marxist-socialist tradition. For more on this, see Cohen's encyclopedic *Self-Ownership, Freedom, and Equality*, passim. Nozick's argument is concerned with a basic theoretical question pertaining to action or a work, which Hegel formulates in the thesis that a work is not merely "self-expression of individuality" [Tr. – translation modified]: "The work produced is the reality which consciousness gives itself; it is that in which the individual is explicitly for himself what he is implicitly or *in himself*, and in such a manner that the consciousness, for which the individual becomes explicit in the work, is not the particular, but the universal, consciousness. In his work, he has placed himself altogether in the element of universality, in the quality-less void of being" (G.W.F. Hegel, *Phenomenology of Spirit*, trans. by A.V. Miller [Oxford: Oxford University Press, 1977], 242–3).

52 [Tr. – translation modified] Hegel, *Elements of the Philosophy of Right*, 233 (§ 200). This opportunity for participation is thought to be unequal by Hegel, since he regards it as "conditional" upon (naturally?) occurring wealth already in existence; this is inconsistent.

53 Étienne Balibar, "'Possessive Individualism' Reversed: From Locke to Derrida," *Constellations*, 9.3 (2002), 299–317. [Tr. – Menke's quote here is taken from the substantially longer version of this essay by Balibar available in German translation. The English translation is a much-abbreviated version, and does not seem to include the passage that Menke is citing here.] This argument against possessive individualism is opposed to the one that Rawls develops. Rawls derives his argument from the premise that a subject's abilities are "naturally" given and hence contingent. They cannot justify any claims to a work of one's own (John Rawls, *A Theory of Justice* [Cambridge: Belknap, 1999], 273–7). But this is not merely a false theory of abilities. We cannot even understand the *positive* justification of social rights in this way. This justification is found not even in the social chances for realizing natural abilities, but in the social nature of abilities themselves.

54 Crawford Brough Macpherson, *Democratic Theory: Essays in Retrieval* (Oxford: Oxford University Press, 2014), 136.

55 See the comprehensive account of developments in France in François Ewald, *L'etat providence* (Paris: Bernard Grasset, 1986).

56 Thomas H. Marshall, *Citizenship and Social Class, and Other Essays* (Cambridge: Cambridge University Press, 1950), 27–8. The matrix for this classification forms Jellinek's typology of three kinds of status: negative, active, and positive (Georg Jellinek, *System der subjektiven öffentlichen Rechte* [Darmstadt: Wissenschaftliche Buchgesellschaft, 1963; reprint of the

2nd edn. (Tübingen: 1905)], 89ff.). For a critique of "models of development or phases" of bourgeois configurations of law, see Bernhard Peters,
Rationalität, Recht und Gesellschaft (Frankfurt: Suhrkamp, 1991, 51f.).
57 Marshall, *Citizenship and Social Class*, 21 and 28.
58 Axel Honneth, *The Struggle for Recognition: The Moral Grammar of
Social Conflicts*, trans. by Joel Anderson (Cambridge: MIT Press, 1995),
175. Honneth understands this central theme differently than I am interpreting it here: not as subjective self-will, but as autonomous or universal
will (Honneth, *Struggle for Recognition*, 175f.). For a discussion of this
question, see chapter 11, "Excursus: The Pathology of Rights: Critique of
Liberalism (Dworkin)," in this volume. For the third model of rights that are
listed in this sequence in the classical periodizations (Marshall) or typologies
(Jellinek), the model of political rights, see part IV of this volume. In truth,
political rights exist on a categorically different level: they involve an act that
produces the (form of) rights.
59 Talcott Parsons, *The System of Modern Societies* (Englewood Cliffs: Prentice
Hall, 1971), 83.
60 "Society is obliged to provide for the subsistence of all its members, whether
by procuring them work or by assuring the means of existence to those
who are not in a condition to work" (Maximilien Robespierre, "Draft of
a Declaration of Rights," cited in: François-Alphonse Aulard, *The French
Revolution: A Political History*, vol. 2 [New York: Charles Scribner's Sons,
1910], 176). It is here a matter of providing "certain operations, estab-
lishments, and institutions . . . to prevent or diminish the evils entailed on
our nature" – according to Condorcet (1786); Marie-Jean-Antoine-Nicolas
Caritat, Marquis de Condorcet, *Outlines of an Historical View of the Progress
of the Human Mind* (New York: Lang and Ustick, 1796), 193; cited and discussed in Dieter Thomä, "Leben als Teilnehmen: Überlegungen im Anschluss
an Johann Gottfried Herder," *Deutsche Zeitschrift für Philosophie*, 59
(2011), 5–32, here 5.
61 For a concise summary, see Habermas, "Natural Law and Revolution,"
94–7. Habermas contrasts this ideology with its rival, the construction of
natural law in the French republican tradition, which can be directly linked
to the present welfare-state conception of rights (97–101 and 113–20).
62 See chapter 12, "The Struggle for Law: Critique in Bourgeois Law," in this
volume.

10 The Privatization of the Public: Two Examples

1 In Hegel's sense of civil right [*Recht*] as "*abstract . . . right*" [*Recht*]; cf.
G.W.F. Hegel, *Elements of the Philosophy of Right*, 63 (§ 33).
2 Hans Kelsen, *Pure Theory of Law* (Berkeley: University of California Press,
1967), 138.
3 *The Oldest Code of Laws in the World: The Code of Laws Promulgated
by Hammurabi, King of Babylon B.C. 2285–2242*, trans. by C.H.W. Johns
(Edinburgh: T. & T. Clark, 1911), 1. The second statute states: "If a man
has put a spell upon a man, and has not justified himself, he upon whom the
spell is laid shall go to the holy river, he shall plunge into the holy river, and

if the holy river overcome him, he who wove the spell upon him shall take to himself his house. If the holy river makes that man to be innocent, and has saved him, he who laid the spell upon him shall be put to death. He who plunged into the holy river shall take to himself the house of him who wove the spell upon him" (*Oldest Code of Laws in the World*, 1–2). On the role of taking legal action during the transition from vengeance to law, see the outline sketched in Christoph Menke, *Law and Violence: Christoph Menke in Dialogue*, trans. by Gerrit Jackson (Manchester: Manchester University Press, 2018), 3–76.

4 "The plaintiff, even if he makes his case himself, with his own personal power, even if he *takes action* in person, must at the very least submit to specific rules. The state obliges him to let it regulate and control his *action*" (Michel Villey, *Le droit roman* [Paris: PUF, 1964], 12).

5 Kelsen, *Pure Theory of Law*, 135.

6 Kelsen, *Pure Theory of Law*, 136–7.

7 Karl Larenz, "Zur Struktur 'subjektiver Rechte'," in: *Beiträge zur europäischen Rechtsgeschichte und zum geltenden Zivilrecht: Festgabe für Johannes Sontis*, ed. by Fritz Baur, Karl Larenz, and Franz Wieacker (Munich: Beck, 1977), 129–48, here 135 (with regard to Eugen Bucher and Josef Aichler). "As Raiser puts it," Larenz is thus concerned "with the personhood of the person himself, with his activity as intellectual and ethical being in the community" (145). In an early essay ("Rechtsperson und subjektives Recht," in: Georg Dahm [ed.], *Grundfragen der neuen Rechtswissenschaft* [Berlin: Junker und Dünnhaupt, 1935], 225–60), Larenz still understood this community as the (German) people and thus rejected the concept of the subjective right. For more, see the critique by Heinrich Lange, "Larenz, Karl: Rechtsperon und subjektives Recht," *Archiv für civilistische Praxis*, 23 (1937), 105–7.

8 Larenz, "Zur Struktur 'subjektiver Rechte'," 136.

9 Rudolf von Ihering, *Geist des römischen Rechts auf den verschiedenen Stufen seiner Entwicklung* (1865), unaltered reprint of the 10th edn. (Aalen: Scientia, 1968), part III, 353. "Roman" law must here be understood as Roman Law: as modern private law.

10 Georg Jellinek, *System der subjektiven öffentlichen Rechte* (Darmstadt: Wissenschaftliche Buchgesellschaft, 1963; reprint of the 2nd edn. [Tübingen: 1905]), 70.

11 Bernhard Windscheid, *Die Actio des römischen Zivilrechts vom Standpunkte des heutigen Rechts* (Düsseldorf: Julius Buddeus, 1856), 1. Cf. Jan Schapp, *Das subjektive Recht im Prozeß der Rechtsgewinnung* (Berlin: Duncker & Humblot, 1977), 69–77. Savigny, whom Windscheid is opposed to here, describes the right of action as follows: "Some have wished to view rights of action as an independent class of rights, on the same level with the rights of family, to property, etc., and the contradiction that was mentioned above (§ 59), which tells against this conception, must here be recalled. These rights are better characterized as the outcome of a developmental process, or even a metamorphosis, that can occur in any respective class of rights. They should thus be considered in the same light as the emergence and decline of rights that likewise should only be conceived as single moments in the life-process of rights, not as separate rights that stand on their own" (Friedrich Carl von Savigny, *System des heutigen römischen Rechts* (Berlin: Veit, 1841), vol. 5, 3).

12 Windscheid, *Die Actio des römischen Zivilrechts*, 3.
13 Windscheid, *Die Actio des römischen Zivilrechts*, 3.
14 Windscheid encourages this misunderstanding when he undermines his thesis that the right of action in Rome was independent from the claim under private law with the – completely different – thesis that here the judge "is above the law" (*Die Actio des römischen Zivilrechts*, 4). The claim that the *actio* is based on a subjective right does not mean that it is not based on law in the objective sense, a system of justice – according to Windscheid himself (in the next citation).
15 Windscheid, *Die Actio des römischen Zivilrechts*, 4f.
16 Helmut Coing, *Zur Geschichte des Privatrechtssystems* (Frankfurt: Klostermann, 1962), 40. Coing thus describes the new understanding of the right of action in the Bolognese glossators to whom, with his objection against Villey (*Zur Geschichte des Privatrechtssystems*, 37–40), he attributes the origins of the subjective right. This specifically modern explanation of the right of action for the most part manifests itself as conceptually self-evident; see Joel Feinberg, "The Nature and Value of Rights," in: *Rights, Justice, and the Bounds of Liberty* (Princeton: Princeton University Press, 1980), 43–158, here 148ff.; Ernst Tugendhat, *Vorlesungen über Ethik* (Frankfurt: Suhrkamp, 1993), 340–2.
17 Cf. Tatjana Sheplyakova, "Das Recht der Klage aus demokratietheoretischer Perspektive," *Deutsche Zeitschrift für Philosophie*, 64.1 (2016), 45–67.
18 Niklas Luhmann, "Subjektive Rechte: Zum Umbau des Rechtsbewußtseins für die moderne Gesellschaft," in: *Gesellschaftsstruktur und Semantik*, vol. 2 (Frankfurt: Suhrkamp, 1981), 45–104, here 66.
19 Cf. chapter 8, "Excursus: The Political Presupposition of Private Law (Savigny)," in this volume.
20 [Tr. – translation modified] Carl Schmitt, *Constitutional Theory*, trans. and ed. by Jeffrey Seitzer (Durham/London: Duke University Press, 2008), 197–8. Schmitt returns to this theme repeatedly; see 202, 205, and 218. The idea that "general freedom of action" was "discovered" by the Federal Constitutional Court in the 1950s (Christoph Möllers, *Das Grundgesetz: Geschichte und Inhalt* [Munich: Beck, 2009], 73–6), is an application of this Schmittean thesis. Alexander Peukert argues explicitly along these lines in *Güterzuordnung als Rechtsprinzip* (Tübingen: Mohr Siebeck, 2008), 74–80.
21 [Tr. – Schmitt, *Constitutional Theory*, 170.]
22 Niklas Luhmann, *Grundrechte als Institution: Ein Beitrag zur politischen Soziologie* (Berlin: Duncker & Humblot, 1999), 79. "For this reason, there cannot be a dogmatic system of constitutional rights" (Luhmann, *Grundrechte als Institution*, 36). Its multiplicity and unity can only be understood through a sociological reconstruction of social differentiation.
23 Luhmann, *Grundrechte als Institution*, 84 and 23.
24 Gunther Teubner, *Constitutional Fragments: Societal Constitutionalism and Globalization*, trans. by Gareth Norbury (Oxford: Oxford University Press, 2012), 134. Teubner understands this to be a result of the development "from rights directed against the state to fundamental rights in society" (Teubner, *Constitutional Fragments*, 134). With Schmitt, we must understand it as a basic definition of bourgeois fundamental rights from the beginning.

25 Dieter Grimm, *Recht und Staat der bürgerlichen Gesellschaft* (Frankfurt: Suhrkamp, 1987), 194 and 29.

26 Hans Kelsen, *Reine Rechtslehre* (2nd edn., Heidelberg: Mohr Siebeck, 2014), 108.

27 Honoré-Gabriel de Riqueti, Graf Mirabeau, "Die Menschenrechte," in: Christoph Menke and Francesca Raimondi (eds.), *Die Revolution der Menschenrechte* (Berlin: Suhrkamp, 2011), 35–40, here 35.

28 Jeremy Waldron, "Between Rights and Bills of Rights," in: *Law and Disagreement* (Oxford: Oxford University Press, 1999), 211–31, here 221. Robert Alexy pleads for a strict juridification of basic rights: "Grundrechte als subjective Rechte und als objektive Normen," in: Markus S. Stepanians (ed.), *Individuelle Rechte* (Paderborn: mentis, 2007), 227–46. Ingeborg Maus criticizes this as a "substantialization and reification of civil liberties" ("Die demokratische Theorie der Freiheitsrechte und ihre Konsequenzen für gerichtliche Kontrollen politischer Entscheidungen," in: *Zur Aufklärung der Demokratietheorie: Rechts- und demokratietheoretische Überlegungen im Anschluß an Kant* [Frankfurt: Suhrkamp, 1992], 298–307). According to Maus, the ability to take legal action via basic rights is at most supposed to be provided only in opposition to state administration, but not in opposition to a democratically elected legislator.

29 Peukert, *Güterzuordnung als Rechtsprinzip*, 77.

30 Ingeborg Maus, "Die Struktur subjektiver Freiheitsrechte im Verfassungssystem der Volkssouveränität," in: *Über Volkssouveränität: Elemente einer Demokratietheorie* (Berlin: Suhrkamp, 2011), 62–72, here 66.

31 Maus, *Über Volkssouveränität*, 64.

32 Maus, *Über Volkssouveränität*, 64.

33 René Descartes, *Discourse on Method and Meditations*, trans. by Donald A. Cress (Indianapolis: Hackett, 1998), 1. Cf. Ludger Schwarte's instructive *Vom Urteilen: Gesetzlosigkeit, Geschmack, Gerechtigkeit* (Berlin: Merve, 2012), 113–16.

34 Thomas Hobbes, *Leviathan or The Matter, Forme, & Power of a Commonwealth, Ecclesiasticall and Civil*, ed. by Richard Tuck (Cambridge: Cambridge University Press, 1996), 110 (§ 13).

35 Benedict de Spinoza, *A Theological-Political Treatise*, trans. by Michael Silverthorne and Jonathan Israel (Cambridge: Cambridge University Press, 2007), 196.

36 Spinoza, *Theological-Political Treatise*, 196.

37 Cf. part I, pp. 38–40 and 59, in this volume.

38 Schmitt, *Constitutional Theory*, 206. Cf. Grimm, *Recht und Staat der bürgerlichen Gesellschaft*, 232 and passim.

39 Jürgen Habermas, *The Structural Transformation of the Public Sphere: An Inquiry into a Category of Bourgeois Society*, trans. by Thomas Burger (Cambridge: MIT Press, 1991), 151.

40 Habermas, *Structural Transformation of the Public Sphere*, 142.

41 Cf. Michel Foucault, "'Omnes et singulatim': Toward a Critique of Political Reason," in: Michel Foucault and Noam Chomsky, *The Chomsky–Foucault Debate: On Human Nature* (New York: New Press, 2006), 172–210.

42 See pp. 168–9 in this volume.

43 Émile Durkheim, *Leçons de sociologie: physique des mœurs et du droit* (online edn., accessed at: https://unige.ch/sciences-societe/socio/files/1214/0533/6006/Durkheim_1950.pdf), 59.
44 Durkheim, *Leçons de sociologie*, 59.
45 See the context on pp. 159–60 in this volume.
46 See p. 169 in this volume.
47 See the more explicit treatment on pp. 202–7 in this volume.
48 Durkheim, *Leçons de sociologie*, 62.
49 Durkheim, *Leçons de sociologie*, 64f.
50 Durkheim, *Leçons de sociologie*, 66.
51 Durkheim, *Leçons de sociologie*, 66.
52 Sonja Buckel, *Subjektivierung und Kohäsion. Zur Rekonstruktion einer materialistischen Theorie des Rechts* (Weilerswist: Velbrück, 2007), 221; Michel Foucault, *The Birth of Biopolitics: Lectures at the Collège de France*, trans. by Graham Burchell (New York: Palgrave Macmillan, 2010), 270.

11 Conclusion: The Bourgeois Subject – Loss of Negativity

1 Robert Alexy, *A Theory of Constitutional Rights*, trans. by Julian Rivers (Oxford: Oxford University Press, 2002), 151.
2 See the brief discussion on p. 160 in this volume; for a more extensive treatment, see pp. 213–21.
3 See pp. 140–1 in this volume.
4 Niklas Luhmann, "Subjektive Rechte: Zum Umbau des Rechtsbewußtseins für die moderne Gesellschaft," in: *Gesellschaftsstruktur und Semantik*, vol. 2 (Frankfurt: Suhrkamp, 1981), 45–104, here 74.
5 Georg Lukács, *History and Class Consciousness: Studies in Marxist Dialectics*, trans. by Rodney Livingstone (Cambridge: MIT Press, 1971), 126.
6 Cf. Thomas Vesting, *Legal Theory and the Media of Law*, trans. by James C. Wagner (Cheltenham: Edward Elgar, 2018), § 15: "The cultural framework of the liberal state."
7 Jürgen Habermas, *Between Facts and Norms: Contributions to a Discourse Theory of Law and Democracy* (Cambridge: MIT Press, 1996), 399. The breakdown of this distinction (between what subjective rights *enable* and what they alone can *guarantee*) is particularly clear in Stephen Holmes' defense of liberalism; see Holmes, *The Anatomy of Antiliberalism* (Cambridge: Harvard University Press, 1993), esp. part II.
8 Axel Honneth, *Freedom's Right: The Social Foundations of Democratic Life* (Cambridge: Polity, 2014), 83.
9 Gunther Teubner, *Law as an Autopoietic System* (Oxford: Blackwell, 1993), 93. Teubner's formulation refers in particular to the way in which law regulates the economy through "contracts and rights," but holds in general for the form of subjective rights.
10 Habermas, *Between Facts and Norms*, 399.
11 John Rawls, "Justice as Fairness: Political not Metaphysical," *Philosophy & Public Affairs*, 14.3 (1985), 223–51, here 245–6.

12 [Tr. – Ronald Dworkin, "Liberalism," in: *A Matter of Principle* (Cambridge: Harvard University Press, 1985), 181–204, here 191.]

13 Dworkin, "Liberalism," 191. On the concept of liberal neutrality, see John Rawls, *Political Liberalism* (New York: Columbia University Press, 2005), 190–6. For a more explicit treatment, see Christoph Menke, "The Problem and Limit of Equality," in: *Reflections of Equality*, trans. by Howard Rouse and Andrei Denejkine (Stanford: Stanford University Press, 2006), 41–8.

14 Dworkin, "Liberalism," 205 and 190.

15 Dworkin, "Liberalism," 191.

16 Dworkin, "Liberalism," 198.

17 The following argument (against Isaiah Berlin's claim for a right to negative freedom) can be found in Dworkin, "What Rights Do We Have?" in: *Taking Rights Seriously* (Cambridge: Harvard University Press, 1977), 266–78, here 267–8.

18 A complete critique of Dworkian liberalism (which is not my concern here) would have to show two things: (i) that and why Dworkin's understanding of dignity and/or autonomy is committed to the form of subjective rights, and (ii) that and how Dworkin is subsequently systematically mistaken about this form. The argument for (i) indicates that the step from the dignity to the autonomy of rights only seems obvious to Dworkin – so obvious that he never justifies it – because he understands autonomy to be private. Subjects accordingly always *have* autonomy for themselves. In other words, autonomy is not political. The fact that Dworkin is then (ii) systematically mistaken about the form of subjective rights, which is introduced without justification and surreptitiously, perhaps most clearly demonstrates his assumption that this form can be considered a basis without thereby having to recognize a right to private property: accordingly, "The argument for any given specific liberty ['the supposed individual right to the free use of property'] may therefore be entirely independent of the argument for any other, and there is no antecedent inconsistency or even implausibility in contending for one while disputing the other" (Dworkin, "What Rights Do We Have?" 277–8). Not only does Dworkin's particular theory show that he has no intention at all of disputing private property; the fact that he does not draw this consequence is also highly significant – since private property is not an arbitrary content of subjective rights but inscribed in their form.

19 Raymond Geuss, "Liberalism and its Discontents," in: *Outside Ethics* (Princeton: Princeton University Press, 2005), 11–28, here 23 and 22. (Geuss here says this with reference to Rawls.)

20 Axel Honneth, *Suffering from Indeterminacy: An Attempt at a Reactualization of Hegel's Philosophy of Right*, trans. by Jack Ben-Levi (Assen: Van Gorcum, 2000), 50.

21 G.W.F. Hegel, *Elements of the Philosophy of Right*, 69 (§ 37).

22 Hegel, *Elements of the Philosophy of Right*, 69 (§ 37).

23 Honneth, *Suffering from Indeterminacy*, 50.

24 Hegel, *Elements of the Philosophy of Right*, 221 (§ 184).

25 *Freedom's Right*, 86–94, here 87.

26 Michel Foucault, *The History of Sexuality*, vol. 1: *An Introduction*, trans. by Robert Hurley (New York: Pantheon, 1978), 144. According to Foucault, what the "continual and clamorous legislative activity" conceals is an

"essentially normalizing power" over the subject (144). For the connection between the authorization of self-will and the normalization of the subject, see pp. 202–7 and 209–11 in this volume.

27 Michel Foucault, *The Birth of Biopolitics: Lectures at the Collège de France*, trans. by Graham Burchell (London: Palgrave Macmillan, 2008), 275. In volume 1 of *The History of Sexuality*, Foucault describes the disappearance of the legal subject as an emergence of life – as he emphasizes: in the form of legal claims (145); cf. pp. 206–7 in this volume.

28 Pierre Legendre, *Le crime du Caporal Lortie* (Paris: Flammarion, 2000), 42. It is obviously Lacanianism, which Legendre has extended to legal theory, that guides even Foucault's definition of the legal subject.

29 Foucault, *History of Sexuality*, vol. 1, 143 and 145.

30 Michel Foucault, *Security, Territory, Population: Lectures at the Collège de France, 1977–78*, trans. by Graham Burchell (London: Palgrave Macmillan, 2009), 453–4.

31 Legendre, *Le crime du Caporal Lortie*, 57.

32 [Tr. – Christoph Menke, *Law and Violence: Christoph Menke in Dialogue*, trans. by Gerrit Jackson (Manchester: Manchester University Press, 2018), 32.] Cf. Menke, "The Curse of Autonomy (King Oedipus)," in: *Law and Violence*, 22–36. For a more extensive discussion, see: Menke, *Tragic Play: Irony and Theater from Sophocles to Beckett*, trans. by James Phillips (New York: Columbia University Press, 2009), part I: "The Excess of Judgment: A Reading of Oedipus Tyrannus."

33 G.W.F. Hegel, *Natural Law: The Scientific Ways of Treating Natural Law, Its Place in Moral Philosophy, and Its Relation to the Positive Sciences of Law*, trans. by T.M. Knox (Philadelphia: University of Pennsylvania Press, 1975), 63. See also pp. 119–21 in this volume. In the first part of his text, Hegel reconstructs the empirical concept of bourgeois natural law.

34 [Tr. –*Natural Law*, 63 (425).]

35 I am here recapitulating the argument of chapter 10 in this volume.

36 Karl Marx, "Contribution to the Critique of Hegel's Philosophy of Law," in: *Marx and Engels Collected Works*, vol. 3 (London: Lawrence & Wishart, 2010), 3–129, here 30–1 [Tr. – translation modified].

12 Subjective Rights and Social Domination: An Outline

1 [Tr. – translation modified] G.W.F. Hegel, *Elements of the Philosophy of Right*, 219 (§ 181).

2 For a critique of the critique of civil society's "egoism" (which the young Marx, among others, discusses; see "On the Jewish Question," in: *Marx and Engels Collected Works*, vol. 3 [London: Lawrence & Wishart, 1996], here 155; cf. pp. 1–4 in this volume), see Karl-Heinz Ladeur, *Negative Freiheitsrechte und gesellschaftliche Selbstorganisation: Die Erzeugung von Sozialkapital durch Institutionen* (Tübingen: Mohr Siebeck, 2000), 57 and passim.

3 For the concept of legal consideration, see chapter 14 in this volume, pp. 251–4 in particular.

4 Therefore, in what follows, it is a matter not of the basic structure of bour-

geois society *as such*, but rather of this structure from a juridical perspective, *insofar* as it is juridically produced.

5 The concept of domination thus has a twofold sense: "I understand by domination institutionalized power. Max Weber also viewed it this way" (Heinrich Popitz, *Phenomena of Power: Authority, Domination, and Power*, trans. by Gianfranco Poggi [New York: Columbia University Press, 2017], 165). To put this in more general terms, domination is "a power relationship" in which "confrontation . . . is . . . at one and the same time its fulfillment and suspension" (Michel Foucault, "The Subject and Power," in: *Power*, trans. by Robert Hurley et al. [New York: New Press, 2000], 326–48, here 347).

6 Karl Marx, "Introduction to a Contribution to the Critique of Political Economy," in: *Preface and Introduction to A Critique of Political Economy* (Peking: Foreign Languages Press, 1976), 1–63, here 14–15. For more on the methodological aspects of Marx's critique of law, which is outlined in what follows, see Christoph Menke, "Law and Domination," in: *Critical Theory in Critical Times*, ed. by Penelope Deutscher and Cristina LaFont (New York: Columbia University Press, 2017), 112–40; see also Menke, "Die 'andre Form' der Herrschaft: Recht und Gesellschaft," in: Rüdiger Schmidt-Grépály, Jan Urbich, and Claudia Wirsing (eds.), *Der Ausnahmezustand als Regel: Eine Bilanz der Kritischen Theorie* (Weimar: Verlag der Bauhaus Universität, 2013), 96–113.

7 "This juridical relation, which thus expresses itself in a contract, whether such contract be part of a developed legal system or not, is a relation between two wills, and is but the reflex of the real economic relation between the two. It is this economic relation that determines the subject matter comprised in each such juridical act" (Karl Marx, *Capital*, vol. 1, in: *Marx and Engels Collected Works*, vol. 35 (London: Lawrence & Wishart, 1996), 95. The figure of law as "different form" rules out understanding this in a simple reductionist sense. If law *in itself splits* into form and content, or is even self-contradictory, this rules out the possibility that law is *nothing but* a reflection of material relations. It is at best a "reflection" of social domination in the sense that it is simultaneously a *reversal* of what is reflected into its opposite.

8 Claude Lefort and Marcel Gauchet, "Sur la démocratie: le politique et l'institution du social," *Textures*, 2.3 (1971), 7–78, here 7. In editing Gauchet, Lefort reformulates the Marxist position. Lefort does not want to abstractly dismiss this position, but wants to call its functional definition into question, due to its exclusivity. The critique of the equation of law and ideology, however, already holds true for this position itself. See Nicos Poulantzas, "Marxist Examination of the Contemporary State and Law and the Question of the 'Alternative'," in: *The Poulantzas Reader*, ed. by James Martin (London: Verso, 2008), 25–46, here 27; Étienne Balibar, "The Elements of the Structure and Their History," in: Louis Althusser and Étienne Balibar, *Reading Capital*, trans. by Ben Brewster (London: Verso, 2009), 252–84, here 255 and 257.

9 This critique of Marx forms the basis of Ewald's great study, *L'état providence* (Paris: Bernard Grasset, 1986), which elaborates on the "concurrence between the social economy, on the one hand, and the liberal juridical economy" (223) that *constitutes* or is immanent to it.

10 I will thus be adopting formulations from Menke, "Die 'andre Form' der Herrschaft."

11 For Marx's relation to the German historical school of jurisprudence, see Paul Wolf, *Marxistische Rechtstheorie als Kritik des Rechts: Intention, Aporien und Folgen des Rechtsdenkens von Karl Marx – Eine kritische Rekonstruktion* (Frankfurt: Athenäum, 1974), 43–84, and the comprehensive overview in: Paul Wolf, "Marx versus Savigny: El primer examen crítico de los fundamentos teóricos y metodológicos de la ciencia jurídica del siglo XIX," *Savigny y la ciencia juridica del siglo XIX: Annales de la catedra Francisco Suarez*, 18.9 (1978/9), 243–69.

12 Karl Marx, *Grundrisse: Introduction to the Critique of Political Economy*, trans. by Martin Nicolaus (New York: Vintage, 1973), 246.

13 [Tr. – translation modified] In Roman law, "the *servus* is therefore correctly defined as one who may not enter into exchange (see the *Institutes*)" (Marx, *Grundrisse*, 245).

14 Marx, *Grundrisse*, 244–5.

15 For an explanation of the difference between classical Roman law and Modern "Roman Law" in Savigny and Hegel, see note 28 to chapter 8 in this volume.

16 Marx, *Capital*, vol. 1, 186.

17 Marx, *Capital*, vol. 1, 540. Cf. Wieacker's remark that in the German tradition of pandectic jurisprudence (which Marx is familiar with), the labor contract simply falls into the general category of freedom of contract (Franz Wieacker, *Privatrechtsgeschichte der Neuzeit unter besonderer Berücksichtigung der deutschen Entwicklung* [Göttingen: Vandenhoek & Ruprecht, 1952], 261); a good critique of this position can be found in (among other places) Otto von Gierke's review (in Wieacker's *Privatrechtsgeschichte der Neuzeit*, 269).

18 Marx, *Grundrisse*, 198.

19 For more on the logic of external limitation by the law of equality, see chapter 2, pp. 38–40, in this volume.

20 Marx, *Grundrisse*, 247. Marx here further develops an argument that he finds in Kant. Kant writes that civil "independence" does *not* belong – *cannot* belong to – a person who "allows others to make use of him" (Immanuel Kant, "On the Common Saying: That may be correct in theory, but it is of no use in practice," in: *Political Writings*, ed. by H.S. Reiss [Cambridge: Cambridge University Press, 1991], 61–92, here 78). This giving of permission is an act of freedom, by which one does not cease to be "his own master" (76 and 78) and thus someone who is equally free: loss of independence signifies having another for a master. For an interpretation of exploitation as domination, see "Excursus: Realization of Freedom as 'Increase of Coercion' (Weber)" in this chapter.

21 Marx, *Grundrisse*, 458. In *Capital*, it will be the same inversion that happens when, "Accompanied by Mr. Moneybags and by the possessor of labour power, we therefore take leave for a time of this noisy sphere [C.M. – of the market or of the sphere of circulation], where everything takes place on the surface and in view of all men, and follow them both into the hidden abode of production, on whose threshold there stares us in the face 'No admittance except on business.'" He goes on to write: "On leaving this sphere of simple circulation or of exchange of commodities, which furnishes the 'Free-trader

Vulgaris' with his views and ideas, and with the standard by which he judges a society based on capital and wages, we think we can perceive a change in the physiognomy of our *dramatis personae*. He, who before was the money owner, now strides in front as capitalist; the possessor of labour power follows as his labourer. The one with an air of importance, smirking, intent on business; the other, timid and holding back, like one who is bringing his own hide to market and has nothing to expect but – a hiding" (Marx, *Capital*, vol. 1, 186).

22 Ulrich K. Preuß, *Die Internalisierung des Subjekts s: Zur Kritik der Funktionsweise des subjektiven Rechts* (Frankfurt: Suhrkamp, 1979), 42. This is confirmed on the basis of entirely different theoretical premises by Hans Kelsen: if private property is understood to be "exclusive dominion of a person over a thing," this conceals "the economically decisive function of this relation – a function which (if it refers to ownership of the means of production) – is, rightly or wrongly, labeled as 'exploitation' by socialist theory; which function certainly is present in the relation of the owner toward all other subjects" (Hans Kelsen, *Pure Theory of Law* [Berkeley: University of California Press, 1967], 131).

23 Oskar Negt, "10 Thesen zur marxistischen Rechtstheorie," in Hubert Rottleuthner (ed.), *Probleme der marxistischen Rechtstheorie* (Frankfurt: Suhrkamp, 1975), 10–71, here 61.

24 Marx, *Grundrisse*, 458.

25 The form of the commodity is thus the basis for law's form: "This necessary presence of 'commodity categories' in the analysis of the process of production explains the necessary presence of the corresponding legal categories" (Balibar, "Elements of the Structure and Their History," 258–9). Sonja Buckel has emphasized that this context cannot be understood to be a structural "analogy" of commodity form and legal form (*Subjektivierung und Kohäsion: Zur Rekonstruktion einer materialischen Theorie des Rechts* [Weilerswist: Velbrück, 2007], 131f.). It is instead a matter of conceiving the "functioning of law" (*Subjektivierung und Kohäsion*, 132) in its systematic connection to precisely those social relations that are defined by labor in the form of a commodity. This connection can only be explicated by an analysis of the specific form – in other words, specific to modernity or the modern era – of subjectification, in which economic and juridical categories coincide; thus Buckel's central thesis in the third part of *Subjektivierung und Kohäsion*.

26 Max Weber, *Economy and Society: An Outline of Interpretive Sociology*, ed. by Guenther Roth and Claus Wittich (Berkeley: University of California Press, 1978), 729.

27 Weber, *Economy and Society*, 729.

28 [Tr. – translation modified] Weber, *Economy and Society*, 729.

29 One example of such a critique, among many: Ernest J. Weinrib, *The Idea of Private Law* (Cambridge: Harvard University Press, 1995), in particular ch. 2: "Legal Formalism," 22–55. For more on this, see the overview by Duncan Kennedy, cited in note 000 to chapter 6 in this volume, and, in chapter 1, "Excursus: The Politics and History of Civil Law (Weinrib)."

30 Weber, *Economy and Society*, 729.

31 Weber, *Economy and Society*, 729–30. In connection with this, Weber

makes a comparison between a socialist and civil legal order. He concludes that "In the event of disobedience, observance will be produced by means of some sort of 'coercion' but not through struggle in the market. Which system would possess more real coercion and which one more real personal freedom cannot be decided, however, by the mere analysis of the actually existing or conceivable formal legal system. So far sociology can only perceive the qualitative differences among the various types of coercion and their incidence among the participants in the legal community" (Weber, *Economy and Society*, 731).

32 Weber, *Economy and Society*, 731.
33 Weber, *Economy and Society*, 731.
34 Weber, *Economy and Society*, 731.
35 Marx, *Preface and Introduction to A Critique of Political Economy*, 2–3.
36 Ewald, *L'etat providence*, 224. The *concept* of law is changed by the introduction of classes of social rights. Even Marshall (see p. 158 of this volume) already understood the sequence of three types of law. For a typological comparison of "liberal" and "welfare-state" models of law, see Bernhard Peters, *Rationalität, Recht und Gesellschaft* (Frankfurt: Suhrkamp, 1991), ch. III.
37 For a comprehensive account of this development in Germany, see Wieacker, *Privatrechtsgeschichte der Neuzeit*, 318–24. For the French situation, see the extensive account by Ewald, *L'etat providence*, esp. part III.
38 Ewald ascribes the basic idea of social law to discussions that took place not only in, but *before*, the French Revolution (see Ewald, *L'etat providence*, pp.158–67, 301–18, and 556) and Habermas traces the twentieth-century social welfare state to another, non-liberal, French "Natural law construction of bourgeois society" from the eighteenth century (see Habermas, "Natural Law and Revolution," in: *Theory and Practice*, trans. by John Viertel [Boston: Beacon, 1973], 82–120, here 105 and 115–20). For more on this context, see also the concise summary in Ernst-Wolfgang Böckenförde, "Fundamental Rights as Constitutional Principles: On the Current State of Interpreting Fundamental Rights," in: *Constitutional and Political Theory: Selected Writings* (Oxford: Oxford University Press, 2017), 266–89, here 266–9.
39 See chapter 4 and chapter 9 in this volume.
40 [Tr. – G.W.F. Hegel, *Elements of the Philosophy of Right*, 221 (§ 183).]
41 [Tr. – Hegel, *Elements of the Philosophy of Right*, 233 (§199).]
42 Constant writes that, in raising children, we "modern . . . human beings . . . need the authorities only to give us the general means of instruction which they can supply" – but, in any case, they are already needed (Benjamin Constant, "The Liberty of the Ancients Compared with That of the Moderns," in: *Political Writings*, trans. by Biancamaria Fontana [Cambridge: Cambridge University Press, 1988], 308–28, here 323).
43 For a paternalistic interpretation of the "right to live" in England at the end of the eighteenth century, see Karl Polanyi, *The Great Transformation* (Boston: Beacon, 2001), 81–5. The emergence of social law is part of the history of the development of the modern state from pastoral power; cf. Michel Foucault, "'*Omnes et singulatim*': Toward a Critique of Political Reason," in: Michel Foucault and Noam Chomsky, *The Chomsky–Foucault*

Debate: On Human Nature (New York: New Press, 2006), 172–210, here 185 and 191ff.

44 Friedrich Engels and Karl Kautsky, "Juridical Socialism," *Politics & Society*, 7.2 (1977), 203–20, here 209.

45 Marx, *Grundrisse*, 248. (This is directed against Proudhon.)

46 [Tr. – Marx, *Grundrisse*, 248.]

47 Marx, *Capital*, vol. 1, 243.

48 Karl Marx, "Critique of the Gotha Programme," in: *Marx and Engels Collected Works* (London: Lawrence & Wishart, 2010), vol. 24, 75–99, here 88: "The vulgar socialists (and from them in turn a section of the Democrats) have taken over from the bourgeois economists the consideration and treatment of distribution as independent of the mode of production and hence the presentation of socialism as turning principally on distribution."

49 Engels and Kautsky, "Juridical Socialism," 209.

50 Axel Honneth emphasizes this when he notes that social law demands start by "politicizing the analysis of the social consequences of the new organization of labour" (Axel Honneth, *Freedom's Right: The Social Foundations of Democratic Life* [Cambridge: Polity, 2014], 227). In particular, social law demands, in their socialist form, thus by no means ignore relations of production. At the same time, however, social law demands refer critically to these relations, with the result that they only externally restrict the freedom of choice guaranteed by private law. To this extent, the objection remains in force: such demands do not significantly change the fact "work will still be . . . sold as a commodity" (Engels and Kautsky, "Juridical Socialism," 210).

51 Michel Foucault, *The History of Sexuality*, vol. 1: *An Introduction*, trans. by Robert Hurley (New York: Pantheon, 1978), 145. For more, see Francesca Raimondi, "'Diese andere Sache': Agamben, Foucault und die Politik der Menschenrechte," in: Maria Muhle and Kathrin Thiele (eds.), *Biopolitische Konstellationen* (Berlin: August Verlag, 2011), 37–59, here 43–53. Raimondi ("'Diese andere Sache'," 44) also refers to the following passage in Foucault: "And I think that one of the greatest transformations political right underwent in the nineteenth century was precisely that, I wouldn't say exactly that sovereignty's old right – to take life or let live – was replaced, but it came to be complemented by a new right which does not erase the old right but which does penetrate it, permeate it. This is the right, or rather precisely the opposite right. It is the power to 'make' live and 'let' die. The right of sovereignty was the right to take life or let live. And then this new right is established: the right to make live and to let die" (Michel Foucault, *Society Must Be Defended: Lectures at the Collège de France, 1975–76*, trans. by David Macey [New York: Picador, 2003], 241). Foucault describes the emergence of a right to life; for more on this, see chapter 11, "Foucault's Diagnosis: The Regression of the Juridical," in this volume.

52 Foucault, *History of Sexuality*, vol. 1, 144.

53 Foucault, *History of Sexuality*, vol. 1, 144. For the concept of value, see pp. 155–8 in this volume. "Fördern und Fordern" [Tr. – "Facilitating and Demanding"] is the title of the First Chapter of the Second Book ("Basic Security for Jobseekers") of the German Social Code [Tr. – accessed online at: http://www.ilo.org/dyn/natlex/docs/ELECTRONIC/76851/81205/F1028 001871/DEU76851.pdf] from May 13, 2011 (commonly known as Hartz

IV). § 1.1 declares: "Basic security for jobseekers should enable beneficiaries to lead a life that is in keeping with human dignity." This is supposed to happen by "'strengthening'" not only the "individual responsibility" of jobseekers, but also those "living with them in a community shaped by needs. The achievement of basic security 'is to be aligned' with this" (§ 1.2). The measures to be taken to this end are stipulated in the so-called "Integration Agreements" (§ 2.1; cf. pp. 212–13 in this volume). Essential mechanisms for enforcement are listed in § 31 as "Sanctions" for "Breaches of Duty."

54 In what follows, I use this term in a broad sense, which includes the "increase of coercion" analyzed by Weber (see pp. 199–202 in this volume). For this reason, exploitation does not here mean only the one-sided absorption of surplus value, but includes all forms of the utilization of asymmetrical positions in the market by classes.

55 John Rawls, "Justice as Fairness: Political not Metaphysical," *Philosophy & Public Affairs*, 14.3 (1985), 223–51, here 243–4.

56 [C.M. – my italics] John Rawls, *A Theory of Justice* (Cambridge: Belknap, 1999), 122; Jürgen Habermas, *Between Facts and Norms: Contributions to a Discourse Theory of Law and Democracy* (Cambridge: MIT Press, 1996), 122. For an extensive discussion (which also considers the differences between Habermas and Rawls), see Christoph Menke, *Tragödie im Sittlichen: Gerechtigkeit und Freiheit nach Hegel* (Frankfurt: Suhrkamp, 1996), 293–8; Christoph Menke, *Reflections of Equality*, trans. by Howard Rouse and Andrei Denejkine (Stanford: Stanford University Press, 2006), 129–50.

57 Rawls, "Justice as Fairness," 244.

58 Jürgen Habermas, *Legitimation Crisis*, trans. by Thomas McCarthy (Boston: Beacon Press, 1975), 36; the citations which follow are found on 36–7.

59 Claus Offe, "Social Policy and the Theory of the State," in: *Contradictions of the Welfare State*, ed. by John Keane (London: Hutchinson, 1984), 88–118, here 92; the following citation is found on 96.

60 "A third function will be added to these two: the function of making functions invisible. Capitalist relations of domination, exploitation and coercion, enter into the social relation between the state and the individual through social policy. When the detrimental consequences [C.M. – and necessary presuppositions] of wage-labor existence come into conflict, wage labor and capital are not opposed, and the dispute is not over the capitalist organization of labor or even the amount of the resulting wages. What could otherwise trigger open class conflicts is transformed into *political* conflicts, or legal disputes" (Offe, "Social Policy and the Theory of the State" [Tr. – it has not been possible to locate the page number for this citation]).

61 This is the argument of chapter 9, "Capacity," in this volume.

62 Offe, "Social Policy and the Theory of the State" [Tr. – it has not been possible to locate the page number for this citation].

63 Claus Offe, "Social Policy and the Theory of the State" [Tr. – it has not been possible to locate the page number for this citation, but see 165–6 of the English translation for the relevant material here]. The "shift . . . [from] the welfare state . . . [to] personal well-being" in the present "neoliberal" transformation of social policy (Stephan Lessenich, "Mobility and Control: On the Dialectic of the 'Active Society'," in: Klaus Dörre, Stephan

344

Lessenich, and Hartmut Rosa, *Sociology, Capitalism, Critique*, trans. by Jan-Peter Hermann and Loren Balhorn [London: Verso, 2015], 98–142, here 130) is thus a reaction to the structural limits of bourgeois social policy in general, a limit to its normalizing domination, behind which, obviously, lies not the realm of freedom of domination, but the paradoxical attempt to establish a *different* form of domination, one of exploitation and coercion, in the (public) relation between the state and the individual via the model of contracts between individuals under private law. For an analysis of this complex, see Ulrich Bröckling, Susanne Krasmann, and Thomas Lemke (eds.), *Glossar der Gegenwart* (Frankfurt: Suhrkamp, 2004), especially the entries "Aktivierung" (Hermann Kocyba), "Empowerment" (Ulrich Bröckling), and "Selbstverantwortung" (Wolfgang Fach).

64 Jean-François Lyotard, *The Differend: Phrases in Dispute*, trans. by Georges Van Den Abbeele (Manchester: Manchester University Press, 1998), xi. Lyotard describes this as a consequence of the general structural difference between conflict and legal dispute. Social struggles between the classes fall into the category of conflict: there is no neutral standard of judgment, according to which they could be decided.

65 [Tr. – translation modified]

66 The bourgeois struggle for law is thus not to be understood in either vitalist or idealist terms: not in vitalist terms, since it has a normative content; not in idealist terms, since it is not a mere dispute over interpretations, not a mere dispute over who has *correctly* understood the "idea" of law. The struggle for law is neither vitalist nor idealist, but political, namely the power to define or interpret.

67 Marx, *Capital*, vol. 1, 95.

68 Friedrich Nietzsche, *On the Genealogy of Morals and Ecce Homo*, trans. by Walter Kaufmann and R.J. Hollingdale (New York: Vintage, 1989), 77–8. The truth of political critique is ontological: it consists of insight into the contingency of social, normative orders; cf. Oliver Marchart, *Post-Foundational Political Thought: Political Difference in Nancy, Lefort, Badiou, and Laclau* (Edinburgh: Edinburgh University Press, 2007), 52–60.

69 An example of this mystery: the inversion of "politics" into "police" in Jacques Rancière (*Disagreement: Politics and Philosophy*, trans. by Julie Rose [Minneapolis: University of Minnesota Press, 1999], 21–42), who for this reason also lacks a theory of law.

70 See p. 204 in this volume.

71 Émile Durkheim, *The Division of Labor in Society* (New York: Free Press, 1984), 316; cf. also 158–80. The idea of "contractual solidarity" thus does not (or not merely) mean a normative demand on how contracts are conducted, a demand that would be opposed to freedom of contract (see pp. 135–7 in this volume), but accounts for contracts with a fundamentally different understanding of what a contract *is*: for Durkheim (read as a theoretician of social law), the contract is the basic form of "organic" solidarity through which a society with a division of labor creates "consensus" and "cooperation."

72 Durkheim, *Division of Labor in Society*, 316 and 321.

73 Durkheim, *Division of Labor in Society*, 319.

74 Kant, "On the Common Saying," 74. In its "postmodern" version, this

critique of the despotism of social welfare politics is offered no longer in the name of individual freedom, but in the name of the "responsiveness of social networks of association as a whole" (Ladeur, *Negative Freiheitsrechte und gesellschaftliche Selbstorganisation*, 302).

75 For a closer account of this characteristic feature, see chapter 13 in this volume.

76 Karl Marx, "Contribution to the Critique of Hegel's Philosophy of Law," in: *Marx and Engels Collected Works*, vol. 3 (London: Lawrence & Wishart, 2010), 3–129, here 91; for more, see p. 4 of this volume.

Part IV Revolution: The Dialectic of Judgment

1 Theodor Adorno, *Minima Moralia*, trans. by E.F.N. Jephcott (London: Verso, 2005), 156–7. The passage, in its entirety, is as follows: "The conception of unfettered activity, of uninterrupted procreation, of chubby insatiability, of freedom as frantic bustle, feeds on the bourgeois concept of nature that has always served solely to proclaim social violence as unchangeable, as a piece of healthy eternity. It was in this, and not in their alleged levelling-down, that the positive blue-prints of socialism, resisted by Marx, were rooted in barbarism. It is not man's lapse into luxurious indolence that is to be feared, but the savage spread of the social under the mask of universal nature, the collective as a blind fury of activity. *Rien faire comme une bête*, lying on water and looking peacefully at the sky, 'being, nothing else, without any further definition and fulfillment', might take the place of process, act, satisfaction, and so truly keep the promise of dialectical logic that it would culminate in its origin."

2 Jürgen Habermas, *Between Facts and Norms: Contributions to a Discourse Theory of Law and Democracy* (Cambridge: MIT Press, 1996), 111–12. For a critique of this thesis, see chapter 6, "The Basis of Rights," in this volume.

3 Kant conceives the "change in the way of thinking," whose revolution consists in the natural sciences, as the awareness that the matter of cognition does not dictate its rules or forms to us, but that these rules or forms precede their matter; Immanuel Kant, *Critique of Pure Reason*, trans. and ed. by Paul Guyer and Allen W. Wood (Cambridge: Cambridge University Press, 1998), 110 (B XVI). This also holds true for the "*revolution* in the disposition of the human being," as "a transition to the maxim of holiness of disposition," as Kant, in his work on religion, describes "rebirth," "as it were a new creation," which takes place so that the human being becomes virtuous; Immanuel Kant, *Religion within the Boundaries of Mere Reason and Other Writings*, trans. and ed. by Allen Wood and George di Giovanni (Cambridge: Cambridge University Press, 1998), 68.

4 Habermas describes the democratic power of the autonomous citizens by which they "are to be capable of applying the discourse principle *for themselves*," in such a way that they thereby become "authors of the rights they submit to as addressees." However, this authorship is limited: "to be sure, as legal subjects, they may no longer choose the medium in which they can actualize their autonomy. They no longer have a choice about which language they might want to use. Rather, the legal code is given to legal subjects

in advance as the only language in which they can express their autonomy" (Habermas, *Between Facts and Norms*, 126). They have "no other alternative" (130): according to Habermas, there is no revolution (of rights).

5 For the concept of legality, see chapter 5 in this volume.

6 Niklas Luhmann, *Political Theory in the Welfare State*, trans. by John Bednarz (Berlin: De Gruyter, 1990), 27. The title of the chapter in which he cites this declaration is "Obsolete Theory."

13 The Aporia of the Bourgeois Constitution

1 Dieter Grimm, *Die Zukunft der Verfassung* (Frankfurt: Suhrkamp, 1991), 69. For more, see chapter 10, "The Declaration of Basic Rights," in this volume.

2 Grimm, *Die Zukunft der Verfassung*, 69. For the historical novelty of civil constitutions, see 31f.

3 According to Harold J. Berman, this redefinition of political power as "legislative, administrative, and judicial authority" is the crucial feature of the "Papal revolution" (*c.*1100), which made the church into the model for the – modern – state. Harold J. Berman, *Law and Revolution: The Formation of the West* (Cambridge: Harvard University Press, 1983), 205–7.

4 Grimm, *Die Zukunft der Verfassung*, 12.

5 Jürgen Habermas, *Between Facts and Norms: Contributions to a Discourse Theory of Law and Democracy* (Cambridge: MIT Press, 1996), 83.

6 Grimm, *Die Zukunft der Verfassung*, 13 [C.M. – my italics]. In contrast to this approach, Carl Schmitt deconstructs the constitution into two separate "elements" (into a "constitutional" element and a "political" one) that are foreign to each other, indeed potentially hostile. The reason for this can be found in the fact that he does not see that basic rights already play a constitutive role in the political element: because they define the bourgeois concept of democracy. In contrast, Schmitt defines democracy as "the identity of ruler and ruled, governing and governed, commander and follower" (Carl Schmitt, *Constitutional Theory*, trans. and ed. by Jeffrey Seitzer [Durham/ London: Duke University Press, 2008], 264), an identity that is not bound to the individual's participation. How the will is "formed" is a secondary "practical question" for this conception of democracy: "The will of the people can be expressed just as well and perhaps better through acclamation, through something taken for granted, an obvious and unchallenged presence, than through the statistical apparatus that has been constructed with such meticulousness in the last fifty years" (Carl Schmitt, *Crisis of Parliamentary Democracy*, trans. by Ellen Kennedy [Cambridge: MIT Press, 1988], 16).

7 Ingeborg Maus, "Der zerstörte Zusammenhang von Freiheitsrechten und Volkssouveränität in der aktuellen nationalstaatlichen und internationalen Politik," in: *Über Volkssouveränität: Elemente einer Demokratietheorie* (Berlin: Suhrkamp, 2011), 359–74, here 363. Maus here sees an aberrant development that contradicts the original political meaning of basic rights. The counter-thesis to this, as Jürgen Habermas puts it, is that the two sides of rights – foundation and limitation of domination – have an "internal relation"; see Jürgen Habermas, "On the Internal Relation between the Rule

of Law and Democracy," in: *The Inclusion of the Other: Studies in Political Theory* (Cambridge: Polity, 2000), 253–64. For more on this, see chapter 6, "The Basis of Rights," in this volume.

8 Grimm, *Die Zukunft der Verfassung*, 72.

9 Ernst-Wolfgang Böckenförde, *Die verfassungstheoretische Unterscheidung von Staat und Gesellschaft als Bedingung der individuellen Freiheit* (Opladen: Westdeutscher Verlag, 1973), 17.

10 Jürgen Habermas, "Natural Law and Revolution," in: *Theory and Practice*, trans. by John Viertel (Boston: Beacon, 1973), 82–120, here 100.

11 Habermas, "Natural Law and Revolution," 105.

12 Habermas, "Natural Law and Revolution," 101.

13 Habermas, "Natural Law and Revolution," 96.

14 Franz Böhm, "Privatrechtsgesellschaft und Marktwirtschaft," *Ordo*, 17 (1966), 75–151, here 121 [C.M. – my italics].

15 Franz Böhm, "Das Problem der privaten Macht: Ein Beitrag zur Monopolfrage," in: *Reden und Schriften* (Karlsruhe: C.F. Müller 1960), 25–45, here 27.

16 Böhm, "Das Problem der privaten Macht," 27.

17 Michael Stolleis, "Die Entstehung des Interventionsstaates und das öffentliche Recht," in: *Konstitution und Intervention: Studien zur Geschichte des öffentlichen Rechts im 19. Jahrhundert* (Frankfurt: Suhrkamp, 2001), 253–82, here 264.

18 Habermas, "Natural Law and Revolution," 115.

19 Böckenförde, *Die verfassungstheoretische Unterscheidung von Staat und Gesellschaft*, 38. As Böckenförde has definitively elaborated, this is equally true for traditional liberal freedoms, and even for social rights: "As we have seen, the idea of fundamental social rights does not seem to be opposed to the preservation of freedom in the bourgeois-liberal constitutional state, but rather seems to be its logical consequence in a transformed social situation." It is based "on the principle of securing freedom itself" (Ernst-Wolfgang Böckenförde, "Die sozialen Grundrechte im Verfassungsgefüge," in: *Staat, Verfassung, Demokratie: Studien zur Verfassungstheorie und zum Verfassungsrecht* [Frankfurt: Suhrkamp, 1991], 146–58, here 149; cf. "Grundrechtstheorie und Grundrechtsinterpretation," in: *Staat, Verfassung, Demokratie*, 115–45, esp. 142–5).

20 Grimm, *Die Zukunft der Verfassung*, 437.

21 Habermas, "Natural Law and Revolution," 119.

22 Gunther Teubner, *Constitutional Fragments: Societal Constitutionalism and Globalization*, trans. by Gareth Norbury (Oxford: Oxford University Press, 2012), 16.

23 Teubner, *Constitutional Fragments*, 6.

24 Teubner, *Constitutional Fragments*, 103.

25 Teubner, *Constitutional Fragments*, 103.

26 Teubner, *Constitutional Fragments*, 107.

27 Teubner, *Constitutional Fragments*, 105. Luhmann emphasizes this with respect to basic rights; see the following note.

28 Niklas Luhmann, *Grundrechte als Institution: Ein Beitrag zur politischen Soziologie* (Berlin: Duncker & Humblot, 1999), 37. "The basic rights that have been discussed to this point [every kind except for political rights] serve

to maintain the structural differentiation of the social order against dangers from the political system" (138). A "postmodern constitutional theory" that views the only task of politics to be that of "enabling the pursuit of individual interests" is helpful in this regard, since it is based on a "civilized society"; cf. Karl-Heinz Ladeur, "Postmoderne Verfassungstheorie," in: Ulrich K. Preuß (ed.), *Zum Begriff der Verfassung* (Frankfurt: Fischer, 1994), 304–31, here 323f.

29 On this question, it seems as though Teubner himself takes the position of "it depends on the case." Thus Teubner takes it to be true that the social autonomy of the economy "requires a huge amount of support from the law for its self-foundation, albeit not to the same extent as politics. As is well known, the institutions of property, contract, competition, and currency form the cornerstones of an economic constitution. These are all based on double reflexivity, that is, on the application of economic operations to economic operations and on the application of secondary norms to primary norms of the legal system" (Teubner, *Constitutional Fragments*, 108). He exempts science from this, however, because "Science requires almost no support at all from stabilizing legal norms to achieve autonomy" (108). Here, it is not just that mechanisms exist, such as patents, copyrights, formal credentials, and so forth, without which science would be unable to function. Rather, science's social autonomy is dependent in an elementary sense on the juridical notion of the freedom of science – as art is dependent on the juridical notion of artistic freedom, and so forth – and thus dependent on the blocking of normative regulations with normative regulations. On the autonomy of the relations of social reproduction, see the comparison between the Marxist model of capital "as automatic subject" and the autopoiesis of functionally differentiated systems in João Paulo Bachur, *Kapitalismus und funktionale Differenzierung: Eine kritische Rekonstruktion* (Baden-Baden: Nomos, 2013), ch. 2.

30 This formulation is based on how Claude Lefort and Marcel Gauchet describe the relation between the division *between* civil society and political power and the division *in* political power; see Claude Lefort and Marcel Gauchet, "Sur la démocratie: le politique et l'institution du social," *Textures*, 2.3 (1971),7–78, esp. 7–14.

31 Teubner, *Constitutional Fragments*, 102–10.

32 Teubner, *Constitutional Fragments*, 115.

33 Teubner, *Constitutional Fragments*, 116.

34 Michel Foucault, *The Birth of Biopolitics: Lectures at the Collège de France*, trans. by Graham Burchell (London: Palgrave Macmillan, 2008), 296. For a more explicit treatment, see Thomas Lemke, *A Critique of Political Reason: Foucault's Analysis of Modern Governmentality*, trans. by Erik Butler (London: Verso, 2019), part 2.

35 Foucault, *Birth of Biopolitics*, 296.

36 Teubner, *Constitutional Fragments*, 53–4.

37 Teubner, *Constitutional Fragments*, 54. Teubner is here discussing "nation-state constitutions" because he is considering constitutionalization on a global scale (which I am not at all doing here).

38 Rudolf Wiethölter, "Materialization and Proceduralization in the Welfare State," in: *Dilemmas of Law in the Welfare State*, ed. by Gunther Teubner

(Berlin: De Gruyter, 2011), 221–49, here 249. See also the following definition: "Proceduralization is – in one phrase – the renewal of linkage with the
history of 'bourgeois' political philosophy, with the intention of reproducing
its 'idealistic' and 'materialistic' transitions in different circumstances as social
learning projects" (Rudolf Wiethölter, "Proceduralization of the Category of
Law," in: Christian Joerges and David Trubek [eds.], *Critical Legal Thought:
An American–German Debate* [Baden-Baden: Nomos, 1989], 501–10, here
510).

39 [Tr. – my translation] Rudolf Wiethölter, cited by Andreas Fischer-Lescano
and Gunther Teubner, "Prozedurale Rechtstheorie: Wiethölter," in: Sonja
Buckel, Ralph Christensen, and Andreas Fischer-Lescano (eds.), *Neue
Theorien des Rechts* (Stuttgart: Lucius & Lucius, 2006), 79–96, here 82.

40 Fischer-Lescano and Teubner, "Prozedurale Rechtstheorie: Wiethölter," 82.

41 Wiethölter, "Materialization and Proceduralization in the Welfare State,"
239. Gunther Teubner has further developed this argument for fundamen-
tal rights; see Gunther Teubner, "The Anonymous Matrix: Human Rights
Violations by 'Private' Transnational Actors," *Modern Law Review*, 69.3
(2006), 327–46. See also Isabell Hensel and Gunther Teubner, "Horizontal
Fundamental Rights as Conflicts of Laws Rules: How Transnational
Pharmagroups Manipulate Scientific Publications," in: Kerstin Blome,
Andreas Fischer-Lescano, Hannah Franzki, Nora Markard, and Stefan Oeter
(eds.), *Contested Regime Collisions: Norm Fragmentation in World Society*
(Cambridge: Cambridge University Press, 2016), 139–68.

42 Rudolf Wiethölter, "Recht-Fertigungen eines Gesellschafts-Rechts," in:
Christian Joerges and Gunther Teubner (eds.), *Rechtsverfassungsrecht:
Recht-Fertigung zwischen Privatrechtsdogmatik und Gesellschaftstheorie*
(Baden-Baden: Nomos, 2003), 13–24.

43 [Tr. – "keep to the subject matter" is in English in the original.] Wiethölter,
"Materialization and Proceduralization in the Welfare State," 238.

44 Habermas, *Between Facts and Norms*, 412.

45 Gunther Teubner, "Reflexives Recht: Entwicklungsmodelle des Rechts in
vergleichender Perspektive," *Archiv für Rechts- und Sozialphilosophie*, 68
(1982), 13–59, here 49. [C.M. – I have omitted the italics in the original
here.]

14 Slave Revolt: Critique and Affirmation

1 Friedrich Nietzsche, *Beyond Good and Evil*, trans. by Judith Norman
(Cambridge: Cambridge University Press, 2002), 45 (§ 46).

2 See chapter 9 in this volume.

3 Karl Marx, "Contribution to the Critique of Hegel's Philosophy of Law,"
in: *Marx and Engels Collected Works*, vol. 3 (London: Lawrence & Wishart,
2010), 3–129, here 117.

4 Marx, "Contribution to the Critique of Hegel's Philosophy of Law," 30.

5 This is not Marx's own terminology in this early text. For why Marx still
rejects the term "communism" here, see Miguel Abensour, *Democracy
Against the State: Marx and the Machiavellian Moment*, trans. by Max
Blechman (Cambridge: Polity, 2011), 69. According to Abensour, the com-

munism that Marx here rejects is the idea of "a species-community that would exist beyond politics, beyond the political realm" (69). The explanation of the relation between politics and society in the "true democracy" without rights that I propose in what follows will distinguish this form of communism from others. It is communism as "the *real* movement which abolishes the present state of things" (Karl Marx and Friedrich Engels, "The German Ideology," in: *Marx and Engels Collected Works*, vol. 5 [London: Lawrence & Wishart, 1976], 19–539, here 49). For the different meanings of "communism" in Marx, see the concise overview in Kenneth A. Megill, "The Community in Marx's Philosophy," *Philosophy and Phenomenological Research*, 30 (1970), 382–93.

6 Marx, "Contribution to the Critique of Hegel's Philosophy of Law," 30.

7 [Tr. – translation modified] Marx, "Contribution to the Critique of Hegel's Philosophy of Law," 30 and 118.

8 Alasdair MacIntyre, *After Virtue* (Notre Dame: University of Notre Dame Press, 1984), 148f. For more, see Rahel Jaeggi, *Critique of Forms of Life*, trans. by Ciaran Cronin (Cambridge: Harvard University Press, 2018), 63–72. The Aristotelian conception of practice that MacIntyre reconstructs is also an essential point of reference for the young Marx's critique of society.

9 [Tr. – translation modified] G.W.F. Hegel, *Elements of the Philosophy of Right*, 219 (§ 181) and 161 (§ 157). In contrast to this approach, Simmel emphasizes the achievement (of freedom) in the alienated loss of practice: the fact that ("on the one hand") practical contexts portray themselves as a matter of natural law enables "the objective necessity of events" to "emerge more clearly and distinctly, while on the other we see the emphasis upon the independent individuality, upon personal freedom, upon independence in relation to all external and natural forces becoming more and more acute and increasingly stronger" (Georg Simmel, *The Philosophy of Money*, trans. by Tom Bottomore and David Frisby [London: Routledge, 2011], 326). I am here taking up this argument for an affirmation of the loss of practice; cf. pp. 263–6 in this volume.

10 Hegel characterizes the form of civil society in these terms: *Elements of the Philosophy of Right*, 181 (§ 183). Habermas reformulates this difference as one of system and lifeworld; see Jürgen Habermas, *Theory of Communicative Action*, vol. 2, *Lifeworld and System: Toward a Critique of Functionalist Reason*, trans. by Thomas McCarthy (Boston: Beacon, 1987), 113–98.

11 MacIntyre, *After Virtue*, 150.

12 Hegel, *Elements of the Philosophy of Right*, 275 (§ 257). This is Hegel's definition of the state, which Durkheim reformulates by stating that "Its central function is thought" (Émile Durkheim, *Leçons de sociologie: physique des mœurs et du droit* [online edn., accessed at: https://unige.ch/sciences-societe/socio/files/1214/0533/6006/Durkheim_1950.pdf], 73–4). Cf. also Hegel in *Phenomenology of Spirit*: "This spirit can be called the human law, because it is essentially in the form of a reality that is conscious of itself. In the form of universality it is the *known* law, and the prevailing custom; in the form of individuality it is the actual certainty of itself in the individual as such, and the certainty of itself as a simple individuality is that Spirit as government" (G.W.F. Hegel, *Phenomenology of Spirit*, trans. by A.V. Miller [Oxford: Oxford University Press, 1977], 267–8, § 448). Government here means

"reflexive government" or reflexivity *as* government. Martin Saar argues along similar lines in *Die Immanenz der Macht: Politische Theorie nach Spinoza* (Berlin: Suhrkamp, 2013), 254–9.

13 Marx, "Contribution to the Critique of Hegel's Philosophy of Law," 117.
14 Marx, "Contribution to the Critique of Hegel's Philosophy of Law," 32.
15 Marx, "Contribution to the Critique of Hegel's Philosophy of Law," 31.
16 Marx, "Contribution to the Critique of Hegel's Philosophy of Law," 31.
17 Marx, "Contribution to the Critique of Hegel's Philosophy of Law," 117.
18 Abensour is thus right: Marx's concept of true democracy does not dissolve politics *into* the social: "in democracy the political moment remains a particular moment" (Abensour, *Democracy Against the State*, 64). At the same time, however, it operates in the social: the social is its basis and content.
19 Karl Marx, "On the Jewish Question," in: *Marx and Engels Collected Works*, vol. 3, 165. See also pp. 1–6 in this volume ("Marx's Puzzle").
20 This is not entirely correct: he uses this term here and there, but mostly to speak about that to which he, Nietzsche, has a right or does not have a right. In the Preface to *On the Genealogy of Morals*, he thus writes: "We [sc. "men of knowledge"] have no right to *isolated* acts of any kind." Or: "I might almost have the right to call it [sc. "a scruple peculiar to me"] my '*a priori*'" (Friedrich Nietzsche, *On the Genealogy of Morals and Ecce Homo*, trans. by Walter Kaufmann and R.J. Hollingdale [New York: Vintage, 1989], 16).
21 Nietzsche, *On the Genealogy of Morals*, 25–6. In connection with his discussion of Foucault's concept of rights, Paul Patton ("Foucault, Critique and Rights," *Critical Horizons*, 6 [2005], 267–87, here 270–2) refers to Nietzsche's definition in *Daybreak*: "That is how rights originate: recognized and guaranteed degrees of power" (Friedrich Nietzsche, *Daybreak*, trans. by R.J. Hollingdale [Cambridge: Cambridge University Press, 1997], 112). This shows that the conception of power operative in rights allows quantitative gradations and thus a precarious intersubjective balance: "If our power is materially diminished, the feeling of those who have hitherto guaranteed our rights changes: they consider whether they can restore us to the full possession we formerly enjoyed – if they feel unable to do so, they henceforth deny our 'rights'" (Nietzsche, *Daybreak*, 112f.).
22 Nietzsche, *On the Genealogy of Morals*, 45 (§ 13).
23 See chapter 1, p. 14, in this volume.
24 Alexandre Kojève, *Outline of a Phenomenology of Right*, trans. by Bryan-Paul Frost and Robert Howse (Lanham: Rowman & Littlefield, 2000), 371–2.
25 Friedrich Nietzsche, *On the Genealogy of Morals*, 36 (§ 10).
26 Kojève, *Outline of a Phenomenology of Right*, 118. Kojève thus characterizes the "bourgeois *Droit*," which he conceives as the "Justice of equivalence" (251–62), as follows: in bourgeois law, justice demands equivalence for the respective position of the person affected, his or her "involvement."
27 Stephen Darwall, *The Second-Person Standpoint: Morality, Respect, and Accountability* (Cambridge: Harvard University Press 2009), 4. Darwall calls this reason "second-personal." We can thus also say that the slave revolt creates the right to justification – the right of the other to my justification vis-à-vis him. Cf. Rainer Forst, *The Right to Justification: Elements of a*

Constructivist Theory of Justice, trans. by Jeffry Flynn (New York: Columbia University Press, 2014).

28 Gilles Deleuze, *Nietzsche and Philosophy*, trans. by Hugh Tomlinson (London: Continuum, 1983), 60–1.

29 From the perspective of the "suffering, deprived, sick, ugly": Nietzsche, *On the Genealogy of Morals*, 34 (§ 7).

30 Aristotle, *On Sophistical Refutations, On Coming-to-Be and Passing Away, On the Cosmos*, trans. by E.S. Forster and D.J. Furley (London: Heinemann, 1955), 227–35 (I.7, 323b–324b). For the reception of this Aristotelian doctrine, see Jean Starobinski, *Action and Reaction: The Life and Adventures of a Couple* (New York: Zone, 2003), 23–8.

31 Aristotle, *Metaphysics*, trans. by Hugh Tredennick (Cambridge: Harvard University Press, 1933), 431 (IX.1, 1046a). See the discussion in Dirk Setton, *Unvermögen: Die Potentialität der praktischen Vernunft* (Zurich: Diaphanes, 2012), 34–41.

32 Immanuel Kant, *Critique of Pure Reason*, trans. and ed. by Paul Guyer and Allen W. Wood (Cambridge: Cambridge University Press, 1998), 212 (A 80, B 106).

33 Kant, *Critique of Pure Reason*, 318–20 (A 213–16, B 260–3). Reciprocity is defined in terms of causality. The difference between Aristotle and Kant is obvious (it concerns the concept of causality), but this is not relevant to the point at issue here.

34 The typical definition of acting as intentional effectuation is therefore not neutral: it presupposes that the relation between the one and the other is constituted in such a way that there *can* be causal interactions between them. This entails that their relation can be described as a *commercium* of the one acting and the one suffering.

35 Immanuel Kant, *The Metaphysics of Morals* (Cambridge: Cambridge University Press, 1996), 56.

36 Kant, *Metaphysics of Morals*, 58.

37 The claim that legal consideration is not a form of recognition is merely another formulation of the same thesis. The crucial presupposition for any demand for recognition – the presupposition that puts it in stark contrast to the demand for consideration – consists in the claim to being worthy of recognition, the claiming of merit and thus of a good. Anyone who demands recognition conceives himself, in so doing, not as a sufferer, but as an agent who has or is able to do something that earns recognition because it is good. The demand for recognition refers to an achievement or an accomplishment (or the capacity for such). Recognition can only be demanded in the name of a good. And it is in the name of the *same* good, where one demands recognition and another gives it to him. Recognition and that to which it refers are linked to each other in such a way that they express the same judgment concerning the good. In other words, they are elements and features of *one* practice that realizes an intrinsic good through their constitutive rules. For this reason, both the one who demands recognition and the one who gives it to him are participants in the same practice. Recognition is an action that is "indivisibly the action of one as well as of the other" (Hegel, *Phenomenology of Spirit*, 112 [§ 183]); its community is *communio*. Cf. Christoph Menke, "Das Nichtanerkennbare: Oder warum das moderne Recht keine 'Sphäre

der Anerkennung' ist," in: Rainer Forst, Martin Hartmann, Rahel Jaeggi, and Martin Saar (eds.), *Sozialphilosophie und Kritik* (Frankfurt: Suhrkamp, 2009), 87–108.

38 [Tr. – translation modified] Alain Badiou, *Ethics: An Essay on the Understanding of Evil*, trans. by Peter Hallward (London: Verso, 2001), 13. Badiou connects Marx to Nietzsche: the "ethics" that he is examining is nothing but slave morality, whose present form he detects in the theory and practice of human rights.

39 A different version of this paradox is described by Wendy Brown, when she notes that the "turn away from the political" that is the consequence of the form of rights is itself the result of the political function "to emancipate": Wendy Brown, "Rights and Losses," in: *States of Injury: Power and Freedom in Late Modernity* (Princeton: Princeton University Press, 1995), 96–134, here 115 and 100.

40 Nietzsche, *On the Genealogy of Morals*, 38 (§ 10).

41 Nietzsche, *On the Genealogy of Morals*, 47 (§ 14).

42 Marx, "Contribution to the Critique of Hegel's Philosophy of Law," 30; see p. 245 in this volume.

43 Benjamin Constant, "The Liberty of the Ancients Compared with That of the Moderns," in: *Political Writings*, trans. by Biancamaria Fontana (Cambridge: Cambridge University Press, 1988), 308–28, here 317.

44 For the "eminent" governability of the private discussed by Michel Foucault, see chapter 10, "The Government of Subjects," in this volume.

45 Nietzsche, *On the Genealogy of Morals*, 46 (§ 13).

46 Odo Marquard, "Indicted and Unburdened Man in Eighteenth-Century Philosophy," in: *Farewell to Matters of Principle: Philosophical Studies*, trans by Robert M. Wallace (Oxford: Oxford University Press, 1989), 38–63, here 46 and 50.

47 [Tr. – Marquard, "Indicted and Unburdened Man in Eighteenth-Century Philosophy," 53.]

48 Marquard, "Indicted and Unburdened Man in Eighteenth-Century Philosophy," 53.

49 Hegel, *Outlines of the Philosophy of Right*, 228 (§ 190).

50 Marx, "Contribution to the Critique of Hegel's Philosophy of Law," 117.

51 Claude Lefort and Marcel Gauchet, "Sur la démocratie: le politique et l'institution du social," *Textures*, 2.3 (1971), 7–78, here 29.

52 John Rawls, *Political Liberalism* (New York: Columbia University Press, 1996), 37. Rawls pursues this insight, but not far enough. To be sure, he is correct in saying that even "A society united on a reasonable form of utilitarianism, or on the reasonable liberalisms of Kant or Mill, would likewise require the sanctions of state power to remain so" (37). However, he wishes to see his so-called political liberalism free of this problem. For an attempt to turn Rawls against Rawls, see Christoph Menke, *Reflections of Equality*, trans. by Howard Rouse and Andrei Denejkine (Stanford: Stanford University Press, 2006), 130–47.

53 Lefort and Gauchet, "Sur la démocratie," 37. The authors characterize this as the moment of "governance." For an analysis of decision as an irreducible (and irreducibly particularizing) moment of the particular, see Francesca Raimondi, *Die Zeit der Demokratie: Politische Freiheit nach Carl*

Schmitt und Hannah Arendt (Konstanz: Konstanz University Press, 2014), 37–43.

54 V.I. Lenin, "The State and Revolution," in: *Collected Works*, vol. 25 (Moscow: Progress, 1964), 385–498, here 463.

55 Rawls, *Political Liberalism*, 36.

56 Rawls, *Political Liberalism*, 37.

57 For more on the concept of political opinion, see chapter 10, "Excursus: Freedom of Opinion, for Example (Spinoza, Habermas)," in this volume.

58 Niklas Luhmann, "Die Tücke des Subjekts und die Frage nach dem Menschen," in: *Soziologische Aufklärung* (Opladen: Westdeutscher Verlag, 1970), 155–68, here 158. For an interpretation of this theory in terms of legal theory, see Christoph Menke, "Subjektive Rechte: Zur Paradoxie der Form," in: *Nach Jacques Derrida und Niklas Luhmann: Zur (Un-)Möglichkeit einer Gesellschaftstheorie der Gerechtigkeit* (Stuttgart: Lucius & Lucius, 2008), 81–108.

59 Albrecht Wellmer, "Models of Freedom in the Modern World," in: *Endgames: The Irreconcilable Nature of Modernity: Essays and Lectures*, trans. by David Midgley (Cambridge: MIT Press, 1998), 29.

60 Nietzsche, *On the Genealogy of Morals*, 26.

61 Friedrich Nietzsche, *The Portable Nietzsche*, trans. by Walter Kaufmann (New York: Viking, 1954), 458. On the relation of force and will, see Deleuze, *Nietzsche and Philosophy*, 61–5.

62 Yirmiyahu Yovel, *Dark Riddle: Hegel, Nietzsche and the Jews* (Cambridge: Polity, 1998), part 2.

63 Badiou, *Ethics*, 12.

64 Marx, "On the Jewish Question," 168.

15 A New Right

1 Aristotle, *Politics*, trans. by H. Rackham (Cambridge: Harvard University Press, 1944), 11 (I.2, 1253a).

2 Ernst Tugendhat, *Egocentricity and Mysticism: An Anthropological Study*, trans. by Alexei Procyshyn (New York: Columbia University Press, 2016), 5–6. Tugendhat introduces his theory of judgment as an elucidation of the just-cited passage in Aristotle; see 4f.

3 [Tr. – translation modified] Tugendhat, *Egocentricity and Mysticism*, 6.

4 Hannah Arendt, *Lectures on Kant's Political Philosophy*, ed. by Ronald Beiner (Chicago: University of Chicago Press, 1992), 67.

5 Aristotle, *Politics*, 23 (I.2, 1254b).

6 [Tr. – Tugendhat, *Egocentricity and Mysticism*, 18.]

7 Aristotle, *Politics*, 23 (I.2, 1254b).

8 Jacques Rancière, *Disagreement: Politics and Philosophy*, trans. by Julie Rose (Minneapolis: University of Minnesota Press, 1999), 22. For what follows (the self-distinction of logos from the perceptible voice), see Rancière's concept of the "account" established by politics: "Politics exists because the logos is never simply speech, because it is always indissolubly the *account* that is made of this speech: the account by which a sonorous admission is understood as speech, capable of enunciating what is just, whereas some

other emission is merely perceived as a noise signaling pleasure or pain, consent or revolt" (Rancière, *Disagreement*, 22).

9   Rancière, *Disagreement*, 24.

10 This interpretation, which I am calling the communist one, is formulated by Rancière, *Disagreement*, 24f. To be sure, Rancière says that the revolt of servants establishes "another order, another partition of the perceptible" (24). If servants wish to become *like* masters, however, then this is not another order, but another way of separating the two sides that distinguishes them: *phonē* and *logos*, the perceptible and the conceptual. Rancière's application of the category of the human being – human beings are (like) masters, because they can judge like the latter – corresponds to Tugendhat's reconstruction of the Aristotelian distinction as a neutral anthropological truth, through which "the fundamental differences between humans and other animals could be formulated" and can be explained "evolutionarily" by the "gain in the adaptability of social organizations to new environmental conditions" (Tugendhat, *Egocentricity and Mysticism*, 4f.). Both Rancière and Tugendhat thus anthropologize and depoliticize the difference between *phonē* and *logos*.

11 Juliane Rebentisch formulates this in her critical reading of Plato's critique of democracy as follows: "Not only does a theatrocracy grant everybody the authority to judge, more importantly it transforms the concept of judgment itself" (*The Art of Freedom: On the Dialectics of Democratic Existence* [Cambridge: Polity, 2016], 48).

12 Theodor Adorno, *Negative Dialectics*, trans. by E.B. Ashton (New York: Continuum, 1973), 193. For a more extensive treatment of this thought, see Christoph Menke, *Reflections of Equality*, trans. by Howard Rouse and Andrei Denejkine (Stanford: Stanford University Press, 2006), chs. 3 and 4; Christoph Menke, *Die Kraft der Kunst* (Berlin: Suhrkamp, 2013), chs. I.3 and II.1.

13 Aristotle, *Metaphysics*, trans. by Hugh Tredennick (Cambridge: Harvard University Press, 1933), 431 (IX.1, 1046a). A close interpretation of this thesis is central to chs. 1 and 2 of Dirk Setton's *Unvermögen: Die Potentialität der praktischen Vernunft* (Zurich: Diaphanes, 2012). I here limit myself to drawing a metaphorical connection.

14 Theodor Adorno, *Minima Moralia*, trans. by E.F.N. Jephcott (London: Verso, 2005), 156.

15 Adorno, *Negative Dialectics*, 187 and 182. Adorno understands "the materialist moment in Schelling" (*Negative Dialectics*, 182) in this way. Alexander García Düttmann, in considering the art of the aphorism in *Minima Moralia*, has defined this as the "so-it-is that is not found at the end of a logically connected series of inferences and for this reason ought not to be confused with a cognitive judgment" (Düttmann, *So ist es: Ein philosophischer Kommentar zu Adornos Minima Moralia* [Frankfurt: Suhrkamp, 2004], 41).

16 The first citation: Martin Seel, "Sich bestimmen lassen: Ein revidierter Begriff von Selbstbestimmung," in: *Sich bestimmen lassen: Studien zur theoretischen und praktischen Philosophie* (Frankfurt: Suhrkamp, 2002), 279–98, here 294. Seel now calls this "active passivity;" cf. Seel, *Aktive Passivität: Über den Spielraum des Denkens, Handelns und anderer Künste* (Frankfurt: Fischer, 2014). The second citation: Adorno, *Negative Dialectics*, 40. Adorno says of

this immediacy: "To dialectics, immediacy does not maintain its immediate pose."

17 Adorno, *Negative Dialectics*, 172 and 184 [Tr. – translation modified].
18 Adorno, *Negative Dialectics*, 194.
19 Adorno, *Negative Dialectics*, 194. "By tailoring its categories, traditional philosophy has bewitched what is heterogeneous to it."
20 Adorno, *Negative Dialectics*, 203.
21 Frank Ruda, "Père-Version des Passiven," in: Kathrin Busch and Helmut Draxler (eds.), *Theorien der Passivität* (Munich: Fink, 2013), 258–75, here 275.
22 Cf. Setton, *Unvermögen*, 101–7.
23 Perceptible affection has a structurally unconscious moment. For a more extensive treatment of this, see Christoph Menke, *Force: A Fundamental Concept of Aesthetic Anthropology*, trans. by Gerrit Jackson (New York: Fordham University Press, 2013), chs. 1 and 3.
24 Adorno, *Negative Dialectics*, 172.
25 Rancière, *Disagreement*, 27. (According to Michel Villey, division, *partage*, is the basic operation of justice in traditional law; see chapter 2 in this volume.)
26 Rancière, *Disagreement*, 28.
27 Rancière, *Disagreement*, 30.
28 Rancière, *Disagreement*, 33.
29 Rancière, *Disagreement*, 33.
30 Étienne Balibar, "Citizen Subject," in: Eduardo Cadava, Peter Connor, and Jean-Luc Nancy (eds.), *Who Comes after the Subject?* (New York: Routledge, 1991), 33–57, here 50–1.
31 Rancière, *Disagreement*, 30–31.
32 Alain Badiou, *Theory of the Subject*, trans. by Bruno Bosteels (New York: Continuum, 2009), 162.
33 Badiou, *Theory of the Subject*, 165 and 164.
34 Badiou, *Theory of the Subject*, 166.
35 Badiou, *Theory of the Subject*, 158 and 173.
36 Jacques Rancière, "Who is the Subject of the Rights of Man?" *South Atlantic Quarterly*, 103.2/3 (2004), 297–310. In contrast, in *Disagreement*, Rancière still exclusively treats the rights of man under the chapter heading "Politics in Its Nihilistic Age." The central thesis of that chapter is that "Human rights are no longer experienced as political capacities" (126).
37 Étienne Balibar, "What is a Politics of the Rights of Man?," in: *Masses, Classes, Ideas: Studies on Politics and Philosophy Before and After Marx* (New York: Routledge, 1994), 205–25; Étienne Balibar, "'Rights of Man' and 'Rights of the Citizen': The Modern Dialectic of Equality and Freedom," in: *Masses, Classes, Ideas*, 39–59.
38 Rancière, "Who is the Subject of the Rights of Man?" 302–3.
39 Rancière, "Who is the Subject of the Rights of Man?" 303f.
40 Claude Lefort, "Human Rights and Politics," in: *The Political Forms of Modern Society: Bureaucracy, Democracy, Totalitarianism*, trans. by Alan Sheridan (Cambridge: MIT Press, 1986), 239–72, here 257–8.
41 Balibar, "What is a Politics of the Rights of Man?" 224.
42 In fact, they do not *analyze* this form at all – as though it were neutral. Like

the bourgeois revolution itself, whose (critical) theory they wish to write, they identify the declaration of equality with equal rights; for more on this see pp. 1–6, "Marx's Puzzle."

43 Balibar, "'Rights of Man' and 'Rights of the Citizen'," 51.

44 Wendy Brown, "Suffering Rights as Paradoxes," *Constellations*, 7.2 (2000), 208–29. See p. 183 in this volume.

45 Axel Honneth, *Freedom's Right: The Social Foundations of Democratic Life* (Cambridge: Polity, 2014), 5.

46 Alexandre Kojève, *Outline of a Phenomenology of Right*, trans. by Bryan-Paul Frost and Robert Howse (Lanham: Rowman & Littlefield, 2000), 164.

47 Because they are rights to the natural, and the natural to which they entitle us is given in equal measure to all human beings – in contrast to virtue or reason, which forms the content of traditional rights: thus Hobbes' basic argument; see chapter 2, pp. 38–40, in this volume.

48 See chapter 4 and chapter 9 in this volume.

49 Michel Foucault, *Society Must Be Defended: Lectures at the Collège de France, 1975–76*, trans. by David Macey (New York: Picador, 2003), 40.

50 Foucault, *Society Must Be Defended*, 40.

51 Jacques Derrida, "Force of Law: The 'Mystical Foundation of Authority'," in: *Deconstruction and the Possibility of Justice*, ed. by Drucilla Cornell, Michael Rosenfeld, and David Gray Carlson (New York: Routledge, 1992), 3–67, here 23.

52 Derrida, "Force of Law," 23.

Law and Violence

1 Immanuel Kant, *The Metaphysics of Morals* (Cambridge: Cambridge University Press, 1996), 68.

2 Niklas Luhmann, *Trust and Power*, trans. by Howard Davies, John Raffan, and Kathryn Rooney (Cambridge: Polity, 2017), 71. In what follows, I am summarizing an argument that I made in *Law and Violence: Christoph Menke in Dialogue*, trans. by Gerrit Jackson (Manchester: Manchester University Press, 2018), part 1.

3 Luhmann, *Trust and Power*, 170.

4 Jürgen Habermas, *Between Facts and Norms: Contributions to a Discourse Theory of Law and Democracy* (Cambridge: MIT Press, 1996), 21.

5 Violence in this sense no longer primarily refers to potential and how powerful an effect that wrongs is, but is a violence that operates within normative logic.

6 See chapter 5, "Gap, Violence, Exception," in this volume.

7 Walter Benjamin, "The Critique of Violence," in: *Reflections: Essays, Aphorisms, Autobiographical Writings*, trans. by Edmund Jephcott (New York: Schocken, 1986), here 295.

8 Benjamin, "Critique of Violence," 294.

9 See chapter 5, "Self-Reflection," in this volume.

10 Franz Neumann, *The Rule of Law: Political Theory and the Legal System in Modern Society* (Oxford: Berg, 1986), 215.

11 [Tr. – translation modified] Karl Marx, "Contribution to the Critique of

Hegel's Philosophy of Law," in: *Marx and Engels Collected Works*, vol. 3 (London: Lawrence & Wishart, 2010), 3–129, here 30–1; Karl Marx, "On the Jewish Question," in: *Marx and Engels Collected Works*, vol. 3, 167.

12 [Tr. – translation modified] Theodor Adorno, *Negative Dialectics*, trans. by E.B. Ashton (New York: Continuum, 1973), 190.

13 V.I. Lenin, "The State and Revolution," in: *Collected Works*, vol. 25 (Moscow: Progress, 1964), 385–498, here 411.

INDEX